An IBM® SPSS® Companion to Political Analysis

Fifth Edition

SAGE was founded in 1965 by Sara Miller McCune to support the dissemination of usable knowledge by publishing innovative and high-quality research and teaching content. Today, we publish more than 850 journals, including those of more than 300 learned societies, more than 800 new books per year, and a growing range of library products including archives, data, case studies, reports, and video. SAGE remains majority-owned by our founder, and after Sara's lifetime will become owned by a charitable trust that secures our continued independence.

Los Angeles | London | New Delhi | Singapore | Washington DC

An IBM® SPSS® Companion to Political Analysis

Fifth Edition

Philip H. Pollock III
University of Central Florida

Los Angeles | London | New Delhi
Singapore | Washington DC

Los Angeles | London | New Delhi
Singapore | Washington DC

FOR INFORMATION:

CQ Press
An Imprint of SAGE Publications, Inc.
2455 Teller Road
Thousand Oaks, California 91320
E-mail: order@sagepub.com

SAGE Publications Ltd.
1 Oliver's Yard
55 City Road
London EC1Y 1SP
United Kingdom

SAGE Publications India Pvt. Ltd.
B 1/I 1 Mohan Cooperative Industrial Area
Mathura Road, New Delhi 110 044
India

SAGE Publications Asia-Pacific Pte. Ltd.
3 Church Street
#10-04 Samsung Hub
Singapore 049483

Acquisitions Editor: Sarah Calabi
Associate Editor: Natalie Konopinski
Editorial Assistant: Katie Lowry
eLearning Editor: Allison Hughes
Production Editor: Kelly DeRosa
Copy Editor: Christina West
Typesetter: C&M Digitals (P) Ltd.
Proofreader: Jennifer Grubba
Cover Designer: Anupama Krishnan
Marketing Manager: Amy Whitaker

Copyright © 2016 by CQ Press, an Imprint of SAGE Publications, Inc. CQ Press is a registered trademark of Congressional Quarterly, Inc.

All rights reserved. No part of this book may be reproduced or utilized in any form or by any means, electronic or mechanical, including photocopying, recording, or by any information storage and retrieval system, without permission in writing from the publisher.

All trademarks depicted within this book, including trademarks appearing as part of a screen figure, or other image are included solely for the purpose of illustration and are the property c their respective holders. The use of the trademarks in no way indicates any relationship with, endorsement by, the holders of said trademarks. SPSS is a registered trademark of Internation Business Machines Incorporated.

Printed in the United States of America

Library of Congress Cataloging-in-Publication Data

Pollock, Philip H., III.

An IBM SPSS companion to political analysis / Philip H. Pollock, III, University of Ce Florida. — Fifth Edition.

pages cm
System requirements: System requirements: Microsoft Windows-based computer; CD-ROM drive.

Companion text to: Essentials of political analysis/Philip H. Pollock.
Previous edition title: An SPSS companion to political analysis.

Includes bibliographical references.

ISBN 978-1-5063-0579-0 (paperback: acid-free paper)

1. Political science—Research—Handbooks, manuals, etc. 2. Political statistics—Comp programs—Handbooks, manuals, etc. 3. Analysis of variance—Computer programs—Handbooks, manuals, etc. 4. SPSS (Computer file)—Handbooks, manuals, etc. I. Pollo Philip H., III. Essentials of political analysis. II. Title. III. Title: International Business Machines statistical package for the social sciences companion to political analysis.

JA86.P64 2015

320.0285'555—dc22 2015023736

This book is printed on acid-free paper.

SFI label applies to text stock

18 19 10 9 8 7 6 5 4 3 2

Contents

Figures

Preface

Since I began teaching research methods nearly forty years ago, I have introduced my students to the joys of doing their own political analysis. In my experience, students who appreciate the practical side of research are better prepared to contribute to class discussions of methodological concepts and problems. Moreover, students often develop a usable skill they can hone as they continue their academic careers or pursue employment opportunities. Whatever their professional goals, students need a solid foundation in basic political analysis techniques. They should learn to manipulate variables, explore patterns, and graph relationships. They also need a working knowledge of powerful yet easy-to-learn software, such as IBM® SPSS® Statistics.* This book instructs students in using SPSS to construct meaningful descriptions of variables and to perform substantive analysis of political relationships. The chapters cover all major topics in data analysis, from descriptive statistics to logistic regression. A final chapter describes several doable research projects, shows how to find analyzable data, and lays out a framework for a well-organized research paper.

In its essential features—multiple datasets, guided examples, screenshots, graphics instruction, and end-of-chapter exercises—this book continues in the tradition of previous editions. However, previous adopters will find some changes and improvements.

DATASETS AND EXERCISES

The SPSS datasets have been thoroughly revised and updated. There are four downloadable datasets: selected variables from the 2012 General Social Survey (dataset GSS2012) and the 2012 American National Election Study (NES2012), as well as datasets on the 50 states (States) and 167 countries of the world (World). As before, each chapter is written as a step-by-step tutorial, taking students through a series of guided examples and providing many annotated screenshots. Because of the revised and updated datasets, all of the examples are fresh and all of the screenshots are new.

This book contains fifty-three end-of-chapter exercises. The exercises are designed to give students opportunities to apply their new skills and to engage students in discovering the meaning of their findings and learning to interpret them. I have included exercises that reflect current scholarly debates in American political behavior and issues in comparative politics. The exercises test a full range of competencies, and most chapters include at least one more-challenging exercise. In a change from previous editions, I have augmented or replaced many of the "check the correct box" response choices with expansive answer lines: "Explain, making specific reference to the results." (In recent years, I have observed a growing student reluctance to write paragraph-length justifications for their answers.) As before, I continue to assume that students using this workbook have never heard of SPSS and have never used a computer to analyze data. After completing this book, students will have become competent SPSS users, and they will have learned a fair amount about substantive political science, too.

*SPSS is a registered trademark of International Business Machines Corporation.

Any student who has access to SPSS—the full version or the student version (technically referred to as the IBM® SPSS® Statistics Base Integrated Student Edition)—can use this book. When students analyze the States and World datasets using the student version, their results will be identical to full-version output. Because NES2012 and GSS2012 exceed student version limitations, I created student-version compatible sets (NES2012_Student_A, NES2012_Student_B, GSS2012_Student_A, and GSS2012_Student_B) by drawing random samples from the full datasets. SPSS output from these sets will be similar to, but not the same as, output from the full-version datasets. To perform logistic regression, covered in Chapter 10, students will need access to the full version of SPSS.

Different Releases of SPSS

SPSS 22 is featured here, but anyone running release 12 or later can profitably use this book. There are many commonalities across post-12 releases, including the graphic dialogs and the Chart Editor. There are currently three ways to obtain unedited charts: Chart Builder, Graphboard Template Chooser, and Legacy Dialogs. Although I have attempted to migrate to the more recent tools—for how many more releases will SPSS support routines labeled "legacy"?—the Legacy Dialogs still offer superior intuitiveness and flexibility. (One notable exception: bubble plots, which can only be created in Graphboard Template Chooser. Although bubble plots are not covered in this book, a screencast, available as an ancillary, demonstrates how to create this graphic form.) In any event, this edition carries forward the emphasis on elegant graphic display to complement and clarify empirical results. I have sought to instruct students in using the Chart Editor to emulate the techniques advocated by Edward R. Tufte and other experts on the visual display of data.

CHAPTER ORGANIZATION

Chapter organization follows that of the previous edition. The "Getting Started" introduction describes the datasets, alerts students to differences between the full and student versions, and describes how to install the student version software. Chapter 1 introduces the SPSS Data Editor, discusses the output Viewer, and illustrates the print procedure. Chapter 2 covers central tendency and dispersion and guides students in using the Frequencies routine. This chapter also includes coverage of Case Summaries, which can be quite useful for providing insights into small datasets, such as States and World. Chapter 2 also shows how a frequency distribution, examined in conjunction with a bar chart or histogram, can enrich the description of a variable. Chapter 3 describes the main SPSS data transformation procedures, Recode and Compute. This chapter also discusses Visual Binning, which is a powerful and efficient alternative to Recode, especially for collapsing interval variables into ordinal categories of roughly equal size. In Chapter 4, which covers Crosstabs and Compare Means, students learn bivariate analysis. This chapter introduces line charts and bar charts, and—new in this edition—box plots. Chapter 4 also gives students an initial tour of the Chart Editor. In Chapter 5 students use Crosstabs and Compare Means to obtain and interpret controlled comparisons. This chapter also discusses graphic support for controlled relationships. Chapter 6 uses One-Sample T Test and Independent-Samples T Test to demonstrate statistical significance for interval-level dependent variables. Chapter 6 is the most thoroughly rewritten chapter in the book. Gone is the unloved discussion of one-tailed versus two-tailed tests of significance. Instead, Chapter 6 focuses exclusively on two-tailed tests and on the 95 percent confidence interval. Chapter 7 covers chi-square and measures of association for nominal and ordinal variables. In Chapter 8 students work through guided examples to learn Correlate (Bivariate) and Regression (Linear). Chapter 8 discusses advanced editing using the Chart Editor. Chapter 9 shows how to create dummy variables (essentially an application of Recode, which students learned in Chapter 3), perform dummy variable regression analysis, and model interaction in multiple regression. Chapter 10 covers binary logistic regression, including a reworked discussion of how to present logistic regression results in terms of probabilities: marginal effects at the means (MEMs) and marginal effects at representative values (MERs). Chapter 11 guides students as they analyze their own data.

These chapters are organized in the way that I typically teach my methods courses. I prefer to cover the logic of description and hypothesis testing before introducing inferential statistics and statistical significance. However, with a little rearranging of the chapters, this book will prove useful for instructors who do things differently. For example, after covering basic data transformations (Chapter 3) and discussing cross-tabulation analysis (Chapter 4), an instructor could assign Chapter 7, which covers chi-square and bivariate measures of association for categorical variables. Instructors who prefer using the regression approach to evaluating the statistical significance of mean differences might decide to skip Chapter 6 and move on to Chapters 8 and 9.

Screencasts

This book has always taken a two-step approach to skill-set learning: (1) Perform the guided examples. (2) Work the exercises. To augment the first step, I have produced a set of screencasts that cover all of the guided examples—plus some other topics of interest, such as creating bubble plots and producing nicely formatted SPSS tables in Microsoft Word. Students can access the screencasts here: **edge.sagepub.com/Pollock**

ACCOMPANYING CORE TEXT

Instructors will find that this book makes an effective supplement to any of a variety of methods textbooks. However, it is a particularly suitable companion to my own core text, *The Essentials of Political Analysis*. The textbook's substantive chapters cover basic and intermediate methodological issues and ideas: measurement, explanations and hypotheses, univariate statistics and bivariate analysis, controlled relationships, sampling and inference, statistical significance, correlation and linear regression, and logistic regression.

Each chapter also includes end-of-chapter exercises. Students can read the textbook chapters, do the exercises, and then work through the guided examples and exercises in *An IBM® SPSS® Companion to Political Analysis*. The idea is to get students in front of the computer, experiencing political research firsthand, fairly early in the academic term. An instructor's solutions manual, available for download online at edge.sagepub .com/Pollock and free to adopters, provides solutions for all of the textbook and workbook exercises.

ACKNOWLEDGMENTS

I received more than a few friendly e-mails suggesting ways to improve this book, and I am grateful for this advice. I also thank current and past reviewers for pointing me in the right direction: Holly Brasher, University of Alabama at Birmingham; Matthew Davis, University of Delaware; Jason Kehrberg, University of Kentucky; Thad Kousser, University of California, San Diego; Nancy Martorano, University of Dayton; Matthew Streb, Northern Illinois University; Brian Vargus, Indiana University–Purdue University Indianapolis; Julian Westerhout, Illinois State University; Lindsay Benstead, Portland State University; William Field, Rutgers, The State University of New Jersey; Rob Mellen, Mississippi State University; Brian Frederick, Bridgewater State College; Krista Jenkins, Fairleigh Dickinson University; Renato Corbetta, University of Alabama at Birmingham; Changkuk Jung, SUNY College at Geneseo; and Wesley Hussey, California State University, Sacramento. I thank my University of Central Florida colleagues Bruce Wilson and Kerstin Hamann for helping me with ideas for exercises on comparative politics. I also give special thanks to my friend and fellow University of Minnesota alum, Bill Claggett of Florida State University, for sharing his SPSS know-how with me. It was Claggett who reminded me of an ancient flaw in Compute: Multiply 0 times missing, and SPSS interprets the product as 0, not as missing. This flaw—a serious defect, in my opinion—is discussed in Chapter 9. Many encouraging people have helped me make this a better book. Any remaining errors, however, are mine.

I gratefully acknowledge the encouragement and professionalism of everyone associated with the College Division of CQ Press: Sarah Calabi, acquisitions editor; Natalie Konopinski, associate editor; Allison Hughes, elearning editor; Kelly DeRosa, production editor; Christina West, copy editor; and Katie Lowry, editorial assistant. I owe an enduring debt to Charisse Kiino, editorial director—without her commitment, this entire project would still be an incoherent jumble of datasets and syntax files lying fallow on my hard drive.

Getting Started

To get started with this book you will need

- Access to a Microsoft Windows–based computer with an Internet connection

As you have learned about political research and explored techniques of political analysis, you have studied many examples of other people's work. You may have read textbook chapters that present frequency distributions, or you may have pondered research articles that use cross-tabulation, correlation, or regression analysis to investigate interesting relationships between variables. As valuable as these learning experiences are, they can be enhanced greatly by performing political analysis firsthand—handling and modifying social science datasets, learning to use data analysis software, obtaining your own descriptive statistics for variables, setting up the appropriate analysis for interesting relationships, and running the analysis and interpreting your results.

This book is designed to guide you as you learn these valuable practical skills. In this volume you will gain a working knowledge of SPSS, a data analysis package used widely in academic institutions and business environments. SPSS has been in use for many years (it first appeared in 1968), and it contains a great variety of statistical analysis routines—from basic descriptive statistics to sophisticated predictive modeling. It is extraordinarily user friendly. In fact, although this book assumes that you have practical knowledge of the Windows operating system and that you know how to perform elemental file-handling tasks, it also assumes that you have never heard of SPSS and that you have never used a computer to analyze data of any kind. By the time you complete the guided examples and the exercises in this book, you will be well on your way to becoming an SPSS aficionado. The skills you learn will be durable, and they will serve you well as you continue your educational career or enter the business world.

This book's chapters are written in tutorial fashion. Each chapter contains several guided examples, and each includes exercises at the end. You will read each chapter while sitting in front of a computer, doing the analyses described in the guided examples, and analyzing the datasets that accompany this text. Each data analysis procedure is described in step-by-step fashion, and the book has many figures that show you what your computer screen should look like as you perform the procedures. Thus, the guided examples allow you to develop your skills and to become comfortable with SPSS. The end-of-chapter exercises allow you to apply your new skills to different substantive problems.

This book will provide you with a solid foundation in data analysis. You will learn to obtain and interpret descriptive statistics (Chapter 2), to collapse and combine variables (Chapter 3), to perform cross-tabulation and mean comparison analysis (Chapter 4), and to control for other factors that might be affecting your results (Chapter 5). Techniques of statistical inference (Chapters 6 and 7) are covered, too. On the more advanced side, this book introduces correlation and linear regression (Chapter 8), and it teaches you how to use dummy variables and how to model interaction effects in regression analysis (Chapter 9). If you are running the full version of SPSS, Chapter 10 provides an introduction to logistic regression, an analytic technique that has gained wide currency in recent years. Chapter 11 shows you how to read data into SPSS, and it provides guidance on writing up your results.

DOWNLOADING THE DATASETS

To access the datasets that you will analyze in this book, navigate to this site:

edge.sagepub.com/Pollock

In the left navigation pane of the site, click on the dataset link below *An IBM® SPSS® Companion to Political Analysis, 5th edition*. This page for the datasets has two links: (1) Full Version SPSS and (2) Student Version SPSS (technically referred to as the IBM® SPSS® Statistics Base Integrated Student Edition) (Figure I-1). If you are a Full Version user, click the Full Version link (Figure I-2), making sure that the Save File option is selected, click OK to download the data sets. If you are a Student Version user, click the Student Version link (Figure I-3), making sure that the Save File option is selected, click OK to download the data sets. Even though the Student Version link contains six datasets, the Student Version datasets are based on the four Full Version sets. (The major differences between versions are discussed below.)

Download the datasets to a USB drive or other portable media. (Or download the datasets to the default location, and then copy them to a USB drive.) There are four datasets.

1. **GSS2012** (for Student Version users: GSS2012_Student_A and GSS2012_Student_B). This dataset has selected variables from the 2012 General Social Survey, a random sample of 1,974 adults aged ≥18 years, conducted by the National Opinion Research Center and made available through the Inter-university Consortium for Political and Social Research (ICPSR) at the University of Michigan.[1]

2. **NES2012** (for Student Version users: NES2012_Student_A and NES2012_Student_B). This dataset includes selected variables from the 2012 American National Election Study, a random sample of 5,916 citizens of voting age, conducted by the University of Michigan's Institute for Social Research and made available through the ICPSR.[2]

3. **States.** This dataset includes variables on each of the fifty states. These variables were compiled by the author from various sources, including Americans United for Life (http://aul.org/featured-images/AUL-1301_DL13%20Book_FINAL.pdf), the Brady Campaign (http://www.bradycampaign.org/), the Bureau of Alcohol, Tobacco, Firearms and Explosives (https://www.atf.gov/), Gallup (http://www.gallup.com; Gallup-Healthways Well-Being Index; Gallup State of the States), the Guttmacher Institute (http://www.guttmacher.org), the Marijuana Policy Project (http://www.mpp.org/), the National Conference of State Legislatures (http://www.ncsl.org/legislatures-elections/elections/statevote-charts.aspx; http://www.ncsl.org/legislatures-elections/wln/women-in-state-legislatures-2011.aspx), the *National Journal* (http://www.nationaljournal.com/2011voteratings), Survey USA (http://surveyusa.com), the U.S. Census Bureau (http://census.gov), and the Williams Institute (http://williamsinstitute.law.ucla.edu/).

4. **World.** This dataset includes variables on 167 countries of the world. Many of these variables are based on data compiled by Pippa Norris, John F. Kennedy School of Government, Harvard University, and are made available to the scholarly community through her Web site.[3] Other variables were compiled by the author from various sources, including the Association of Religion Data Archives (http://www.thearda.com), the Center for Systemic Peace (http://www.systemicpeace.org/polity/polity4.htm), the CIA World Factbook, (https://www.cia.gov/library/publications/the-world-factbook/), Freedom House (http://freedomhouse.org), the Heritage Foundation (http://www.heritage.org/index/), Inter-Parliamentary Union (http://ipu.org), the United Nations (http://data.un.org), and the World Bank (http://data.worldbank.org).

Figure I-1 Data Website

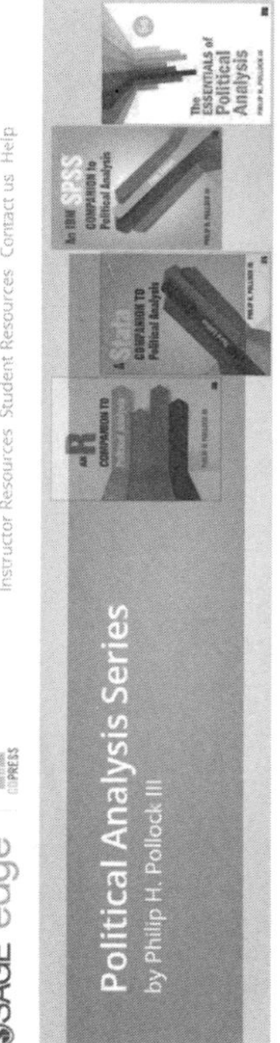

Instructor Resources Student Resources Contact us Help

Student Resources

The Essentials of Political Analysis, 5th edition
1. Introduction
2. The Definition and Measurement of Concepts
3. Measuring the Describing Variables
4. Proposing Explanations, Framing Hypotheses, and Making Comparisons
5. Research Design and the Logic of Control
6. Making Controlled Comparisons
7. Foundations of Statistical Inference
8. Tests of Significance and Measures of Association
9. Correlation and Linear Regression
10. Logistic Regression
11. Thinking Empirically, Thinking Probabilistically

An IBM SPSS® Companion to Political Analysis, 5th edition
Datasets
Tables and Figures
Video

An R Companion to Political Analysis
A Stata Companion to Political Analysis, 3rd edition

Datasets

Download the applicable dataset to a USB or other portable media. (Or download the datasets to the default location, and then copy them to a USB drive.) If you are a Full Version user, click the Full Version link. If you are a Student Version user, click the Student Version link.

Full Version full version.zip

- GSS2012.sav
- NES2012.sav
- States.sav
- World.sav

Student Version student version.zip

- GSS2012_Student_A.sav
- GSS2012_Student_B.sav
- NES2012_Student_A.sav
- NES2012_Student_B.sav
- States_Student.sav
- World_Student.sav

Author: Philip Pollock III
Pub date: Nov. 2015
Buy the book
Order Review Copy

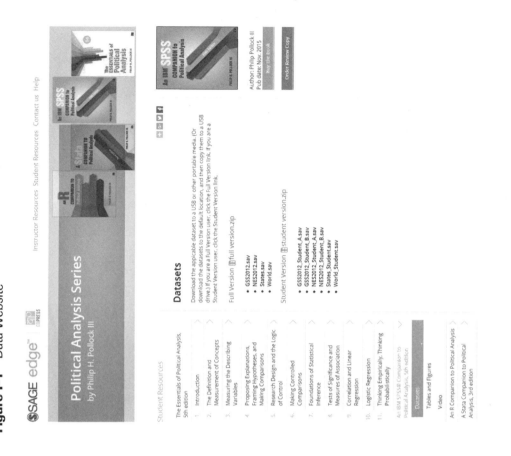

Figure I-2 Full Version Datasets

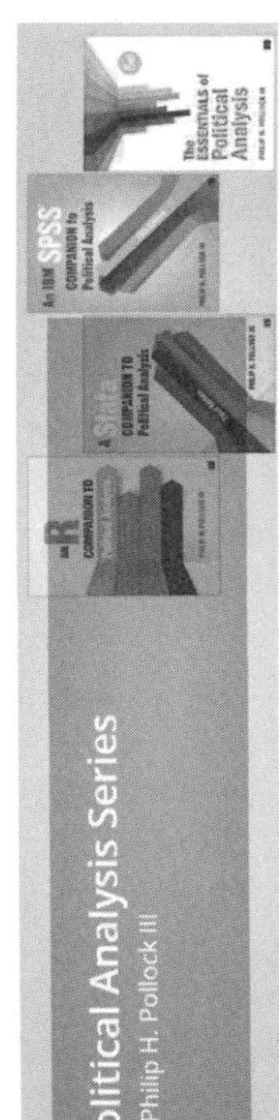

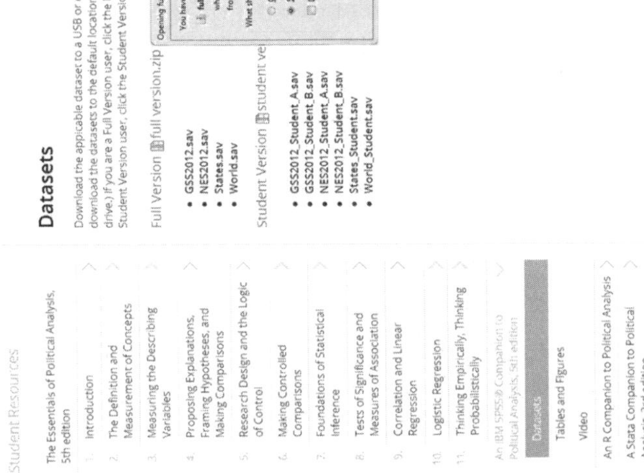

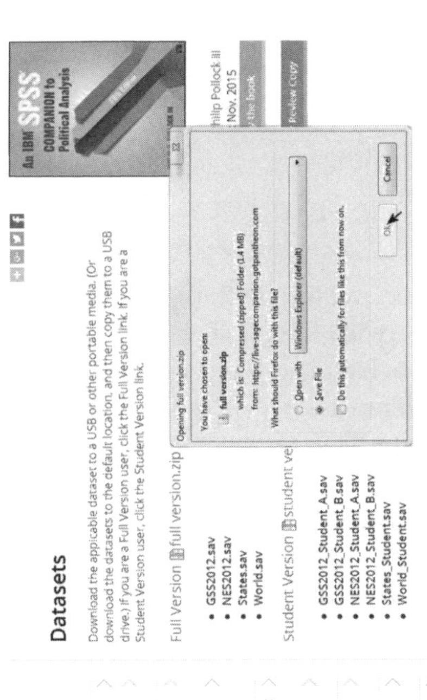

Student Resources

Datasets

Full Version full version.zip

- GSS2012.sav
- NES2012.sav
- States.sav
- World.sav

- GSS2012_Student_A.sav
- GSS2012_Student_B.sav
- NES2012_Student_A.sav
- NES2012_Student_B.sav
- States_Student.sav
- World_Student.sav

© 2015 SAGE Publications Terms of Service • Copyright Notice • Privacy Policy

Figure I-3 Student Version Datasets

As you work your way through this book, you will modify these datasets—recoding some variables, computing new variables, and otherwise tailoring the datasets to suit your purposes. You will need to make personal copies of the datasets and store them on a removable drive, such as a USB flash drive.

When you begin each chapter's guided examples, or when you do the exercises, you will want to insert your personal media into the appropriate computer drive. SPSS will read the data from the drive. (Chapter 1 covers this operation in detail.) If you make any changes to a dataset, you can save the newly modified dataset directly to your drive. Alternatively, your computer lab's administrator may permit you to work on datasets that have been copied to the lab computer's desktop or to a folder designated for such a purpose. In any case, if you have modified a dataset during a data analysis session, it is important that you copy the dataset to your personal drive and take the datasets with you.

SPSS FULL VERSION AND STUDENT VERSION: WHAT IS THE DIFFERENCE?

Campus computer labs run Full Version SPSS. Your institution may offer Full Version SPSS as an app, or you may have rented it. Alternatively, along with this workbook, you may have purchased Student Version SPSS. After you install Student Version, you can run SPSS from your PC or laptop.

In terms of the guided examples and exercises in this book, how does Student Version compare with Full Version? Here are four facts worth knowing:

1. Chapter 1 through Chapter 9: Student Version users will analyze States_Student or World_Student. Output will be identical in every respect to Full Version output.
2. Chapter 1 through Chapter 5: Student Version users will analyze NES2012_Student_A or GSS2012_Student_A. Student Version output will not be the same as Full Version output.
3. Chapter 6 through Chapter 9: Student Version users will analyze NES2012_Student_B or GSS2012_Student_B. Student Version output will not be the same as Full Version output.
4. Student Version will not perform logistic regression, covered in Chapter 10.[4]

These similarities and differences are summarized in the table that follows:

Version of SPSS				
Full Version		Student Version		
Dataset	*Chapters*	*Dataset*	*Chapters*	*Same output as Full Version?*
GSS2012	All	GSS2012_Student_A	1 through 5	No
		GSS2012_Student_B	6 through 9	No
NES2012	All	NES2012_Student_A	1 through 5	No
		NES2012_Student_B	6 through 9	No
States	All	States_Student	1 through 9	Yes
World	All	World_Student	1 through 9	Yes

NOTES

1. GSS2012 was created from the General Social Survey 1972–2012 Cumulative Data File. Tom W. Smith, Michael Hout, and Peter V. Marsden. General Social Survey, 1972–2012 [Cumulative File], ICPSR34802-v1 (Storrs, Conn.: Roper Center for Public Opinion Research, University of Connecticut; Ann Arbor, Mich.: Inter-university Consortium for Political and Social Research [distributors], 2013-09-11). http://doi.org/10.3886/ICPSR34802.v1.
2. The American National Election Studies (ANES; http://www.electionstudies.org). The ANES 2012 Time Series Study [dataset]. Stanford University and the University of Michigan [producers]. These materials are based on work supported by the National Science Foundation under grants SES-0937727 and SES-0937715, Stanford University, and the University of Michigan. Any opinions, findings, and conclusions or recommendations expressed in these materials are those of the author and do not necessarily reflect the views of the funding organizations.
3. http://www.pippanorris.com.
4. Student Version will not handle datasets containing more than 50 variables or having more than 1,500 cases. To get around these limitations, the author split NES2012 into two sets (NES2012_Student_A and NES2012_Student_B) and split GSS2012 into two sets (GSS2012_Student_A and GSS2012_Student_B), each of which contains fewer than 50 variables and no more than 1,500 cases. Cases were selected by taking random samples from the full datasets. The Full Version States and World datasets have more than 50 variables. States_Student and World_Student were created by deleting variables that are not used in this book's guided examples or exercises.

1 Introduction to SPSS

Watch a screencast of the guided examples in this chapter.
edge.sagepub.com/pollock

Suppose you were hired by a telephone-polling firm to interview a large number of respondents. Your job is to find out and record three characteristics of each person you interview: age, educational attainment, and ideological leanings. The natural human tendency would be to record these attributes in words. For example, you might describe a respondent this way: "The respondent is 22 years old, has a college degree, and is ideologically moderate." This would be a good thumbnail description, easily interpreted by another person. To SPSS, though, it would make no sense at all. Whereas people excel at recognizing and manipulating words, SPSS excels at recognizing and manipulating numbers. This is why researchers devise a *coding system*, a set of numeric identifiers for the different values of a variable. For one of the above variables, age, a coding scheme would be straightforward: Simply record the respondent's age in number of years, 22. In recording information about education and ideology, however, a different set of rules is needed. For example, the General Social Survey (GSS) applies these codes for education (named educ_4 in the dataset) and ideology (polviews):

Variable (GSS2012 variable name)	Response	Code
Education (educ_4)	Less than high school	1
	High school	2
	Some college	3
	College degree or higher	4
Ideological views (polviews)	Extremely liberal	1
	Liberal	2
	Slightly liberal	3
	Moderate	4
	Slightly conservative	5
	Conservative	6
	Extremely conservative	7

Thus, the narrative profile "the respondent is 22 years old, has a college degree, and is moderate" becomes "22 4 4" to SPSS. SPSS doesn't really care what the numbers stand for. As long as SPSS has numeric data, it will crunch the numbers—telling you the mean age of all respondents or the modal level of educational attainment. It is important, therefore, to provide SPSS with labels for each code so that the software's analytic work makes sense to the user. Accordingly, the SPSS Data Editor has two "views." The Data View shows the codes that SPSS recognizes and analyzes. The Variable View, among other useful features, shows the word labels that the researcher has assigned to the numeric codes.

THE DATA EDITOR

Open the 2012 General Social Survey, GSS2012, and see how this works. (If you are using Student Version, open GSS2012_Student_A. You will use GSS2012_Student_A through Chapter 5.) Locate GSS2012 in the folder where you saved it. Double-click the file to open it. SPSS opens the data file and displays the Data Editor (Figure 1-1). Notice the two tabs at the bottom of the window: Data View and Variable View. Turn your attention to the Data View. (Make sure the Data View tab is clicked.) This shows how all the cases are organized for analysis. Information for each case occupies a separate row. The variables, given brief yet descriptive names, appear along the columns of the editor. You can tell that the first respondent in the dataset is 22 years old. You can also see that this respondent has a college degree (coded 4 on the variable named educ_4) and is a moderate (coded 4 on polviews). To paint a more complete word-portrait of this respondent, however, you need to see how all the variables are coded. To reveal this information, click the Variable View tab (Figure 1-2). This view shows complete information on the meaning and measurement of each variable in the dataset. (You can adjust the width of a column by clicking, holding, and dragging the column border.)

The most frequently used variable information is contained in Name, Label, Values, and Missing. Name is the brief descriptor recognized by SPSS when it does analysis. Names can be up to 64 characters in length, although they need to begin with a letter (not a number). Plus, names must not contain any special characters, such as dashes or commas, although underscores are okay. You are encouraged to make good use of Label, a long descriptor

Figure 1-1 SPSS Data Editor: Data View

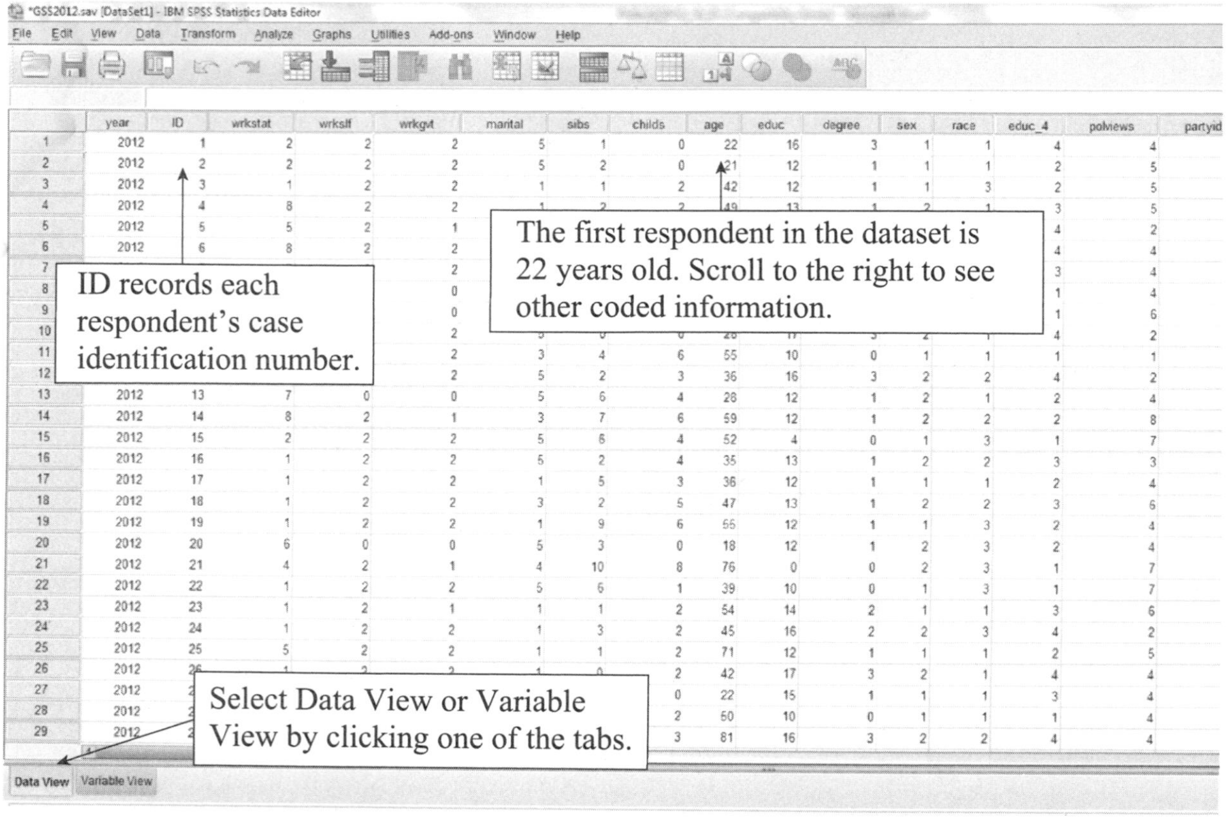

*GSS2012.sav [DataSet1] - IBM SPSS Statistics Data Editor

File Edit View Data Transform Analyze Graphs Utilities Add-ons Window Help

	year	ID	wrkstat	wrkslf	wrkgvt	marital	sibs	childs	age	educ	degree	sex	race	educ_4	polviews	partyid
1	2012	1	2	2	2	5	1	0	22	16	3	1	1	4	4	
2	2012	2	2	2	2	5	2	0	21	12	1	1	1	2	5	
3	2012	3	1	2	2	1	1	2	42	12	1	1	3	2	5	
4	2012	4	8	2	2	1	2	2	49	13	1	2	1	3	5	
5	2012	5	5	2	1									4	2	
6	2012	6	8	2	2									4	4	
7					2									3	4	
8					0									1	4	
9					0									1	6	
10					2									4	2	
11					2	3	4	6	55	10	0	1	1	1	1	
12					2	5	2	3	36	16	3	2	2	4	2	
13	2012	13	7	0	0	5	6	4	28	12	1	2	1	2	4	
14	2012	14	8	2	1	3	7	6	59	12	1	2	2	2	8	
15	2012	15	2	2	2	5	6	4	52	4	0	1	3	1	7	
16	2012	16	1	2	2	5	2	4	35	13	1	2	2	3	3	
17	2012	17	1	2	2	1	5	3	36	12	1	1	1	2	4	
18	2012	18	1	2	2	3	2	5	47	13	1	2	2	3	6	
19	2012	19	1	2	2	1	9	6	66	12	1	1	3	2	4	
20	2012	20	6	0	0	5	3	0	18	12	1	2	3	2	4	
21	2012	21	4	2	1	4	10	8	76	0	0	2	3	1	7	
22	2012	22	1	2	2	5	6	1	39	10	0	1	3	1	7	
23	2012	23	1	2	1	1	1	2	54	14	2	1	1	3	6	
24	2012	24	1	2	2	1	3	2	45	16	2	2	3	4	2	
25	2012	25	5	2	2	1	1	2	71	12	1	1	1	2	5	
26	2012							2	42	17	3	2	1	4	4	
27	2012							0	22	15	1	1	1	3	4	
28	2012							2	60	10	0	1	1	1	4	
29	2012							3	81	16	3	2	2	4	4	

Data View | Variable View

ID records each respondent's case identification number.

The first respondent in the dataset is 22 years old. Scroll to the right to see other coded information.

Select Data View or Variable View by clicking one of the tabs.

Figure 1-2 SPSS Data Editor: Variable View

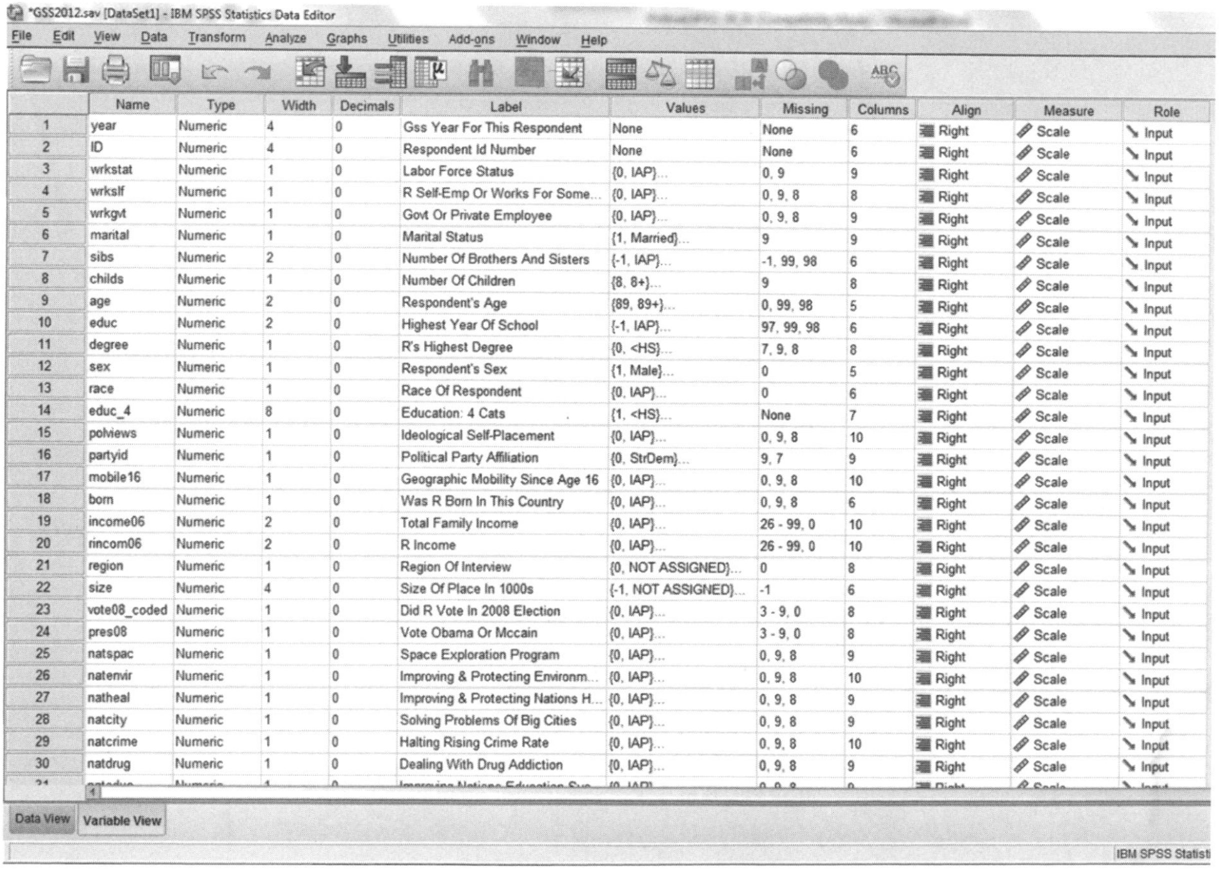

*GSS2012.sav [DataSet1] - IBM SPSS Statistics Data Editor

File Edit View Data Transform Analyze Graphs Utilities Add-ons Window Help

	Name	Type	Width	Decimals	Label	Values	Missing	Columns	Align	Measure	Role
1	year	Numeric	4	0	Gss Year For This Respondent	None	None	6	Right	Scale	Input
2	ID	Numeric	4	0	Respondent Id Number	None	None	6	Right	Scale	Input
3	wrkstat	Numeric	1	0	Labor Force Status	{0, IAP}...	0, 9	9	Right	Scale	Input
4	wrkslf	Numeric	1	0	R Self-Emp Or Works For Some...	{0, IAP}...	0, 9, 8	8	Right	Scale	Input
5	wrkgvt	Numeric	1	0	Govt Or Private Employee	{0, IAP}...	0, 9, 8	9	Right	Scale	Input
6	marital	Numeric	1	0	Marital Status	{1, Married}...	9	9	Right	Scale	Input
7	sibs	Numeric	2	0	Number Of Brothers And Sisters	{-1, IAP}...	-1, 99, 98	6	Right	Scale	Input
8	childs	Numeric	1	0	Number Of Children	{8, 8+}...	9	8	Right	Scale	Input
9	age	Numeric	2	0	Respondent's Age	{89, 89+}...	0, 99, 98	5	Right	Scale	Input
10	educ	Numeric	2	0	Highest Year Of School	{-1, IAP}...	97, 99, 98	6	Right	Scale	Input
11	degree	Numeric	1	0	R's Highest Degree	{0, <HS}...	7, 9, 8	8	Right	Scale	Input
12	sex	Numeric	1	0	Respondent's Sex	{1, Male}...	0	5	Right	Scale	Input
13	race	Numeric	1	0	Race Of Respondent	{0, IAP}...	0	6	Right	Scale	Input
14	educ_4	Numeric	8	0	Education: 4 Cats	{1, <HS}...	None	7	Right	Scale	Input
15	polviews	Numeric	1	0	Ideological Self-Placement	{0, IAP}...	0, 9, 8	10	Right	Scale	Input
16	partyid	Numeric	1	0	Political Party Affiliation	{0, StrDem}...	9, 7	9	Right	Scale	Input
17	mobile16	Numeric	1	0	Geographic Mobility Since Age 16	{0, IAP}...	0, 9, 8	10	Right	Scale	Input
18	born	Numeric	1	0	Was R Born In This Country	{0, IAP}...	0, 9, 8	6	Right	Scale	Input
19	income06	Numeric	2	0	Total Family Income	{0, IAP}...	26 - 99, 0	10	Right	Scale	Input
20	rincom06	Numeric	2	0	R Income	{0, IAP}...	26 - 99, 0	10	Right	Scale	Input
21	region	Numeric	1	0	Region Of Interview	{0, NOT ASSIGNED}...	0	8	Right	Scale	Input
22	size	Numeric	4	0	Size Of Place In 1000s	{-1, NOT ASSIGNED}...	-1	6	Right	Scale	Input
23	vote08_coded	Numeric	1	0	Did R Vote In 2008 Election	{0, IAP}...	3 - 9, 0	8	Right	Scale	Input
24	pres08	Numeric	1	0	Vote Obama Or Mccain	{0, IAP}...	3 - 9, 0	8	Right	Scale	Input
25	natspac	Numeric	1	0	Space Exploration Program	{0, IAP}...	0, 9, 8	9	Right	Scale	Input
26	natenvir	Numeric	1	0	Improving & Protecting Environm...	{0, IAP}...	0, 9, 8	10	Right	Scale	Input
27	natheal	Numeric	1	0	Improving & Protecting Nations H...	{0, IAP}...	0, 9, 8	9	Right	Scale	Input
28	natcity	Numeric	1	0	Solving Problems Of Big Cities	{0, IAP}...	0, 9, 8	9	Right	Scale	Input
29	natcrime	Numeric	1	0	Halting Rising Crime Rate	{0, IAP}...	0, 9, 8	10	Right	Scale	Input
30	natdrug	Numeric	1	0	Dealing With Drug Addiction	{0, IAP}...	0, 9, 8	9	Right	Scale	Input

Data View | Variable View

IBM SPSS Statisti

(up to 256 characters are allowed), for each variable name. For example, when SPSS analyzes the variable mobile16, it will look in the Variable View for a label. If it finds one, then it will label the results of its analysis by using Label instead of Name. So mobile16 shows up as "Geographic Mobility Since Age 16"—a bit more descriptive than "mobile16." Just as Label permits a wordier description for Name, Values attaches word labels to the numeric value codes. To find out the value labels for mobile16, click the mouse anywhere in the Values cell and then click the gray button that appears. A Value Labels window opens, revealing the labels that SPSS will attach to the numeric codes of mobile16 (Figure 1-3). Unless you instruct it to do otherwise, SPSS will apply these labels to its analysis of mobile16. (Click the Cancel button in the Value Labels window to return to the Variable View.)

Finally, a word about Missing. Sometimes a dataset does not have complete information for some variables on a number of cases. In coding the data, researchers typically give a special numeric code to these missing values. In coding mobile16, for example, the GSS coders entered a value of 0, 8, or 9 for respondents who were not asked the question ("IAP"), did not know ("DK"), or for whom the information is otherwise not available ("NA"). Because these numeric codes have been set to missing (and thus appear in the Missing column), SPSS does not recognize them as valid codes and will not include them in an analysis of mobile16. In many cases, the author has set most missing values in the datasets to *system-missing*, which SPSS automatically removes from the analysis. However, when you use an existing variable to create a new variable, SPSS may not automatically transfer missing values on the existing variable to missing values on the new variable. Later in this volume, we discuss how to handle such situations.

A MUST-DO: SETTING OPTIONS FOR VARIABLE LISTS

Now you have a feel for the number-oriented side and the word-oriented side of SPSS. Before looking at how SPSS produces and handles output, you must do one more thing. To ensure that all the examples in this workbook correspond to what you see on your screen, you will need to follow the steps given in this section when you open each dataset for the first time.

Figure 1-3 Value Labels Box

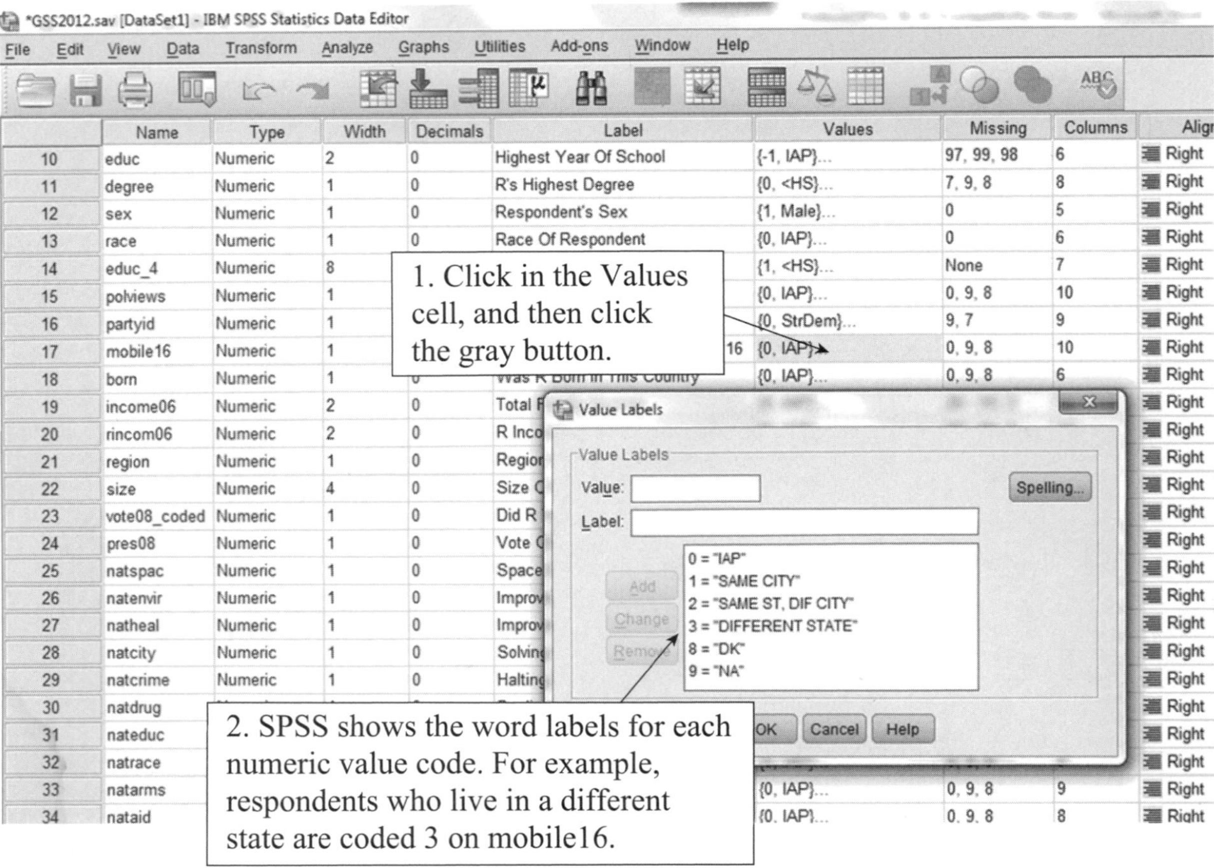

DO THIS NOW: In the main menu bar of the Data Editor, click Edit → Options. Make sure that the General tab is clicked. (See Figure 1-4.) If the radio button Display names *and* the radio button Alphabetical were already selected when you opened the Options menu, you are set to go. Click Cancel. If, however, Display names and/or Alphabetical were not already selected when you opened the Options menu, select them (as in Figure 1-4). Click Apply. Click OK, returning to the Data Editor. When you open a new dataset for the first time, go to Edit → Options and ensure that Display names/Alphabetical are selected and applied.

THE VIEWER

We will run through a quick analysis and see how SPSS handles variables and output. On the main menu bar, click Analyze → Descriptive Statistics → Frequencies. The Frequencies window appears (Figure 1-5). There are two panels. On the right is the (currently empty) Variable(s) panel. This is the panel where you enter the variables you want to analyze. On the left you see the names of all the variables in GSS2012 in alphabetical order, just as you specified in the Options menu. Although the names are not terribly informative, complete coding information is just a (right) mouse click away. Suppose you want to analyze educ_4. Scroll the alphabetized list until you find educ_4. (*Hint*: Select any variable in the variable list. Type "e" on the keyboard. SPSS will go to the first e's in the list.) Put the mouse pointer on the variable, educ_4, and right-click. Then click on Variable Information. As shown in Figure 1-6, SPSS retrieves and displays the label (Education: 4 Cats), name (educ_4), and, most usefully, the value labels for the numeric codes. (To see all the codes, click the drop-down arrow in the Value Labels box.)

Return the mouse to the Frequencies window and click educ_4 into the Variable(s) panel. (Click on educ_4 and then click the arrow between the panels.) Click OK. SPSS runs the analysis and displays the results in the Viewer (Figure 1-7). The Viewer has two panes. In the Outline pane, SPSS keeps a running log of the analyses you are performing. The Outline pane references each element in the Contents pane, which reports the results of your analyses. In this book we are interested exclusively in the Contents pane. Reduce the size of the Outline

Figure 1-4 Setting Options for Variable Lists

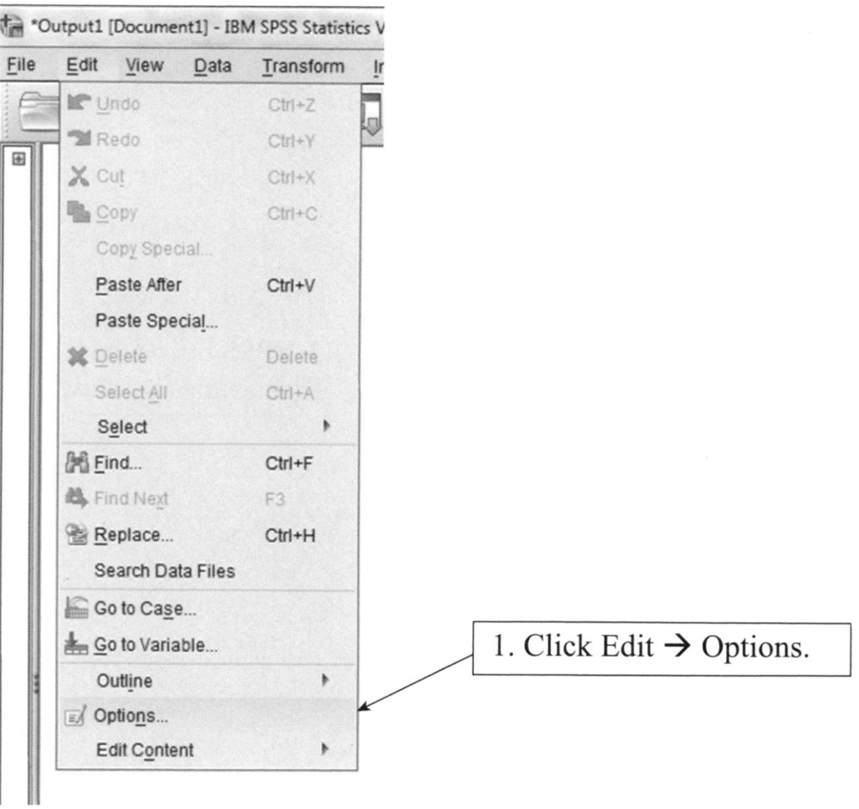

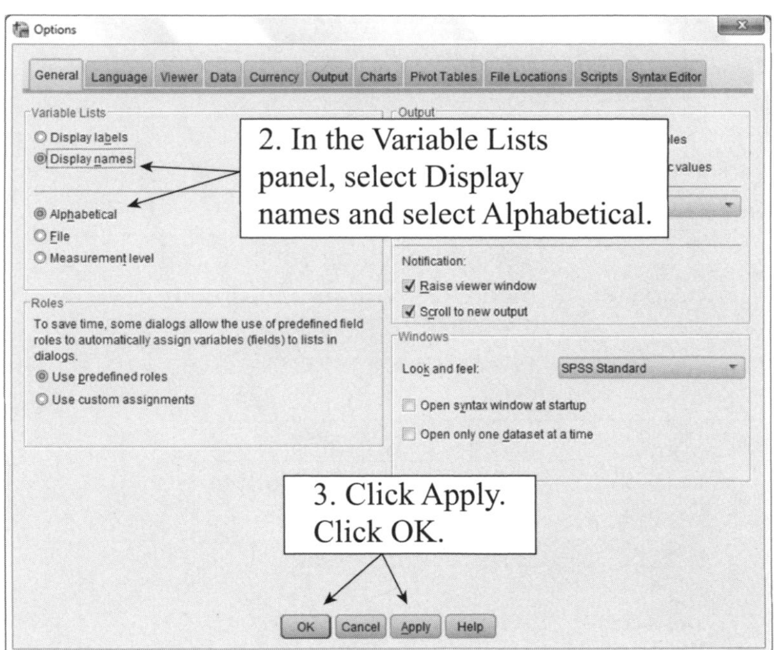

pane by first placing the cursor on the Pane divider. Click and hold the left button of the mouse and then move the Pane divider over to the left-hand border of the Viewer. The Viewer should now look like Figure 1-8. The output for educ_4 shows you the frequency distribution, with value codes labeled. In Chapter 2 we discuss frequency analysis in more detail. Our immediate purpose is to become familiar with SPSS output.

Here are some key facts about the Viewer. First, the Viewer is a separate file, created by you during your analysis of the data. It is completely distinct from the data file. Whereas SPSS data files all have the file extension *.sav, Viewer files have the file extension *.spv. The output can be saved, under a name that you choose, and then

Figure 1-5 Requesting Frequencies

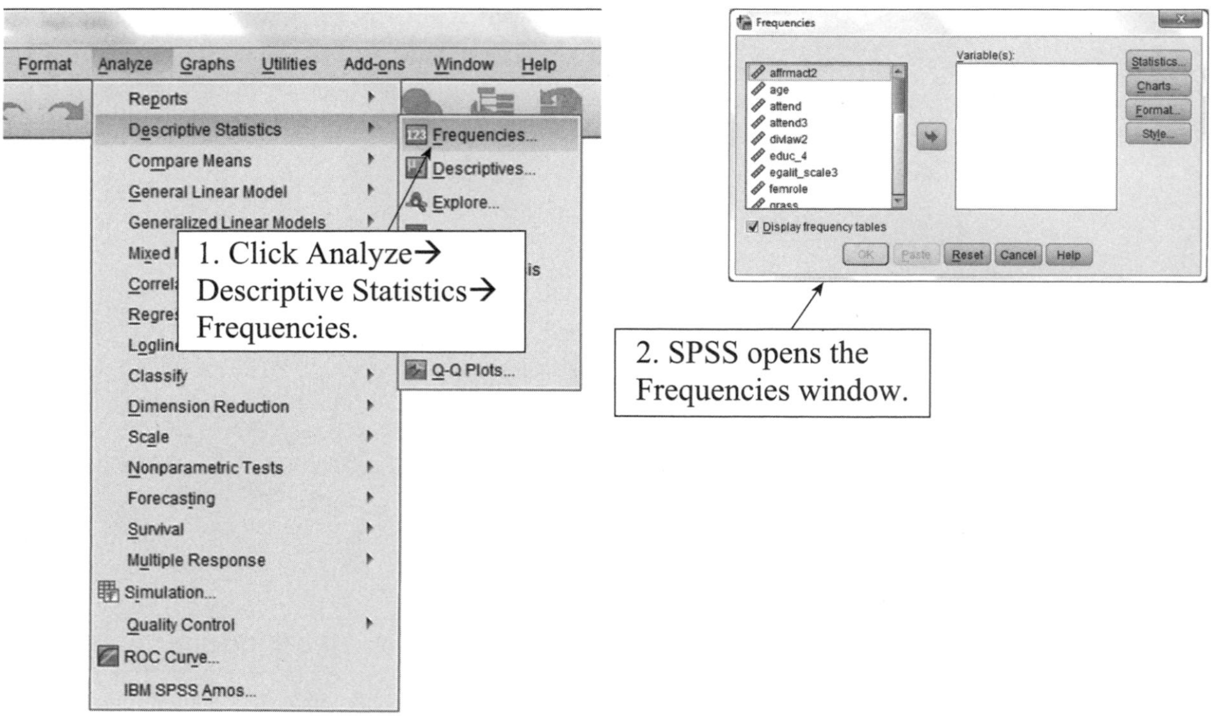

Figure 1-6 Retrieving Coding Information

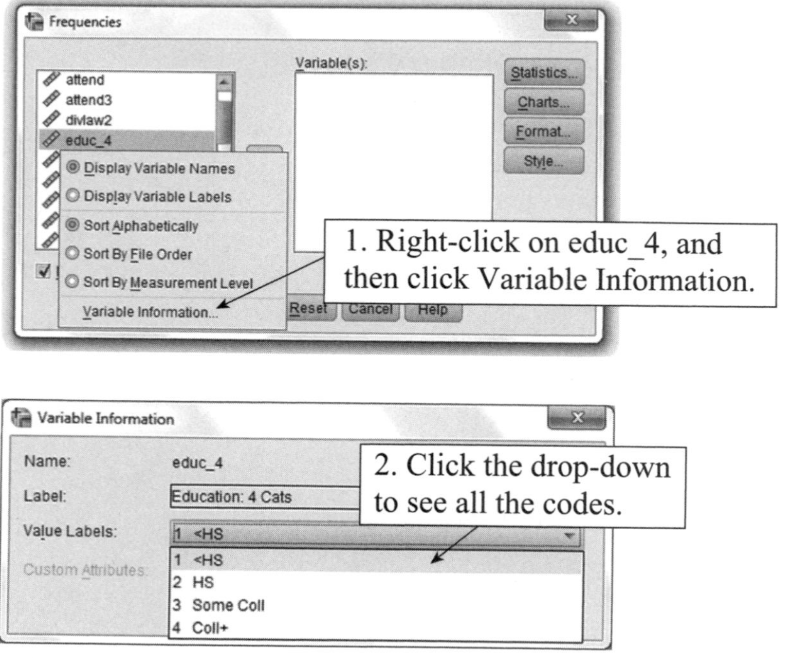

reopened later. Second, the output from each succeeding analysis does not overwrite the file. Rather, it appends new results to the Viewer file. If you were to run another analysis for a different variable, SPSS would dump the results in the Viewer below the analysis you just performed. Third, the quickest way to return to the Data Editor is to click the starred icon on the menu bar, as shown in Figure 1-8. And, of course, Windows accumulates icons for all open files along the bottom Taskbar. Finally, you may select any part of the output file, print it, or copy and paste it into a word processing program.

Figure 1-7 SPSS Viewer: Outline Pane and Contents Pane

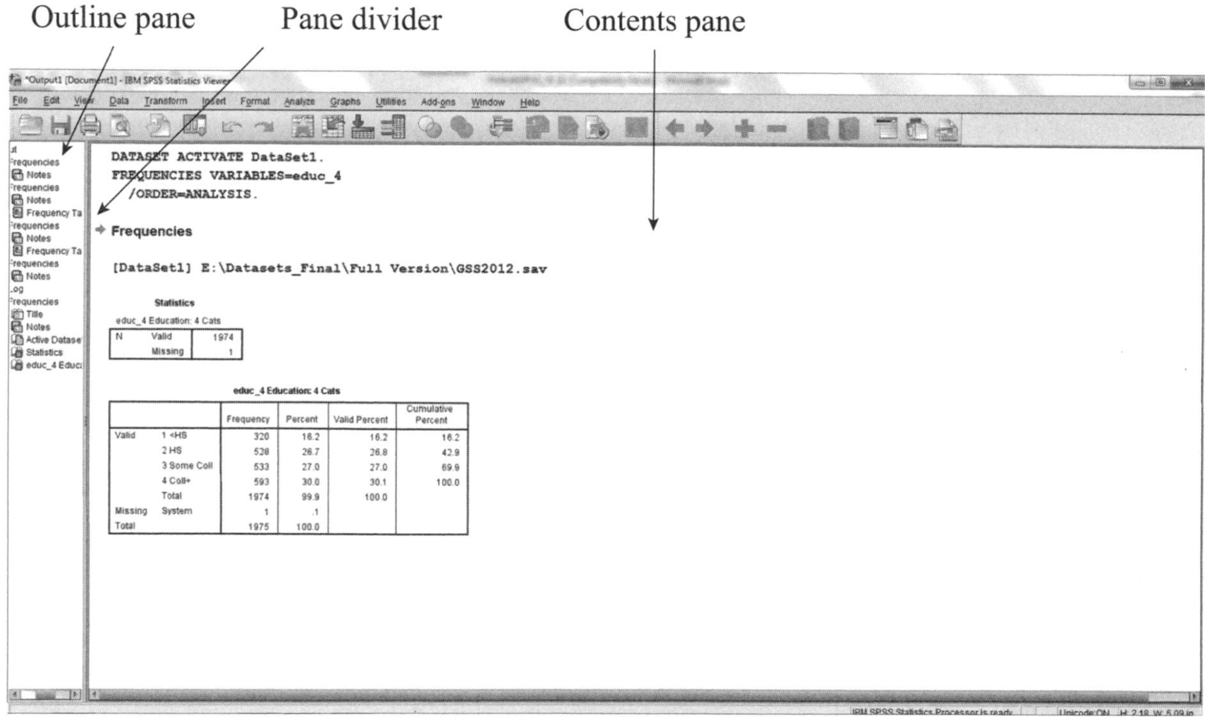

Figure 1-8 SPSS Viewer: Outline Pane Minimized

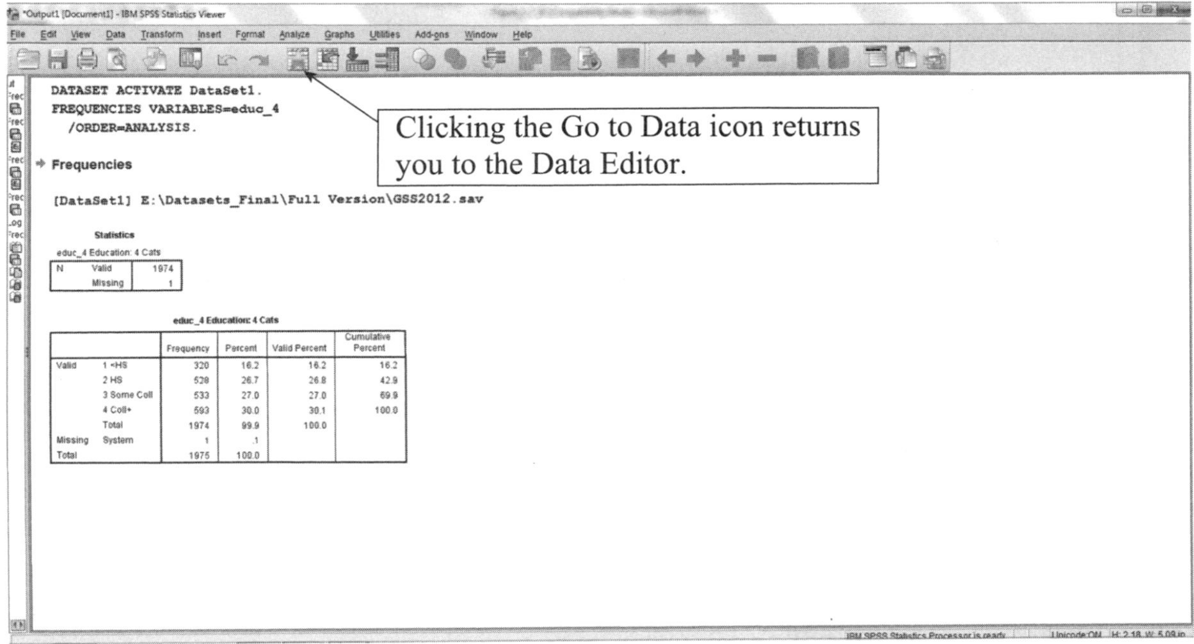

Many of the exercises in this workbook will ask you to print the results of your SPSS analyses, so let's cover the print procedure. We'll also address a routine necessity: saving output.

Selecting, Printing, and Saving Output

Printing desired results requires, first, that you select the output or portion of output you want to print. A quick and easy way to select a single table or chart is to place the cursor anywhere on the desired object and click once.

For example, if you want to print the educ_4 frequency distribution, place the cursor on the frequency table and click. A red arrow appears in the left-hand margin next to the table (Figure 1-9). Now click the Printer icon on the Viewer menu bar. The Print window opens. In the window's Print Range panel, the radio button next to "Selected output" should already be clicked. Clicking OK would send the frequency table to the printer. To select more than one table or graph, hold down the Control key (Ctrl) while selecting the desired output with the mouse. Thus, if you wanted to print the frequency table and the statistics table, first click on one of the desired tables. While holding down the Ctrl key, click on the other table. SPSS will select both tables.

To save your output, simply click the familiar Save icon on the Viewer menu bar (refer to Figure 1-9). Browse for an appropriate location. Invent a file name (but preserve the .spv extension), such as "chap1.spv," and click Save. SPSS saves all of the information in the Viewer to the file chap1.spv. Saving your output protects your work. Plus, the output file can always be reopened later. Suppose you are in the middle of a series of SPSS analyses and you want to stop and return later. You can save the Viewer file, as described here, and exit SPSS. When you return, you start SPSS and load a data file (like GSS2012) into the Data Editor. In the main menu bar of the Data Editor, you click File → Open → Output, find your .spv file, and open it. Then you can pick up where you left off.

Figure 1-9 Selecting, Printing, and Saving Output

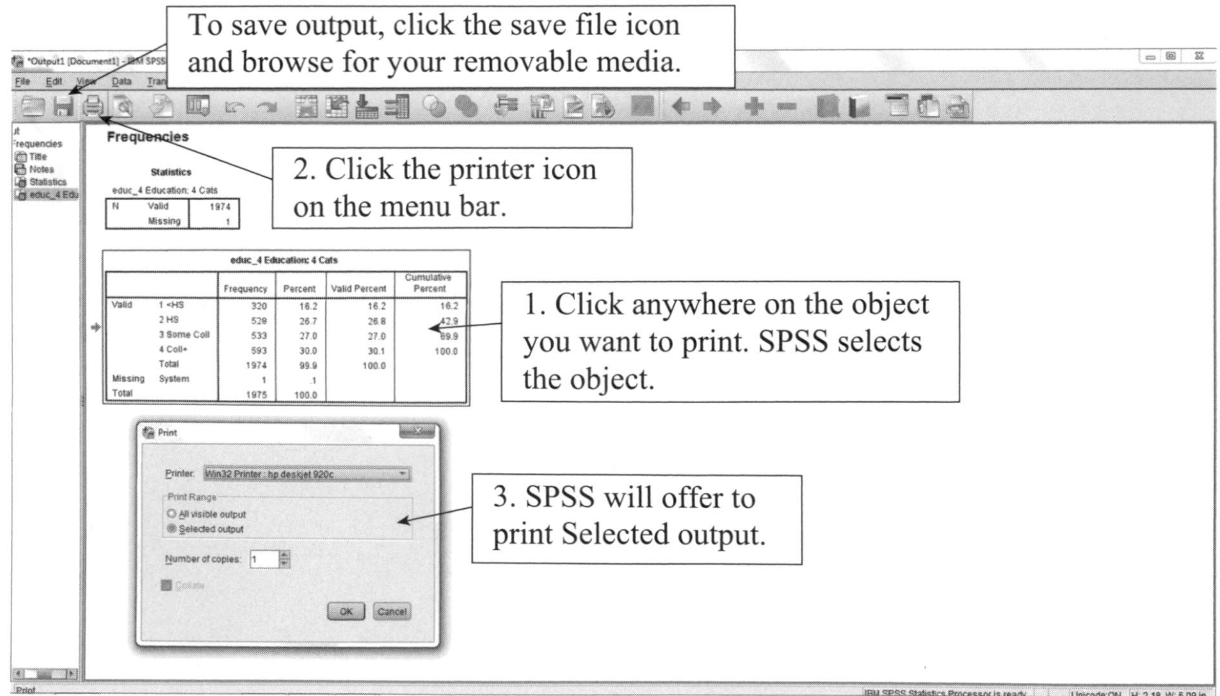

EXERCISES

1. (Dataset: GSS2012. Variables: income06, attend.) Earlier we spent some time using the Data View and the Variable View to describe the first respondent in the GSS2012 dataset. In this exercise you will use your familiarity with the Data Editor to find out this respondent's income (income06) and how often this respondent attends religious services (attend).

   A. With GSS2012 open, go to the Data View. What numeric code does the first respondent have on income06? A code of (fill in the blank) ______________. Go to the Variable View. Just as you did earlier in this chapter, find income06 and click in the Values cell. What is this respondent's income? (circle one)

   $25,000 to $29,999 $60,000 to $74,999 $150,000 or over

B. Return to the Data View. What is this respondent's code on the variable attend? A code of (fill in the blank) ______________. Go to the Variable View. How often does this respondent attend religious services? (circle one)

Never　　　　Once a year　　　　2–3 times a month

2. Suppose that you have just opened the World, States, or NES2012 dataset for the first time. The first thing you do is to click Edit → Options and consider the Variable Lists panel of the General tab. You must make sure that which two choices are selected and applied? (check two)

❑ Display labels

❑ Display names

❑ Alphabetical

❑ File

❑ Measurement level

2 Descriptive Statistics

Watch a screencast of the guided examples in this chapter.
edge.sagepub.com/pollock

Procedures Covered

Analyze → Descriptive Statistics → Frequencies

Analyze → Reports → Case Summaries

Analyzing descriptive statistics is the most basic—and sometimes the most informative—form of analysis you will do. Descriptive statistics reveal two attributes of a variable: its typical value (central tendency) and its spread (degree of dispersion or variation). The precision with which you can describe central tendency for any given variable depends on the variable's level of measurement. For nominal-level variables you can identify the *mode,* the most common value of the variable. For ordinal-level variables, those whose categories can be ranked, you can find the mode and the *median*—the value of the variable that divides the cases into two equal-size groups. For interval-level variables you can obtain the mode, median, and arithmetic *mean,* the sum of all values divided by the number of cases.

In this chapter you will use Analyze → Descriptive Statistics → Frequencies to obtain appropriate measures of central tendency, and you will learn to make informed judgments about variation. With the correct prompts, the Frequencies procedure also provides valuable graphic support—bar charts and (for interval variables) histograms. These tools are essential for distilling useful information from datasets having hundreds of anonymous cases, such as the American National Election Study (NES2012) or the General Social Survey (GSS2012). For smaller datasets with aggregated units, such as the States and World datasets, SPSS offers an additional procedure: Analyze → Reports → Case Summaries. Case Summaries lets you see firsthand how specific cases are distributed across a variable that you find especially interesting.

INTERPRETING MEASURES OF CENTRAL TENDENCY AND VARIATION

Finding a variable's central tendency is ordinarily a straightforward exercise. Simply read the computer output and report the numbers. Describing a variable's degree of dispersion or variation, however, often requires informed judgment.[1] Here is a general rule that applies to any variable at any level of measurement: A variable has no dispersion if all the cases—states, countries, people, or whatever—fall into the same value of the variable. A variable has maximum dispersion if the cases are spread evenly across all values of the variable. In other words, the number of cases in one category equals the number of cases in every other category.

Central tendency and variation work together in providing a complete description of any variable. Some variables have an easily identified typical value and show little dispersion. For example, suppose you were to ask a large number of U.S. citizens what sort of economic system they believe to be the best: capitalism, communism, or socialism. What would be the modal response, or the economic system preferred by most people? Capitalism. Would there be a great deal of dispersion, with large numbers of people choosing the alternatives, communism or socialism? Probably not.

In other instances, however, you may find that one value of a variable has a more tenuous grasp on the label *typical.* And the variable may exhibit more dispersion, with the cases spread out more evenly across the variable's other values. For example, suppose a large sample of voting-age adults were asked, in the weeks preceding a presidential election, how interested they are in the campaign: very interested, somewhat interested, or not very interested. Among your own acquaintances you probably know a number of people who fit into each category. So even if one category, such as "somewhat interested," is the median, many people will likely be found at the extremes of "very interested" and "not very interested." In this instance, the amount of dispersion in a variable—its degree of spread—is essential to understanding and describing it.

These and other points are best understood by working through some guided examples. For the next several analyses, you will use GSS2012. Open the dataset by double-clicking the GSS2012 icon. (If you are using SPSS Student Version, open GSS2012_Student_A.) In the Data Editor, click Edit → Options and then click on the General tab. Just as you did with NES2012 in Chapter 1, make sure that the radio buttons in the Variable Lists area are set for Display names and Alphabetical. (If these options are already set, click Cancel. If they are not set, select them, click Apply, and then click OK. Now you are ready to go.)

DESCRIBING NOMINAL VARIABLES

First, you will obtain a frequency distribution and bar chart for a nominal-level variable, zodiac, which records respondents' astrological signs. Click Analyze → Descriptive Statistics → Frequencies. Scroll down to the bottom

Figure 2-1 Obtaining Frequencies and a Bar Chart (nominal variable)

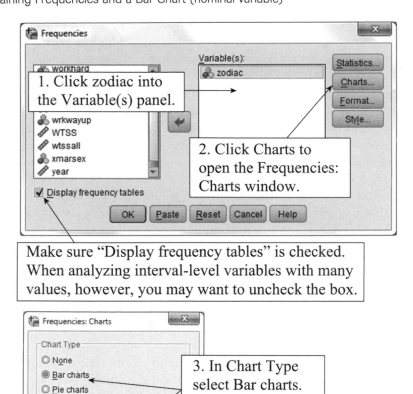

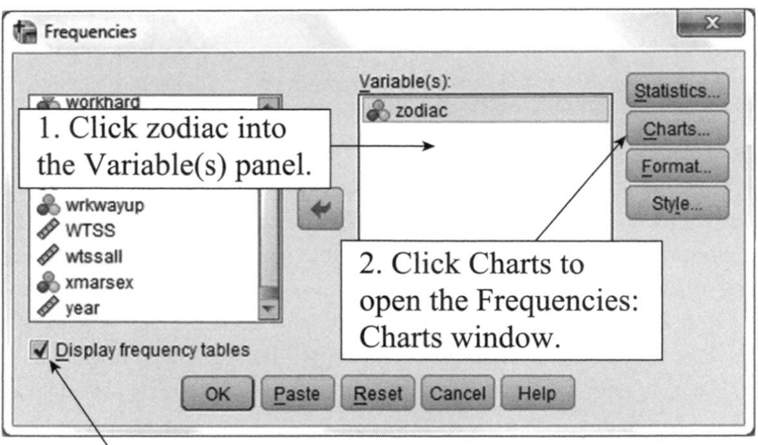

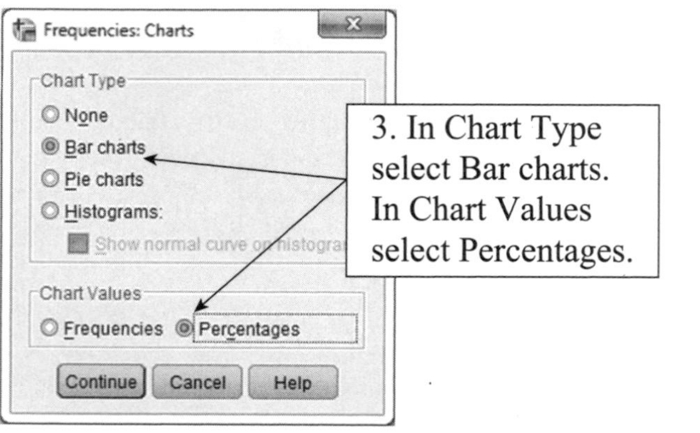

of the left-hand list until you find zodiac. Click zodiac into the Variable(s) panel. To the right of the Variable(s) panel, click the Charts button (Figure 2-1). The Frequencies: Charts window appears. In Chart Type, select Bar charts. In Chart Values, select Percentages. Click Continue, which returns you to the main Frequencies window. Click OK. SPSS runs the analysis.

SPSS has produced two items of interest in the Viewer: a frequency distribution of respondents' astrological signs and a bar chart of the same information. Examine the frequency distribution (Figure 2-2). The value labels for each astrological code appear in the leftmost column, with Aries occupying the top row of numbers and Pisces occupying the bottom row. There are four numeric columns: Frequency, Percent, Valid Percent, and Cumulative Percent. The Frequency column shows raw frequencies, the actual number of respondents having each zodiac sign. Percent is the percentage of *all* respondents, including missing cases, in each category of the variable. Ordinarily the Percent column can be ignored, because we generally are not interested in including missing cases in our description of a variable. Valid Percent is the column to focus on. Valid Percent tells us the percentage of nonmissing responses in each value of zodiac. Finally, Cumulative Percent reports the percentage of cases that fall in *or below* each value of the variable. For ordinal or interval variables, as you will see, the Cumulative Percent column can provide valuable clues about how a variable is distributed. But for nominal variables, which cannot be ranked, the Cumulative Percent column provides no information of value.

Now consider the Valid Percent column more closely. Scroll between the frequency distribution and the bar chart, which depicts the zodiac variable in graphic form (Figure 2-3). What is the mode, the most common astrological sign? For nominal variables, the answer to this question is (almost) always an easy call: Simply find the value with the highest percentage of responses. Leo is the mode. Does this variable have little dispersion or a

Figure 2-2 Frequencies Output (nominal variable)

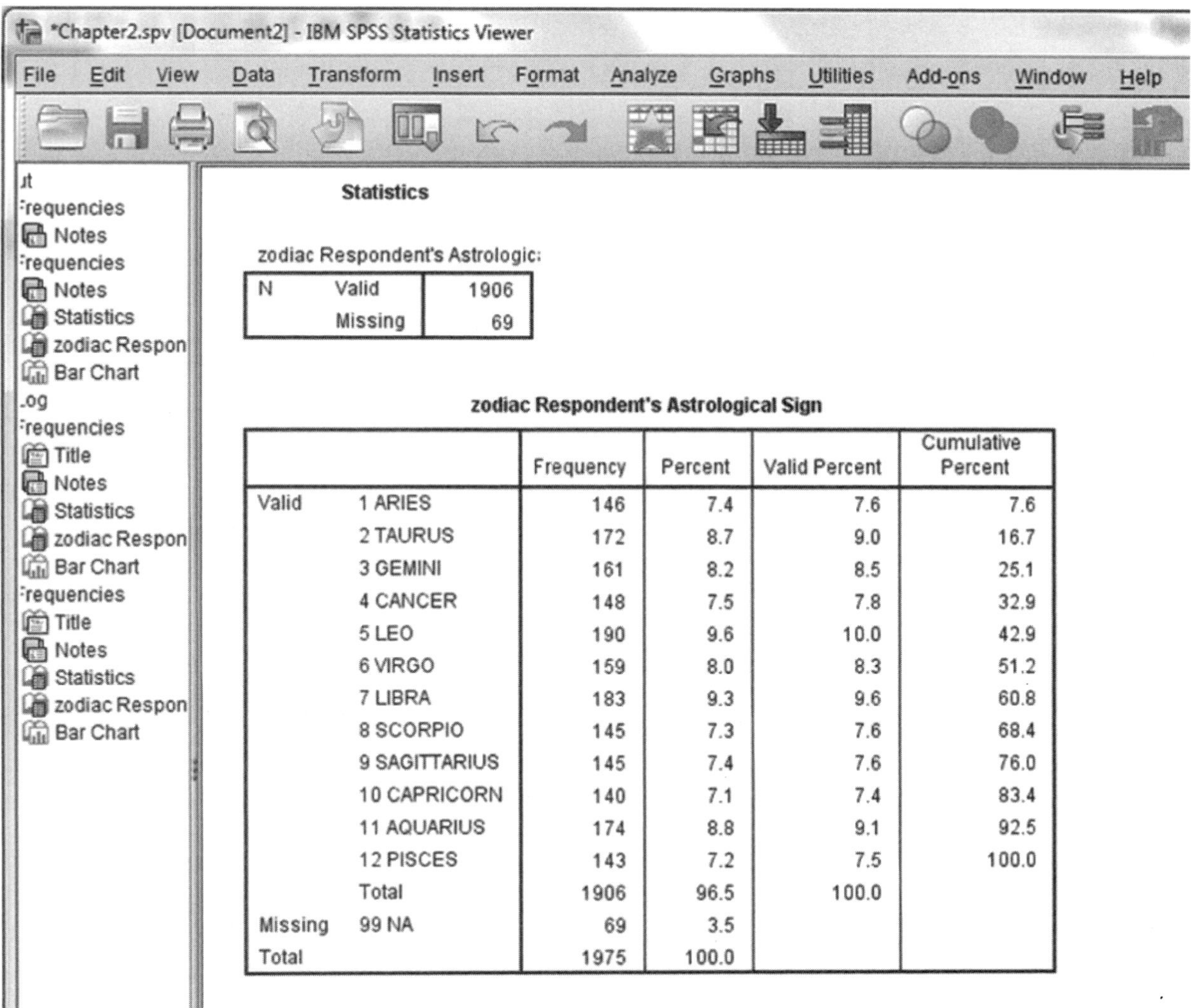

Statistics

zodiac Respondent's Astrologic:

N	Valid	1906
	Missing	69

zodiac Respondent's Astrological Sign

		Frequency	Percent	Valid Percent	Cumulative Percent
Valid	1 ARIES	146	7.4	7.6	7.6
	2 TAURUS	172	8.7	9.0	16.7
	3 GEMINI	161	8.2	8.5	25.1
	4 CANCER	148	7.5	7.8	32.9
	5 LEO	190	9.6	10.0	42.9
	6 VIRGO	159	8.0	8.3	51.2
	7 LIBRA	183	9.3	9.6	60.8
	8 SCORPIO	145	7.3	7.6	68.4
	9 SAGITTARIUS	145	7.4	7.6	76.0
	10 CAPRICORN	140	7.1	7.4	83.4
	11 AQUARIUS	174	8.8	9.1	92.5
	12 PISCES	143	7.2	7.5	100.0
	Total	1906	96.5	100.0	
Missing	99 NA	69	3.5		
Total		1975	100.0		

Figure 2-3 Bar Chart (nominal variable)

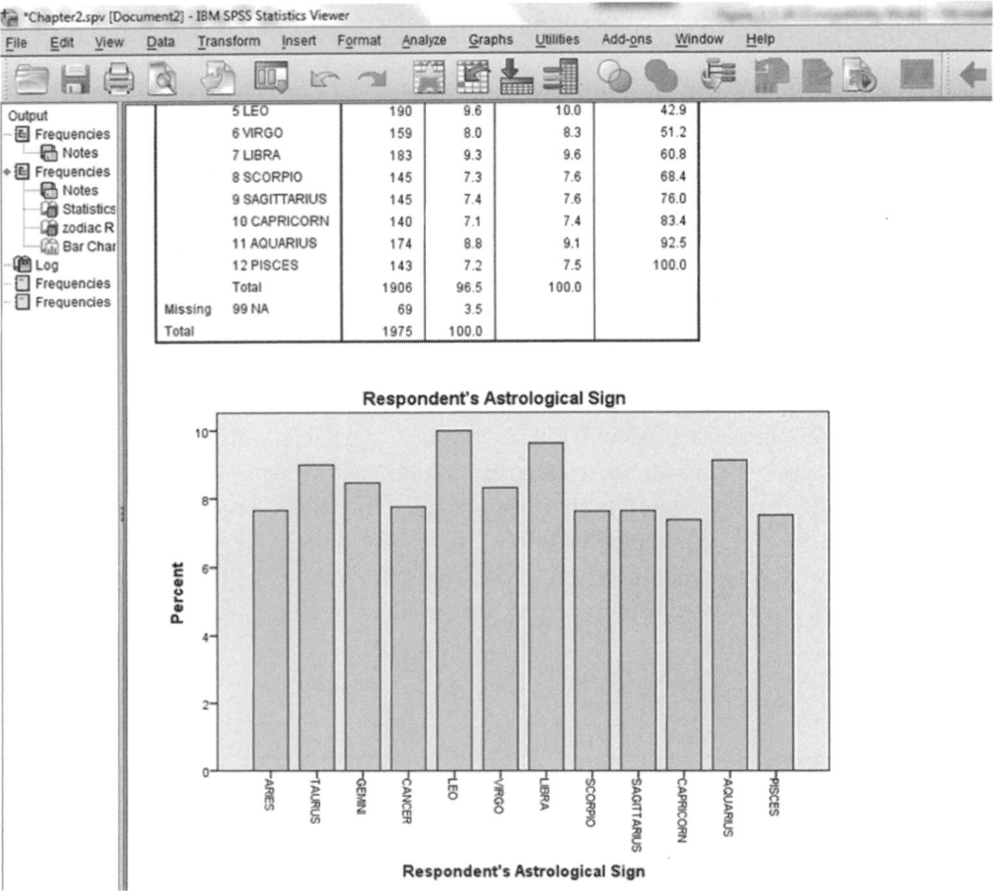

lot of dispersion? Again study the Valid Percent column and the bar chart. Apply the following rule: *A variable has no dispersion if the cases are concentrated in one value of the variable; a variable has maximum dispersion if the cases are spread evenly across all values of the variable.* Are most of the cases concentrated in Leo, or are there many cases in each value of zodiac? Because respondents are spread out—all astrological signs are about equally represented—you would conclude that zodiac has a high level of dispersion.

DESCRIBING ORDINAL VARIABLES

Next, you will analyze and describe two ordinal-level variables, one of which has little variation and the other of which is more spread out. Along the top menu bar of the Viewer, click Analyze → Descriptive Statistics → Frequencies. SPSS remembers the preceding analysis, so zodiac is still in the Variable(s) list. Click zodiac back into the left-hand list. Scroll through the list until you find these variables: helppoor and helpsick. Each of these is a 5-point ordinal scale. Helppoor asks respondents to place themselves on a scale between 1 ("The government should take action to help poor people") and 5 ("People should help themselves"). Helpsick, using a similar 5-point scale, asks respondents about government responsibility or individual responsibility for medical care. Click helppoor and helpsick into the Variable(s) list. SPSS retained your earlier settings for Charts, so accompanying bar charts will appear in the Viewer. Click OK.

SPSS runs the analysis for each variable and produces two frequency distributions, one for helppoor and one for helpsick, followed by two bar charts of the same information. First, focus on helppoor. Scroll back and forth between the frequency distribution (Figure 2-4) and the bar chart (Figure 2-5). Because helppoor is an ordinal variable, you can report both its mode and its median. Its mode, clearly enough, is the response "Agree with both," which contains 44.6 percent of the cases. What about the median? This is where the Cumulative Percent column of the frequency distribution comes into play. *The median for any ordinal (or interval) variable is the*

Figure 2-4 Frequencies Output (ordinal variables)

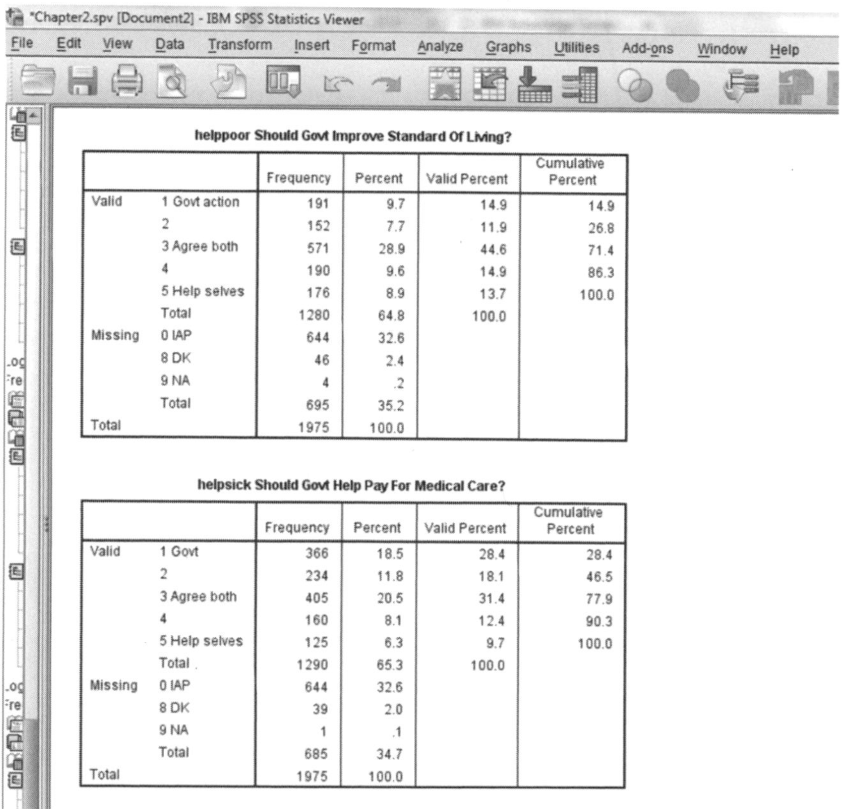

helppoor Should Govt Improve Standard Of Living?

		Frequency	Percent	Valid Percent	Cumulative Percent
Valid	1 Govt action	191	9.7	14.9	14.9
	2	152	7.7	11.9	26.8
	3 Agree both	571	28.9	44.6	71.4
	4	190	9.6	14.9	86.3
	5 Help selves	176	8.9	13.7	100.0
	Total	1280	64.8	100.0	
Missing	0 IAP	644	32.6		
	8 DK	46	2.4		
	9 NA	4	.2		
	Total	695	35.2		
Total		1975	100.0		

helpsick Should Govt Help Pay For Medical Care?

		Frequency	Percent	Valid Percent	Cumulative Percent
Valid	1 Govt	366	18.5	28.4	28.4
	2	234	11.8	18.1	46.5
	3 Agree both	405	20.5	31.4	77.9
	4	160	8.1	12.4	90.3
	5 Help selves	125	6.3	9.7	100.0
	Total	1290	65.3	100.0	
Missing	0 IAP	644	32.6		
	8 DK	39	2.0		
	9 NA	1	.1		
	Total	685	34.7		
Total		1975	100.0		

Figure 2-5 Bar Chart (ordinal variable with low dispersion)

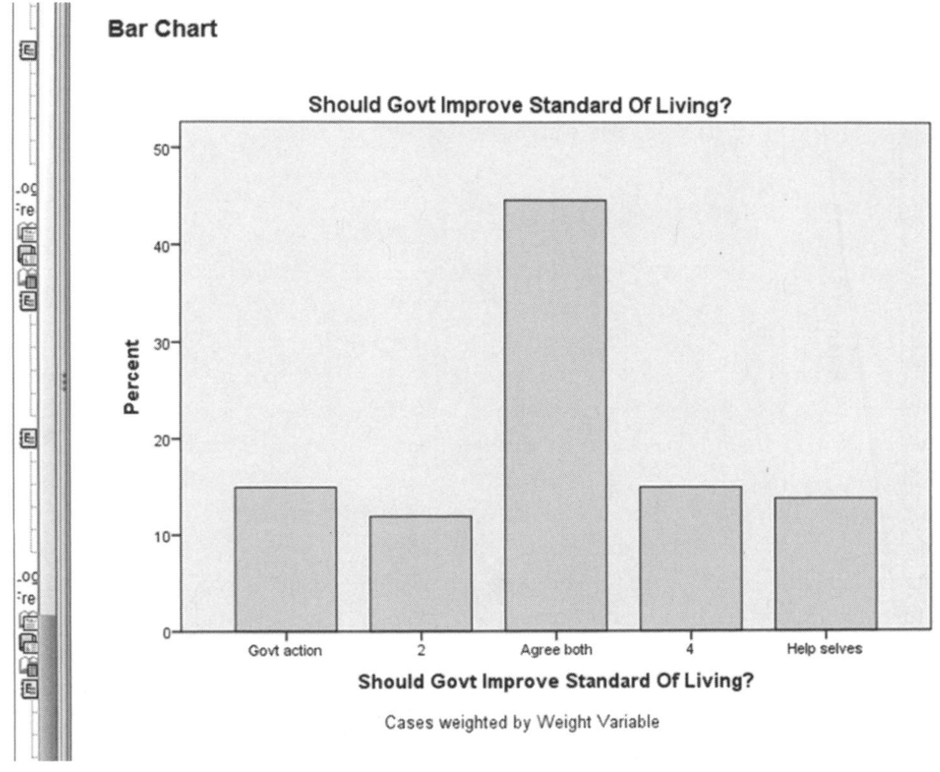

category below which 50 percent of the cases lie. Is the first category, "Govt action," the median? No, this code contains fewer than half of the cases. How about the next higher category? No, again. The Cumulative Percent column still has not reached 50 percent. The median occurs in the "Agree with both" category (cumulative percentage, 71.4).

Now consider the question of whether helppoor has a high degree of dispersion or a low degree of dispersion. If helppoor had a high level of variation, then the percentages of respondents in each response category would be roughly equal, much like the zodiac variable that you analyzed earlier. So, roughly one-fifth of the cases would fall into each of the five response categories: 20 percent in "Govt," 20 percent in response category "2," 20 percent in "Agree with both," 20 percent in response category "4," and 20 percent in "Help selves." If helppoor had no dispersion, then all the cases would fall into one value. That is, one value would have 100 percent of the cases, and each of the other categories would have 0 percent. Which of these two scenarios comes closest to describing the actual distribution of respondents across the values of helppoor? The equal-percentages-in-each-category, high variation scenario? Or the 100-percent-in-one-category, low variation scenario? It seems clear that helppoor is a variable with a relatively low degree of dispersion. "Agree with both," with 44.6 percent of the cases, contains nearly three times as many cases as its nearest rival ("Govt"), and more than three times as many cases as any of the other response categories.

Now contrast helppoor's distribution with the distribution of helpsick (Figure 2-6). Interestingly, helpsick has the same mode as helppoor ("Agree with both," with 31.4 percent of the cases), and the same median (again, "Agree with both," where the cumulative percentage exceeds 50.0). Yet, with helppoor it seemed reasonable to say that "Agree with both" was the typical response. Would it be reasonable to say that "Agree with both" is helppoor's typical response? No, it would not. Notice that, unlike helppoor, respondents' values on helpsick are more spread out, with sizable numbers of cases falling in the first value ("Govt," with 28.4 percent), making it a close rival to "Agree with both" for the distinction of being the modal opinion on this issue. Clearly, the public is more divided—more widely dispersed—on the question of medical assistance than on the question of assistance to the poor.

Figure 2-6 Bar Chart (ordinal variable with high dispersion)

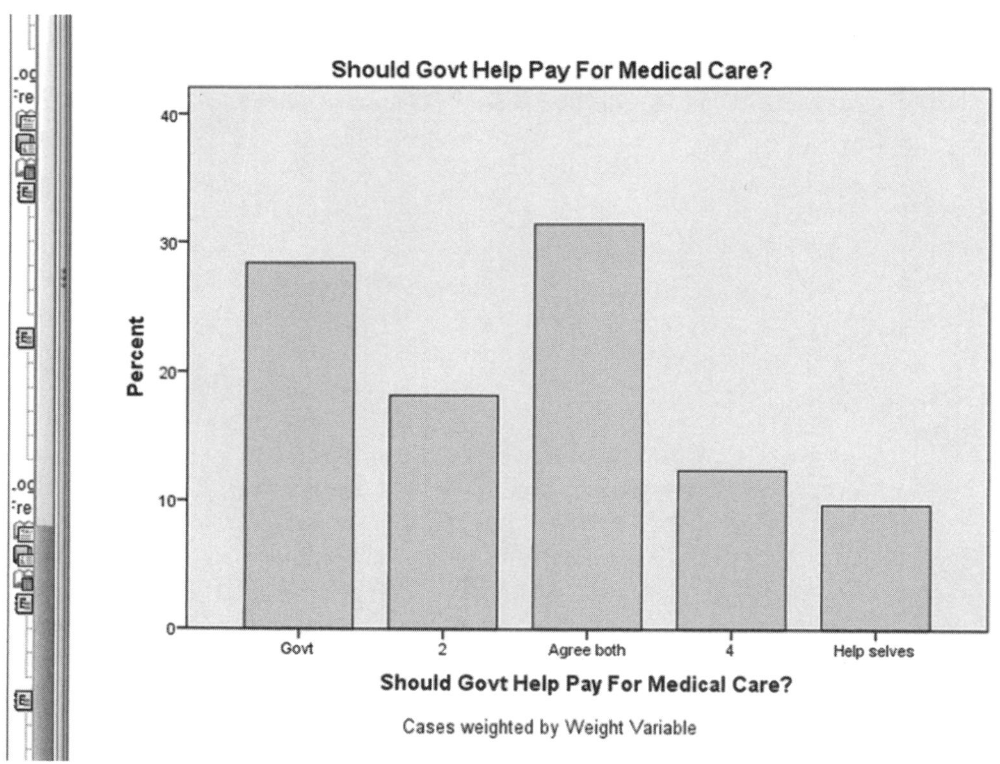

DESCRIBING INTERVAL VARIABLES

Let's now turn to the descriptive analysis of interval-level variables. An interval-level variable represents the most precise level of measurement. Unlike nominal variables, whose values stand for categories, and ordinal variables, whose values can be ranked, the values of an interval variable *tell you the exact quantity of the characteristic being measured.* For example, age qualifies as an interval-level variable because its values impart each respondent's age in years.

Because interval variables have the most precision, they can be described more completely than can nominal or ordinal variables. For any interval-level variable, you can report its mode, median, and arithmetic average, or *mean.* In addition to these measures of central tendency, you can make more sophisticated judgments about variation. Specifically, you can determine if an interval-level distribution is *skewed.*

Skewness refers to the symmetry of a distribution. If a distribution is not skewed, the cases tend to cluster symmetrically around the mean of the distribution, and they taper off evenly for values above and below the mean. If a distribution is skewed, by contrast, one tail of the distribution is longer and skinnier than the other tail. Distributions in which some cases occupy the higher values of an interval variable—distributions with a skinnier right-hand tail—have a *positive skew.* By the same token, if the distribution has some cases at the extreme lower end—the distribution has a skinnier left-hand tail—then the distribution has a *negative skew.* Skewness affects the mean of the distribution. A positive skew tends to "pull" the mean upward; a negative skew pulls it downward. However, skewness has less effect on the median. Because the median reports the middlemost value of a distribution, it is not tugged upward or downward by extreme values. *For badly skewed distributions, it is a good practice to use the median instead of the mean in describing central tendency.*

A step-by-step analysis of a GSS2012 variable, age, will clarify these points. Click Analyze → Descriptive Statistics → Frequencies. If helppoor and helpsick are still in the Variable(s) list, click them back into the left-hand list. Click age into the Variable(s) list. Click the Charts button. Make sure that Bar charts (under Chart Type) and Percentages (under Chart Values) are selected. Click Continue, which returns you to the main Frequencies window (Figure 2-7).

So far, this procedure is the same as in your analysis of zodiac, helppoor, and helpsick. When running a frequencies analysis of an interval-level variable, however, you need to do two additional things. One of these is a must-do. The other is a may-want-to-do. The must-do: Click the Statistics button in the Frequencies window, as shown in Figure 2-7. The Frequencies: Statistics window appears. In the Central Tendency panel, click the boxes next to Mean, Median, and Mode. In the Distribution panel, click Skewness. Click Continue, returning to the main Frequencies window. The may-want-to-do: *Un*check the box next to Display frequency tables, appearing at the foot of the left-hand list.[2] Click OK.

SPSS runs the analysis of age and dumps the requested statistics and bar chart into the Viewer (Figure 2-8). Most of the entries in the Statistics table are familiar to you: valid number of cases; number of missing cases; and mean, median, and mode. In addition, SPSS reports values for skewness and a statistic called standard error of skewness. When a distribution is perfectly symmetrical—no skew—it has skewness equal to 0. If the distribution has a skinnier right-hand tail—positive skew—then skewness will be a positive number. A skinnier left-hand tail, logically enough, returns a negative number for skewness. For the age variable, the skewness statistic is positive (.338). This suggests that the distribution has a skinnier right-hand tail—a feature that is confirmed by the shape of the bar chart. Note also that the mean (46.1 years) is higher than the median (45 years), a situation that often—although not always—indicates a positive skew.[3] Even so, the mean and median are only about 1 year apart. You have to exercise judgment, but in this case it would not be a distortion of reality to use the mean instead of the median to describe the central tendency of the distribution.[4]

All the guided examples thus far have used bar charts for graphic support. For nominal and ordinal variables, a bar chart should always be your choice. For interval variables, however, you may want to ask SPSS to produce a histogram instead. What is the difference between a bar chart and a histogram? A bar chart displays each value of a variable and shows you the percentage (alternatively, the raw number) of cases that fall into each category. A histogram is similar, but instead of displaying each discrete value, it collapses categories into ranges (called bins), resulting in a compact display. Histograms are sometimes more readable and elegant than bar charts. Most of the time a histogram will work just as well as a bar chart in summarizing an interval-level variable. For interval variables with a large number of values, a histogram is the graphic of choice. (Remember: For nominal or ordinal variables, you always want a bar chart.)

Figure 2-7 Requesting Statistics for an Interval Variable

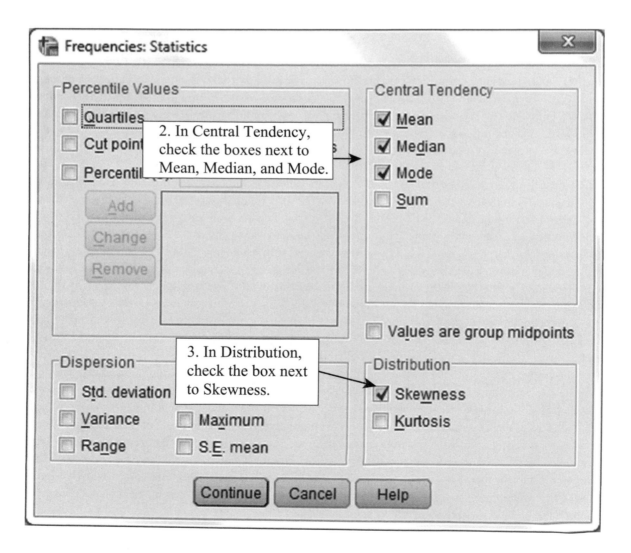

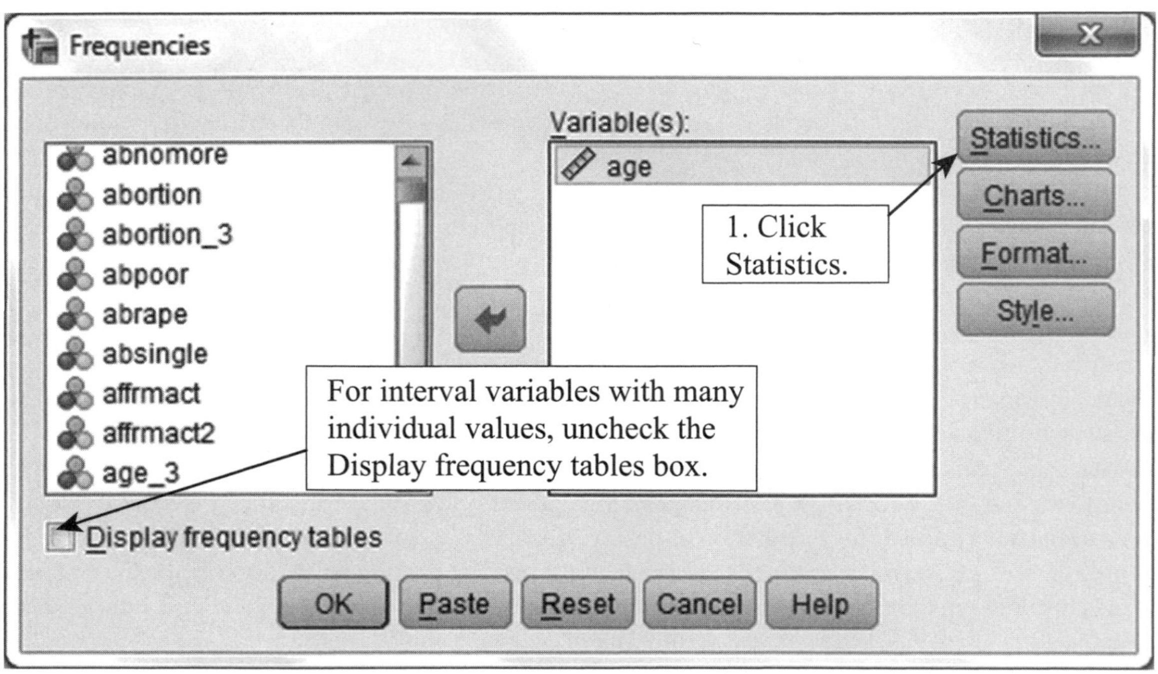

So that you can become familiar with histograms, run the analysis of age once again—only this time ask SPSS to produce a histogram instead of a bar chart. Click Analyze → Descriptive Statistics → Frequencies. Make sure age is still in the Variable(s) list. Click Statistics, and then uncheck all the boxes: Mean, Median, Mode, and Skewness. Click Continue. Click Charts, and then select the Histograms radio button in Chart Type. Click Continue. For this analysis, we do not need a frequency table. In the Frequencies window, uncheck the Display frequency tables box. (Refer to Figure 2-7.) Click OK.

This is a bare-bones run. SPSS reports its obligatory count of valid and missing cases, plus a histogram for age (Figure 2-9). On the histogram's horizontal axis, notice the hash marks, which are spaced at 20-year intervals. SPSS has compressed the data so that each bar represents about 2 years of age rather than 1 year of age. Now scroll up the Viewer to the bar chart of age, which you produced in the preceding analysis. Notice that the histogram has smoothed out the nuance and choppiness of the bar chart, though it still captures the essential qualities of the age variable.

Figure 2-8 Statistics and Bar Chart (interval variable)

Statistics

age Respondent's Age

N	Valid	1970
	Missing	5
Mean		46.10
Median		45.00
Mode		55
Skewness		.338
Std. Error of Skewness		.055

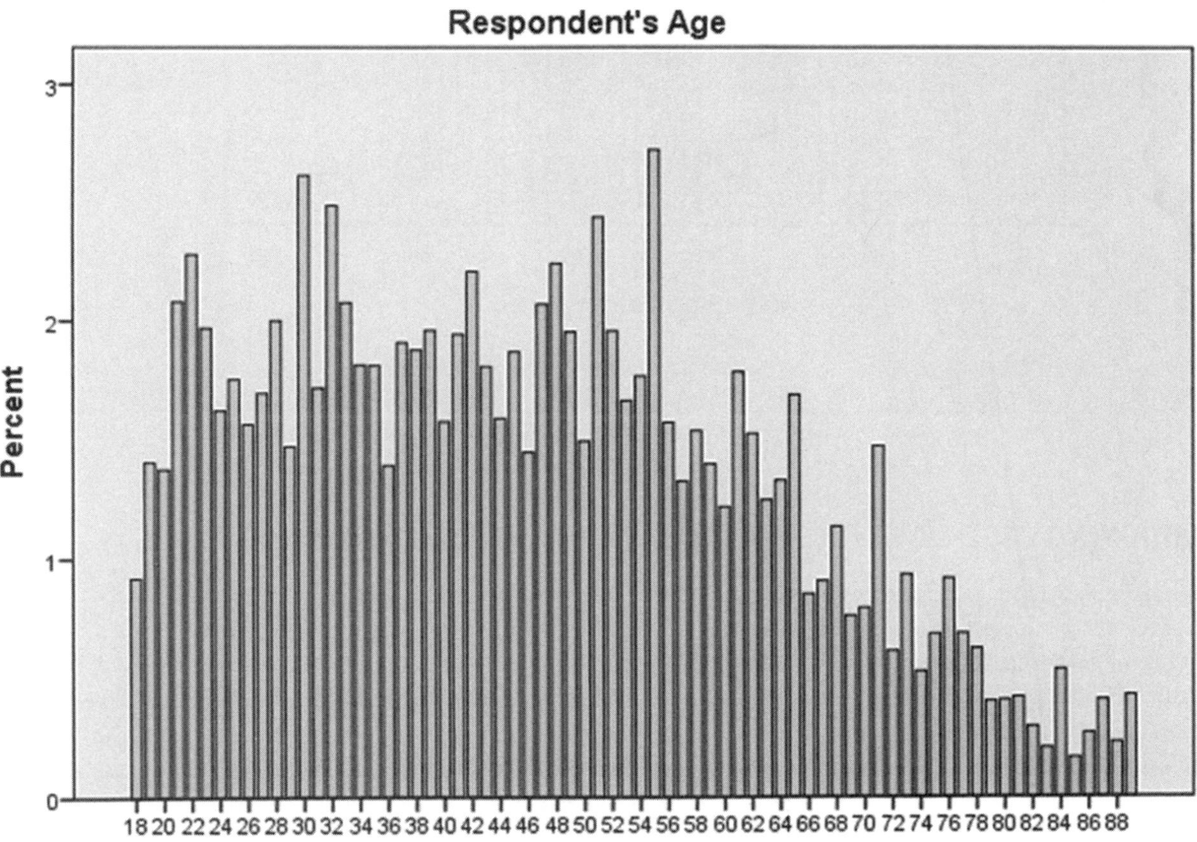

Figure 2-9 Histogram (interval variable)

Statistics

age Respondent's Age

N	Valid	1970
	Missing	5

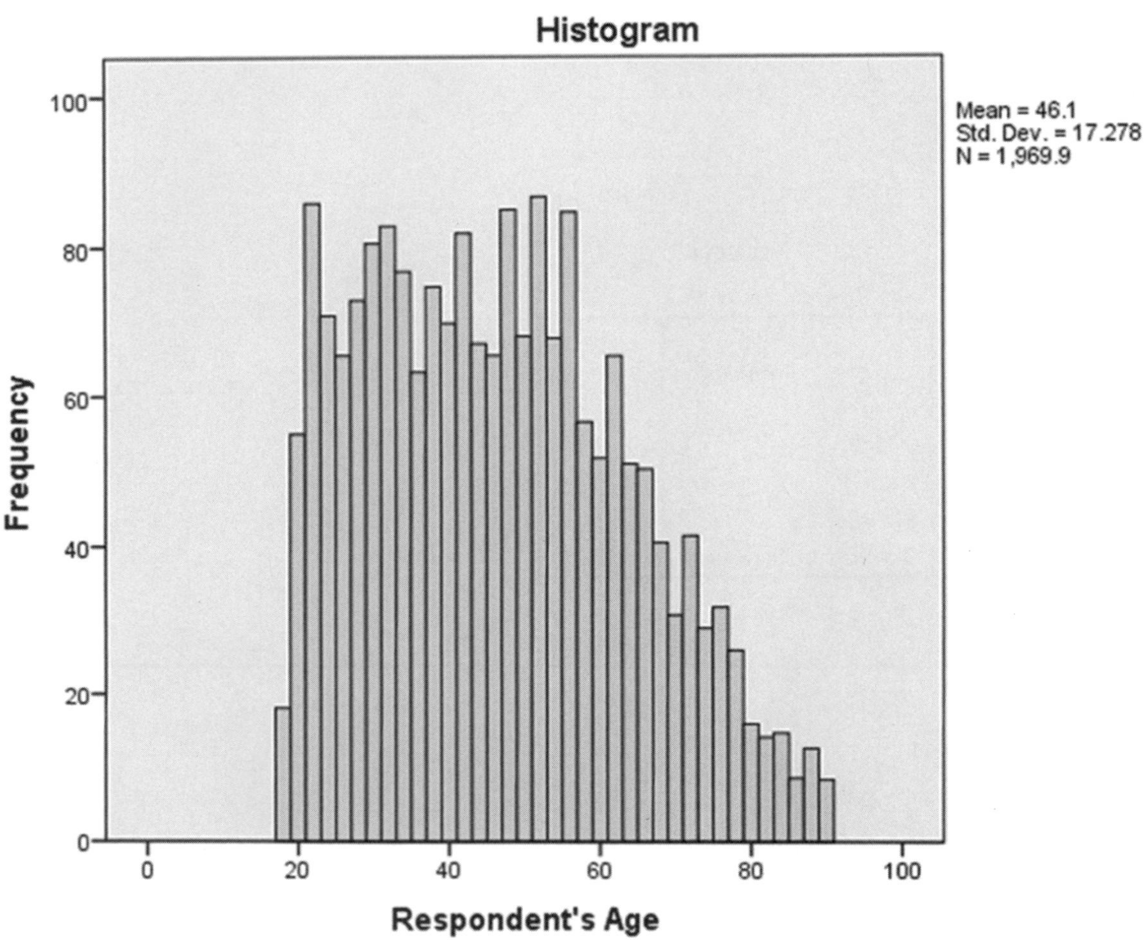

OBTAINING CASE-LEVEL INFORMATION WITH CASE SUMMARIES

When you analyze a large survey dataset, as you have just done, you generally are not interested in how respondent x or respondent y answered a particular question. Rather, you want to know how the entire sample of respondents distributed themselves across the response categories of a variable. Sometimes, however, you gather data on particular cases because the cases are themselves inherently important. The States dataset (50 cases) and World dataset (167 cases) are good examples. With these datasets, you may want to push the descriptions beyond the relative anonymity of Frequencies analysis and find out where particular cases "are" on an interesting variable. Analyze → Reports → Case Summaries is readymade for such elemental insights. Before beginning this guided example, close GSS2012 and open World.

Figure 2-10 Obtaining Case Summaries

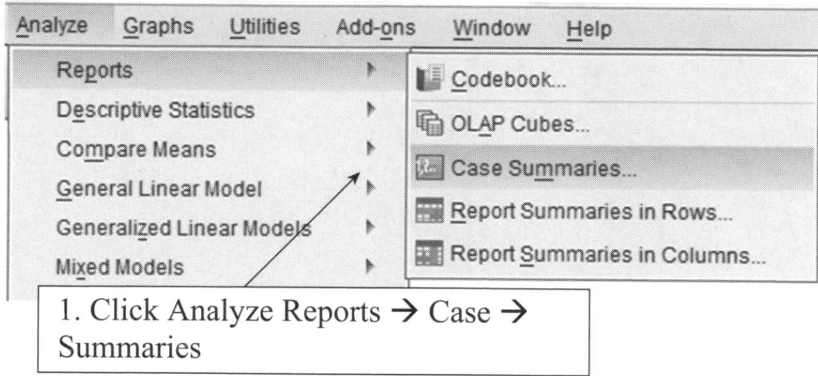

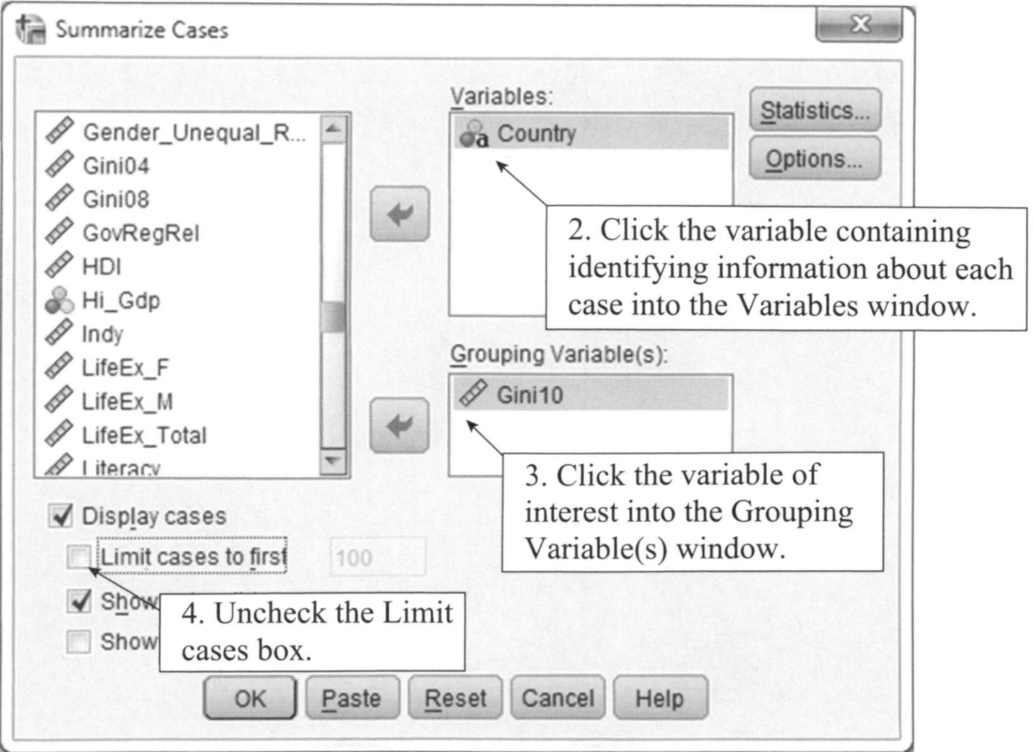

Suppose you are interested in identifying the countries that have the most equitable distribution of wealth, as well as those in which wealth is more concentrated in the hands of a few. The World dataset contains Gini10, the Gini coefficient for each country. The Gini coefficient measures wealth distribution on a scale that ranges from 0 (wealth is distributed equitably) to 100 (wealth is distributed inequitably). Exactly which countries are the most equitable? Which are the least equitable? Where does the United States fall on the list? Case Summaries can quickly answer questions like these. SPSS will sort the countries on the basis of a "grouping variable" (in this example, Gini10) and then produce a report telling you which countries are in each group.

With the World dataset open, click Analyze → Reports → Case Summaries. The Summarize Cases window opens (Figure 2-10). You need to do three things here:

1. Click the variable containing the cases' identities into the Variables window. In the World dataset, this variable is named Country, an alphabetic descriptor of each country's name.

Figure 2-11 Case Summaries Output

Case Summaries

				Country Country/territory name
Gini10 Income Gini coefficient, 2000-2010 (UN)	24.70	1		Denmark
		Total	N	1
	24.90	1		Japan
		Total	N	1
	25.00	1		Sweden
		Total	N	1
	25.80	1		Czech Republic
		2		Norway
		3		Slovakia
		Total	N	3
	26.00	1		Luxembourg
		Total	N	1
	26.30	1		Iceland
		Total	N	1
	26.90	1		Finland
		Total	N	1
	27.40	1		Malta
		Total	N	1
	27.60	1		Ukraine
		Total	N	1
	28.20	1		Serbia
		Total	N	1
	28.30	1		Germany
		Total	N	1
	28.80	1		Belarus
		Total	N	1
	29.00	1		Croatia
		2		Cyprus
		Total	N	2
	29.10	1		Austria

SPSS sorts the cases by the grouping variable, Gini10, and displays results for each country. Denmark, Japan, and Sweden are the three countries with the lowest values on Gini10.

[Output omitted]

		Total	N	1
	54.90	1		Panama
		Total	N	1
	55.00	1		Brazil
		Total	N	1
	55.30	1		Honduras
		Total	N	1
	57.20	1		Bolivia
		Total	N	1
	57.80	1		South Africa
		Total	N	1
	58.50	1		Colombia
		Total	N	1
	58.60	1		Angola
		Total	N	1
	59.50	1		Haiti
		Total	N	1
	61.00	1		Botswana
		Total	N	1
	64.30	1		Comoros
		Total	N	1
	74.30	1		Namibia
		Total	N	1
	Total	N		153

Namibia, Comoros, and Botswana are the three countries with the highest values on Gini10.

2. Click the variable you are interested in analyzing, Gini10, into the Grouping Variable(s) window.
3. Uncheck the Limit cases box. This is important. If this box is left checked, SPSS will limit the analysis to the first 100 cases, which in many instances, such as the World dataset, will produce an incomplete analysis.

Click OK and consider the output (Figure 2-11). SPSS sorts the cases on the grouping variable, Gini10, and tells us which country is associated with each value of Gini10. For example, Denmark, with a Gini coefficient of

24.70, is the country having the most equitable wealth distribution. Which countries rank highest on Gini10? Scroll to the bottom of the tabular output. With a Gini coefficient of 74.30, Namibia is the country having the least equitable distribution of wealth.

EXERCISES

1. (Dataset: World. Variables: Women13, Country.) What percentage of members of the U.S. House of Representatives are women? In 2013 the number was 17.8 percent, according to the Inter-Parliamentary Union, an international organization of parliaments.[5] How does the United States compare to other democratic countries? Is 17.8 percent comparatively low, comparatively high, or average for a typical national legislature? World contains Women13, the percentage of women in the lower house of the legislature in each of 90 democracies. Perform a frequencies analysis on Women13. In Statistics, obtain the mean and the median. In Charts, Chart Type, select Histogram. In the main Frequencies window, make sure that the Display frequency tables box is checked.

   A. The mean of Women13 is equal to (fill in the blank) ____________. The median is equal to ____________.

   B. Analysts generally prefer to use the mean to summarize a variable's central tendency, except in cases where the mean gives a misleading indication of the true center of the distribution. Make a considered judgment. For Women13, can the mean be used, or should the median be used instead? (circle your answer)

   Mean Median

   Explain your answer. ____

   ____

   ____

   C. Recall that 17.8 percent of U.S. House members are women. Suppose a women's advocacy organization vows to support female congressional candidates so that the U.S. House might someday "be ranked among the top one-fourth of democracies in the percentage of female members." According to the frequencies analysis, to meet this goal, women would need to constitute what percentage of the House? (circle one)

   About 21 percent About 25 percent About 28 percent

   D. Print the histogram. Basing your answer on the shape of the histogram, would you say that Women13 has a negative skew or a positive skew? (circle your answer)

   Negative skew Positive skew

   Briefly explain your answer.

   ____

   ____

   E. Run Analyze → Reports → Case Summaries. Click Country into the Variables box and Women13 into the Grouping Variable(s) box. Make sure to uncheck the box next to Limit cases to first 100. Examine the output. Which five countries have the lowest percentages of women in their legislatures?

   1.__________ 2. __________ 3. __________ 4.__________ 5.__________

   Which five countries have the highest percentages of women in their legislatures?

   1.__________ 2. __________ 3. __________ 4.__________ 5.__________

2. (Dataset: GSS2012. Variables: science_quiz, wordsum.) The late Carl Sagan once lamented: "We live in a society exquisitely dependent on science and technology, in which hardly anyone knows anything about

science and technology." Do the data support Sagan's pessimistic assessment? How does the public's grasp of scientific facts compare with other skills, such as word recognition and vocabulary?

GSS2012 contains science_quiz, which was created from 10 questions testing respondents' knowledge of basic scientific facts. Values on science_quiz range from 0 (the respondent did not answer any of the questions correctly) to 10 (the respondent correctly answered all 10).[6] GSS2012 also contains wordsum, which measures respondents' knowledge of the meanings of 10 words. Like science_quiz, wordsum ranged from 0 (the respondent did not know any of the words) to 10 (the respondent knew all 10 words).

A. Obtain frequency distributions and bar charts for science_quiz and wordsum. In Statistics, request mean, median, and mode. In Charts, request bar charts with percentages. Fill in the following table:

	science_quiz	wordsum
Mean	?	?
Median	?	?
Mode	?	?

B. Consider the following Sagan-esque statement: "The public knows more about words than about science." Based on your results in part A, is this statement correct or incorrect? (circle one)

Correct Incorrect

Explain your reasoning, making specific reference to the statistics you reported in A.

____

____

____

____

C. Examine the frequency distributions. According to conventional academic standards, scores of 9 or 10 on a 10-point quiz would be A's. What percentage of respondents would receive a grade of A on science_quiz? (fill in the blank) ____________. What percentage of respondents would receive a grade of A on wordsum? (fill in the blank) ____________.

D. Now turn your attention to the bar charts. Compare the science_quiz chart with the wordsum chart and think about the variation—how respondents are dispersed across the values of each variable. Consider this statement: "Science_quiz has a greater degree of dispersion than wordsum." Is this statement correct or incorrect? (circle one)

Correct Incorrect

Explain your reasoning, making specific reference to the bar charts.

____

____

____

____

E. Print the bar charts that you created for this exercise.

3. (Dataset: GSS2012. Variable: femrole.) Two pundits are arguing about how the general public views the role of women in the home and in politics.

Pundit 1: "Our society has a sizable minority of traditionally minded individuals who think that the proper 'place' for women is taking care of the home and caring for children. This small but vocal group of traditionalists aside, the typical adult supports the idea that women belong outside the home and in the workplace."

Pundit 2: "Poppycock! It's just the opposite. The extremist 'women's liberation' crowd has distorted the overall picture. The typical view among most citizens is that women should be in the home, not in the workplace."

A. GSS2012 contains femrole, an interval-level variable that measures respondents' attitudes toward women in society and politics. Scores can range from 0 (women belong in traditional roles) to 9 (women belong in nontraditional roles).

If Pundit 1 is correct, femrole will have (circle one)

a negative skew.   no skew.   a positive skew.

If Pundit 2 is correct, femrole will have (circle one)

a negative skew.   no skew.   a positive skew.

If Pundit 1 is correct, femrole's mean will be (circle one)

lower than its median.   the same as its median.   higher than its median.

If Pundit 2 is correct, femrole's mean will be (circle one)

lower than its median.   the same as its median.   higher than its median.

B. Perform a frequencies analysis of femrole. Obtain the mean, median, and mode, as well as skewness. Obtain a bar chart with percentages. Fill in the table that follows:

Female role: home, work (femrole)	
Mean	?
Median	?
Mode	?
Skewness	?

C. Based on your analysis, whose assessment is more accurate? (circle one)

Pundit 1's   Pundit 2's

Explain your reasoning, making specific reference to the statistics and chart.

____

____

____

____

4. (Dataset: GSS2012. Variable: attend.) The General Social Survey provides a rich array of variables that permit scholars to study religiosity among the adult population. GSS2012 contains attend, a 9-point ordinal scale that measures how often respondents attend religious services. Values can range from 0 ("Never attend") to 8 ("Attend more than once a week").

A. The shell of a bar chart is given below. The categories of attend appear along the horizontal axis. What would a bar chart of attend look like if this variable had maximum dispersion? Sketch inside the axes a bar chart that would depict maximum dispersion.

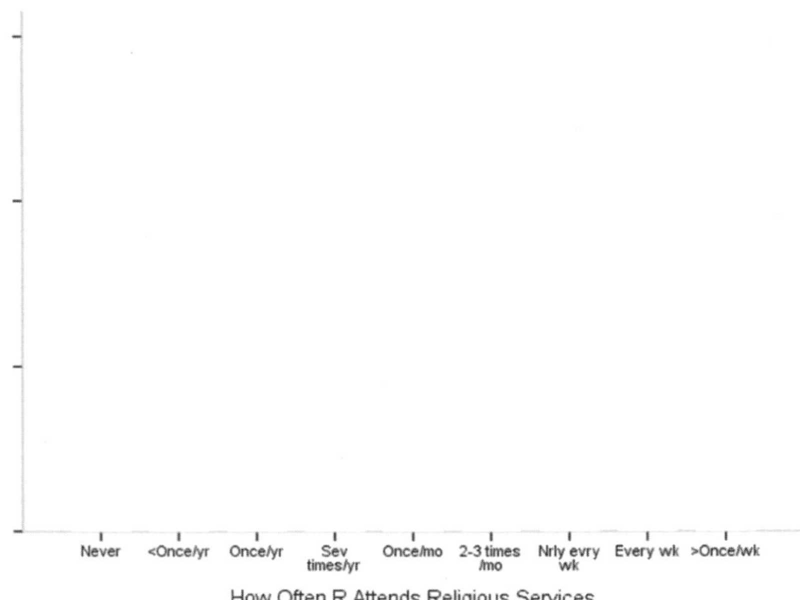

B. What would a bar chart of attend look like if this variable had no dispersion? Sketch inside the axes a bar chart that would depict no dispersion.

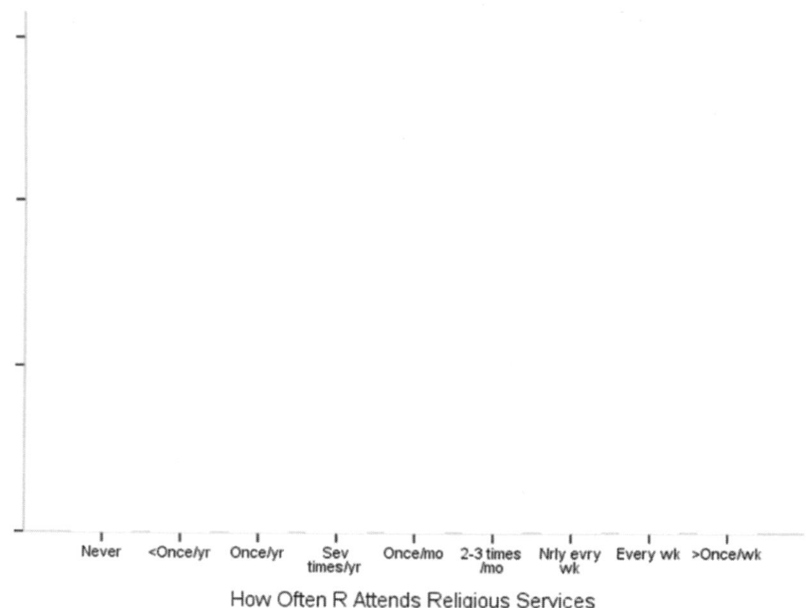

C. Obtain frequencies output and a bar chart for attend. In the main Frequencies window, make sure that the Display frequencies table box is checked. In Statistics, see that all the boxes are unchecked. In Charts, request a bar chart with percentages. Based on your examination of the frequency distribution,

the mode of attend is ____.

the median of attend is ____.

D. Based on your examination of the frequency distribution and bar chart, you would conclude that attend has (circle one)

low dispersion. high dispersion.

Explain your reasoning, making specific reference to the frequency distribution and bar chart.

____

____

____

____

E. Print the bar chart you obtained for this exercise.

5. (Dataset: NES2012. Variables: budget_deficit_x, inspre_self, presapp_scale.) We frequently describe public opinion by referring to how citizens distribute themselves on a political issue. *Consensus* is a situation in which just about everyone, 80–90 percent of the public, holds the same position, or very similar positions, on an issue. *Dissensus* is a situation in which opinion is spread out pretty evenly across all positions on an issue. *Polarization* refers to a configuration of opinion in which people are split between two extreme poles of an issue, with only a few individuals populating the more moderate, middle-of-the-road positions.

In this exercise you will decide whether consensus, dissensus, or polarization best describes public opinion, as measured by three NES2012 variables: opinions about reducing the federal budget deficit (budget_deficit_x), opinions on whether medical insurance should be provided by the government or by the private sector (inspre_self), and opinions about how well the president is performing his job (presapp_scale). The deficit reduction question is measured by a 7-point scale, from "Favor strongly" (point 1) to "Oppose strongly" (point 7). The medical insurance question also uses a 7-point scale, from "Favor government plan" (point 1) to "Favor private plan" (point 7). Presidential approval is measured by a 6-point scale, from "Disapprove" (point 0) to "Approve" (point 5).

A. Obtain frequency distributions and bar charts for budget_deficit_x, inspre_self, and presapp_scale. In the table that follows, write the appropriate percentage next to each question mark (?):

Favor reducing federal budget deficit	Valid percent	Medical insurance scale, self-placement	Valid percent
Favor strongly	?	Government plan	?
Favor weakly	?	2	?
Favor, leaning	?	3	?
Neither	?	4	?
Oppose, leaning	?	5	?
Oppose weakly	?	6	?
Oppose strongly	?	Private plan	?
	100.0		100.0

Presidential approval scale	Valid percent
Disapprove	?
1	?
2	?
3	?
4	?
Approve	?
	100.0

B. Examine the percentages in part A. Of the three issues, which one *most closely approximates* consensus? (Circle one.)

Favor reducing federal budget deficit | Medical insurance scale, self-placement | Presidential approval scale

Explain your reasoning, making specific reference to the distributions you reported in A.

____

____

C. Of the three issues, which one *most closely approximates* dissensus? (circle one)

Favor reducing federal budget deficit | Medical insurance scale, self-placement | Presidential approval scale

Explain your reasoning, making specific reference to the distributions you reported in A.

____

____

D. Of the three issues, which one *most closely approximates* polarization? (circle one)

Favor reducing federal budget deficit | Medical insurance scale, self-placement | Presidential approval scale

Explain your reasoning, making specific reference to the distributions you reported in A.

____

____

E. Print the bar chart of the variable you chose in part D.

6. (Dataset: NES2012. Variables: congapp_job_x, hseinc_approval_x.) Pedantic pontificator believes he has discovered how voters evaluate the performance of House incumbents: "I call it my 'guilt by association' theory. When voters disapprove of the way Congress has been handling its job, they transfer that negative evaluation to their House incumbent. My theory is eminently plausible and surely correct. The distribution of opinions about House incumbents will be very similar to the distribution of opinion about Congress as a whole."

   NES2012 contains congapp_job_x, which gauges respondent approval or disapproval of "the way the U.S. Congress has been handling its job." The dataset also has hseinc_approval_x, which measures approval or disapproval of the way each respondent's House incumbent "has been handling his or her job."

   A. To test pedantic pontificator's theory, perform a frequencies analysis of congapp_job_x and hseinc_approval_x. Obtain bar charts with percentages. Refer to the Valid Percent column of the frequency distributions. In the table that follows, write the appropriate valid percent next to each question mark (?):

	Approve/disapprove Congress handling job	Approve/disapprove House incumbent
	Valid percent	Valid percent
Approve strongly	?	?
Approve weakly	?	?
Disapprove weakly	?	?
Disapprove strongly	?	?
Total	100.0	100.0

B. Consider the tabular and graphic evidence. Does pedantic pontificator's theory appear to be correct or incorrect? (circle one)

Correct Incorrect

Explain your reasoning, making specific reference to the distributions in A and to the bar charts.

____

____

____

____

____

7. (Dataset: States. Variables: defexpen.) Here is the conventional political wisdom: Well-positioned members of Congress from a handful of states are successful in getting the federal government to spend revenue in their states—defense-related expenditures, for example. The typical state, by contrast, receives far fewer defense budget dollars.

   A. Suppose you had a variable that measured the amount of defense-related expenditures in each state. The conventional wisdom says that, when you look at how all 50 states are distributed on this variable, a few states would have a high amount of defense spending. Most states, however, would have lower values on this variable.

      If the conventional wisdom is correct, the distribution of defense-related expenditures will have (circle one)

      a negative skew. a positive skew.

   B. States contains the variable defexpen, defense expenditures per capita for each of the 50 states. Perform a frequencies analysis of defexpen. In Statistics, obtain the mean and median, as well as skewness. (You do not need to obtain the mode for this exercise.) In the main Frequencies window, uncheck the Display frequency tables box. In Charts, request a histogram. Examine the results. Examine the histogram. Record the mean, median, and skewness next to the question marks in the table that follows.

Federal defense expenditures per capita (defexpen)	
Mean	?
Median	?
Skewness	?

C. Analysts generally prefer to use the mean to summarize a variable's central tendency, except in cases where the mean gives a misleading indication of the true center of the distribution. Make a considered judgment. For defexpen, can the mean be used, or should the median be used instead? (circle your answer)

Mean Median

Explain your answer. ____

____

____

D. Based on your analysis, would you say that the conventional wisdom is accurate or inaccurate? (check one)

- ❑ The conventional wisdom is accurate.
- ❑ The conventional wisdom is inaccurate.

Explain your answer, making specific reference to the evidence you have obtained.

____

____

____

____

E. Print the histogram you produced in part B.

8. (Dataset: States. Variables: blkpct10, hispanic10, state.) Two demographers are arguing over how best to describe the racial and ethnic composition of the "typical" state.

Demographer 1: "The typical state is 11.26 percent black and 10.61 percent Hispanic."

Demographer 2: "The typical state is 8.25 percent black and 8.20 percent Hispanic."

A. Run frequencies for blkpct10 (the percentage of each state's population that is African American) and hispanic10 (the percentage of each state's population that is Hispanic). In Statistics, obtain the mean and median, as well as skewness. (You do not need to obtain the mode for this exercise.) In Charts, obtain histograms. In the main Frequencies window, uncheck the Display frequency tables box. Record the appropriate statistics for each variable in the table that follows:

	Percent black, 2010 (blkpct10)	Percent Hispanic, 2010 (hispanic10)
Mean	?	?
Median	?	?
Skewness	?	?

B. Based on your analysis, which demographer is more accurate? (circle one)

Demographer 1 Demographer 2

Explain your reasoning, making specific reference to the statistics in part A and to the histograms.

____

____

____

____

C. Run Case Summaries. Click state into Variables and click hispanic10 into Grouping Variable(s).

Which five states have the lowest percentages of Hispanics?

1.________________ 2. ________________ 3. ________________ 4.________________ 5.________________

Which five states have the highest percentages of Hispanics?

1.________________ 2. ________________ 3. ________________ 4.________________ 5.________________

That concludes the exercises for this chapter.

NOTES

1. In this chapter we use the terms *dispersion, variation,* and *spread* interchangeably.
2. For interval-level variables that have a large number of categories, as does age, a frequency distribution can run to several output pages and is not very informative. Unchecking the Display frequency tables box suppresses the frequency distribution. A general guide: If the interval-level variable you are analyzing has 15 or fewer categories, go ahead and obtain the frequency distribution. If it has more than 15 categories, suppress the frequency distribution.
3. Paul T. von Hippel, "Mean, Median, and Skew: Correcting a Textbook Rule," *Journal of Statistics Education* 13, no. 2 (2005). "Many textbooks teach a rule of thumb stating that the mean is right of the median under right skew, and left of the median under left skew. This rule fails with surprising frequency." See http://www.amstat.org/publications/jse/v13n2/vonhippel.html.
4. For demographic variables that are skewed, median values rather than means are often used to give a clearer picture of central tendency. One hears or reads reports, for example, of median family income or the median price of homes in an area.
5. See the Inter-Parliamentary Union Web site, http://www.ipu.org/english/home.htm.
6. Science_quiz was created by summing the number of correct responses to the following questions (all are in true-false format, except for earthsun): The center of the Earth is very hot (General Social Survey variable, hotcore); It is the father's gene that decides whether the baby is a boy or a girl (boyorgrl); Electrons are smaller than atoms (electron); The universe began with a huge explosion (bigbang); The continents on which we live have been moving their locations for millions of years and will continue to move in the future (condrift); Human beings, as we know them today, developed from earlier species of animals (evolved); Does the Earth go around the Sun, or does the Sun go around the Earth? (earthsun); All radioactivity is man-made (radioact); Lasers work by focusing sound waves (lasers); Antibiotics kill viruses as well as bacteria (viruses).

3 Transforming Variables

Watch a screencast of the guided examples in this chapter.
edge.sagepub.com/pollock

Procedures Covered

Transform → Recode into Different Variables

Transform → Visual Binning

Transform → Compute Variable

Transform → Recode into Same Variables

Political researchers sometimes must modify the variables they want to analyze. Generally speaking, such *variable transformations* become necessary or desirable in two common situations. Often a researcher wants to collapse a variable, combining its values or codes into a smaller number of useful categories. The researcher can do so through the Recode transformation feature or the Visual Binning procedure. In other situations a dataset may contain several variables that provide similar measures of the same concept. In these instances the researcher may want to combine the codes of different variables, creating a new and more precise measure. The Compute transformation feature is designed for this task.

In this chapter you will learn how to use the Recode, Visual Binning, and Compute commands. The chapter contains four guided examples, all of which use NES2012. The variables you modify or create in this chapter (and in this chapter's exercises) will become permanent variables in the datasets. After you complete each guided example, be sure to save the dataset.

USING RECODE

With Recode, you can manipulate any variable at any level of measurement—nominal, ordinal, or interval. But you should exercise vigilance and care. Follow these three guidelines:

1. Before using Recode, obtain a frequency distribution of the variable you intend to manipulate.
2. After using Recode, check your work.
3. Properly label the new variable and its values.

Open NES2012, and we will work through the first example.

Recoding a Categorical Variable

NES2012 contains dem_marital, a demographic variable (hence, the "dem" prefix) that measures marital status in six categories: married: spouse present (code 1), married: spouse absent (code 2), widowed (code 3), divorced (code 4), separated (code 5), and never married (code 6). Suppose we want to create a new variable that collapses respondents into two categories: married (codes 1 and 2) or not married (codes 3 through 6). SPSS Recode will accomplish this goal. Following the first rule of data transformations, we will run Frequencies on dem_marital, which will tell us what the new, collapsed variable should look like. A Frequencies analysis dem_marital produced the following result:

		Frequency	Percent	Valid Percent	Cumulative Percent
Valid	1. Married: spouse present	3043	51.4	51.5	51.5
	2. Married: spouse absent {VOL}	320	5.4	5.4	57.0
	3. Widowed	629	10.6	10.6	67.6
	4. Divorced	347	5.9	5.9	73.5
	5. Separated	1042	17.6	17.7	91.1
	6. Never married	524	8.9	8.9	100.0
	Total	5905	99.8	100.0	
Missing	System	11	.2		
Total		5916	100.0		

According to the Cumulative Percent column, 57.0 percent of the sample falls into the two married codes of dem_marital. This of course means that the rest of the sample, 43.0 percent, must fall into the other four values of dem_marital. The two numbers, 57.0 and 43.0, will help us verify that we performed the recode correctly.

On the main menu bar, click Transform and consider the array of choices (Figure 3-1). Notice that SPSS presents two recoding options: Recode into Same Variables and Recode into Different Variables. When you recode a variable into the same variable, SPSS replaces the original codes with the new codes. The original information is lost. When you recode a variable into a different variable, SPSS uses the original codes to create a new variable. The original variable is retained. In some situations (discussed later) you will want to pick Recode into Same Variables. Most of the time, however, you should use the second option, Recode into Different Variables.

Figure 3-1 Transform Drop-down Menu

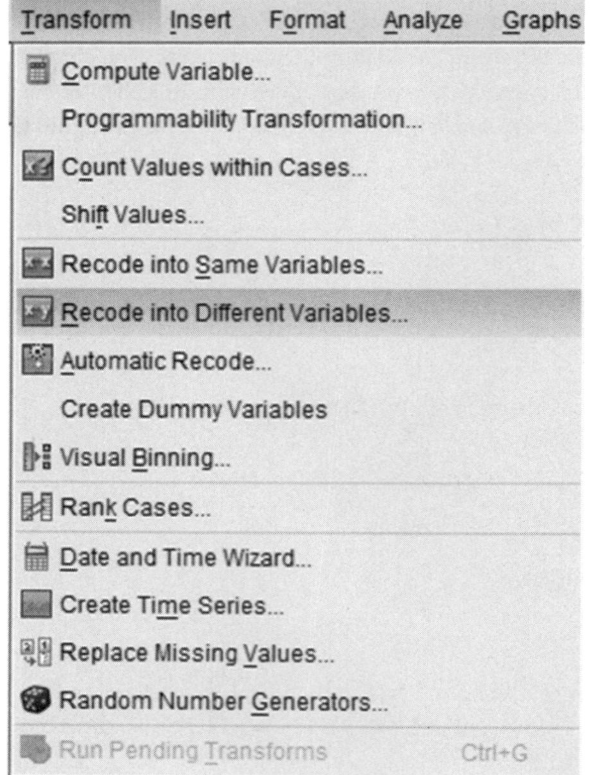

Click Recode into Different Variables. The Recode into Different Variables window opens (Figure 3-2). Scroll down the left-hand variable list and find dem_marital. Click dem_marital into the Input Variable → Output Variable box. SPSS puts dem_marital into the box, with this designation: "dem_marital→?" This is SPSS-speak for "What do you want to name the new variable you are creating from dem_marital?" Click in the Name box and type "married" (without quotation marks). Let's take this opportunity to give the new variable, married, a descriptive label. Click in the Label box and type "Is R married?" Click the Change button. The Recode into Different Variables window should now look like Figure 3-3.

Click Old and New Values. The Recode into Different Variables: Old and New Values window

Figure 3-2 Recode into Different Variables Window

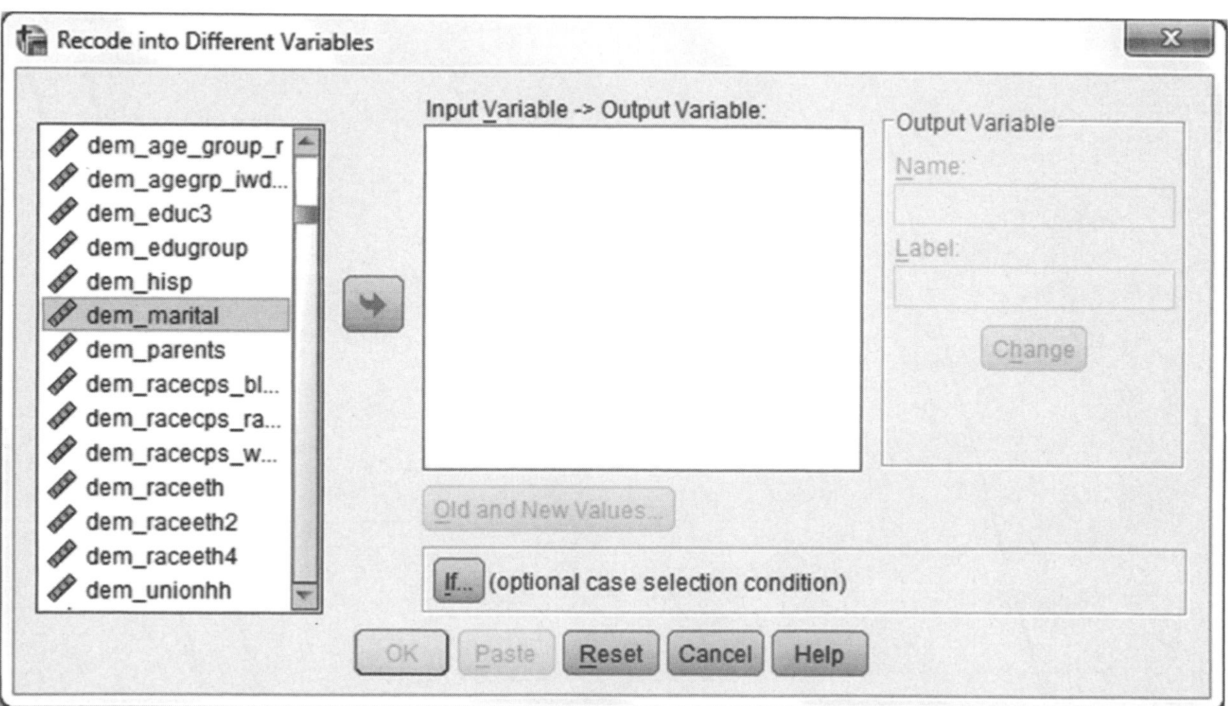

Figure 3-3 Recoding a Categorical Variable

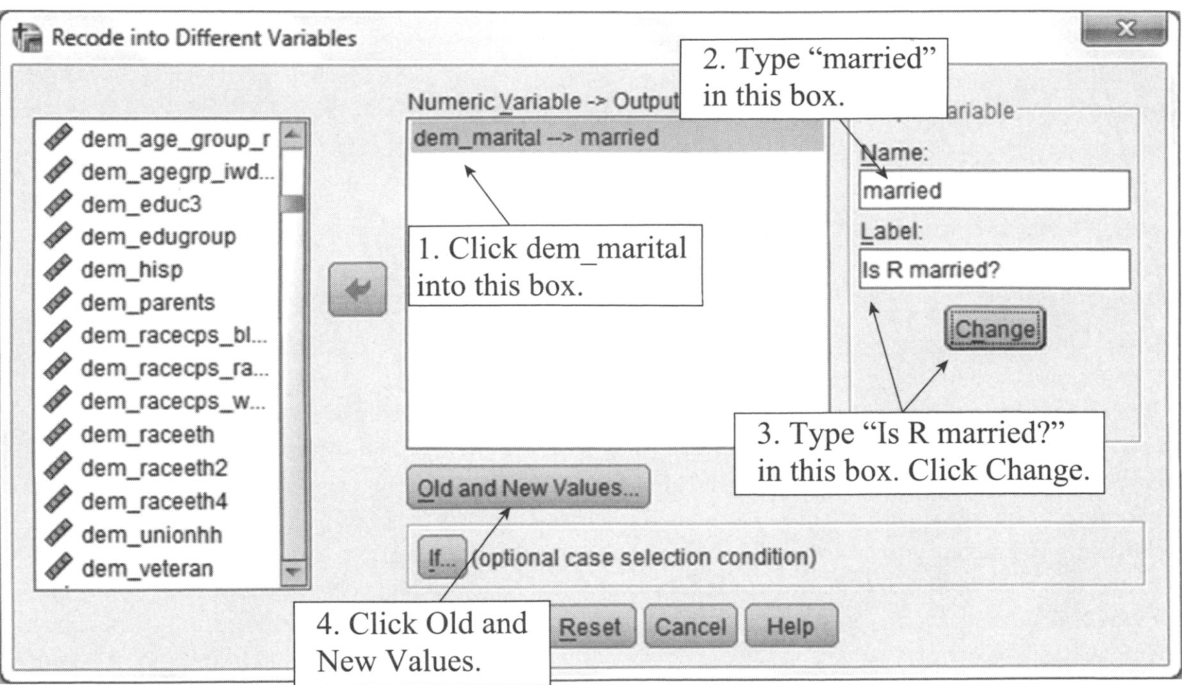

pops up (Figure 3-4). There are two main panels. In the left-hand, Old Value panel, we will tell SPSS how to combine the original codes for dem_marital. In the right-hand, New Value panel, we will assign codes for the new variable, which we have named married.

Let's say that we want the new variable, married, to have two codes: code 1 for married respondents and code 0 for unmarried respondents. Plus, we need to make sure that any respondents who have missing

Figure 3-4 Recode into Different Variables: Old and New Values Window (default)

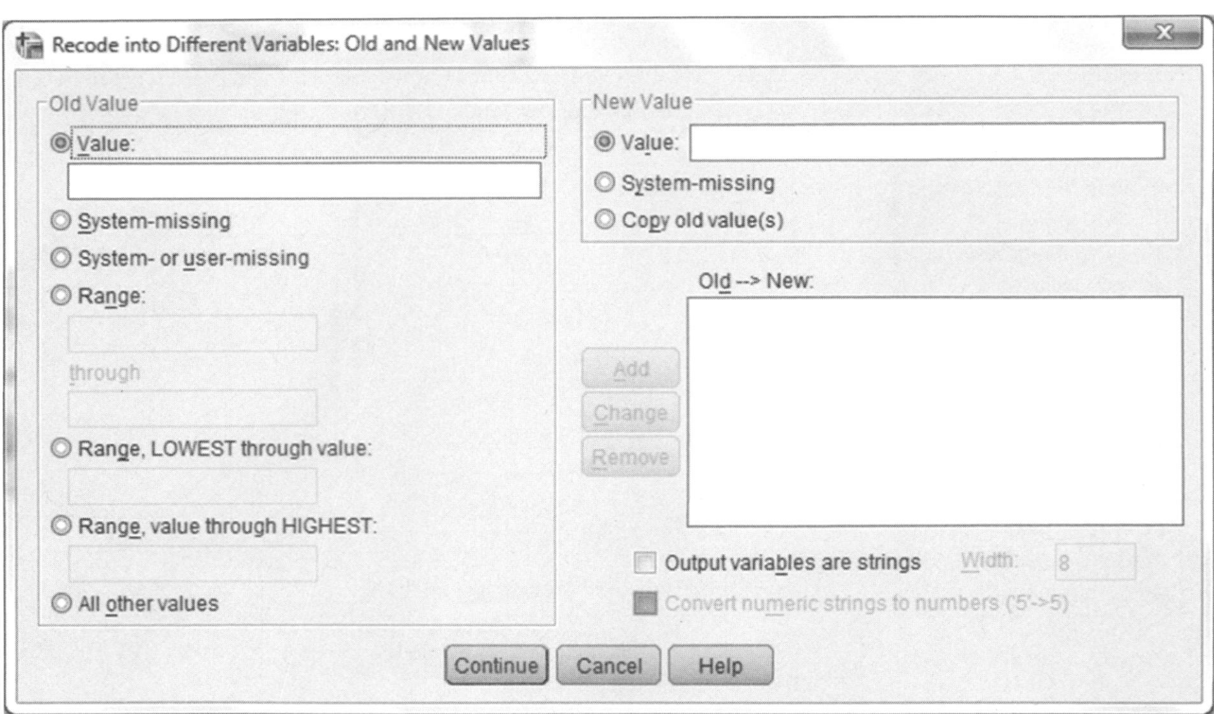

values on dem_marital also have missing values on married. So we need to instruct SPSS to follow this recoding protocol:

Marital status	Old value (dem_marital)	New value (married)
Married: spouse present	1	1
Married: spouse absent	2	1
Widowed	3	0
Divorced	4	0
Separated	5	0
Never married	6	0
	Missing	Missing

By default, SPSS assumes that we want to recode each old value into each new value, one at a time. For example, we could recode dem_marital's old value 1 into married's new value 1, dem_marital's old value 2 into married's new value 1, and so on. But notice that, in the currently grayed-out area of the Old Value panel, SPSS will permit us to specify a *range* of old values to be recoded into a single new value. So that you can become comfortable with both approaches, we will use the default to collapse the married codes (dem_marital's codes 1 and 2) and the range option to collapse the unmarried codes (dem_marital's codes 3 through 6).

In the Old Value, click the cursor in the box next to "Value," and type "1." Move the cursor directly across to the right-hand, New Value panel and type "1" in the Value box. Click the Add button. In the Old → New box, SPSS records your instruction with "1 → 1," meaning "All respondents coded 1 on dem_marital will be coded 1 on married." Now return to the left-hand, Old Value panel and type "2" in the Value box. Again move to the right-hand, New Value panel and type "1" in the Value box. Click Add. SPSS responds, "2 → 1," meaning "All respondents coded 2 on dem_marital will be coded 1 on married." Now for the range option. In the Old Value panel, select the uppermost Range button, the one simply labeled "Range." The two boxes beneath "Range" are activated. In the upper Range box, type "3." In the lower Range box, type "6." Move the cursor to the New Value panel and type "0" in the Value box. Click Add. SPSS responds, "3 thru 6 → 0," letting you know that all respondents coded 3, 4, 5, or 6 on dem_marital will be coded 0 on married. One last loose end: In the Old

Value panel, click the radio button next to "System- or user-missing." In the New Value panel, click the radio button next to "System-missing." Click Add. SPSS records your instruction as "MISSING → SYSMIS," meaning that any respondents having missing values on dem_marital will be assigned missing values on married. The Recode into Different Variables: Old and New Values window should now look like Figure 3-5. Click Continue, returning to the main Recode into Different Variables window. Click OK. SPSS runs the recode.

Figure 3-5 Collapsing a Categorical Variable into Fewer Categories

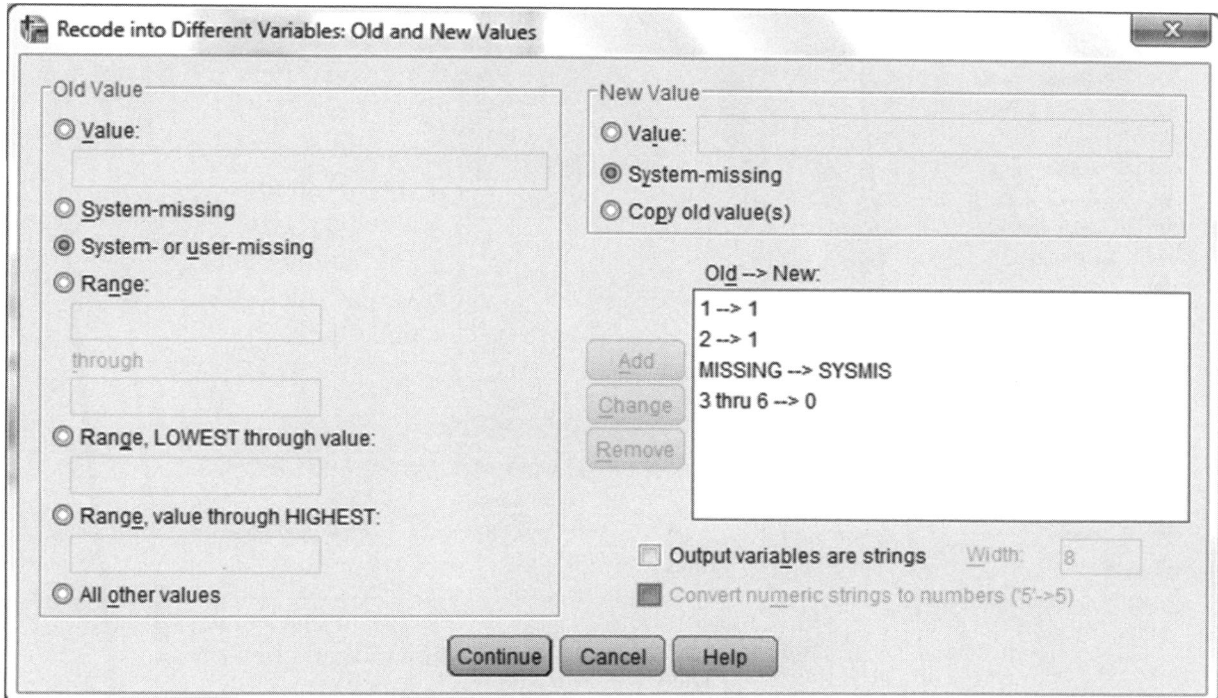

Did the recode work correctly? This is where the check-your-work rule takes effect. Run Frequencies on married to ensure that you did things right:

married Is R married?

		Frequency	Percent	Valid Percent	Cumulative Percent
Valid	.00	2542	43.0	43.0	43.0
	1.00	3363	56.8	57.0	100.0
	Total	5905	99.8	100.0	
Missing	System	11	.2		
Total		5916	100.0		

The frequency table displays the label for the newly minted variable. More important, the valid percentages check out: 43.0 percent coded 0 (not married) and 57.0 percent coded 1 (married). The recode worked as planned. However, we still need to make sure that the numeric codes are labeled properly: "No" for numeric code 0 and "Yes" for numeric code 1. To complete the recoding process, one more step is required.

In the Data Editor, make sure that the Variable View tab is clicked. Scroll down to the bottom of the Data Editor, where you will find married (Figure 3-6). (SPSS always puts newly created variables on the bottom row of the Variable View.) While we are doing the essential work of assigning value labels, we will also tidy up the formatting of the variable we just created. Click in the Decimals cell, which shows "2," and change this value to "0." Next, click in the Values cell (which currently says "None"), and then click on the button that appears. The Value Labels window presents itself. In the box next to "Value," type "0." In the box next to "Label," type "No." Click Add. Repeat the process for code 1, typing "1" in the Value box and "Yes" in the Label box. Click Add. Click OK.

Figure 3-6 Assigning Value Labels to a Recoded Variable

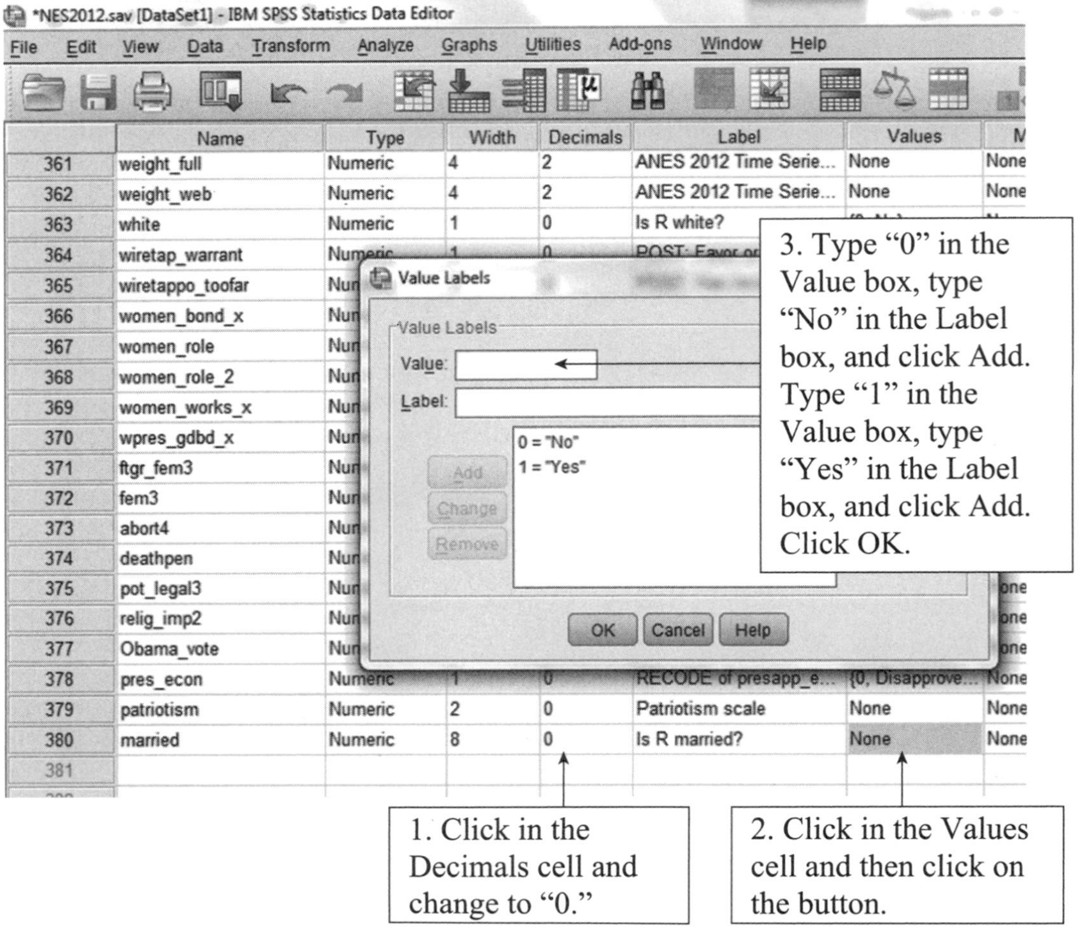

A final Frequencies run will confirm that the labeling worked as planned:

married Is R married?

		Frequency	Percent	Valid Percent	Cumulative Percent
Valid	No	2542	43.0	43.0	43.0
	Yes	3363	56.8	57.0	100.0
	Total	5905	99.8	100.0	
Missing	System	11	.2		
Total		5916	100.0		

You have just invested your time in recoding an original variable into a new variable and, in the process, made NES2012 better and more usable. Before going on to the next example, make sure you save the dataset.

Recoding an Interval-level Variable

Collapsing the values of a categorical variable, as you have just done, is perhaps the most common use of the Recode transformation feature. The original variable may be nominal level, such as dem_marital. Or it may be ordinal level. For example, it might make sense to collapse four response categories such as "strongly agree," "agree," "disagree," and "strongly disagree" into two, "agree" and "disagree." At other times the original variable is interval level, such as age or income. In such cases you could use Recode to create a new variable having, say, three or four ordinal-level categories. Let's pursue this route.

NES2012 contains the variable ftgr_fedgov, which measures respondents' attitudes toward "the federal government in Washington." Ftgr_fedgov is one of the many "feeling thermometer" scales used by the American National Election Studies to record respondents' ratings of groups, political personalities, and other political objects. Scale scores can range from 0 (cold or negative feelings) to 100 (warm or positive feelings). Consider the frequency output for ftgr_fedgov (Figure 3-7).

Suppose we want to use ftgr_fedgov to create a new variable, ftgr_fedgov3, by classifying respondents into three ordinal categories—those who rated the federal government at 30 degrees or lower, those giving ratings of 31 through 50, and those who rated the government at 51 or higher. The two cumulative percentage markers (which are circled in Figure 3-7) will help us verify that we performed the recode correctly: 33.8 percent will fall into the first category, and 70.2 percent will fall into the first *and* second categories of the transformed variable.

Click Transform → Recode into Different Variables. Click Reset to clear the panels. Click ftgr_fedgov into the Input Variable → Output Variable box. Type "ftgr_fedgov3" in the Name box. Type "Ratings of Fed Govt" in the Label box and click Change (Figure 3-8). Click Old and New Values. First create the lowest category for ftgr_fedgov3. In the Old Value panel, select the radio button next to "Range, LOWEST through value"; doing so activates the box. Type "30" in the box. In the New Value panel, type "1" in the Value box and click Add. SPSS translates the instruction as "Lowest thru 30 → 1," lumping all respondents between the lowest value of ftgr_fedgov (a value equal to 0) and a value of 30 on ftgr_fedgov into code 1 of the new variable, ftgr_fedgov3. In the Old Value panel, select the "Range" button and type "31" in the upper box and "50" in the lower box. Type "2" in the Value box in the New Value panel and click Add. That's the middle category, now coded 2 on ftgr_fedgov3. In the Old Value panel, select the radio button next to "Range, value through HIGHEST" and type "51" in the box. Type "3" in the Value box in the New Value panel and click Add. That puts the highest values of ftgr_fedgov into code 3 on ftgr_fedgov3. Complete the recode by clicking the System- or user-missing button in the Old Value panel and the System-missing button in the New Value panel. Click Add. The Recode into Different Variables: Old and New Values window should now look like Figure 3-9. Click Continue. Click OK. Check your work by running Frequencies on ftgr_fedgov3 and examining the output:

ftgr_fedgov3 Ratings of Fed Govt

		Frequency	Percent	Valid Percent	Cumulative Percent
Valid	1.00	1839	31.1	33.8	33.8
	2.00	1981	33.5	36.4	70.2
	3.00	1624	27.4	29.8	100.0
	Total	5444	92.0	100.0	
Missing	System	472	8.0		
Total		5916	100.0		

The cumulative percent markers, 33.8 percent and 70.2 percent, are just where they are supposed to be. Ftgr_fedgov3 checks out. Before proceeding, scroll to the bottom of the Variable View in the Data Editor and make two changes to ftgr_fedgov3. First, change Decimals to 0. Second, click in the Values cell and label ftgr_fedgov3's values with the following labels: 1, "Low"; 2, "Medium"; and 3, "High." Run Frequencies on ftgr_fedgov3 one more time, just to make sure:

ftgr_fedgov3 Ratings of Fed Govt

		Frequency	Percent	Valid Percent	Cumulative Percent
Valid	Low	1839	31.1	33.8	33.8
	Medium	1981	33.5	36.4	70.2
	High	1624	27.4	29.8	100.0
	Total	5444	92.0	100.0	
Missing	System	472	8.0		
Total		5916	100.0		

Figure 3-7 Frequency Distribution of an Interval-level Variable

ftgr_fedgov POST: Feeling thermometer: FEDERAL GOVERNMENT IN WASHINGTON

		Frequency	Percent	Valid Percent	Cumulative Percent
Valid	0	511	8.6	9.4	9.4
	1	10	.2	.2	9.6
	2	11	.2	.2	9.8
	3	5	.1	.1	9.9
	4	9	.1	.2	10.0
	5	33	.6	.6	10.6
	6	1	.0	.0	10.6
	7	1	.0	.0	10.7
	9	0	.0	.0	10.7
	10	90	1.5	1.6	12.3
	12	0	.0	.0	12.3
	15	448	7.6	8.2	20.6
	16	0	.0	.0	20.6
	20	56	.9	1.0	21.6
	22	2	.0	.0	21.6
	23	2	.0	.0	21.7
	25	50	.8	.9	22.6
	27	3	.0	.1	22.6
	30	608	10.3	11.2	33.8
	32	1	.0	.0	33.8
	33	3	.1	.1	33.9
	34	1	.0	.0	33.9
	35	59	1.0	1.1	35.0
	38	2	.0	.0	35.0
	39	0	.0	.0	35.0
	40	979	16.5	18.0	53.0
	42	1	.0	.0	53.0
	43	6	.1	.1	53.1
	44	2	.0	.0	53.2
	45	84	1.4	1.5	54.7
	47	6	.1	.1	54.8
	48	2	.0	.0	54.8
	49	3	.1	.1	54.9
	50	832	14.1	15.3	70.2
	51	3	.0	.1	70.2
	52	2	.0	.0	70.3
	53	2	.0	.0	70.3
	55	51	.9	.9	71.2
	58	1	.0	.0	71.3
	59	3	.0	.0	71.3
	60	660	11.2	12.1	83.4
	61	2	.0	.0	83.4
	62	0	.0	.0	83.5
	65	53	.9	1.0	84.4
	67	1	.0	.0	84.4
	68	2	.0	.0	84.5
	69	2	.0	.0	84.5
	70	411	6.9	7.5	92.1
	73	0	.0	.0	92.1
	75	67	1.1	1.2	93.3
	77	1	.0	.0	93.3
	78	1	.0	.0	93.3
	80	54	.9	1.0	94.3
	84	3	.0	.1	94.4
	85	214	3.6	3.9	98.3
	87	0	.0	.0	98.3
	88	0	.0	.0	98.3
	89	1	.0	.0	98.3
	90	11	.2	.2	98.5
	95	1	.0	.0	98.5
	97	1	.0	.0	98.6
	100	79	1.3	1.4	100.0
	Total	5444	92.0	100.0	
Missing	System	472	8.0		
Total		5916	100.0		

Figure 3-8 Recoding an Interval-level Variable

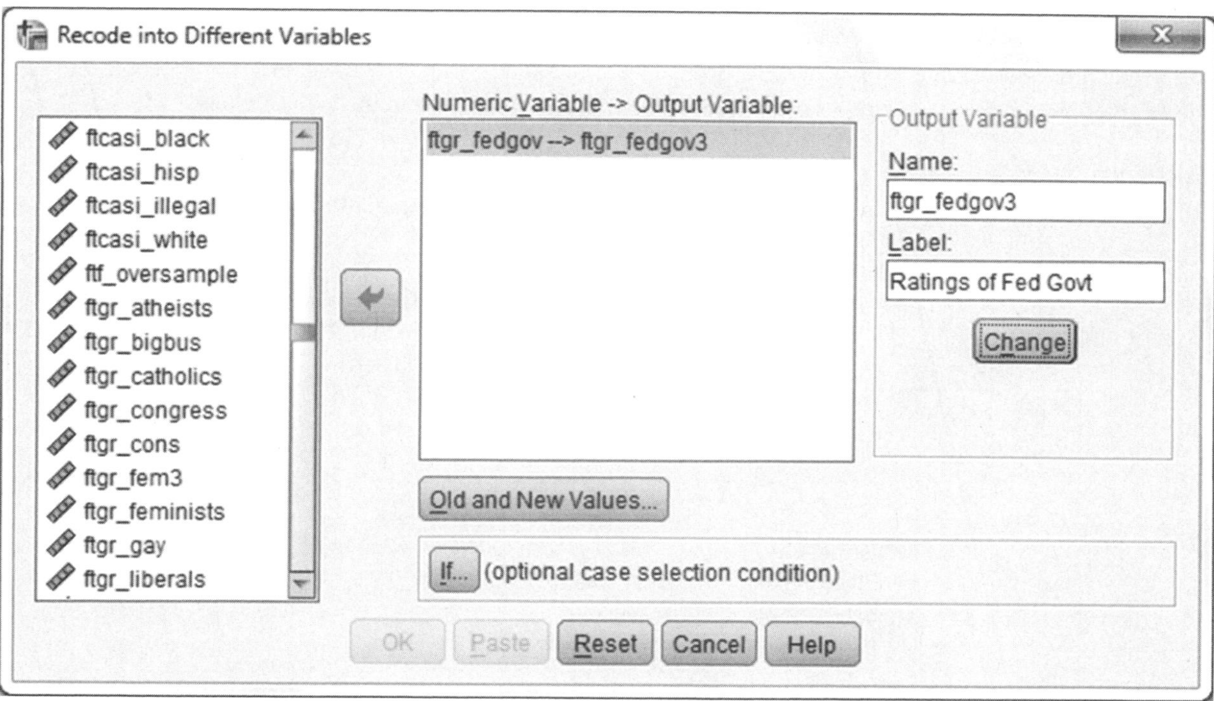

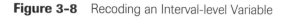

Figure 3-9 Collapsing an Interval-level Variable into Categories

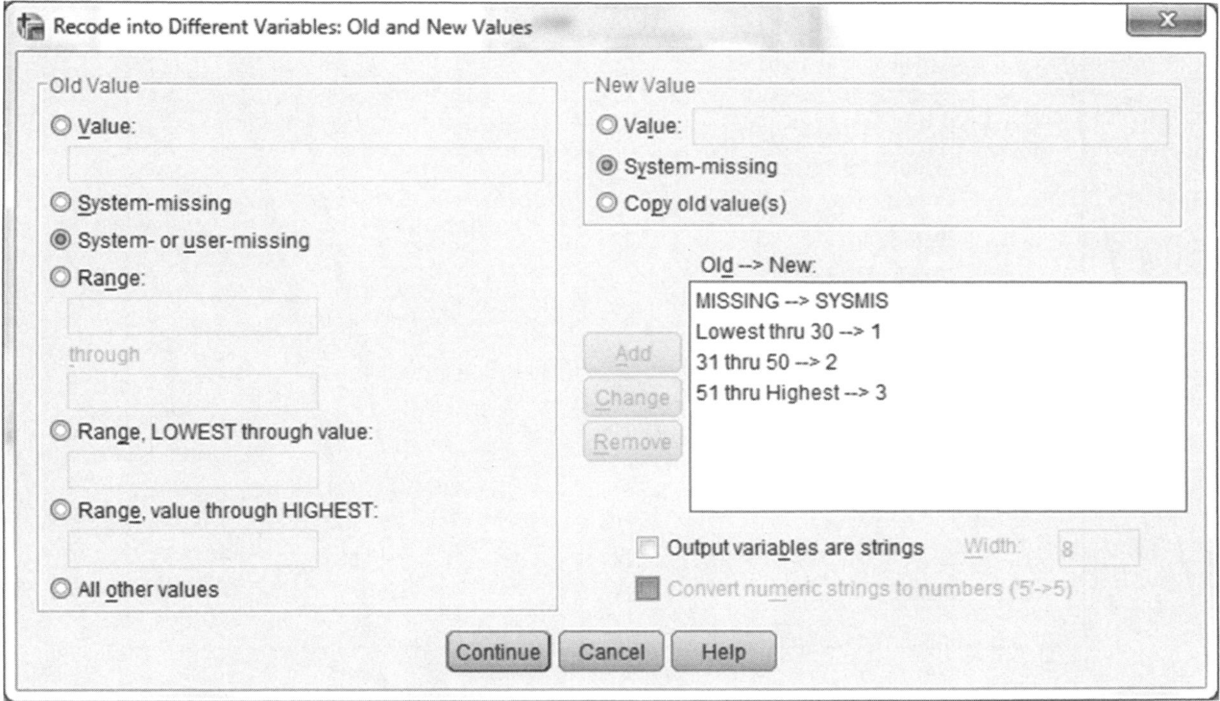

USING VISUAL BINNING

For nominal and ordinal variables, Recode is fast and easy to use. However, for interval variables, as we have just seen, it can be a bit more cumbersome. For collapsing interval variables, SPSS's more obscure Visual Binning procedure provides an attractive alternative to Recode. Visual Binning is as good as Recode for creating variables, such as ftgr_fedgov3, for which the researcher has selected theoretically meaningful cutpoints for defining the categories of the new variable. And it is superior to Recode for situations in which you want to quickly collapse an interval-level variable into a handful of values, each containing roughly equal numbers of cases. Let's work through a guided example using NES2012's incgroup_prepost, a measure of each respondent's income. You will use Visual Binning to create a three-category ordinal, incgroup3. Incgroup3 will break incgroup_prepost into thirds or terciles: the lowest tercile ("Low"), the middle tercile ("Middle"), and the highest tercile ("High").

Collapsing an Interval-level Variable with Visual Binning

An obligatory Frequencies run on incgroup_prepost produces the following output:

incgroup_prepost CASI/WEB: PREPOST SUMMARY- Family income

		Frequency	Percent	Valid Percent	Cumulative Percent
Valid	01. Under $5,000	545	9.2	9.6	9.6
	02. $5,000-$9,999	157	2.7	2.8	12.3
	03. $10,000-$12,499	170	2.9	3.0	15.3
	04. $12,500-$14,999	70	1.2	1.2	16.5
	05. $15,000-$17,499	154	2.6	2.7	19.2
	06. $17,500-$19,999	95	1.6	1.7	20.9
	07. $20,000-$22,499	191	3.2	3.4	24.2
	08. $22,500-$24,999	100	1.7	1.8	26.0
	09. $25,000-$27,499	221	3.7	3.9	29.9
	10. $27,500-$29,999	81	1.4	1.4	31.3
	11. $30,000-$34,999	333	5.6	5.8	37.1
	12. $35,000-$39,999	270	4.6	4.7	41.9
	13. $40,000-$44,999	272	4.6	4.8	46.6
	14. $45,000-$49,999	173	2.9	3.0	49.7
	15. $50,000-$54,999	320	5.4	5.6	55.3
	16. $55,000-$59,999	145	2.5	2.5	57.8
	17. $60,000-$64,999	253	4.3	4.4	62.3
	18. $65,000-$69,999	174	2.9	3.0	65.3
	19. $70,000-$74,999	190	3.2	3.3	68.6
	20. $75,000-$79,999	202	3.4	3.5	72.2
	21. $80,000-$89,999	297	5.0	5.2	77.4
	22. $90,000-$99,999	203	3.4	3.6	80.9
	23. $100,000-$109,999	262	4.4	4.6	85.5
	24. $110,000-$124,999	188	3.2	3.3	88.8
	25. $125,000-$149,999	217	3.7	3.8	92.6
	26. $150,000-$174,999	145	2.5	2.5	95.2
	27. $175,000-$249,999	171	2.9	3.0	98.2
	28. $250,000 or more	104	1.8	1.8	100.0
	Total	5701	96.4	100.0	
Missing	System	215	3.6		
Total		5916	100.0		

If you were using Recode to collapse this variable into three equally sized groups, you could create the "Low" group by collapsing codes 1 through 11 (cumulative percent, 37.1), the "Middle" group by combining codes 12 through 19 (cumulative percent, 68.6), and the "High" group by collapsing codes 20 through 28. That's a fair amount of Recode drudgery. Visual Binning will accomplish the same task with fewer clicks and less typing.

Click Transform → Visual Binning, opening the Visual Binning window. Scroll the variable list, find incgroup_prepost, and click it into the Variables to Bin panel, as shown in Figure 3-10. Click Continue. To light up the panels, click on incgroup_prepost in the Scanned Variable List (Figure 3-11). There are three

Figure 3-10 Visual Binning Opening Window

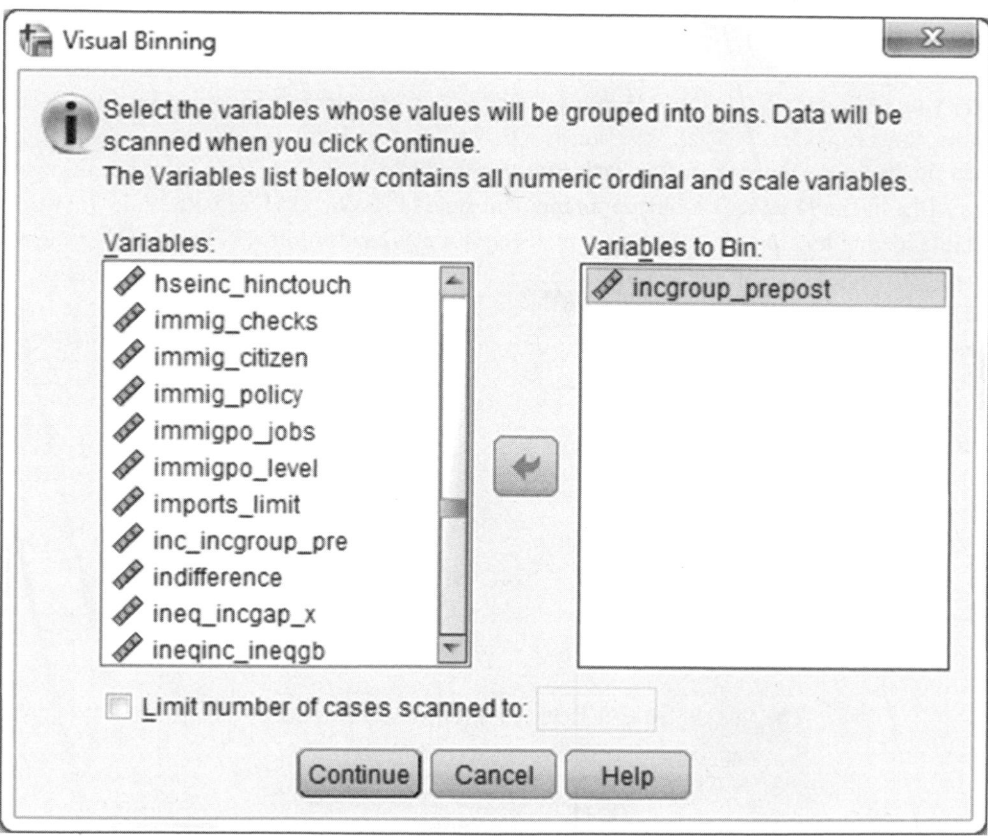

Figure 3-11 Visual Binning Continuation Window

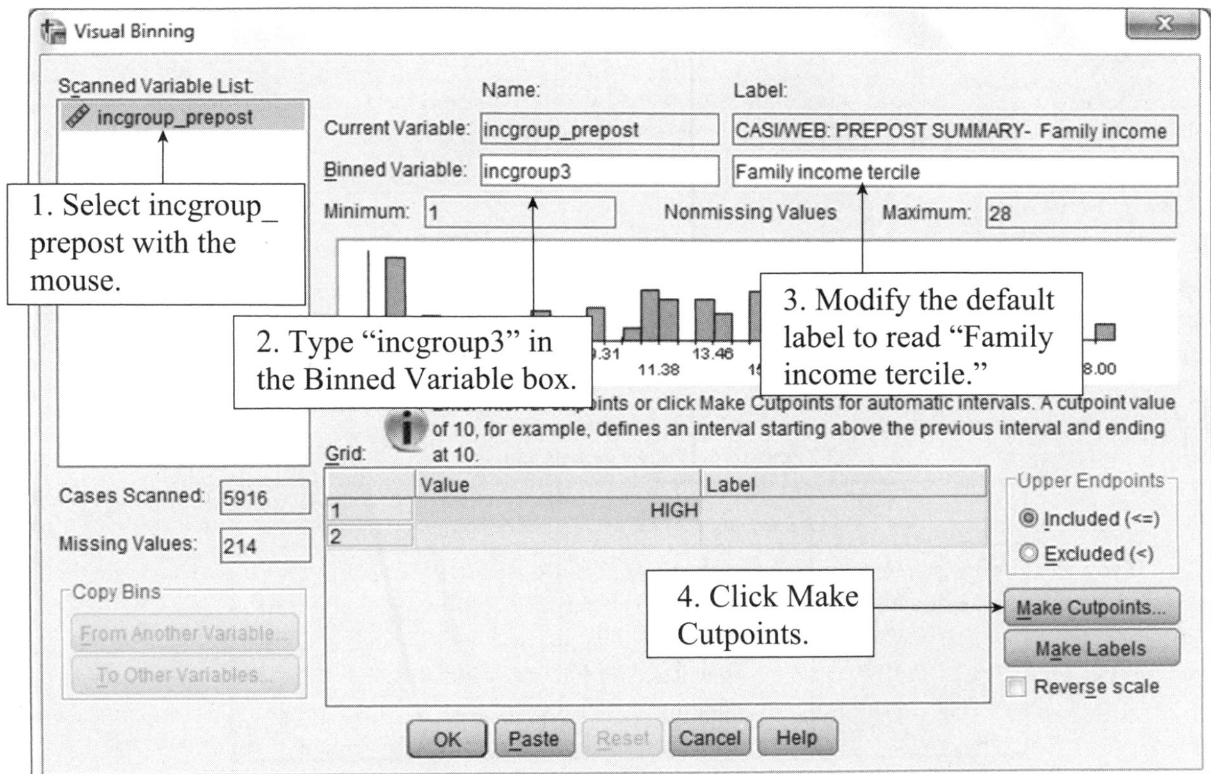

panels to the right of the Scanned Variable List: the Name panel (top), a graphic display of the selected variable (middle), and the Grid panel (bottom). Click in the Binned Variable box in the Name panel. This is where you provide a name for the variable you are about to create. Type "incgroup3." Click in the box beneath Label, where SPSS has supplied a wordy default name. Modify the label to read, "Family income tercile." Later you will attend to the Grid panel, but first you need to create incgroup3's categories. Click Make Cutpoints and consider the Make Cutpoints window (Figure 3-12). Because you want equal-sized groups, select the radio button next to Equal Percentiles Based on Scanned Cases. And because you want three groups, click in the Number of Cutpoints box and type "2." Why 2? Here is the rule: If you wish to create a variable having k categories, then you must request k – 1 cutpoints. (Reassuringly, after you type "2," SPSS automatically puts "33.3" in the Width(%) box.) Click Apply, returning to the continuation window (Figure 3-13). Now, notice the values "11.0," "19.0," and "HIGH" that SPSS has entered in the Grid panel. Earlier, when we inspected the frequency distribution of incgroup_prepost, we knew that these cutpoints would divide respondents into nearly equal groups.[1]

Figure 3-12 Visual Binning: Make Cutpoints Window

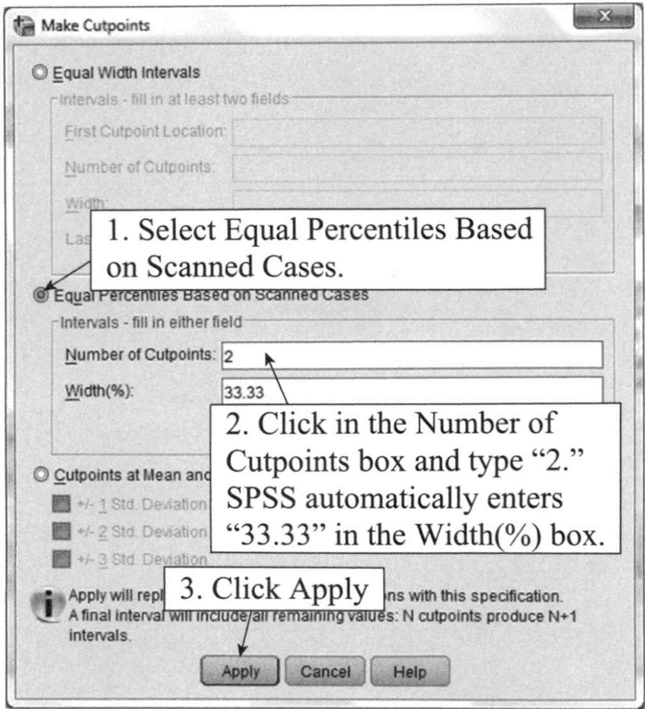

Let's finish the job by typing labels in the Values cells next to each cutpoint number, as shown in Figure 3-13: "Low" next to "11.0," "Middle" next to "19.0," and "High" next to "HIGH."[2] Click OK. (Click OK again when SPSS issues the warning, "Binning specifications will create 1 variables.") Check your work by running Frequencies on incgroup3:

incgroup3 Family income tercile

		Frequency	Percent	Valid Percent	Cumulative Percent
Valid	Low	2117	35.8	37.1	37.1
	Middle	1796	30.4	31.5	68.6
	High	1788	30.2	31.4	100.0
	Total	5701	96.4	100.0	
Missing	System	215	3.6		
Total		5916	100.0		

Figure 3-13 Labeling Values of a Collapsed Variable in the Visual Binning Continuation Window

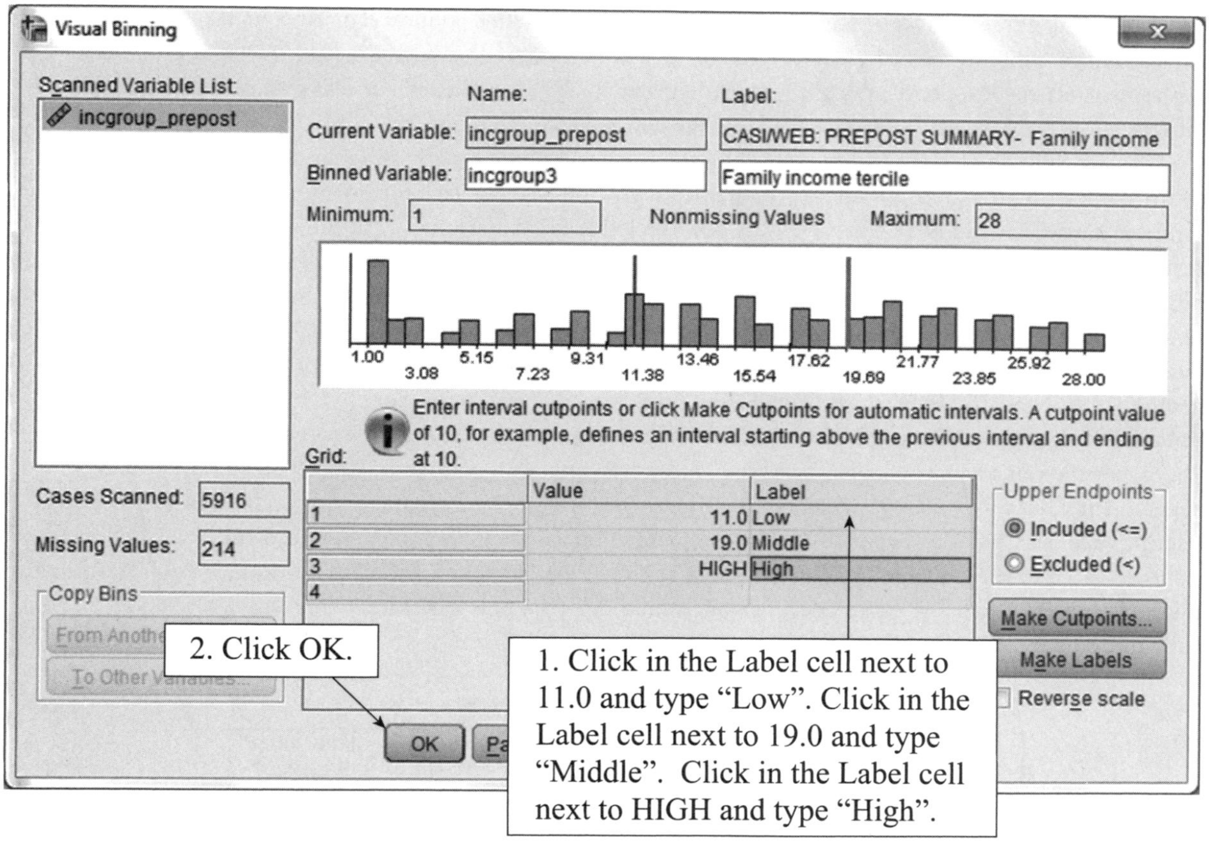

1. Click in the Label cell next to 11.0 and type "Low". Click in the Label cell next to 19.0 and type "Middle". Click in the Label cell next to HIGH and type "High".

2. Click OK.

This is a nice-looking three-category ordinal. Save the dataset, and let's move to the next topic.

USING COMPUTE

Although SPSS permits the creation of new variables through a dizzying variety of complex transformations, the typical use of Compute is pretty straightforward. By and large, Compute is typically used to create a simple *additive index* from similarly coded variables. Consider a simple illustration. Suppose you have three variables, each of which measures whether or not a respondent engaged in each of the following activities during an election campaign: tried to convince somebody how to vote, put a campaign bumper sticker on his or her car, or gave money to one of the candidates or parties. Each variable is coded identically: 0 if the respondent did not engage in the activity and 1 if he or she did. Now, each of these variables is interesting in its own right, but you might want to add them together, creating an overall measure of campaigning: People who did not engage in any of these activities would end up with a value of 0 on the new variable; those who engaged in one activity, a code of 1; two activities, a code of 2; and all three activities, a code of 3.

Here are some suggested guidelines to follow in using Compute to create a simple additive index. First, before running Compute, make sure that each of the variables is coded identically. In the preceding illustration, if the "bumper sticker" variable were coded 1 for no and 2 for yes, and the other variables were coded 0 and 1, the resulting additive index would be incorrect. Second, make sure that the variables are all coded in the same *direction*. If the "contribute money" variable were coded 0 for yes and 1 for no, and the other variables were coded 0 for no and 1 for yes, the additive index would again be incorrect.[3] Third, after running Compute, obtain a frequency distribution of the newly created variable. Upon examining the frequency distribution, you may decide to use Recode to collapse the new variable into more useful categories.

These points are best understood firsthand. The 2012 National Election Study asked respondents whether they had engaged in each of the following activities in the past four years: contacted a member of congress (NES2012 variable, involv_contact), sent a political message on Facebook or Twitter (involv_message), given money to a political organization (involv_org), or signed an Internet petition (involv_petition). For each of these variables, a

"No, have not done this" response is coded 0 and a "Yes, have done this" response is coded 1. We are going to add these variables together, using the expression, "involv_contact + involv_message + involv_org + involv_petition." Think about this expression for a moment. Perhaps a respondent shuns political activism and has not engaged in any of the activities. What would be his or her score on an additive index? It would be $0 + 0 + 0 + 0 = 0$. Another, involvement-oriented respondent might have participated in all four activities. For that respondent, $1 + 1 + 1 + 1 = 4$. Thus we know from the get-go that the values of the new variable will range from 0 to 4.

Let's get SPSS to compute a new variable, which we will name involv_scale, by summing the codes of involv_contact, involv_petition, involv_org, and involv_message. Click Transform → Compute, invoking the Compute Variable window (Figure 3-14). A box labeled "Target Variable" is in the window's upper left-hand corner. This is where we name the new variable. Click in the Target Variable box and type "involv_scale" (as shown in Figure 3-15). The large box on the right side of the window, labeled "Numeric Expression," is where we tell SPSS which variables to use and how to combine them. Scroll down the left-hand variable list until you find involv_contact. Click involv_contact into the Numeric Expression box. Using the keyboard (or the calculator pad beneath the Numeric Expression box), type or click a plus sign (+) to the right of involv_contact. Returning to the variable list, click involv_message into the Numeric Expression box. Repeat this process for the remaining variables, until the Numeric Expression box reads, "involv_contact + involv_message + involv_org + involv_petition" (see Figure 3-15). Before we create involv_scale, let's give it a descriptive label. Click the Type & Label button, which opens the Compute Variable: Type and Label window, as shown in Figure 3-15. Type "Pol involvement scale" in the Label box and click Continue. You are ready to run the compute. Click OK. SPSS does its work. What does the new variable, involv_scale, look like? To find out, run Frequencies on involv_scale:

involv_scale Pol involvement scale

		Frequency	Percent	Valid Percent	Cumulative Percent
Valid	.00	2792	47.2	50.9	50.9
	1.00	1300	22.0	23.7	74.6
	2.00	779	13.2	14.2	88.9
	3.00	444	7.5	8.1	97.0
	4.00	167	2.8	3.0	100.0
	Total	5481	92.6	100.0	
Missing	System	435	7.4		
Total		5916	100.0		

Political activism has an asymmetric quality: heavily populated at lower levels, and thinly populated at higher levels. Half of the sample (50.9 percent) did not engage in any of the activities, and about a quarter (23.7 percent) engaged in one. Although a fair number of respondents (14.2 percent) reported two activities, only a bit more than 10 percent engaged in three or four. Let's collapse this variable into a four-category ordinal. We will keep codes 0 through 2 as they are, but we will combine codes 3 and 4 into one category.

This is a situation in which Recode into Same Variables is appropriate.[4] Click Transform → Recode into Same Variables. In the Recode into Same Variables window, click involv_scale into the Numeric Variables box, as shown in Figure 3-16. Click Old and New Values. Follow this recoding protocol:

Old value	New value
0	0
1	1
2	2
Range 3 through 4	3
System- or user-missing	System-missing

Figure 3-14 Compute Variable Window

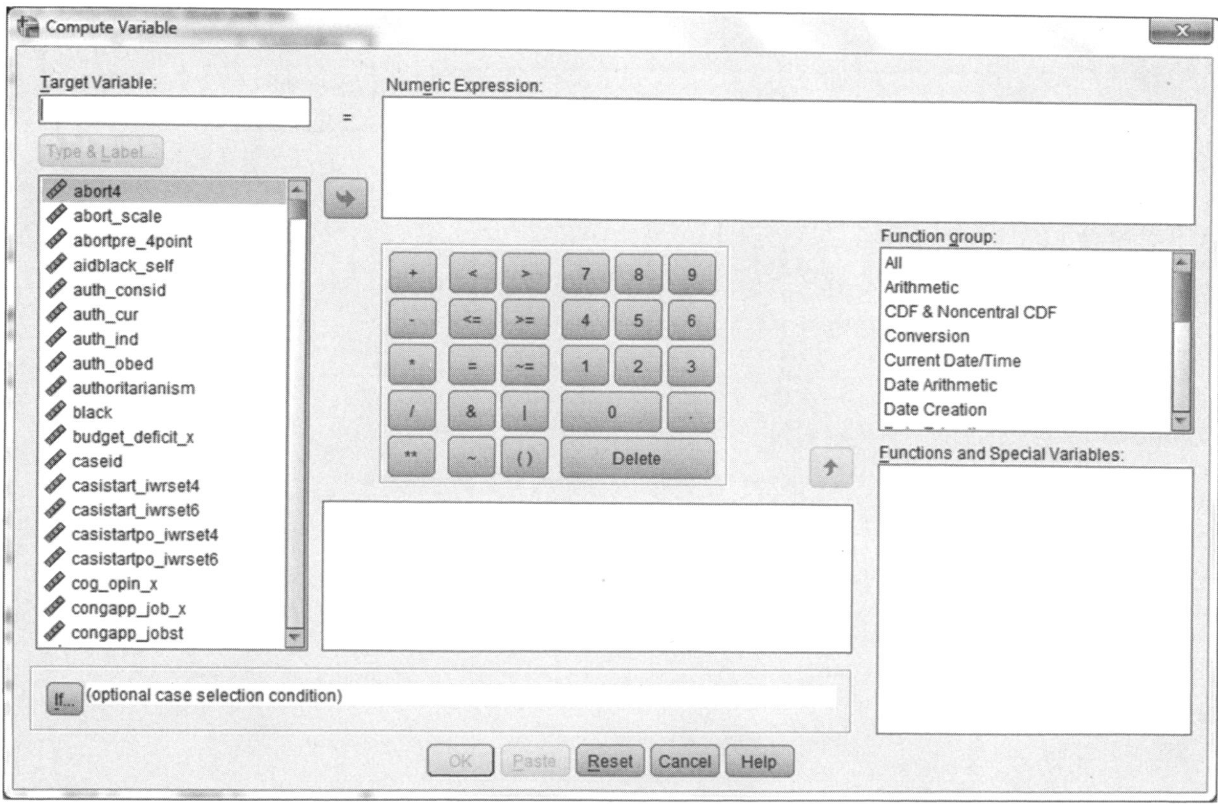

Figure 3-15 Computing a New Variable

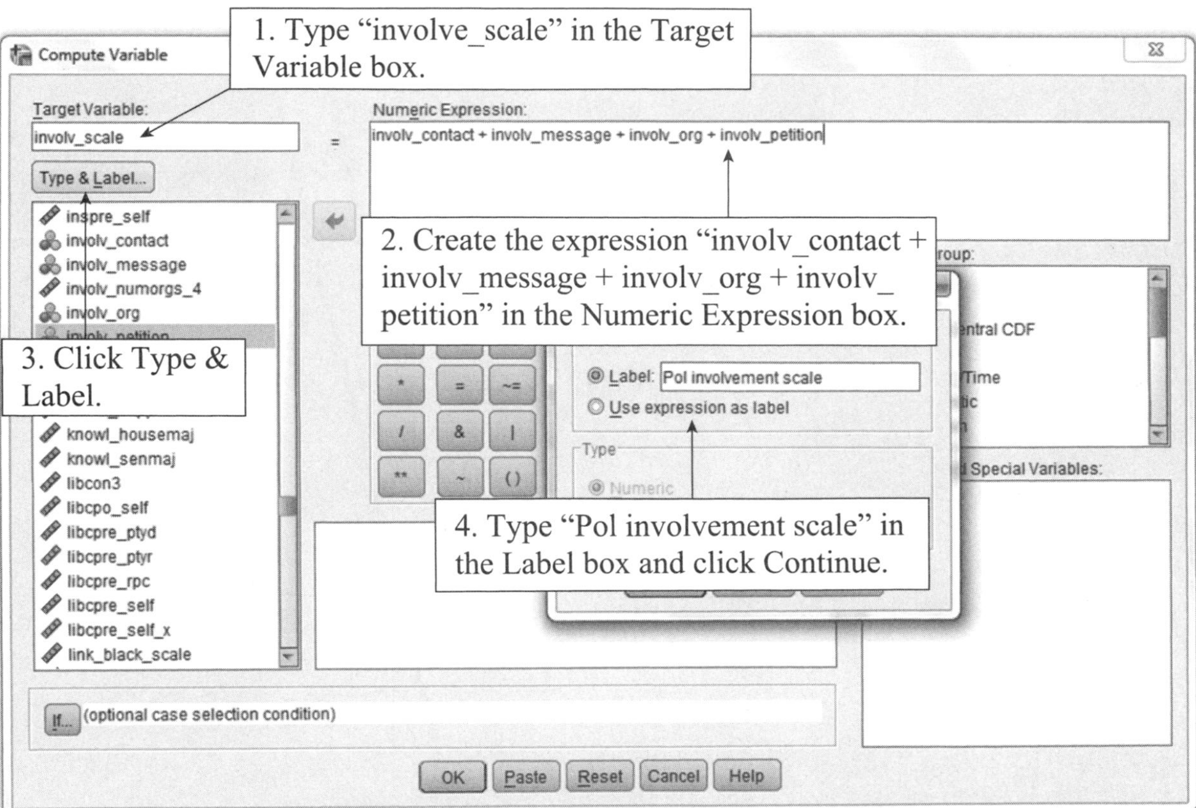

The Recode into Same Variables: Old and New Values window should look like Figure 3-17. Click Continue. Click OK. Again run Frequencies on involv_scale to check the recode:

involv_scale Pol involvement scale

		Frequency	Percent	Valid Percent	Cumulative Percent
Valid	.00	2792	47.2	50.9	50.9
	1.00	1300	22.0	23.7	74.6
	2.00	779	13.2	14.2	88.9
	3.00	611	10.3	11.1	100.0
	Total	5481	92.6	100.0	
Missing	System	435	7.4		
Total		5916	100.0		

Figure 3-16 Recoding a New Variable

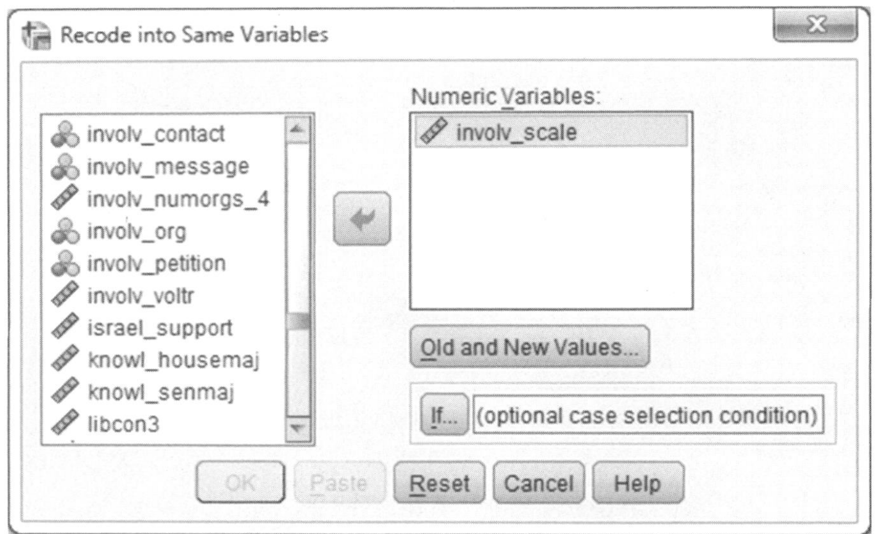

Figure 3-17 Collapsing a New Variable into Categories

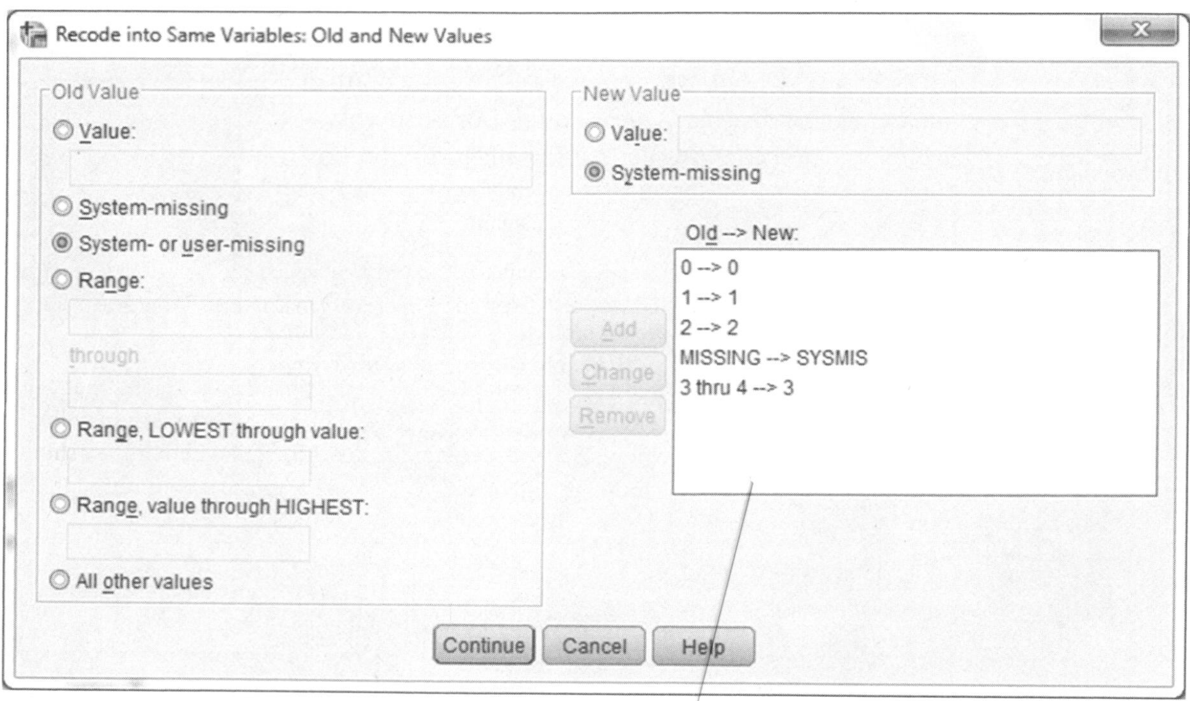

A flawless recode is a thing of beauty. Scroll to the bottom of the Variable View of the Data Editor and perform the usual housekeeping tasks with involv_scale. First, change Decimals to 0. Second, click in the Values cell and assign these value labels: 0, "Low"; 1, "Med-low"; 2 "Med-high"; and 3, "High."

Before proceeding with the exercises, be sure to save the dataset.

EXERCISES

1. (Dataset: GSS2012. Variable: polviews.) GSS2012 contains polviews, which measures political ideology—the extent to which individuals "think of themselves as liberal or conservative." Here is how polviews is coded:

Value	Value label
1	Extremely liberal
2	Liberal
3	Slightly liberal
4	Moderate
5	Slightly conservative
6	Conservative
7	Extremely conservative

A. Run Frequencies on polviews.

The percentage of respondents who are either "extremely liberal," "liberal," or "slightly liberal" is (fill in the blank) ________________ percent.

The percentage of respondents who are "moderate" is (fill in the blank) ________________ percent.

B. Use polviews and Recode into Different Variables to create a new variable named polview3. Give polview3 this label: "Ideology: 3 categories." Collapse the three liberal codes into one category (coded 1 on polview3), put the moderates into their own category (coded 2 on polview3), and collapse the three conservative codes into one category (coded 3 on polview3). (Don't forget to recode missing values on polviews into missing values on polview3.) Run Frequencies on polview3.

The percentage of respondents who are coded 1 on polview3 is (fill in the blank) ____________ percent.

The percentage of respondents who are coded 2 on polview3 is (fill in the blank) ____________ percent.

Make sure that the two percentages you wrote down in part B match the percentages you recorded in part A. The numbers may be slightly different and may still be considered a match. If the two sets of numbers match, proceed to part C. If they do not match, you performed the recode incorrectly. Review this chapter's discussion of Recode, and try the recode again.

C. In the Variable View of the Data Editor, change Decimals to 0, and then click in the Values cell and supply the appropriate labels: "Liberal" for code 1, "Moderate" for code 2, and "Conservative" for code 3. Run Frequencies on polview3. Print the Frequencies output.

2. (Dataset: GSS2012. Variables: mslm_col, mslm_lib, mslm_spk.) GSS2012 contains three variables that gauge tolerance toward "anti-American Muslim clergymen"—whether they should be allowed to teach in college (mslm_col), whether their books should be removed from the library (mslm_lib), and whether they should be allowed to preach hatred of the United States (mslm_spk). For each variable, a less-tolerant response is coded 0, and a more-tolerant response is coded 1.

A. Imagine creating an additive index from these three variables. The additive index would have scores that range between what two values?

Between a score of ______________ and a score of ______________

B. Suppose a respondent takes the more-tolerant position on two questions and the less-tolerant position on the third question. What score would this respondent have?

A score of ______________________________

C. Use Compute to create an additive index from mslm_col, mslm_lib, and mslm_spk. Name the new variable muslim_tol. Give muslim_tol this label: "Tolerance twrd Muslim clergy." Run Frequencies on muslim_tol. Referring to your output, fill in the table that follows:

Tolerance toward Muslim clergy (muslim_tol)		
Score on muslim_tol	Frequency	Valid Percent
?	?	?
?	?	?
?	?	?
?	?	?
Total	?	100.0

D. Use Recode into Same Variables to collapse muslim_tol into three categories, following this recoding protocol:

Old value	New value
0	0
Range: 1 through 2	1
3	2
System- or user-missing	System-missing

In the Variable View of the Data Editor, apply these value labels: 0, "Low"; 1, "Middle"; and 2, "High."

E. Run a frequencies analysis of muslim_tol. Examine the output to ensure that the recode worked properly. Print the Frequencies output.

3. (Dataset: GSS2012. Variable: income06.) In this chapter you learned to use Visual Binning by collapsing an NES2012 measure of income into three terciles. In this exercise, you will use Visual Binning to collapse a very similar variable from GSS2012, income06. Just as you did with incgroup_prepost, you will collapse income06 into income06_3, a three-category ordinal measure of income.

A. Refer to this chapter's visual binning guided example and retrace the steps. Here is new information you will need:

Variable to bin	income06
Binned variable name	income06_3
Binned variable label	Income tercile
Number of cutpoints	2
Labels for Value cells	Low, Middle, High

B. Run Frequencies on income06_3. Refer to your output. Fill in the table that follows:

Income tercile (income06_3)		
income06_3	Frequency	Valid Percent
1 Low	?	?
2 Middle	?	?
3 High	?	?
Total	?	100.0

By performing the exercises in this chapter, you have added three variables to GSS2012: polview3, muslim_tol, and income06_3. Be sure to save the dataset.

That concludes the exercises for this chapter.

NOTES

1. Suppose you wanted to collapse ftgr_fedgov into ftgr_fedgov3 using Visual Binning instead of Recode. You would follow these steps: (1) Click Transform → Visual Binning and scan ftgr_fedgov. (2) In the Scanned Variable List of the continuation window, select ftgr_fedgov. (3) In the Name panel, supply the name "ftgr_fedgov3" and the label "Ratings of Fed Govt." (4) In the Value cells of the Grid panel, type "30" in the topmost cell and "50" in the next lower cell. (SPSS automatically supplies the word "HIGH" in the lowest of the three cells.) (5) In the Label cells of the Grid panel, supply value labels for each value ("Low" goes with "30," "Medium" goes with "50," and "High" goes with "HIGH"). (6) Click OK. ftgr_fedgov3 will be created and labeled correctly.
2. The SPSS-supplied numbers in the Value cells of the Grid panel are not the numeric codes that SPSS assigns to the categories. The numeric codes are numbered sequentially, beginning with 1. So incgroup3 has numeric codes 1 ("Low"), 2 ("Middle"), and 3 ("High").
3. Survey datasets are notorious for reverse-coding. Survey designers do this so that respondents don't fall into the trap of response-set bias, or automatically giving the same response to a series of questions.
4. Recode into Same Variables is an appropriate choice because the original variables are not being replaced or destroyed in the process. If the recode goes badly, you can always use the original variables to compute involv_scale again.

4 Making Comparisons

Watch a screencast of the guided examples in this chapter.
edge.sagepub.com/pollock

Procedures Covered

Analyze → Descriptive Statistics → Crosstabs

Analyze → Compare Means → Means

Graphs → Legacy Dialogs → Line

Graphs → Legacy Dialogs → Bar

Graphs → Legacy Dialogs → Boxplot

All hypothesis testing in political research follows a common logic of comparison. The researcher separates subjects into categories of the independent variable and then compares these groups on the dependent variable. For example, suppose you think that gender (independent variable) affects opinions about gun control (dependent variable) and that women are more likely than men to favor gun control. You would divide subjects into two groups on the basis of gender, women and men, and then compare the percentage of women who favor gun control with the percentage of men who favor gun control. Similarly, if you hypothesize that Republicans have higher incomes than do Democrats, you would divide subjects into partisanship groups (independent variable), Republicans and Democrats, and compare the average income (dependent variable) of Republicans with that of Democrats.

Although the logic of comparison is always the same, the appropriate method depends on the level of measurement of the independent and dependent variables. In this chapter you will learn to address two common hypothesis-testing situations: those in which both the independent and the dependent variables are categorical (nominal or ordinal) and those in which the independent variable is categorical and the dependent variable is interval level. You will also learn to add visual support to your hypothesis testing by creating and editing bar charts and line charts.

CROSS-TABULATION ANALYSIS

Cross-tabulations are the workhorse vehicles for testing hypotheses for categorical variables. When setting up a cross-tabulation, you must observe the following three rules:

1. Put the independent variable on the columns and the dependent variable on the rows.

2. Always obtain column percentages, not row percentages.

3. Test the hypothesis by comparing the percentages of subjects who fall into the same category of the dependent variable.

Consider this hypothesis: In a comparison of individuals, people who have lower incomes will be more likely to identify with the Democratic Party than those who make higher incomes. NES2012 contains pid_3, which measures respondents' partisanship in three categories: Democrat ("Dem"), Independent ("Ind"), and Republican ("Rep"). This will serve as the dependent variable. One of the variables that you created in Chapter 3, incgroup3, is the independent variable. Recall that incgroup3 classifies individuals by terciles of income: the lowest one-third ("Low"), the middle third ("Middle"), and the highest one-third ("High").

In the Data Editor, click Analyze → Descriptive Statistics → Crosstabs. The Crosstabs window appears, sporting four panels. For now, focus on the two upper right-hand panels: Row(s) and Column(s). (The oddly labeled Layer 1 of one panel comes into play in Chapter 5.) This is where we apply the first rule for a properly constructed cross-tabulation: The independent variable defines the columns, and the dependent variable defines the rows. Because pid_3 is the dependent variable, click it into the Row(s) panel, as shown in Figure 4-1. Find incgroup3 in the left-hand variable list and click it into the Column(s) panel.

Figure 4-1 Crosstabs Window (modified)

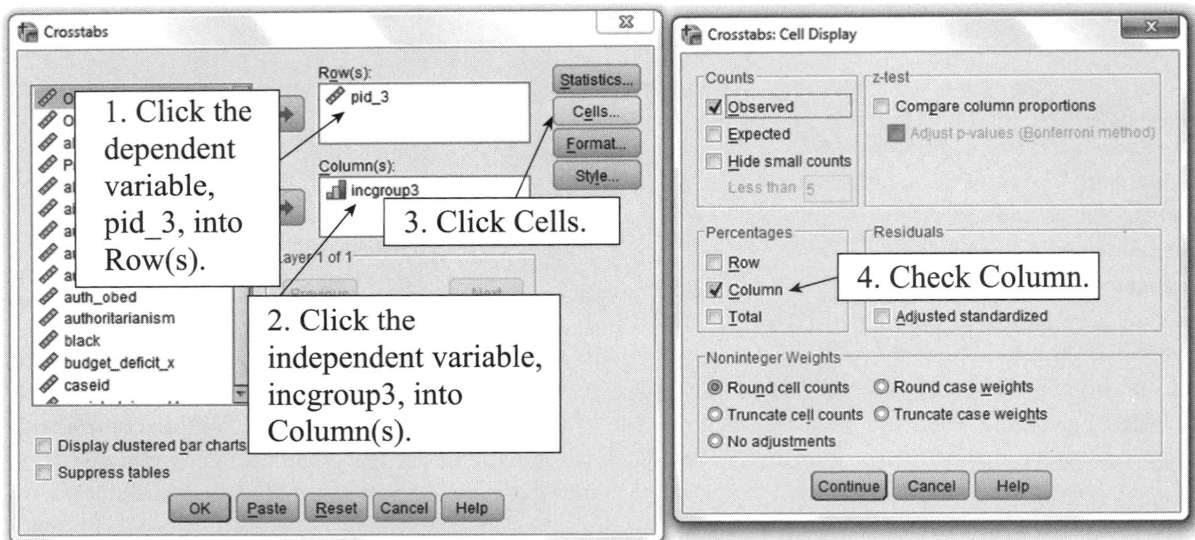

Now for the second rule of cross-tab construction: Always obtain column percentages. On the right-hand side of the Crosstabs window, click the Cells button (refer to Figure 4-1). SPSS displays the available options for Counts, Percentages, and Residuals. Left to its own defaults, SPSS will produce a cross-tabulation showing only the number of cases ("observed" counts) in each cell of the table. That's fine. But to follow the second rule, we also want column percentages—the percentage of each category of the independent variable falling into each category of the dependent variable. Check the Column box in the Percentages panel. Click Continue, which returns you to the Crosstabs window. Click OK.

SPSS runs the analysis and displays the results in the Viewer—a case-processing summary followed by the requested cross-tabulation:

When SPSS runs Crosstabs, it produces a set of side-by-side frequency distributions of the dependent variabl e—one for each category of the independent variable—plus an overall frequency distribution for all analyzed cases. Accordingly, the table has four columns of numbers: one for low-income individuals, one for those in the middle-income tercile, one for those in the highest income group, and a total column showing the distribution

pid_3 Party ID: 3 cats * incgroup3 Family income tercile Crosstabulation

			incgroup3 Family income tercile			Total
			1 Low	2 Middle	3 High	
pid_3 Party ID: 3 cats	1 Dem	Count	829	617	530	1976
		% within incgroup3 Family income tercile	39.3%	34.5%	29.6%	34.7%
	2 Ind	Count	847	634	672	2153
		% within incgroup3 Family income tercile	40.2%	35.4%	37.6%	37.9%
	3 Rep	Count	432	540	586	1558
		% within incgroup3 Family income tercile	20.5%	30.2%	32.8%	27.4%
Total		Count	2108	1791	1788	5687
		% within incgroup3 Family income tercile	100.0%	100.0%	100.0%	100.0%

of all cases across the dependent variable. And, as requested, each cell shows the number (count) and column percentage.

What do you think? Does the cross-tabulation fit the hypothesis? The third rule of cross-tabulation analysis is easily applied. Focusing on the "Dem" value of the dependent variable, we see a pattern in the hypothesized direction. A comparison of respondents in the "Low" column with those in the "Middle" column reveals a decline from 39.3 to 34.5 in the percentage who are Democrats, a drop of about 5 percentage points. Moving from the "Middle" column to the "High" column, we find another decrease, from 34.5 percent to 29.6 percent, about another 5-point drop. Are lower-income people more likely to be Democrats than middle-income and higher-income people? Yes. Across the full range of the independent variable, from "Low" to "High" income, the percentage of Democrats declines by about 10 percentage points.

MEAN COMPARISON ANALYSIS

We now turn to another common hypothesis-testing situation: when the independent variable is categorical and the dependent variable is interval level. The logic of comparison still applies—divide cases on the independent variable and compare values of the dependent variable—but the method is different. Instead of comparing percentages, we now compare means.

To illustrate, let's say that you are interested in explaining this dependent variable: attitudes toward Hillary Clinton. Why do some people have positive feelings toward her, whereas others harbor negative feelings? Here is a plausible (if not self-evident) idea: Partisanship (independent variable) will have a strong effect on attitudes toward Hillary Clinton (dependent variable). The hypothesis: In a comparison of individuals, Democrats will have more favorable attitudes toward Hillary Clinton than will Republicans.

NES2012 contains ft_hclinton, a 100-point feeling thermometer. Each respondent was asked to rate Hillary Clinton on this scale, from 0 (cold or negative) to 100 (warm or positive). This is the dependent variable. NES2012 also has pid_x, which measures partisanship in seven categories, from Strong Democrat (coded 1) to Strong Republican (coded 7). The intervening codes capture gradations between these poles: Weak Democrat (coded 2), Independent-Democrat (coded 3), Independent (coded 4), Independent-Republican (coded 5), and Weak Republican (coded 6). This is the independent variable. If the hypothesis is correct, we should find that Strong Democrats have the highest mean scores on ft_hclinton and that mean scores decline systematically across categories of pid_x, hitting a low point among respondents who are Strong Republicans. Is this what happens?

Click Analyze → Compare Means → Means. The Means window pops into view. Scroll down the left-hand variable list until you find ft_hclinton, and then click it into the Dependent List panel, as shown in Figure 4-2. Now scroll to pid_x and click it into the Independent List panel. In the Means window, click Options. The Means: Options window (also shown in Figure 4-2) permits you to select desired statistics from the left-hand Statistics panel and click them into the right-hand Cell Statistics panel. Alternatively, you can remove statistics from Cell Statistics by clicking them back into the left-hand panel. Unless instructed otherwise, SPSS will always report the mean, number of cases, and standard deviation of the dependent variable for each category of the independent variable. Because at present we are not interested in obtaining the standard deviation, select it with the mouse and click it back into the left-hand Statistics panel. Our mean comparison table will report only the mean value of ft_hclinton and the number of cases for each category of pid_x. Click Continue, returning to the Means window. Click OK.

Compared with cross-tabulations, mean comparison tables are models of minimalism:

ft_hclinton PRE: Feeling Thermometer: H

pid_x Party ID	Mean	N
1 StrDem	82.98	1154
2 WkDem	69.38	889
3 IndepDem	71.59	688
4 Indep	55.16	823
5 IndepRep	44.40	721
6 WkRep	45.99	730
7 StrRep	31.98	867
Total	58.83	5871

The independent variable, pid_x, defines the leftmost column, which shows all seven categories, from Strong Democrat at the top to Strong Republican at the bottom. Beside each category, SPSS has calculated the mean of ft_hclinton and reported the number of respondents falling into each value of partisanship. (The bottom row, "Total," gives the mean for the whole sample.)

Among Strong Democrats, the mean Clinton rating is quite warm—about 83 degrees. Do ratings of Clinton decrease as attachment to the Democratic Party weakens and identification with the Republican Party strengthens? Notice that the mean drops sharply among Weak Democrats (who average about 69 degrees), and remains essentially unchanged (although increasing slightly) among Independent-Democratic Leaners (about 72). The mean declines through the Independent category, and then (interestingly) gets "sticky" again among Independent-Republican Leaners and Weak Republicans (44–46 degrees) before ending at a chilly 32 degrees among Strong Republicans. Interesting hiccups aside, we can see that, on the whole, the data support the hypothesis.

Figure 4-2 Means Window (modified)

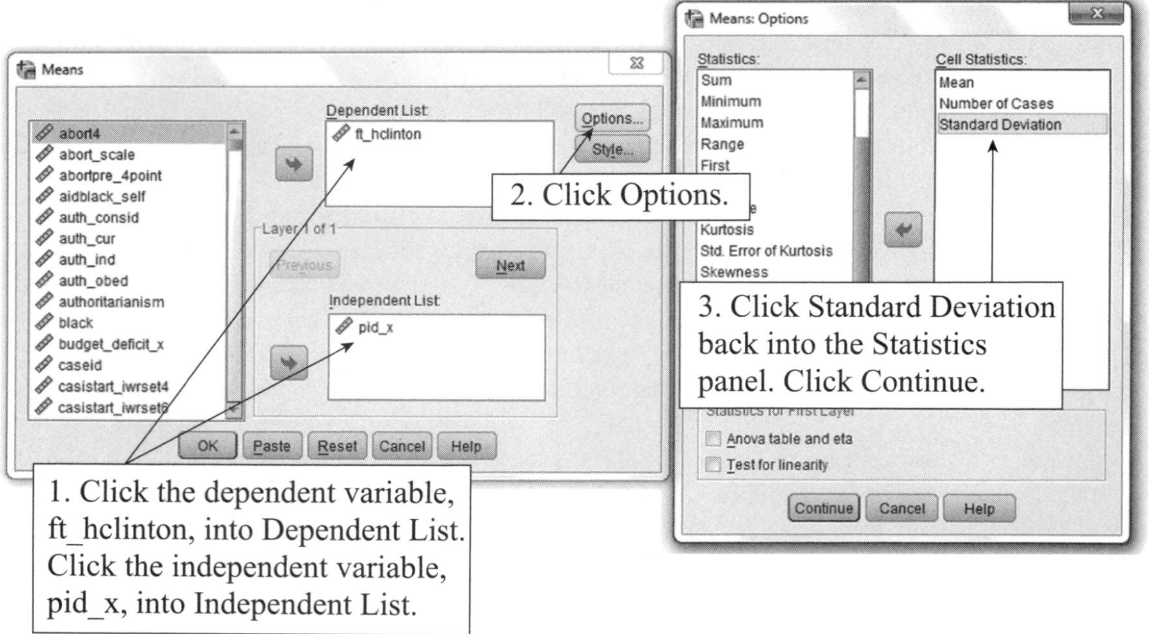

GRAPHING RELATIONSHIPS

We have already seen that bar charts and histograms can be a great help in describing the central tendency and dispersion of a *single* variable. SPSS graphic procedures are also handy for illustrating relationships *between* variables. It will come as no surprise that SPSS supports a large array of graphic styles. To get a flavor of this variety, click Graphs → Legacy Dialogs and consider the choices (Figure 4-3). The legacy charts, as the name implies, use interfaces developed in earlier releases of SPSS. Even so, the Legacy Dialogs are still the best way to create graphics in SPSS. In this chapter you will learn to use Bar, Line, and Boxplot. (In Chapter 6, you will work with Error Bar, and in Chapter 8 you use Scatter/Dot.) A bar chart is useful for summarizing the relationship between two categorical variables. A line chart adds clarity to the relationship between a categorical independent variable and an interval-level dependent variable. Line charts are elegant and parsimonious, and they can be used to display the relationship between two categorical variables as well. Boxplots are especially useful for small-*N* datasets, such as States or World.

To get an idea of how SPSS produces a line chart, let's begin by creating one of our own, using the results from the Hillary Clinton–party identification example. Turn your attention to Figure 4-4, an empty graphic shell. The horizontal axis, called the *category axis,* displays values of the independent variable, party identification. Each partisanship category is represented by a hash mark, from Strong Democrat on the left to Strong Republican on the right. The vertical axis, called the *summary axis,* represents mean values of the dependent variable, Hillary Clinton thermometer ratings. Now, with a pen or pencil, make a dot directly above each category of the independent variable, recording the mean of the Clinton thermometer for each partisan category. Above the Strong Democrat hash mark, for example, place a dot at 83 on the summary axis. Go to the right along the category axis until you reach the hash mark for Weak Democrat and make a dot directly above the hash mark, at about 69. Do the same for the remaining partisan groups, placing a dot vertically above each hash mark at the mean value of ft_hclinton. (Don't worry about being precise. Just get the dots close to the mean values.) Using a straight edge, connect the dots. You've created a line chart for the relationship, a visual summary that is easy to interpret and present.

Figure 4-3 Graphs Drop-down Menu

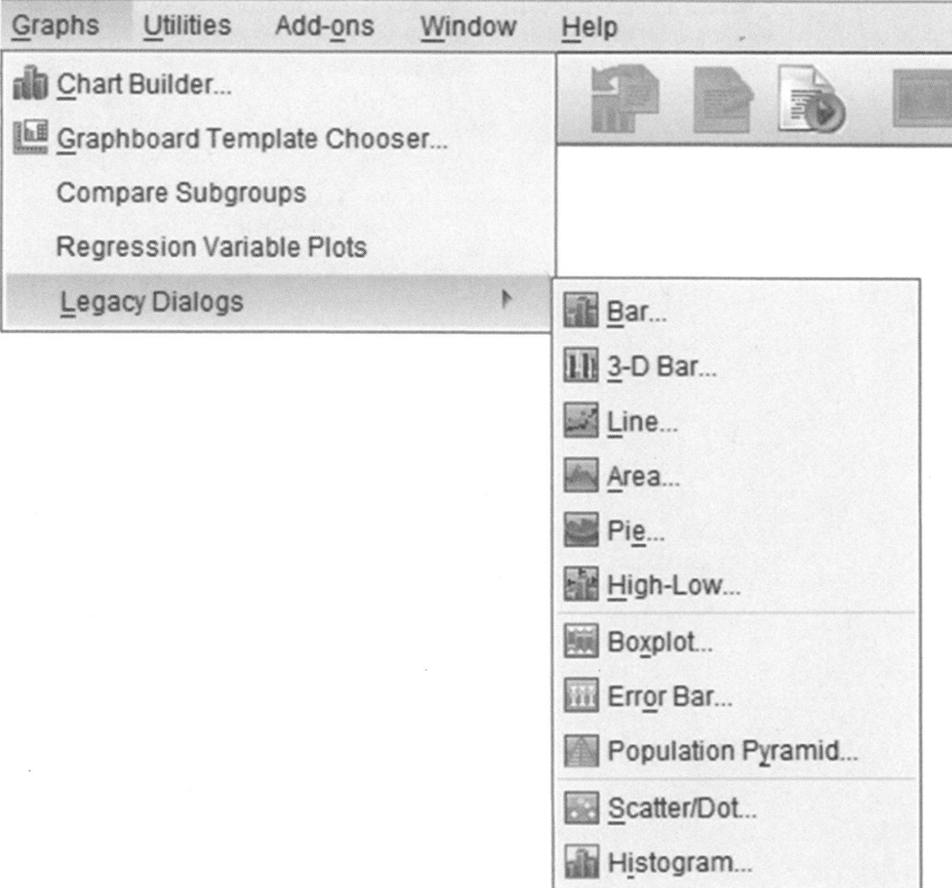

Using Line Chart

Now we will ask SPSS to do the work for us. Click Graphs → Legacy Dialogs → Line. The Line Charts window opens (Figure 4-5). Make sure that the icon next to "Simple" is clicked and that the radio button next to "Summaries for groups of cases" is selected.[1] Click Define. The Define Simple Line window appears (Figure 4-6). The two topmost boxes—the (currently inactive) Variable box in the Line Represents panel and the Category Axis box—are where we tailor the line chart to our specifications. (There are two additional boxes in the Panel by area, one labeled "Rows" and one labeled "Columns," as shown in Figure 4-6. For our purposes in this book, these boxes may be safely ignored.)

Figure 4-4 Line Chart Shell: Mean Values of Hillary Clinton Thermometer, by Party Identification

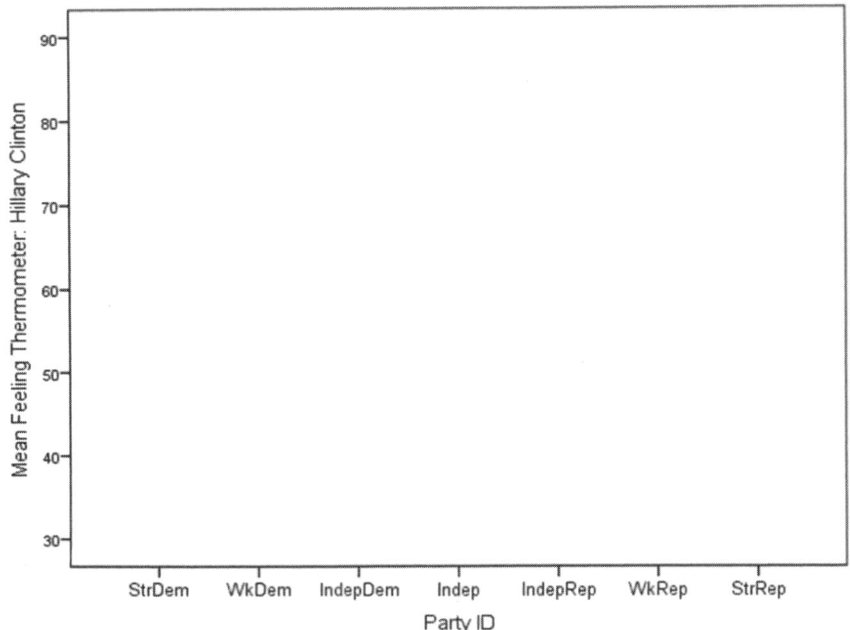

Figure 4-5 Line Charts Window (default)

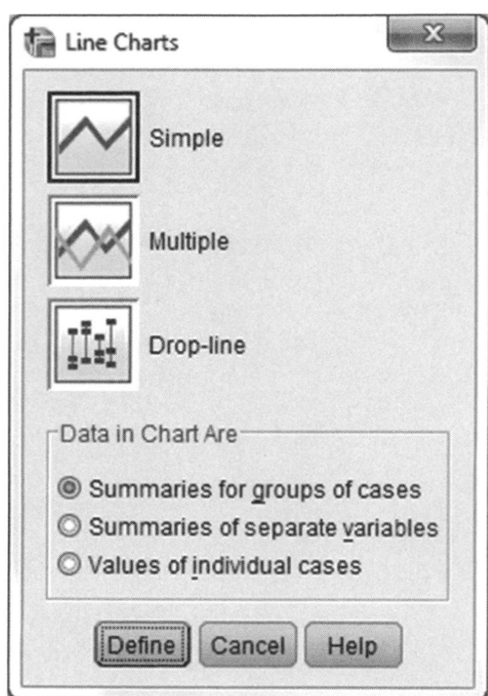

Figure 4-6 Define Simple Line Window (default)

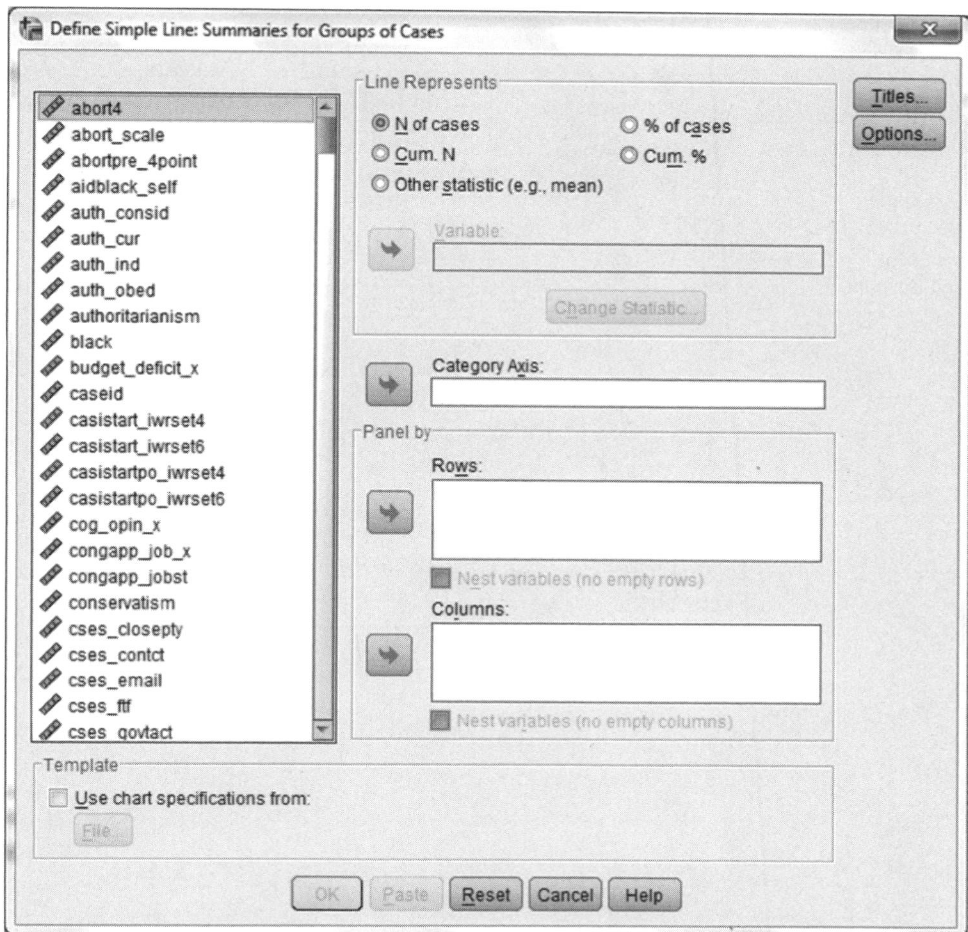

In SPSS idiom, "category axis" means *x*-axis or horizontal axis—the axis that represents values of the independent variable. Because, in the current example, pid_x is the independent variable, scroll down to pid_x and click it into the Category Axis box. We also want to graph the mean values of ft_hclinton for each category of pid_x. To do this, SPSS requires instruction.[2] In the Line Represents panel, select the Other statistic radio button, as shown in Figure 4-7. The Variable box is activated. Now scroll the left-hand variable list until you find ft_hclinton, and then click ft_hclinton into the Variable box. SPSS moves ft_hclinton into the Variable box and gives it the designation "MEAN(ft_hclinton)." In Line Chart, whenever you request Other statistic and click a variable into the Variable box (as we have just done), SPSS assumes that you want to graph the mean values of the requested variable (as, in this case, we do).[3] So this default serves our current needs. Click OK.

A line chart of the Hillary Clinton–party identification relationship appears in the Viewer (Figure 4-8). Line charts are at once simple and informative. You can see immediately the negative linear relationship between the independent and dependent variables. Note, too, the curious "blips" between Weak Democrats and Independent-Democratic Leaners—and between Independent-Republican Leaners and Weak Republicans.

Using Bar Chart

In most respects, Bar Chart is similar to Line Chart. However, a key difference between the two exists. In this guided example, you will obtain a bar chart of the relationship you analyzed earlier between party identification (the dependent variable pid_3) and income (the independent variable incgroup3). In the next section, we will take an excursion into the Chart Editor, which allows you to enhance the appearance and content of the charts you create.

Click Graphs → Legacy Dialogs → Bar. The Bar Charts window gives you the same set of choices as the Line Charts window. (See Figure 4-9.) Ensure that the same choices are selected: Simple and Summaries for groups of cases. Click Define. The Define Simple Bar window opens, and it, too, is identical to the Define Simple Line window in every detail. Because incgroup3 is the independent variable, it goes in the Category Axis box. Scroll to

Figure 4-7 Define Simple Line Window (modified)

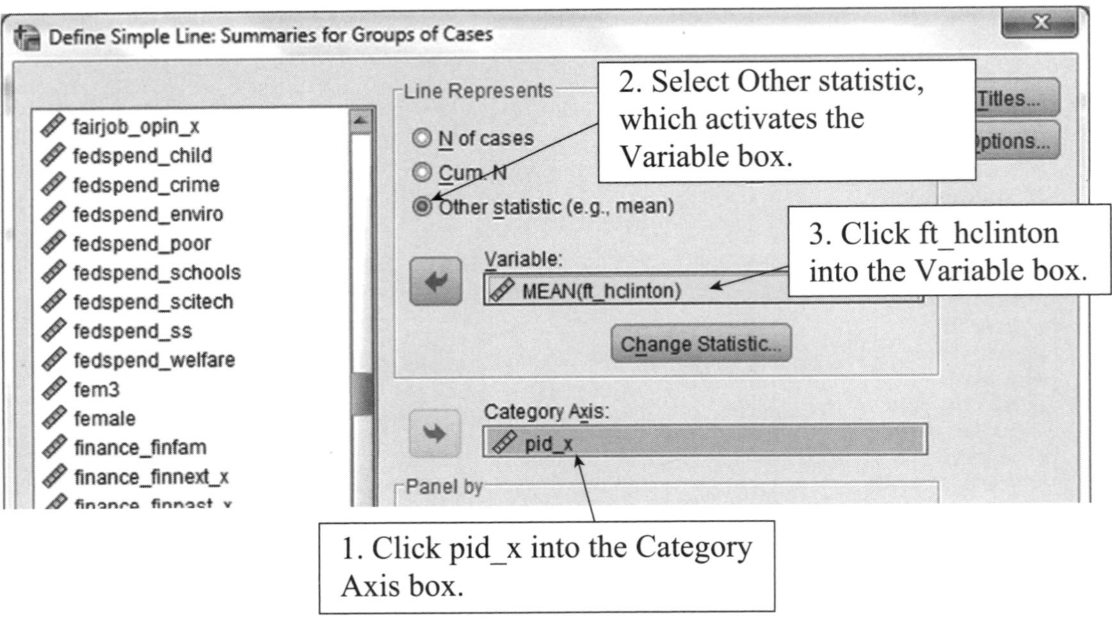

Figure 4-8 Line Chart Output: Mean Values of Hillary Clinton Thermometer by Party Identification

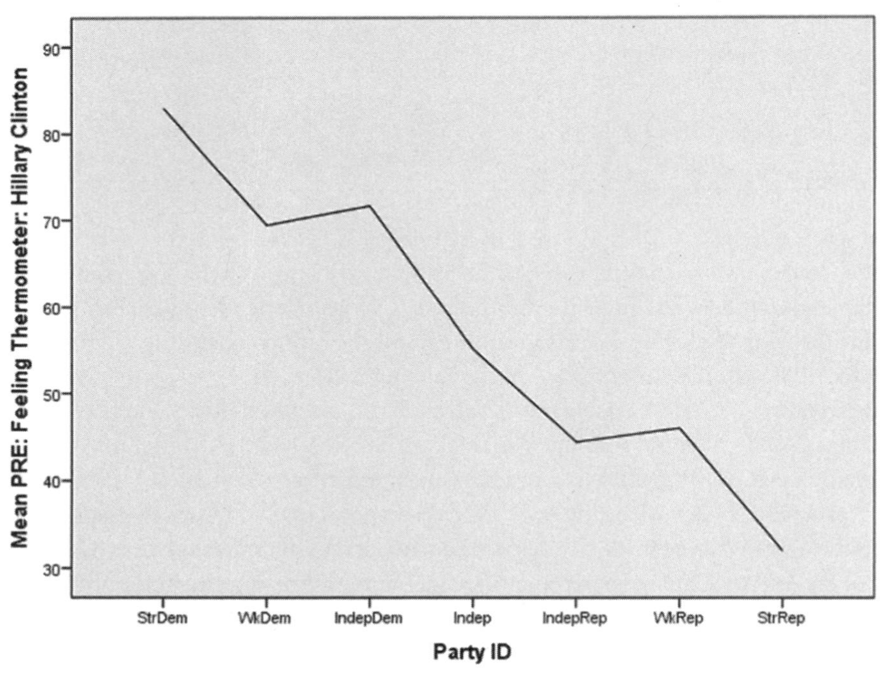

incgroup3 and click it over, as shown in Figure 4-9. So far, this is the same as before. At this point, however, the peculiarities of Bar Chart require that we refamiliarize ourselves with specific coding information about the dependent variable, pid_3. Why so? As a substantive matter, we want to depict the percentage of respondents in each category of incgroup3 who are Democrats. To accomplish this, Bar Chart will need specific coding information. Find pid_3 in the left-hand variable list, place the cursor pointer on it, and then *right*-click. Click on Variable Information and review the numeric codes. Respondents who are Democrats are coded 1, Independents are coded 2, and Republicans are coded 3. Commit this fact to short-term memory: Democrats are coded 1 on the dependent variable, pid_3.

Figure 4-9 Preparing to Create a Bar Chart

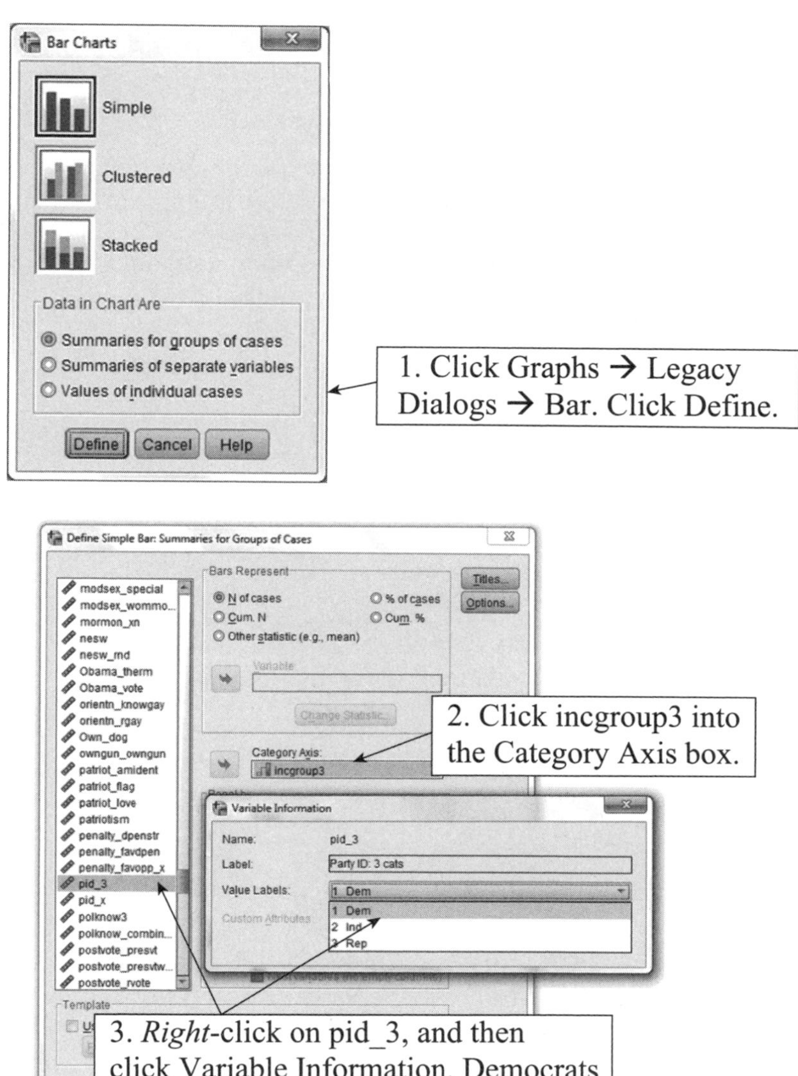

Now return to the Bars Represent panel. Select the Other statistic radio button, and click pid_3 into the Variable box, as shown in Figure 4-10. The designation "MEAN(pid_3)" appears in the Variable box, as shown in Figure 4-10. Just as it did in Line Chart, SPSS assumes that we are after the mean of pid_3. This default is fine for mean comparisons, but in this case it won't do. Click the Change Statistic button.[4]

The Statistic window presents itself (Figure 4-10). The radio button for the default, Mean of values, is currently selected. However, we are interested in obtaining the percentage of cases in code 1 ("Democrat") on pid_3. How do we get SPSS to cooperate with this request? Click the radio button at the bottom on the left, the one labeled "Percentage inside," as shown in Figure 4-11. The two boxes, one labeled "Low" and the other labeled "High," go active. Our request is specific and restrictive: We want the percentage of respondents in code 1 only. Expressed in terms that SPSS can understand, we want the percentage of cases "inside" a coded value of 1 on the low side and a coded value of 1 on the high side. Click the cursor in the Low box and type a "1." Click the cursor in the High box and type a "1." The Statistic window should now look like Figure 4-11. Click Continue, returning to the Define Simple Bar window. The Define Simple Bar window should now look like Figure 4-12. Click OK.

Our special instructions have paid off. SPSS displays a bar chart of the relationship between income and party identification (Figure 4-13). The category axis is labeled nicely, and the heights of the bars clearly depict this pattern: As incomes increase from low to high, the percentage of Democrats declines. At least *we* know what the bars represent, because we did the analysis. An interested observer, however, might do a double-take at the title on the vertical axis, "%in(1,1) Party ID: 3 cats." SPSS is relentlessly literal. We asked it to graph the percentages of people between code 1 and code 1 on pid_3, so that is how SPSS has titled the axis. We need to give the vertical axis a more descriptive title, and perhaps make other appearance-enhancing changes.

Figure 4-10 Define Simple Bar Window and Statistic Window (default)

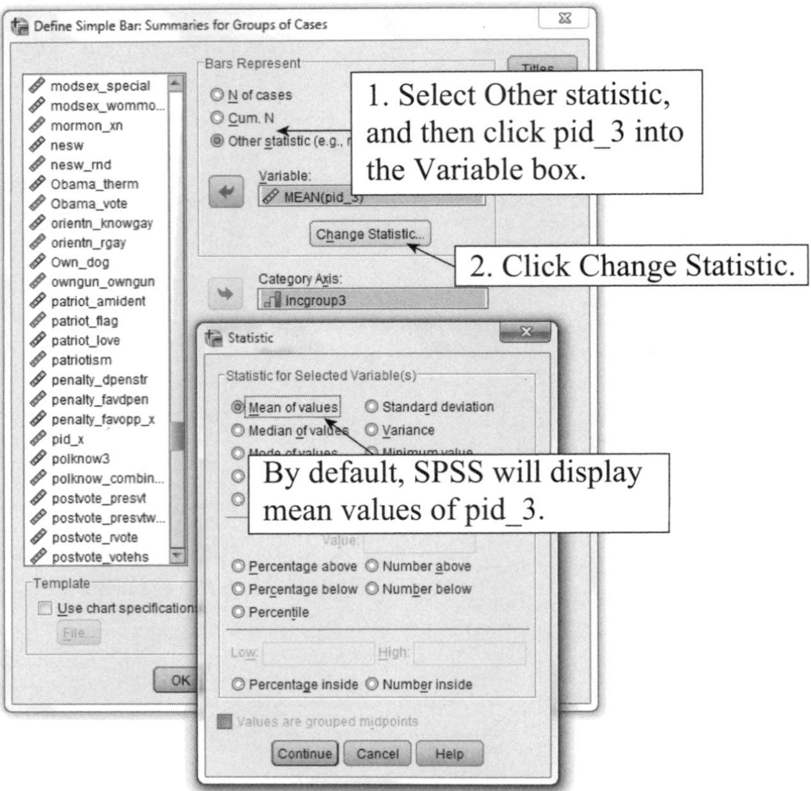

Figure 4-11 Statistic Window (modified)

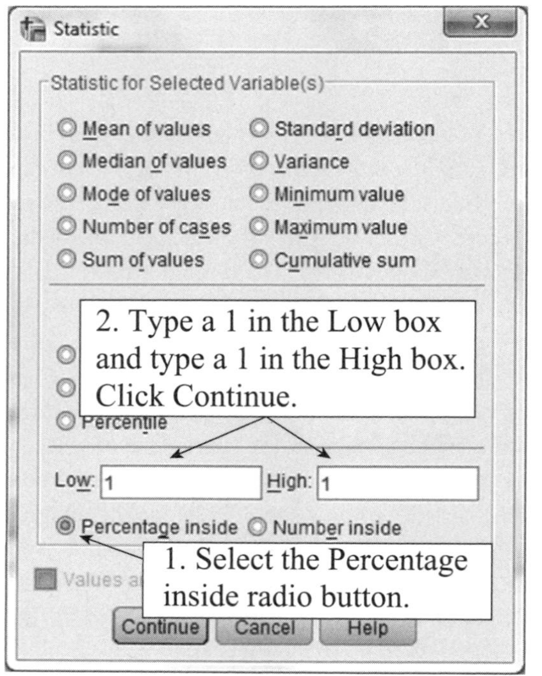

Figure 4-12 Define Simple Bar Window (modified)

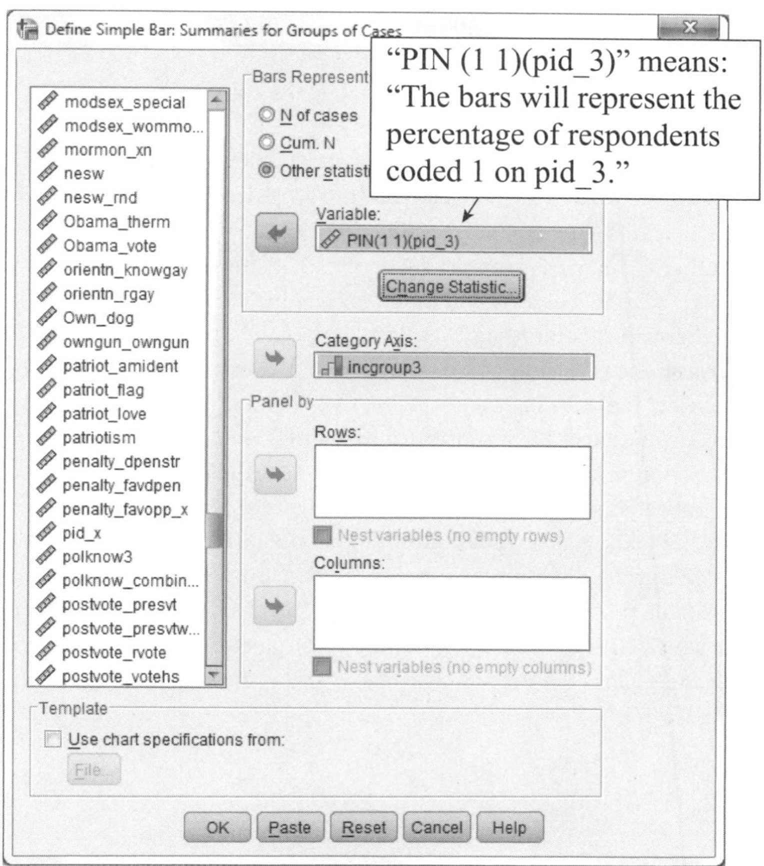

Figure 4-13 Bar Chart Output

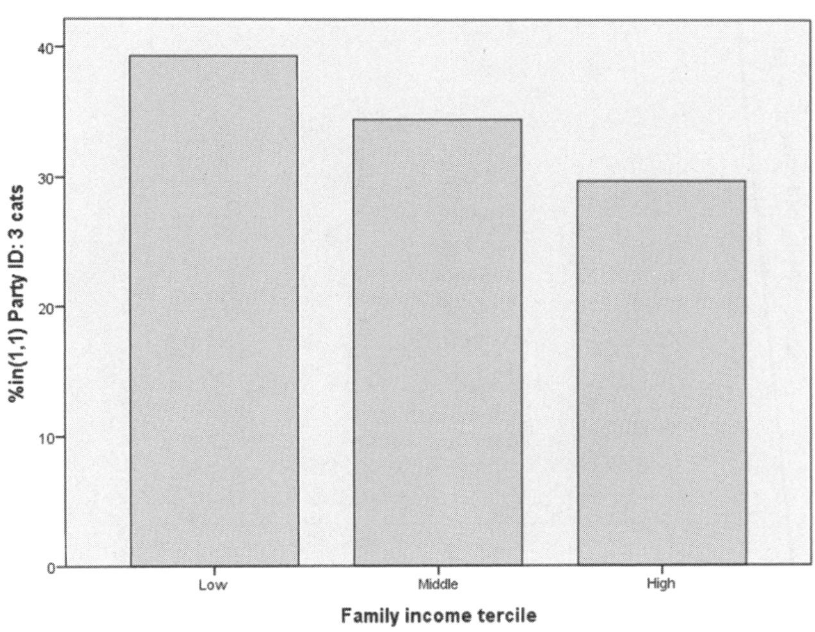

Using the Chart Editor

SPSS permits the user to modify the content and appearance of any tabular or graphic object it produces in the Viewer. The user invokes the Editor, makes any desired changes, and then returns to the Viewer. The changes made in the Chart Editor are recorded automatically in the Viewer. In this section we describe how to retitle the vertical axis of the bar chart you just created. We'll also change the color of the bars. (The default color is rather uninspired, and it doesn't print well.)

In the Viewer, place the cursor anywhere on the bar chart and double-click. SPSS opens the Chart Editor (Figure 4-14). As with any editing software, the Chart Editor recognizes separate elements within an object. It recognizes some elements as text. These elements include the axis titles and the value labels for the categories of incgroup3. It recognizes other elements as graphic, such as the bars in the bar chart. First we will edit a text element, the title on the vertical axis. Then we will modify a graphic element, the color of the bars.

Place the cursor anywhere on the title "%in(1,1) Party ID: 3 cats" and single-click. SPSS selects the axis title. With the cursor still placed on the title, single-click again. SPSS moves the text into editing mode inside the chart (Figure 4-15). Delete the current text. In its place type the title "Percent Democratic." Now click on one of the bars. (As soon as you click off the axis title, it returns to its rightful position in the chart.) The editor selects all the bars (see Figure 4-16). Click on the Properties icon located near the upper-left corner of the Chart Editor window. This opens the Properties window, the most powerful editing tool in the Chart Editor's arsenal. (*Special note:* If you plan to do a lot of editing, it is a good idea to open the Properties window soon after you enter the Chart Editor. Each time you select a different text or graphic element with the mouse, the Properties window changes, displaying the editable properties of the selected element.) Click on the Fill & Border tab, as shown in Figure 4-16. In the Color panel, click in the Fill box. In the color palette, click on a desirable hue, and then click Apply. SPSS makes the change. Close the Properties window and exit the Chart Editor. The finished product appears in the Viewer (Figure 4-17).

Figure 4-14 Chart Editor

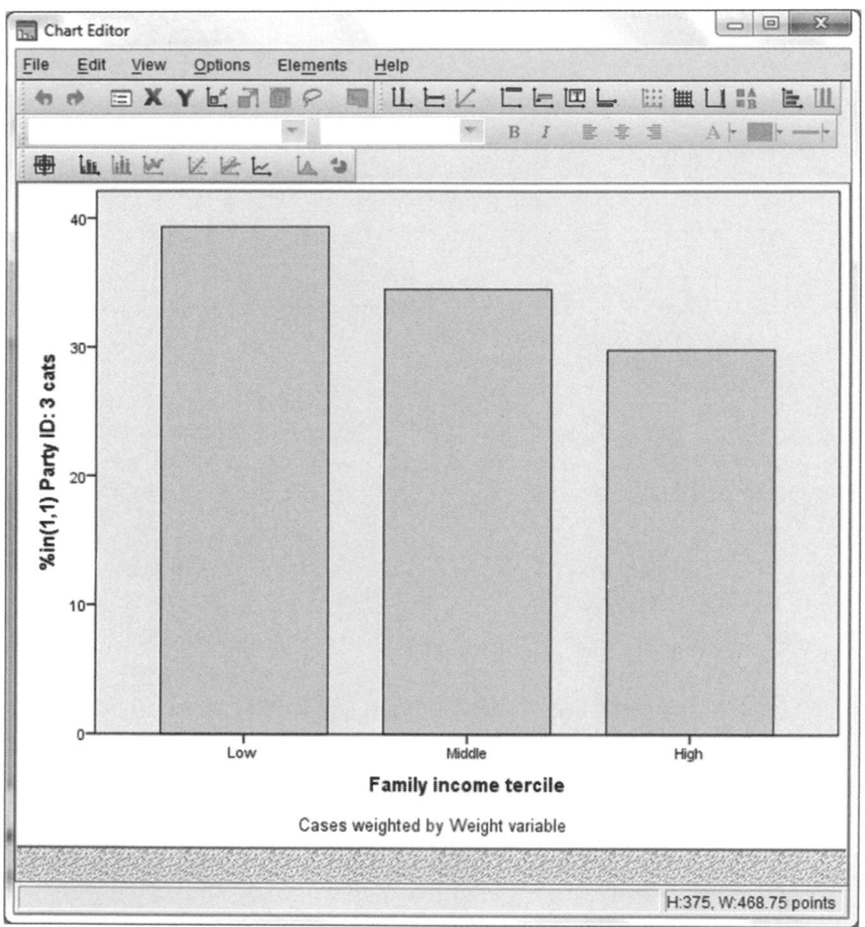

Figure 4-15 Bar Chart Axis Title Ready for Editing

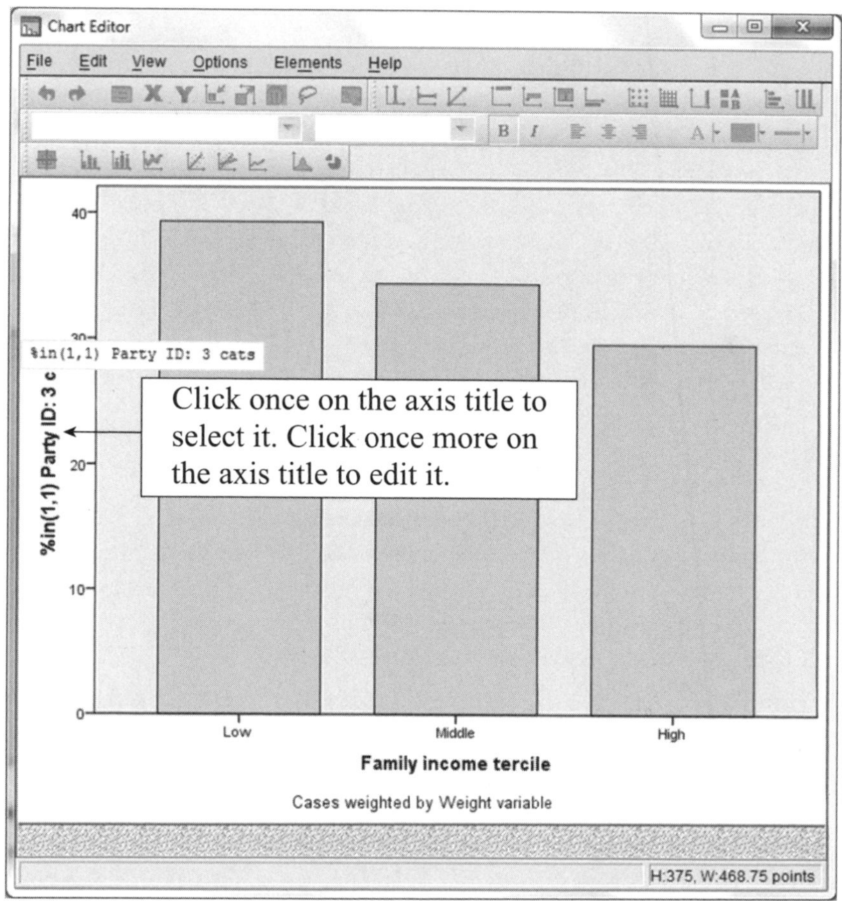

Figure 4-16 Using the Properties Window to Change the Bar Color

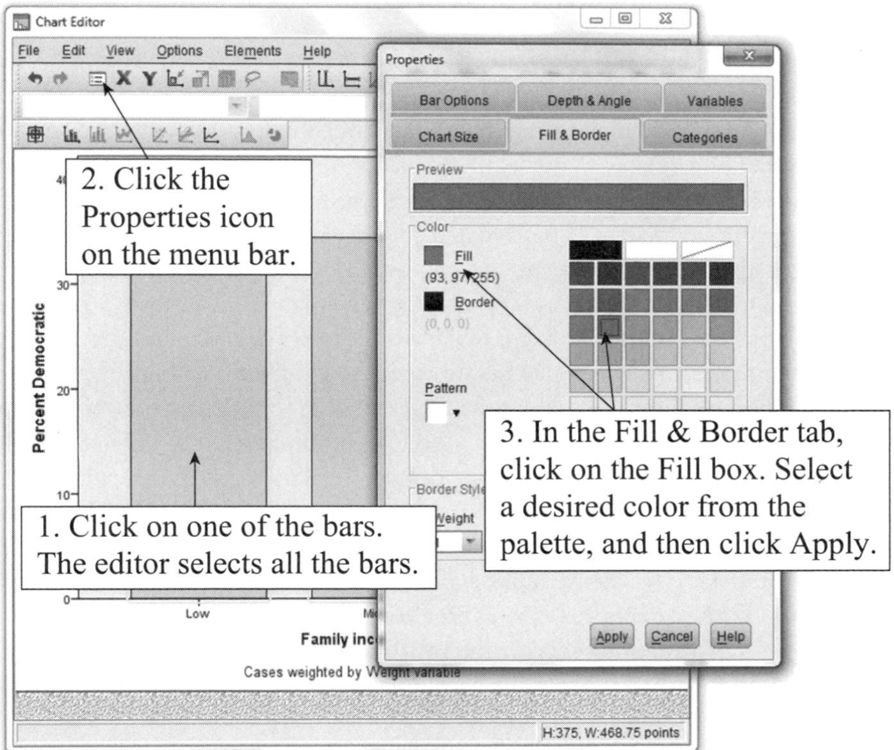

Figure 4-17 Edited Bar Chart in the Viewer

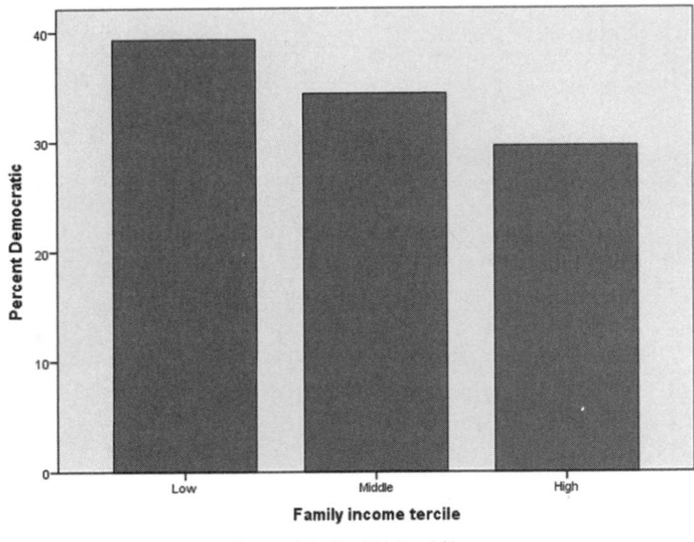

Using Boxplot

We have seen that a line chart, which plots the mean of a dependent variable across the values of an independent variable, is aimed squarely at visualizing mean comparisons by reexpressing them in graphic form. A box plot favors the display of dispersion over central tendency, providing an additional graphic complement to mean comparisons. Box plots describe an interval-level variable by graphing a five-number summary: minimum, lower quartile, median, upper quartile, and maximum. Box plots also reveal outliers.[5] Box plots are particularly useful for graphing relationships in datasets with intrinsically interesting cases, such as States or World. To learn about this type of chart, we will work through an example from States.

Consider Figure 4-18, a box plot of the relationship between region (the independent variable, displayed along the horizontal axis) and the percentage of states' adult population who frequently attend religious services (the dependent variable, displayed on the vertical axis). Each box communicates three values: the lower quartile (the value below which 25 percent of the cases fall), the median (the value that splits the cases into two equal-size groups), and the upper quartile (the value below which 75 percent of the cases fall). Thus, the distance between the bottom and top of the box defines the interquartile range (IQR), the range of a variable that encompasses the "middle half" of a distribution. For example, notice how spread out Southern states are: Their median level of religious attendance is rather high (about 48 percent), but half of them fall in the long interval between about 42 percent and 52 percent. Contrast this with the cohesiveness of Western states, whose median (about 32 percent) is tightly bounded between approximately 29 percent and 34 percent. In the Northeast, low-attendance states are so numerous that, when lumped together, they define the lower quartile. The lower and upper hinges of each box connect the minimum and maximum values, as long as those values fall in the interval between one and a half IQRs above the upper quartile and one and a half IQRs below the lower quartile. Outliers are defined as cases that fall outside those boundaries. SPSS distinguishes two species of outlier. If an outlier falls in the interval between one and a half IQRs and three IQRs above the upper quartile (or below the lower quartile), it is symbolized by a small circle. If the outlier is "extreme"—if it lies beyond three IQRs above the upper quartile (or below the lower quartile)—it is symbolized by a star. By default, SPSS uses case numbers to identify outliers.

To obtain a box plot, click Charts → Legacy Dialogs → Boxplot, opening the Boxplot window (Figure 4-19). Click Define and consider the Define Simple Boxplot window (Figure 4-20). As with the other charts you have produced, the independent variable (in the example, region) goes in the Category Axis box, and the dependent variable (attend_pct) goes in the Variable box. The Label Cases by box allows you to identify outliers with an alphabetic variable. In States, there are two choices: the variable state (states' full names) and StateID (the two-letter state abbreviation). Click StateID into the Label Cases by box and click OK. The box plot appears in the Viewer (Figure 4-21). Among the Western states, Alaska is the outlier at the lower end of attendance; Idaho and Utah are outliers at the higher end.

Figure 4-18 Box Plot

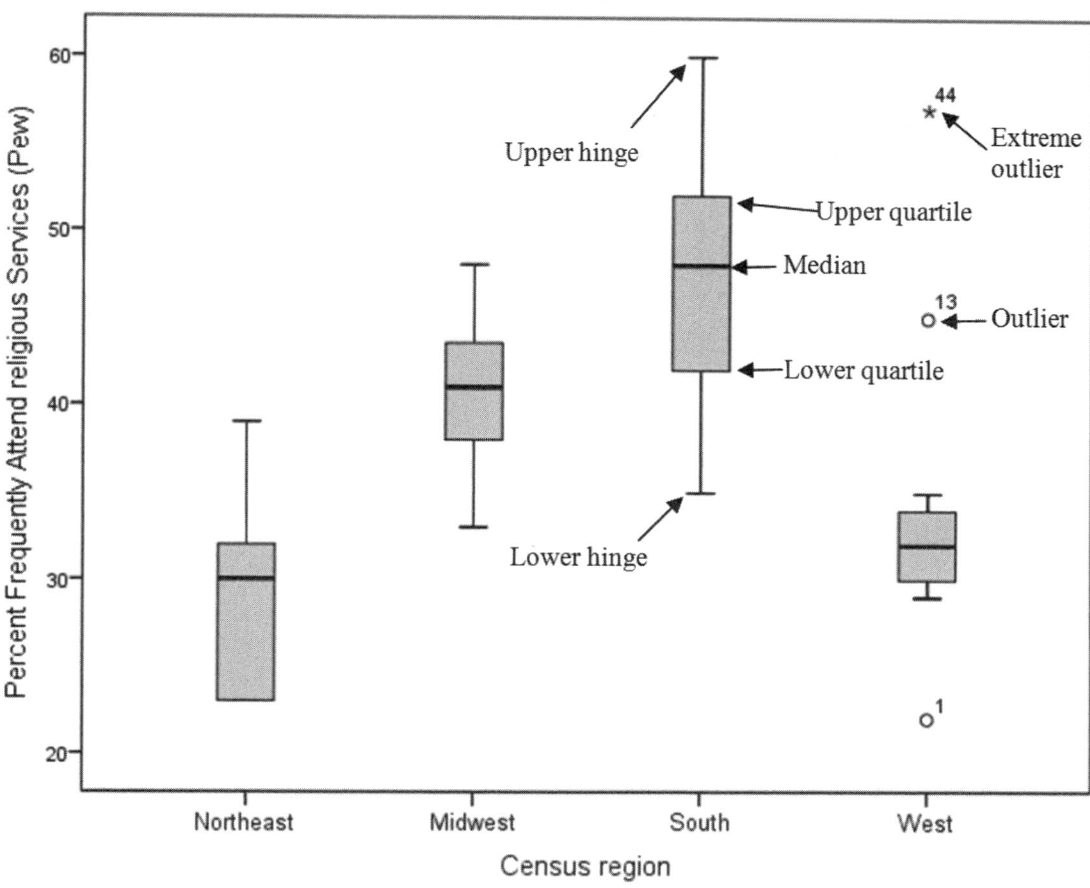

Figure 4-19 Box Plot Window

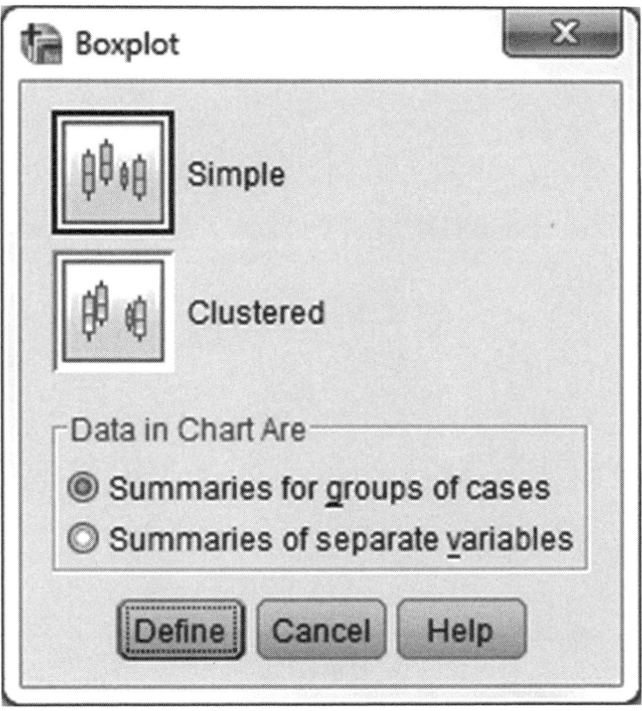

Figure 4-20 Creating a Box Plot

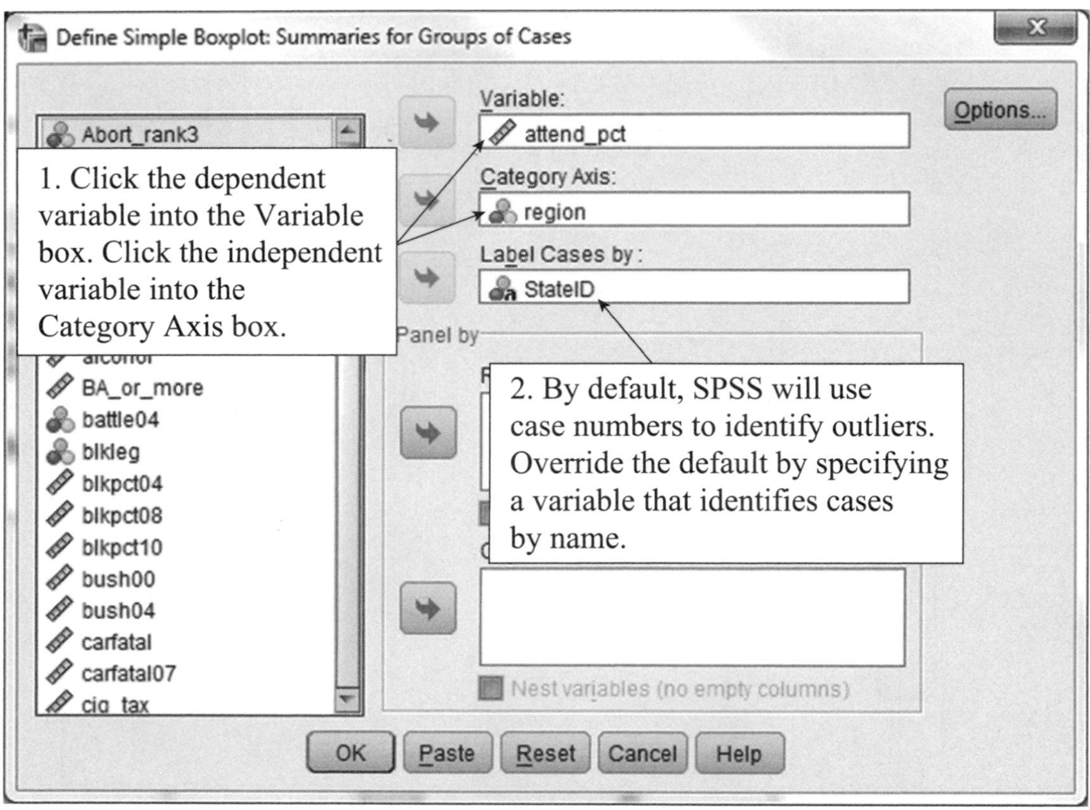

Figure 4-21 Box Plot with Outliers Identified

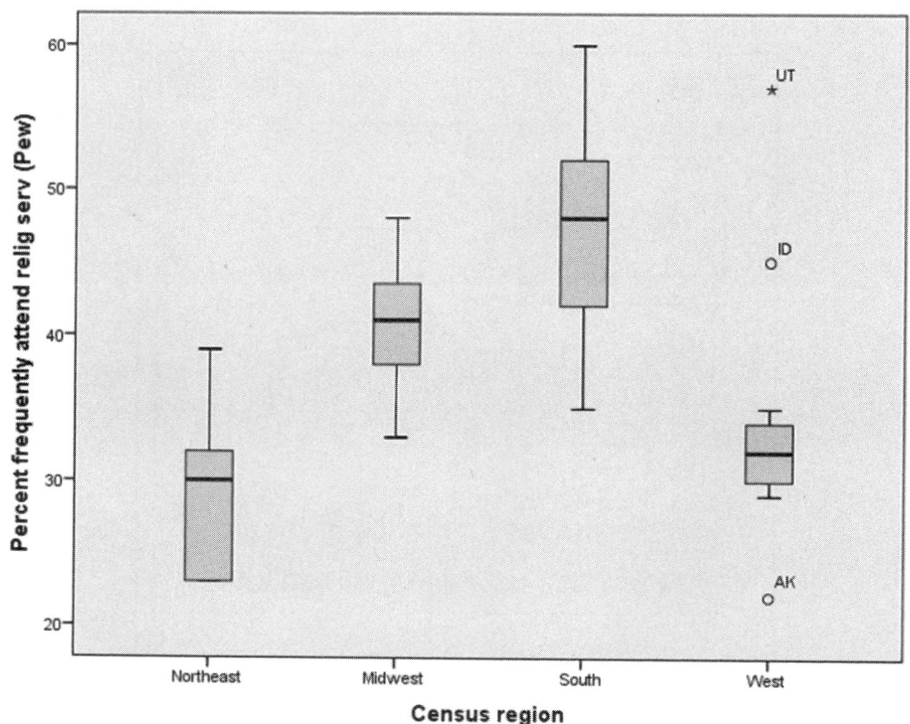

EXERCISES

1. (Dataset: NES2012. Variables: inspre_self, pid_x.) Here is a widely observed difference between Democrats and Republicans: Democrats favor government-funded medical insurance and Republicans prefer private insurance plans. Is this difference borne out by the data? Dataset NES2012 contains the variable inspre_self, a 7-point scale that measures respondents' opinions on this issue. Respondents indicate their opinions by choosing any position on this scale, from 1 (government plan) at one end to 7 (private plan) at the other end. This is the dependent variable. Use the 7-point party identification scale (pid_x) as the independent variable.

   A. If Democrats are more likely than Republicans to favor government-funded medical insurance, then Democrats will have (check one):

   ❑ a higher mean on inspre_self than do Republicans.

   ❑ about the same mean on inspre_self as do Republicans.

   ❑ a lower mean on inspre_self than do Republicans.

   B. Using Analyze → Compare Means → Means, obtain a mean comparison that shows the mean score on the dependent variable, inspre_self, for each category of the independent variable, pid_x. Write the results in the table that follows:

Government/private medical insurance scale: self-placement		
Party ID	Mean	*N*
Strong Democrat	?	?
Weak Democrat	?	?
Independent-Democrat	?	?
Independent	?	?
Independent-Republican	?	?
Weak Republican	?	?
Strong Republican	?	?
Total	?	?

   C. Does your analysis support the idea that Democrats are more likely than Republicans to support government-funded medical insurance? (circle one)

   Yes No

   Explain your answer, making specific reference to the results you obtained in part A.

   ____

   ____

   ____

   ____

   D. Suppose you overheard someone making this claim: "People might say they're 'Independent-Republicans,' but when it comes to opinions about medical insurance, they're closer to 'Independent' than to 'Republican.'" Based on your analysis, is this claim correct? (circle one)

   Yes No

   Explain your answer.

   ____

   ____

   ____

   ____

E. Obtain a line chart of the relationship. Remember to put the independent variable, pid_x, on the Category Axis and the dependent variable, inspre_self, in the Variable box of the Line Represents panel. Print the line chart.

2. (Dataset: NES2012. Variables: gay_marry, relig_import, gender, libcon3.) Should same-sex couples be legally permitted to marry? This controversial issue has gained center stage in American politics. One can imagine several characteristics that divide people on this issue. People for whom religious beliefs are more important might be less likely to approve same-sex marriage than will those for whom religion is less important. Men may be less likely than women to approve. Or conservatives might be less open to the idea than are liberals.

   Dataset NES2012 contains gay_marry, which is coded 0 (no, do not approve of same-sex marriage) and 1 (yes, approve). This is the dependent variable that you will use to test each of the following hypotheses:

   Hypothesis 1: In a comparison of individuals, people who place less importance on religion will be more likely to favor same-sex marriage than will people who place more importance on religion. (The independent variable is relig_import.)

   Hypothesis 2: In a comparison of individuals, women are more likely than men to favor same-sex marriage. (The independent variable is gender.)

   Hypothesis 3: In a comparison of individuals, liberals are more likely than conservatives to favor same-sex marriage. (The independent variable is libcon3.)

   When using SPSS to obtain a series of cross-tabulations having the same dependent variable but different independent variables, only one Crosstabs run is required. In the Crosstabs window, click gay_marry into the Row(s) panel. Click gender, libcon3, and relig_import into the Column(s) panel. (Make sure to request column percentages in the Crosstabs Cell Display.) Run the analysis. In the following spaces, record the percentages who say "Yes" when asked about same-sex marriage:

<table>
<tr><td></td><td colspan="3">Importance of religion</td></tr>
<tr><td></td><td colspan="2">Important</td><td>Not important</td></tr>
<tr><td>Percentage "Yes"</td><td colspan="2">?</td><td>?</td></tr>
<tr><td></td><td colspan="3">Gender</td></tr>
<tr><td></td><td colspan="2">Male</td><td>Female</td></tr>
<tr><td>Percentage "Yes"</td><td colspan="2">?</td><td>?</td></tr>
<tr><td></td><td colspan="3">Ideology</td></tr>
<tr><td></td><td>Liberal</td><td>Moderate</td><td>Conservative</td></tr>
<tr><td>Percentage "Yes"</td><td>?</td><td>?</td><td>?</td></tr>
</table>

B. These findings (circle one)

support Hypothesis 1. do not support Hypothesis 1.

Explain your reasoning, making specific reference to the percentages in part A.

____

____

____

____

C. These findings: (circle one)

support Hypothesis 2. do not support Hypothesis 2.

Explain your reasoning, making specific reference to the percentages in part A.

D. These findings: (circle one)

support Hypothesis 3. do not support Hypothesis 3.

Explain your reasoning, making specific reference to the percentages in part A.

E. Obtain a bar chart of the relationship between gay_marry and libcon3. You will want the vertical axis to depict the percentage of respondents in the "Yes" category of gay_marry. Remember that those who support same-sex marriage are coded 1 on the dependent variable. Using the Chart Editor, give the vertical axis a more descriptive title, such as "Percentage Favoring Same-sex marriage." Change the default bar color to a color of your choosing. Print the bar chart you created.

3. (Dataset: NES2012. Variables: pres_vote12, econ_ecpast.) What factors determine how people vote in presidential elections? Political scientists have investigated and debated this question for many years. A particularly powerful and elegant perspective emphasizes voters' *retrospective* evaluations. According to this view, for example, voters whose financial situations have gotten better during the year preceding the election are likely to reward the candidate of the incumbent party. Voters whose economic situations have worsened, by contrast, are likely to punish the incumbent party by voting for the candidate of the party not currently in power. As political scientist V. O. Key famously once put it, the electorate plays the role of "rational god of vengeance and reward."[6] Does Key's idea help explain how people voted in the 2008 election?

A. Test this hypothesis: In a comparison of individuals, those who think the economy has improved during the year preceding the 2012 election were more likely to vote for the incumbent, Barack Obama, than were individuals who think the economy has not improved. Use these two variables from NES2012: pres_vote12 (dependent variable) and econ_ecpast (independent variable). Obtain a cross-tabulation of the relationship. Record the percentages voting for Romney and Obama in the table that follows:

	PRE: National economy better/worse in last year			
R Vote, 2012	Better	Same	Worse	Total
Obama	?	?	?	?
Romney	?	?	?	?
Total	100.0	100.0	100.0	100.0

B. What do you think? Are the data consistent with the hypothesis? Write a paragraph explaining your reasoning, making specific reference to the evidence in part A.

C. *Loss aversion* is an interesting psychological phenomenon that can shape the choices people make.[7] One idea behind loss aversion is that losses loom larger than commensurate gains. According to this theory, for example, the psychological pain felt from losing $100 is greater than the pleasure felt from gaining $100. Applied to retrospective voting, loss aversion might suggest that the "vengeance" impulse is stronger than the "reward" impulse—that the anti-incumbent motivation among those who say the economy has worsened will be stronger than the pro-incumbent motivation among those who think it has improved.

With this idea in mind, examine the percentages in the table in part A. What do you think? Do the data suggest that Key's rational god of vengeance is stronger than his rational god of reward? Answer yes or no and explain your reasoning, making specific reference to the evidence in part A.

___

___

___

___

4. (Dataset: NES2012. Variables: libcpre_ptyd, libcpre_ptyr, pid_x.) Partisan polarization can create some interesting perceptual distortions. Do partisans tend to view themselves as more moderate than they view the opposing party? For example, do Democrats think Republicans are ideologically extreme, yet see themselves as more moderate? By the same token, do Republicans view Democrats as liberal "extremists" but perceive themselves as purveyors of middle-of-the-road politics? Where do Independents place the Democrats and Republicans on the left–right continuum? A Pew survey found this thought-provoking asymmetry: All partisans—Democrats, Independents, and Republicans—placed the Republicans at practically the same "conservative" position on the liberal–conservative scale. However, the placement of the Democrats varied widely: Republicans placed Democrats well toward the "liberal" side, Independents saw Democrats as somewhat left-of-center, and Democrats placed themselves squarely at the "moderate" position.[8] In this exercise, you will see if you can replicate the Pew report's findings using NES2012.

The NES2012 variable, libcpre_ptyd, measures respondents' perceptions of the ideological position of the Democratic Party using the standard 7-point scale: 1 ("Extremely liberal"), 2 ("Liberal"), 3 ("Slightly liberal"), 4 ("Moderate"), 5 ("Slightly conservative"), 6 ("Conservative"), and 7 ("Extremely conservative"). Another variable, libcpre_ptyr, asks respondents to place the Republican Party along the same 7-point metric. For the purposes of this exercise, you will treat these two measures as interval-level variables. Thus, lower mean values denote higher perceived liberalism, values around 4 denote perceived moderation, and higher mean values denote higher levels of perceived conservatism. Libcpre_ptyd and libcpre_ptyr are the dependent variables. Our old reliable, pid_x, is the independent variable. If the Pew results are correct, you should find that all partisan groups, from Strong Democrats to Strong Republicans, share very similar "conservative" perceptions of the Republican Party—but they hold very different perceptions of the Democratic Party.

A. Run two mean comparison analyses, one for the libcpre_ptyd-pid_x relationship, and one for the libcpre_ptyr-pid_x relationship. Fill in the means in the following table:

Party identification	Ideological placement of Democrats: Mean	Ideological placement of Republicans: Mean
Strong Democrat	?	?
Weak Democrat	?	?
Independent-Democrat	?	?
Independent	?	?
Independent-Republican	?	?
Weak Republican	?	?
Strong Republican	?	?

B. Examine your findings. Are the Pew findings borne out by the NES2012 data? Answer yes or no and explain your reasoning, making specific reference to the evidence you obtained in part A.

____

____

____

____

5. (Dataset: GSS2012. Variables: polviews, femrole.) Why do some people hold more traditional views about the role of women in society, whereas others take a less traditional stance? General ideological orientations, liberalism versus conservatism, may play an important role in shaping individuals' opinions on this cultural question. Thus it seems plausible to suggest that ideology (independent variable) will affect opinions about appropriate female roles (dependent variable). The hypothesis: In a comparison of individuals, liberals will be more likely than conservatives to approve of nontraditional female roles.

GSS2012 contains femrole, a scale that measures opinions about the appropriate role of women. You analyzed this variable in Chapter 2. Recall that femrole ranges from 0 (women "domestic") to 9 (women in "work"). That is, higher scores denote less traditional beliefs. This is the dependent variable. GSS2012 also has polviews, a 7-point ordinal scale measuring ideology. Scores on polviews can range from 1 ("Extremely liberal") to 7 ("Extremely conservative"). This is the independent variable.

A. According to the hypothesis, as the values of polviews increase, from 1 through 7, mean values of femrole should: (circle one)

decrease. neither decrease nor increase. increase.

B. Test the hypothesis using Compare Means → Means. Write the results in the table that follows:

Female role: home, work		
Ideological self-identification	Mean	*N*
Extremely liberal	?	?
Liberal	?	?
Slightly liberal	?	?
Moderate	?	?
Slightly conservative	?	?
Conservative	?	?
Extremely conservative	?	?
Total	?	?

C. *Overall*, would you say that the results generally support the hypothesis, or do the results not support the hypothesis? (circle one)

The results support the hypothesis. The results do not support the hypothesis.

Explain your reasoning, making specific reference to the evidence in part A.

____

____

____

____

D. Obtain a line chart of this relationship. Print the line chart you created.

6. (Dataset: GSS2012. Variables: egalit_scale3, educ_4.) Pedantic pontificator is offering a group of students his thoughts about the relationship between educational attainment and egalitarianism, the belief that government should do more to make sure resources are more equitably distributed in society: “Educated people have a humanistic world view that is sorely lacking among the self-seeking, less educated classes. Educated citizens see inequality . . . and want to rectify it! Plus, most colleges and universities are populated with liberal faculty, who indoctrinate their students into left-wing ideologies at every opportunity. Thus, it’s really quite simple: As education goes up, egalitarianism increases.”

   GSS2012 contains egalit_scale3, which measures egalitarian beliefs in three categories: “Less egalitarian,” “Middle,” and “More egalitarian.” GSS2012 also has educ_4, which records educational attainment in four categories: less than high school (“<HS”), high school (“HS”), some college (“Some Coll”), and college or graduate degree (“Coll+”).

   A. Run a cross-tabulation analysis that tests pedantic pontificator’s idea about the relationship between education and egalitarianism. Use this table to record the percentages you obtained:

	Less than high school	High school	Some college	College or graduate degree	Total
Less egalitarian	?	?	?	?	?
Middle	?	?	?	?	?
More egalitarian	?	?	?	?	?
Total	100.0%	100.0%	100.0%	100.0%	100.0%

   B. Create a bar chart of the relationship. *Hint*: You might decide to graph, for each value of the independent variable, the percentage of respondents falling into the “Less egalitarian” category of the dependent variable (coded 1 on egalit_scale3). Alternatively, you could graph the percentage of respondents falling into the “More egalitarian” category of the dependent variable (coded 3 on egalit_scale3). In the Graph Editor, give the vertical axis a more descriptive label. Edit the chart for appearance. Print the chart.

   C. Consider all the evidence you have obtained. Does your analysis support the hypothesis that those having higher levels of education are more egalitarian than are those having lower levels of education? Explain, making specific reference to the evidence in parts A and B.

7. (Dataset: GSS2012. Variables: intethn_2, affrmact2, natrace.) Untruthful answers by survey respondents can create big headaches for public opinion researchers. Why might a respondent not tell the truth to an interviewer? Certain types of questions, combined with particular characteristics of the interviewer, can evoke a phenomenon called preference falsification: “the act of misrepresenting one’s genuine wants under perceived social pressures.”[9] For example, consider the difficulty in gauging opinions on affirmative action, hiring policies aimed at giving preference to black applicants. One might reasonably expect that people questioned by an African-American interviewer would express greater support for such programs than would those questioned by a white interviewer. An affirmative action opponent, not wanting to appear racially insensitive to a black questioner, might instead offer a false pro-affirmative action opinion.[10]

   GSS2012 contains intethn_2, coded 1 for respondents questioned by a white interviewer and coded 2 for those questioned by a black interviewer. This is the independent variable that will allow you to test two preference falsification hypotheses:

   Hypothesis 1: In a comparison of individuals, those questioned by a black interviewer will be more likely to express support for affirmative action than will those questioned by a white interviewer. (The dependent variable is affrmact2, coded 1 for “support” and 2 for “oppose.”)

Hypothesis 2: In a comparison of individuals, those questioned by a black interviewer will be more likely to say that we are spending too little to improve the condition of blacks than will those questioned by a white interviewer. (The dependent variable is natrace, which is coded 1 for respondents saying "too little," 2 for those saying "about the right amount," and 3 for "too much.")

A. Run the Crosstabs analysis. In the table that follows, record the percentages that support affirmative action and the percentages that say we are spending too little to improve the condition of blacks:

	Interviewer's race	
	White	Black
Percent "support" affirmative action	?	?
Percent spending "too little" to improve condition of blacks	?	?

B. These findings (circle one)

support Hypothesis 1. do not support Hypothesis 1.

Explain your reasoning, making reference to specific percentages in part A.

____

____

____

____

C. These findings (circle one)

support Hypothesis 2. do not support Hypothesis 2.

Explain your reasoning, making reference to specific percentages in part A.

____

____

____

____

D. Produce a bar chart depicting the relationship between support for affirmative action and interviewer race. Give the vertical axis a more descriptive title and edit the bar color. Make the chart more readable. Print the chart.

8. (Dataset: States. Variables: ProLife, region, state.) In this exercise, you will (i) create and print a box plot of the relationship between ProLife (the percentage of the public holding a "pro-life" position on abortion) and region, (ii) identify outliers within regions, and (iii) use the box plot to determine if two hypothetical claims are correct.

A. Obtain and print a box plot of the relationship between ProLife and region. ProLife goes in the Variable box, and region goes in the Category Axis box. To identify outliers, click the alphabetic variable, state, into the Label Cases by box.

B. The box plot you produced in part A identifies one outlier in the Northeast and two outliers in the West. Which state is the outlier in the Northeast? The state of (fill in the blank) ________________.
Which two states are outliers in the West? The states of ________________________
and ____________________________________.

C. Consider this claim: "As measured by the interquartile range, Southern states are less spread out—that is, have less variation in pro-life opinions—than states in the Midwest." Is this claim correct? Answer yes or no and explain, making reference to specific features of the box plot.

____

____

____

D. Consider this claim: "Ignoring outliers, the Northeastern states are more cohesive in their pro-life opinions than are the Western states." Is this claim correct? Answer yes or no and explain, making reference to specific features of the box plot.

____

____

____

____

9. (Dataset: States. Variables: Smokers12, Cig_tax12_3.) Two policy researchers are arguing about whether higher taxes on cigarettes reduce cigarette consumption.

Policy Researcher 1: "The demand for cigarettes is highly inelastic—smokers need to consume cigarettes, and they will buy them without regard to the cost. Raising taxes on a pack of cigarettes will have no effect on the level of cigarette consumption."

Policy Researcher 2: "Look, any behavior that's taxed is discouraged. If state governments want to discourage smoking, then raising cigarette taxes will certainly have the desired effect. Higher taxes mean lower consumption."

Imagine a line chart of the relationship between cigarette taxes and cigarette consumption. The horizontal axis measures state cigarette taxes in three categories, from lower taxes on the left to higher taxes on the right. The vertical axis records the percentage of the population who are smokers. Below are two graphic shells, A and B. In shell A, you will sketch a line chart depicting what the relationship would look like, if Policy Researcher 1 is correct. In shell B, you will sketch a line chart depicting what the relationship would look like, if Policy Researcher 2 is correct.

A. If Policy Researcher 1 were correct, what would the line chart look like? Sketch a line inside the graphic space, depicting the relationship proposed by Policy Researcher 1.

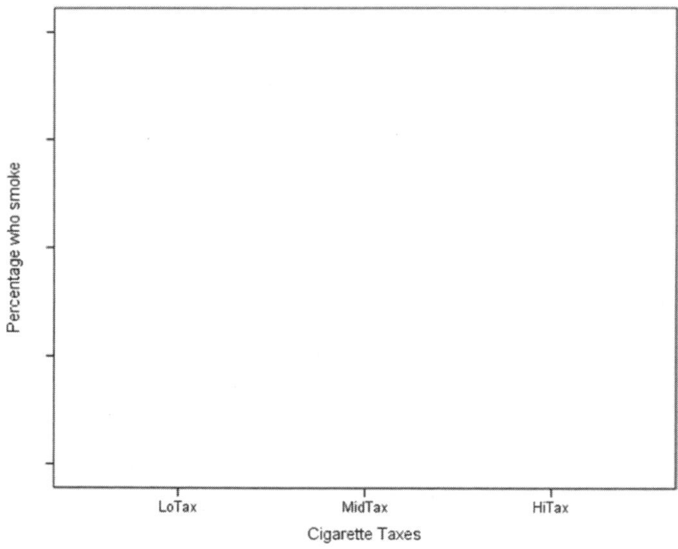

B. If Policy Researcher 2 were correct, what would the line chart look like? Sketch a line inside the graphic space, depicting the relationship proposed by Policy Researcher 2.

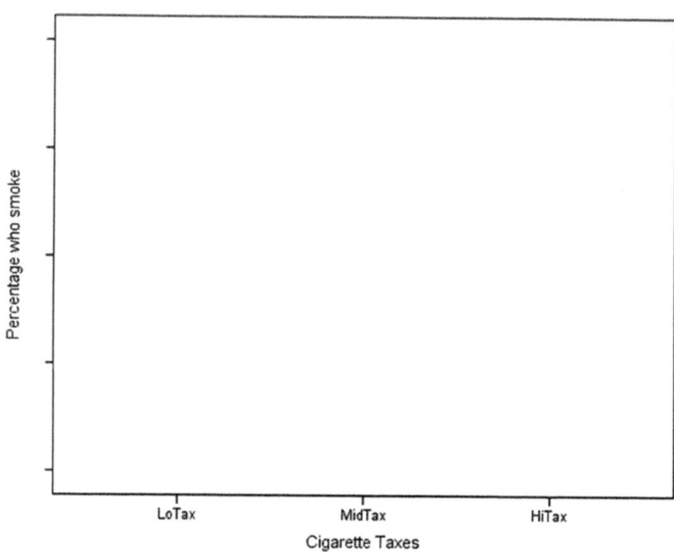

C. The States dataset contains the variables Smokers12 and Cig_tax12_3. Run a mean comparison analysis, using Smokers12 as the dependent variable and Cig_tax12_3 as the independent variable. Record your results in the table that follows:

Percentage who smoke (Smokers12)		
Cigarette taxes	Mean	*N*
Low tax	?	?
Middle tax	?	?
High tax	?	?
Total	?	50

D. Create and print a line chart of the relationship.

E. Examine the mean comparison table and the line chart. Which policy researcher is more correct? (check one)

- ☐ Policy Researcher 1 is more correct.
- ☐ Policy Researcher 2 is more correct.

F. Explain your answer in E, making specific reference to the evidence you obtained in parts C and D.

____

____

____

____

10. (Dataset: World. Variables: Enpp3_democ08, District_size3, Frac_eth3.) Two scholars of comparative politics are discussing possible reasons why some democracies have many political parties and other democracies have only a few.

Scholar 1: "It all has to do with the rules of the election game. Some countries, such as the United Kingdom, have single-member electoral districts. Voters in each district elect only one representative. This militates in favor of fewer and larger parties, since small parties have less chance of winning enough votes to gain the seat. Other countries, like Switzerland, have multimember districts. Because voters choose more than one representative per district, a larger number of smaller parties have a chance to win representation. It doesn't surprise me in the least, then, that the U.K. has fewer political parties than Switzerland."

Scholar 2: "I notice that your explanation fails to mention the single most important determinant of the number of political parties: social structural heterogeneity. Homogeneous societies, those with few linguistic or religious differences, have fewer conflicts and thus fewer parties. Heterogeneous polities, by the same logic, are more contentious and will produce more parties. By the way, the examples you picked to support your case also support mine: the U.K. is relatively homogeneous and Switzerland is relatively heterogeneous. It doesn't surprise me in the least, then, that the U.K. has fewer political parties than Switzerland."

A. Scholar 1's hypothesis: In a comparison of democracies, those having single-member districts will have (circle one)

fewer political parties   more political parties

than democracies electing multiple members from each district.

B. State Scholar 2's hypothesis:

____

____

____

____

C. The World dataset variable Enpp3_democ08 measures, for each democracy, the number of effective parliamentary parties: 1–3 parties (coded 1), 4–5 parties (coded 2), or 6–11 parties (coded 3). Use Enpp3_democ08 as the dependent variable to test each hypothesis. For independent variables, test Scholar 1's hypothesis using District_size3, which measures the number of seats per district: Countries with single-member districts are coded 1, countries that average more than one but fewer than six members are coded 2, and countries with six or more members per district are coded 3. Test Scholar 2's hypothesis using Frac_eth3, which classifies each country's level of ethnic/linguistic fractionalization as low (coded 1), medium (coded 2), or high (coded 3). Countries with higher codes on Frac_eth3 have a higher level of ethnic conflict. Run Crosstabs to test the hypotheses. In the table that follows, record the percentages of cases falling into the lowest code of the dependent variable, 1–3 parties:

	Average number of members per district		
	Single-member	>1–5 members	6 or more members
Percentage having 1–3 parties	?	?	?
	Level of ethnic fractionalization		
	Low	Medium	High
Percentage having 1–3 parties	?	?	?

D. Which of the following statements best summarizes your findings? (check one)

- ❑ Scholar 1's hypothesis is supported by the analysis, but Scholar 2's hypothesis is not supported by the analysis.
- ❑ Scholar 2's hypothesis is supported by the analysis, but Scholar 1's hypothesis is not supported by the analysis.

- ☐ Both hypotheses are supported by the analysis.
- ☐ Neither hypothesis is supported by the analysis.

E. Making specific reference to your findings, write a paragraph explaining your choice in part D.

____

____

____

____

11. (Dataset: World. Variables: Durable, Regime_type3, Country.) The two comparative politics scholars are still arguing, only now they're trying to figure out what sort of institutional arrangement produces the longest-lasting, most stable political system. Also, a third scholar joins the interchange of ideas.

Scholar 1: "Presidential democracies, like the United States, are going to be more stable than are any other type of system. In presidential democracies, the executive and the legislature have separate electoral constituencies and separate but overlapping domains of responsibility. The people's political interests are represented both by the president's national constituency and by legislators' or parliament members' more localized constituencies. If one branch does something that's unpopular, it can be blocked by the other branch. The result: political stability."

Scholar 2: "Parliamentary democracies are by far more stable than presidential democracies. In presidential systems, the executive and the legislature can be controlled by different political parties, a situation that produces deadlock. Since the leaders of the legislature can't remove the president and install a more compliant or agreeable executive, they are liable to resort to a coup, toppling the whole system. Parliamentary democracies avoid these pitfalls. In parliamentary democracies, all legitimacy and accountability resides with the legislature. The parliament organizes the government and chooses the executive (the prime minister) from among its own leaders. The prime minister and members of parliament have strong incentives to cooperate and keep things running smoothly and efficiently. The result: political stability."

Scholar 3: "You two have made such compelling—if incorrect—arguments that I almost hesitate to point this out: Democracies of any species, presidential or parliamentary, are inherently unstable. Any system that permits the clamor of competing parties or dissident viewpoints is surely bound to fail. If it's stability that you value above all else, then dictatorships will deliver. Strong executives, feckless or nonexistent legislatures, powerful armies, social control. The result: political stability."

The World dataset contains the variable Durable, which measures the number of years since the last regime transition. The more years that have passed since the system last failed (higher values on durable), the more stable a country's political system. The variable Regime_type3 captures system type: dictatorship, parliamentary democracy, or presidential democracy.

A. Perform a mean comparison analysis of the relationship between Durable and Regime_type3. Based on a comparison of means, which is the apparently correct ranking of regime types, from most stable to least stable?

- ☐ parliamentary democracies (most stable), presidential democracies, dictatorships (least stable)
- ☐ parliamentary democracies (most stable), dictatorships, presidential democracies (least stable)

B. Create a box plot of the relationship. Use the alphabetic variable, Country, to identify outliers. Closely examine the box plot. In what way does the graphic evidence support the ranking in part A?

____

____

____

____

C. In what way does the graphic evidence NOT support the ranking in part A?

____

____

____

____

D. Print the box plot you created in part B.

12. (Dataset: World. Variables: Dem_score14, Dem_other5.) Why do some countries develop democratic systems, whereas others do not? Certainly the transition toward democracy—or away from it—is a complex process. Some scholars emphasize factors internal to countries, such as educational attainment or economic development. Others look to external factors, such as patterns of governance that are prevalent in a country's region of the world. Perhaps governmental systems are like infectious diseases: Similar systems diffuse among countries in close geographic proximity. According to the democratic diffusion hypothesis, countries in regions having fewer democracies are themselves less likely to be democratic than are countries in regions having more democracies.[11]

A. Suppose you had two variables for a large number of countries: a dependent variable that measured democracy along an interval-level scale, with higher scores denoting higher levels of democracy, and an independent variable measuring the number of democracies in each country's region, from fewer democracies to more democracies. According to the democratic diffusion hypothesis, if you were to compare mean values of the dependent variable for countries having different values on the independent variable, you should find: (check one)

- ☐ a lower mean of the dependent variable for countries in regions having fewer democracies than for countries in regions having more democracies.
- ☐ a higher mean of the dependent variable for countries in regions having fewer democracies than for countries in regions having more democracies.
- ☐ no difference between the means of the dependent variable for countries in regions having fewer democracies and countries in regions having more democracies.

B. The World dataset contains Dem_score14, an interval-level measure of democracy that ranges from 0 to 10, with higher scores denoting a greater level of democracy. This is the dependent variable. World also has Dem_other5, a 5-category ordinal measure that divides countries into five groups, based on the percentage of democracies in each country's geographic region: 10 percent, approximately 40 percent, approximately 60 percent, approximately 90 percent, or 100 percent. This is the independent variable. Run the appropriate mean comparison analysis. Label and record the results in the table that follows:

	Democracy score	
Percentage of other democracies in region	Mean	*N*
10%	?	?
Approximately 40%	?	?
Approximately 60%	?	?
Approximately 90%	?	?
100%	?	?
Total	?	153

C. Create and print a line chart of the relationship you just analyzed.

D. Examine the mean comparison table and the line chart. Which of the following statements are supported by your analysis? (check all that apply)

- ❑ Countries in regions having fewer democracies are more likely to be democratic than are countries in regions having more democracies.
- ❑ The relationship between the independent and dependent variables is positive.
- ❑ The democratic diffusion hypothesis is incorrect.
- ❑ Countries in regions having fewer democracies are less likely to be democratic than are countries in regions having more democracies.
- ❑ The relationship between the independent and dependent variables is negative.

13. (Dataset: World. Variables: Decent08, Effectiveness, Confidence.) Are decentralized governments more effective than centralized governments? In decentralized systems, local officials have politically autonomous authority to raise public money and administer government programs. This leads to more effective governance and, the argument goes, inspires confidence among citizens. Centralized systems, remote from local problems and burdened by red tape, may be both less effective and less likely to be viewed positively by citizens. Given these putative benefits, it is little wonder that "policy makers and politicians have frequently pushed for decentralisation as a panacea for the ills of poor governance."[12]

The World dataset variable Decent08 measures, for each country, the level of decentralization by three ordinal categories: no local elections (coded 1), legislature is elected, but executive is appointed (coded 2), and legislature and executive are locally elected (coded 3). Thus, higher codes on Decent08 denote higher levels of decentralized control. The assessments of a panel of expert observers were used to create the variable effectiveness, which measures government effectiveness on a 100-point scale (higher scores denote greater effectiveness). Confidence, also on a 100-point scale, gauges the degree to which a country's citizens have "a great deal" or "quite a lot" of confidence in state institutions (higher scores denote higher confidence).

A. The World variables will permit you to test two hypotheses about the effects of decentralization on effectiveness and confidence. State the two hypotheses.

Effectiveness hypothesis:

____

____

____

____

Confidence hypothesis:

____

____

____

____

B. Test the hypotheses with Compare Means. Write the results in the table that follows:

Democratic decentralization		Government effectiveness scale	Confidence in institutions scale
No local elections	Mean	?	?
	N	?	?
Legislature is elected but executive is appointed	Mean	?	?
	N	?	?
Legislature and executive are locally elected	Mean	?	?
	N	?	?
Total	Mean	?	?
	N	?	?

C. The effectiveness hypothesis (circle one)

is supported   is not supported by the analysis.

Explain your reasoning, making specific reference to the evidence in part B.

____

____

____

____

D. The confidence hypothesis (circle one)

is supported   is not supported by the analysis.

Explain your reasoning, making specific reference to the evidence in part B.

____

____

____

____

That concludes the exercises for this chapter.

NOTES

1. Because we are graphing one relationship, we want a single line. And because we are comparing groups of partisans, we want SPSS to display a summary measure, the mean, for each group.
2. Unless we modify the Line Represents panel to suit our analysis, SPSS will produce a line chart for the number of cases (*N* of cases) in each category of pid_x.
3. Of course, you will encounter situations in which you do not want mean values. Later in this chapter we review the procedure for Change Statistic.

4. The Change Statistic button will not be available unless the variable in the Variable box is highlighted. A variable is highlighted automatically when you click it into the Variable box. If you are experimenting and lose the highlighting, simply click directly on the variable in the Variable box. This restores the highlighting.
5. Robert I. Kabacoff, *R in Action: Data Analysis and Graphics with R* (Shelter Island, N.Y.: Manning Publications, 2011), 133. Box plots may also be used to describe ordinal-level variables that have many discrete values.
6. V. O. Key, *Politics, Parties, and Pressure Groups,* 5th ed. (New York: Crowell, 1964), 568.
7. George A. Quattrone and Amos Tversky, "Contrasting Rational and Psychological Analyses of Political Choice," *American Political Science Review* 82, no. 3 (September 1988): 719–736.
8. The Pew Research Center for the People and the Press, "Views of Parties' Ideologies: More Now See GOP as Very Conservative," September 12, 2011.
9. Timur Kuran, *Private Truths, Public Lies: The Social Consequences of Preference Falsification* (Cambridge, Mass.: Harvard University Press, 1995), 3.
10. It may have occurred to you that this effect might be greater for white respondents than for black respondents, with white subjects more likely to hide their true preferences in the presence of a black interviewer. An exercise in Chapter 5 will give you a chance to investigate this possibility.
11. See Jeffrey S. Kopstein and David A. Reilly, "Geographic Diffusion and the Transformation of the Postcommunist World," *World Politics,* 53 (2000): 1–37. Noting that "[a]ll of the big winners of postcommunism share the trait of being geographically close to the former border of the noncommunist world" (p. 1), Kopstein and Reilly use geographic proximity to the West as the independent variable in testing the democratic diffusion hypothesis. By and large, the authors find "that the farther away a country is from the West, the less likely it is to be democratic" (p. 10).
12. Conor O'Dwyer and Daniel Ziblatt, "Does Decentralisation Make Government More Efficient and Effective?" *Commonwealth & Comparative Politics,* 44 (November 2006): 1–18. This quote is from page 2. O'Dwyer and Ziblatt use sophisticated multivariate techniques to test the hypothesis that decentralized systems are more effective. Interestingly, they find that decentralization produces a higher quality of governance in richer countries but a lower quality of governance in poorer countries.

Making Controlled Comparisons

Watch a screencast of the guided examples in this chapter.
edge.sagepub.com/pollock

Procedures Covered

Analyze → Descriptive Statistics → Crosstabs (with Layers)

Analyze → Compare Means → Means (with Layers)

Graphs → Legacy Dialogs → Multiple Line

Political analysis often begins by making simple comparisons using cross-tabulation analysis or mean comparison analysis. Simple comparisons allow the researcher to examine the relationship between an independent variable, X, and a dependent variable, Y. However, there is always the possibility that alternative causes—rival explanations—are at work, affecting the observed relationship between X and Y. An alternative cause is symbolized by the letter Z. If the researcher does not control for Z, then he or she may misinterpret the relationship between X and Y.

CROSS-TABULATION ANALYSIS WITH A CONTROL VARIABLE

To demonstrate how to use SPSS Crosstabs to obtain control tables, we will work through an example with GSS2012. Consider this hypothesis: In a comparison of individuals, those who attend religious services less frequently will be more likely to favor the legalization of marijuana than will those who attend religious services more frequently. In this hypothesis, attend3, which categorizes respondents' church attendance as "Low," "Moderate," or "High," is the independent variable. GSS2012 contains the variable grass, which records respondents' opinions on the legalization of marijuana. (Code 1 is "Legal," and code 2 is "Not legal.") To stay acquainted with cross-tabulation analysis, we will start by looking at the uncontrolled relationship between attend3 and grass. In addition to considering whether the hypothesis has merit, we will note the tendency of the relationship, and we will apply a nonstatistical measure of the relationship's strength. By determining tendency and gauging strength, you are better able to interpret relationships involving control variables.

Open GSS2012. Go through the following steps, as covered in Chapter 4: Click Analyze → Descriptive Statistics → Crosstabs. Find the dependent variable, grass, in the left-hand variable list and click it into the Row(s) panel. Find the independent variable, attend3, and click it into the Column(s) panel. Click the Cells button and select the box next to "Column" in the Percentages panel. Click Continue, and then click OK. SPSS reports the results:

grass Should Marijuana Be Made Legal * attend3 Religious Attendance: 3 Cats Crosstabulation

			attend3 Religious Attendance: 3 Cats			Total
			1 Low	2 Moderate	3 High	
grass Should Marijuana Be Made Legal	1 LEGAL	Count	326	149	100	575
		% within attend3 Religious Attendance: 3 Cats	62.3%	45.8%	26.7%	47.0%
	2 NOT LEGAL	Count	197	176	275	648
		% within attend3 Religious Attendance: 3 Cats	37.7%	54.2%	73.3%	53.0%
Total		Count	523	325	375	1223
		% within attend3 Religious Attendance: 3 Cats	100.0%	100.0%	100.0%	100.0%

Clearly the hypothesis has merit. Of the low attenders, 62.3 percent favor legalization, compared with 45.8 percent of moderate attenders and 26.7 percent of the highly observant. And note that, given the way attend3 is coded—increasing values denote increasing church attendance—a negative relationship exists between religiosity and the percentage favoring legalization. As attendance increases, the percentage favoring legalization declines. (If you interpret the cross-tabulation by examining the "Not legal" row, then the tendency is positive. As attendance increases, the percentage opposing legalization increases.) How strong is the relationship? You can arrive at a quick and easy measure of strength by figuring out the percentage-point change in the dependent variable across the full range of the independent variable. At one pole, 62.3 percent of low attenders favor legalization. At the other pole, 26.7 percent of high attenders are in favor. Therefore, the percentage favoring legalization drops by 62.3 – 26.7 = 35.6, or about 36 percentage points. By this rudimentary measure, the relationship's strength is 36. (In Chapter 7, we consider statistical measures of strength.)

What other factors, besides church attendance, might account for differing opinions on marijuana legalization? A plausible answer: whether the respondent has children. Regardless of religiosity, people with children may be less inclined to endorse the legalization of marijuana than are people who do not have children. And here is an interesting (if complicating) fact: People who attend church regularly are substantially more likely to have children than are people who rarely or never attend.[1] Thus, when we compare the marijuana opinions of "High" and "Low" attenders, as we have just done, we are also comparing people who are more likely to have children ("High") with people who are less likely to have children ("Low"). It could be that secular individuals are more inclined to favor legalization, not because they are less religious, but because they are less likely to have children. By the same token, those who go to church more often might oppose legalization for reasons unrelated to their religiosity: They're more likely to have children. The only way to isolate the effect of attendance on marijuana opinions is to compare low attenders who do not have children with high attenders who do not have children, and to compare low attenders who have children with high attenders who have children. In other words, we need to control for the effect of having children by holding it constant. Crosstabs with layers will perform the controlled comparison we are after.

GSS2012 contains the variable kids, which classifies respondents into one of two categories: those with children (coded 1 and labeled "Yes" on kids) or those without (coded 0 and labeled "No" on kids). Let's run the analysis again, this time adding kids as a control variable.

Again click Analyze → Descriptive Statistics → Crosstabs, returning to the Crosstabs window. You will find the dependent variable, grass, and the independent variable, attend3, just where you left them. To obtain a controlled comparison—the relationship between grass and attend3, controlling for kids—scroll down the variable list until you find kids and click it into the box labeled "Layer 1 of 1," as shown in Figure 5-1. SPSS will run a separate cross-tabulation analysis for each value of the variable that appears in the Layer box. And that is precisely what we want: a cross-tabulation of grass and attend3 for respondents without children and a separate analysis for those with children. Click OK. SPSS returns its version of a control table:

grass Should Marijuana Be Made Legal * attend3 Religious Attendance: 3 Cats * kids Does R Have Kids? Crosstabulation

kids Does R Have Kids?				attend3 Religious Attendance: 3 Cats			Total
				1 Low	2 Moderate	3 High	
0 No	grass Should Marijuana Be Made Legal	1 LEGAL	Count	143	43	21	207
			% within attend3 Religious Attendance: 3 Cats	71.9%	55.8%	36.8%	62.2%
		2 NOT LEGAL	Count	56	34	36	126
			% within attend3 Religious Attendance: 3 Cats	28.1%	44.2%	63.2%	37.8%
	Total		Count	199	77	57	333
			% within attend3 Religious Attendance: 3 Cats	100.0%	100.0%	100.0%	100.0%
1 Yes	grass Should Marijuana Be Made Legal	1 LEGAL	Count	183	106	79	368
			% within attend3 Religious Attendance: 3 Cats	56.5%	42.7%	25.0%	41.4%
		2 NOT LEGAL	Count	141	142	237	520
			% within attend3 Religious Attendance: 3 Cats	43.5%	57.3%	75.0%	58.6%
	Total		Count	324	248	316	888
			% within attend3 Religious Attendance: 3 Cats	100.0%	100.0%	100.0%	100.0%
Total	grass Should Marijuana Be Made Legal	1 LEGAL	Count	326	149	100	575
			% within attend3 Religious Attendance: 3 Cats	62.3%	45.8%	26.8%	47.1%
		2 NOT LEGAL	Count	197	176	273	646
			% within attend3 Religious Attendance: 3 Cats	37.7%	54.2%	73.2%	52.9%
	Total		Count	523	325	373	1221
			% within attend3 Religious Attendance: 3 Cats	100.0%	100.0%	100.0%	100.0%

Figure 5-1 Crosstabs with Layers

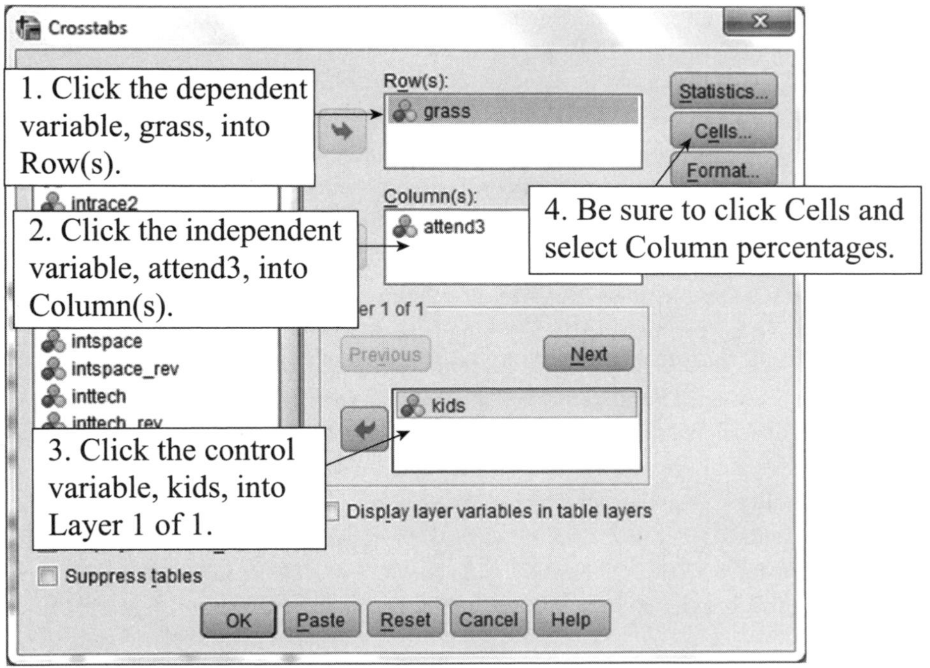

Crosstabs output with layers can be a bit confusing at first, so let's closely consider what SPSS has produced. There are three cross-tabulations, appearing as one table. To the left-hand side of the table you will see the label of the control variable, kids: "Does R Have Kids?" The first value of kids, "No," appears beneath that label. So the top cross-tabulation shows the grass–attend3 relationship for people who do not have children. The next cross-tabulation shows the relationship for respondents with children, respondents with the value "Yes" on the control variable. Finally, the bottom cross-tabulation, labeled "Total," shows the overall relationship between grass and attend3.

First assess the tendency and strength of the relationship between attendance and support for marijuana legalization among respondents who do not have children. Then assess tendency and strength among respondents who have children. Among people without children, the tendency is negative. As the values of attend3 increase from low to high, support for legalization declines: 71.9 percent of the low attenders favor legalization, compared with 55.8 percent of the middle group and 36.8 percent of the high attenders. How large is the drop? Across the full range of religious attendance, the percentage favoring legalization declines from 71.9 to 36.8—an "attendance effect" of about 35 percentage points. Turn your attention to respondents with children. Note that the tendency, once again, is negative: 56.5 percent of the low attenders favor legalization, compared with 42.7 percent of moderate attenders and 25.0 percent of high attenders. Note also that the strength of the relationship is about the same for people who have children as for people who do not have children. Among respondents with kids, the percentage who favor legalization drops from 56.5 among low attenders to 25.0 among high attenders—an "attendance effect" of about 32 points.

To help you make correct interpretations of controlled comparisons, it is a good idea to evaluate the relationship between the control variable and the dependent variable, controlling for the independent variable. In the current example, we would determine the tendency and strength of the relationship between the control variable, kids, and marijuana attitudes, controlling for attendance. This is accomplished by jumping between the "No" cross-tabulation and the "Yes" cross-tabulation, comparing marijuana opinions of people who share the same level of attendance but who differ on the control variable, kids. You can see that "Lows" without kids are more likely to favor legalization than are "Lows" with kids. When the control variable switches from "No" to "Yes," the percentage of marijuana supporters drops, from 71.9 percent to 56.5 percent—a "kid effect" of about 15 percentage points. How about moderate attenders? As with low attenders, the kid effect is negative, 55.8 percent compared with 42.7 percent—about 13 points. This pattern reoccurs among high attenders: 36.8 percent versus 25.0 percent—a kid effect of about 12 points.

How would you characterize this set of relationships? Does a spurious relationship exist between grass and attend3? Or are these additive relationships, with attend3 helping to explain legalization opinions and kids adding to the explanation? Or is interaction going on? If the grass–attend3 relationship were spurious, then the relationship would weaken or disappear after controlling for kids. Among respondents without children, low, moderate, and high attenders would all hold the same opinion about marijuana legalization. Ditto for people with children: Attendance would not play a role in explaining the dependent variable. Because the relationship persists after controlling for kids, we can rule out spuriousness. Now, it is sometimes difficult to distinguish between additive relationships and interaction relationships. In additive relationships, the effect of the independent variable on the dependent variable is the same or quite similar for each value of the control variable. In interaction relationships, by contrast, the effect of the independent variable on the dependent variable varies in tendency or strength for different values of the control variable.

According to the analysis, the grass–attend3 relationship has the same tendency—it "runs in the same direction"—for people with and without children: For both values of the control, as attendance goes up, pro-legalization opinions decline. Tellingly, the grass–attend3 relationships are quite similar in strength for people who do not have children and for people who do have children. For respondents without kids, the ideology effect is 35. For those with kids, the effect is 32. Notice, too, that the kid effect has the same tendency and roughly the same strength (between 12 and 15 points) at all values of attend3. To be sure, the grass–attend3–kids relationships are not paragons of symmetrical perfection—real-world relationships rarely are—but the pattern more closely approximates an additive pattern than an interactive pattern.

Additive relationships always take the same form: The relationship between the independent and dependent variables has the same tendency or direction and the same or very similar strength at all values of the control variable. Interaction relationships are more complex—and they are probably more common. So that you can become comfortable recognizing interaction in cross-tabulations, we will present another example related to the line of analysis we have been pursuing. Does religious attendance affect attitudes toward divorce? Does the strength or tendency of the relationship depend on whether people have children?

GSS2012 contains divlaw2, coded 1 for respondents who think that laws should be changed to make divorce more difficult and coded 0 for those who think that the laws should be kept the same or make divorce easier. Return to the previous Crosstabs window. Click grass back into the Variable list. Find divlaw2 and click it into the Row(s) panel. Click OK. An SPSS cross-tabulation control table is perhaps more familiar this time around.

divlaw2 Shld divorce laws make it more difficult? * attend3 Religious Attendance: 3 Cats * kids Does R Have Kids? Crosstabulation

kids Does R Have Kids?				attend3 Religious Attendance: 3 Cats 1 Low	2 Moderate	3 High	Total
0 No	divlaw2 Shld divorce laws make it more difficult?	0 Same/easier	Count	148	58	38	244
			% within attend3 Religious Attendance: 3 Cats	69.5%	67.4%	55.9%	66.5%
		1 More difficult	Count	65	28	30	123
			% within attend3 Religious Attendance: 3 Cats	30.5%	32.6%	44.1%	33.5%
	Total		Count	213	86	68	367
			% within attend3 Religious Attendance: 3 Cats	100.0%	100.0%	100.0%	100.0%
1 Yes	divlaw2 Shld divorce laws make it more difficult?	0 Same/easier	Count	218	131	130	479
			% within attend3 Religious Attendance: 3 Cats	66.1%	59.3%	43.3%	56.3%
		1 More difficult	Count	112	90	170	372
			% within attend3 Religious Attendance: 3 Cats	33.9%	40.7%	56.7%	43.7%
	Total		Count	330	221	300	851
			% within attend3 Religious Attendance: 3 Cats	100.0%	100.0%	100.0%	100.0%
Total	divlaw2 Shld divorce laws make it more difficult?	0 Same/easier	Count	366	189	168	723
			% within attend3 Religious Attendance: 3 Cats	67.4%	61.6%	45.7%	59.4%
		1 More difficult	Count	177	118	200	495
			% within attend3 Religious Attendance: 3 Cats	32.6%	38.4%	54.3%	40.6%
	Total		Count	543	307	368	1218
			% within attend3 Religious Attendance: 3 Cats	100.0%	100.0%	100.0%	100.0%

To ensure consistency with the analysis of marijuana opinions, we will track the more culturally permissive response, "same/easier." Clearly enough, attendance has an effect on the dependent variable for people without children. As the independent variable changes from low to moderate to high, the percentage of respondents who think that divorce laws should be the same or easier declines by 14 points: from 69.5 percent of low attenders to 55.9 percent of high attenders. So the relationship has a negative tendency or direction, as viewed along the "same/easier" row, and a strength equal to 14. Now shift your attention to the divlaw2–attend3 relationship among respondents who have kids. Notice that the direction of the relationship is the same. Just as with people who do not have children, as attendance increases, the percentage of "same/easier" responses declines. However, the drop is much steeper among respondents with kids, from 66.1 percent to 43.3 percent—nearly 23 percentage points. Thus, the attendance effect is either weaker (14 points) or stronger (23 points), depending on which value of the control variable is in play. This sort of asymmetrical pattern—same tendency, different strengths—is a common form of interaction. To confirm an interaction interpretation, evaluate the kid effect separately at each value of attendance. For low attenders, the effect is only about 3 points: 69.5 percent for those without kids, compared with 66.1 percent for those with kids. Among frequent attenders, by contrast, the kid effect widens to more than 12 points, from 55.9 percent to 43.3 percent.

GRAPHING RELATIONSHIPS WITH A CONTROL VARIABLE

In Chapter 4 you learned how to obtain a bar chart or line chart depicting the relationship between an independent variable and a dependent variable. SPSS also produces two types of graphs for controlled comparisons: clustered bar charts and multiple line charts. For clarifying controlled comparisons, multiple line charts are preferred. Compared with bar charts, line charts are simpler and more elegant, and they have a more favorable data/ink ratio, defined as "the proportion of a graphic's ink devoted to the nonredundant display of data-information."[2] In other words, if one were to "add up" all the ink used in a graph, line charts tend to devote a larger proportion of the total ink to the essential communication of the data.[3] In the following guided example, we produce a multiple line chart for the additive relationship analyzed at the beginning of the chapter, the relationship between grass and attend3, controlling for kids.

Click Graphs → Legacy Dialogs → Line. When the Line Charts window opens, click Multiple and make sure that the Summaries for Groups of Cases radio button is selected (the default). Click Define. The Define Multiple Line: Summaries for Groups of Cases window appears (Figure 5-2). What do we want the line chart to depict? We want to see the percentage of respondents who think marijuana should be legal (code 1 on grass) for each value of the independent variable (attend3). Furthermore, we want to see the grass–attend3 relationship separately for each value of the control variable, kids. In all SPSS charts, the values of the independent variable appear along the axis labeled "Category Axis." Because attend3 is the independent variable, click attend3 into the Category Axis box, as shown in Figure 5-3. For each value of attend3, we want to see the relationship separately for different values of the control variable, kids. In a multiple line chart, the values of the control variable "define" the lines. The variable kids is the control variable, so click kids into the Define Lines by box.

Now we need to make sure that the lines will represent the percentages of respondents saying "legal." In the Lines Represent panel, select the Other statistic radio button, which activates the Variable box. Find grass in the variable list and then click it into the Variable box. By default, SPSS will display the mean value of grass, "MEAN(grass)," which does not suit our purpose (see Figure 5-3). Click Change Statistic. In the Statistic window, click the Percentage inside radio button. Type "1" in the Low box and "1" in the High box. As in Figure 5-3, these instructions tell SPSS to display the percentage of respondents in one category of the dependent variable, the percentage coded 1 on grass. Click Continue, returning to the Define Multiple Line window. The Variable box should now read "PIN(1 1)(grass)," meaning "The lines will display the percentages of respondents inside the value of 1 on grass at the low end and the value of 1 on grass at the high end." Click OK.

The multiple line chart, constructed to our specifications, appears in the Viewer (Figure 5-4). This graphic greatly facilitates interpretation of the relationship. The upper line shows the relationship between grass and attend3 for people without children, and the lower line depicts the relationship for people with children. Trace the effect of the independent variable by moving from left to right along each line, across the values of attend3. As we learned from the cross-tabulation, the lines drop by about the same amount, 35 points for the "No kids" line and 32 points for the "Yes kids" line. Note the effect of the control variable by jumping between the lines, at each value of attend3. As we saw earlier, the kid effect is quite similar, between 12 and 15 points, at each value of the independent variable. This is a beautiful line chart. But let's spruce it up using the Chart Editor.

We will make three changes to the chart: First, we will change the title on the y-axis. Second, we will make the lines thicker. Finally, we will change the style of one of the lines, so that the legend clearly communicates the categories of the control variable, kids. (If you print graphics in black and white, as we do in this book, it is sometimes difficult to distinguish subtle differences in the colors of the lines.)

Place the cursor anywhere on the chart and double-click. This invokes the Chart Editor. To change the y-axis title (Figure 5-5), first select it with a single-click. Single-click again to edit it. Replace the current title with this

Figure 5-2 Opening the Define Multiple Line Window

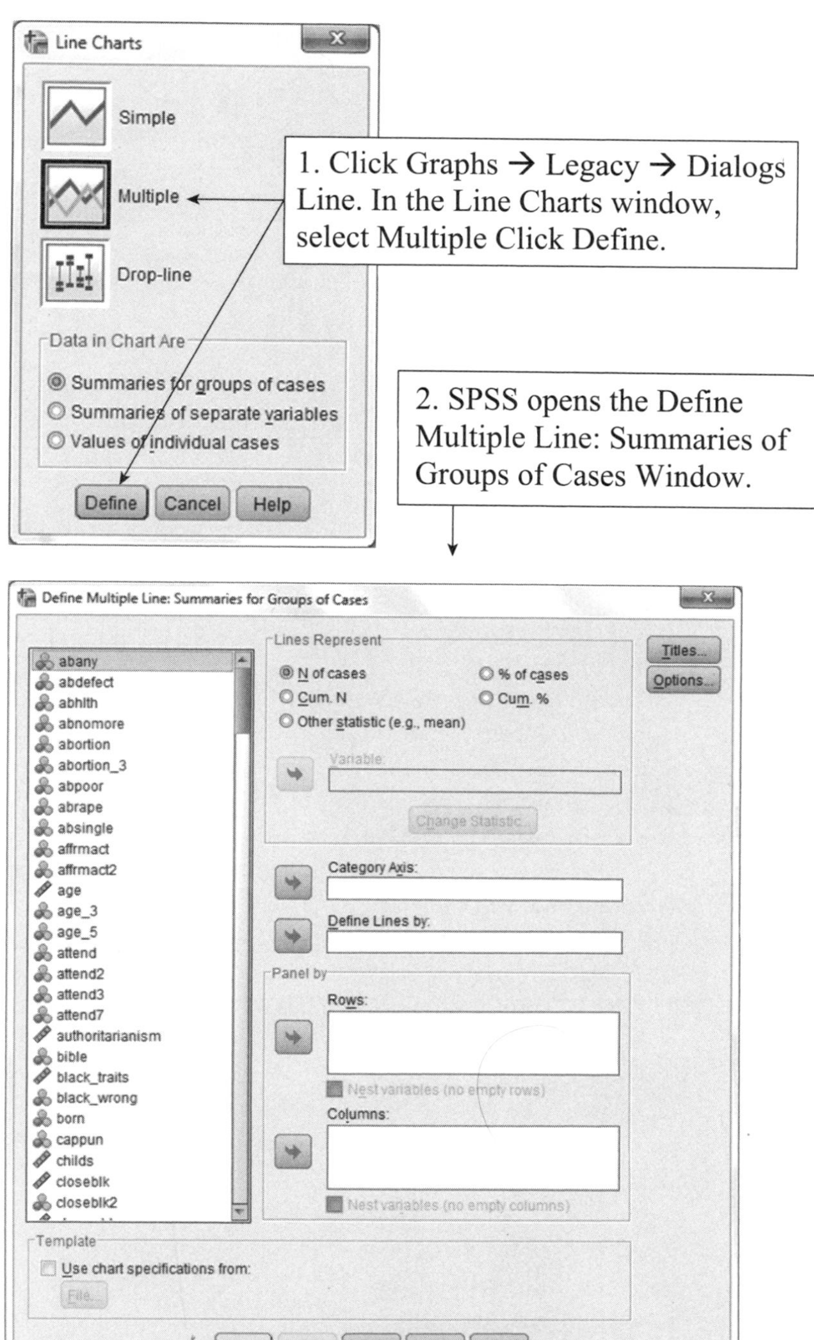

new title: "Percent saying marijuana should be legal." (Clicking anywhere else on the chart returns the axis title to its proper position.) Next let's make the lines thicker. Double-click on one of the lines, as shown in Figure 5-6. The Chart Editor selects both lines and opens the Properties window. In the Lines panel of the Lines tab, click the Weight drop-down and select a heavier weight, such as 2. Click Apply. The Editor makes both lines thicker. To edit the properties of a single line, single-click on the line. The Editor will select only that line. (See Figure 5-7.) To edit the line's style, click the Style drop-down and choose from among the many dashed patterns. When you click Apply, the Editor modifies the line's style and makes a corresponding change in the legend. Close the Properties window and exit the Chart Editor. A newly edited multiple line chart appears in the Viewer (Figure 5-8).

Figure 5-3 Obtaining a Multiple Line Chart

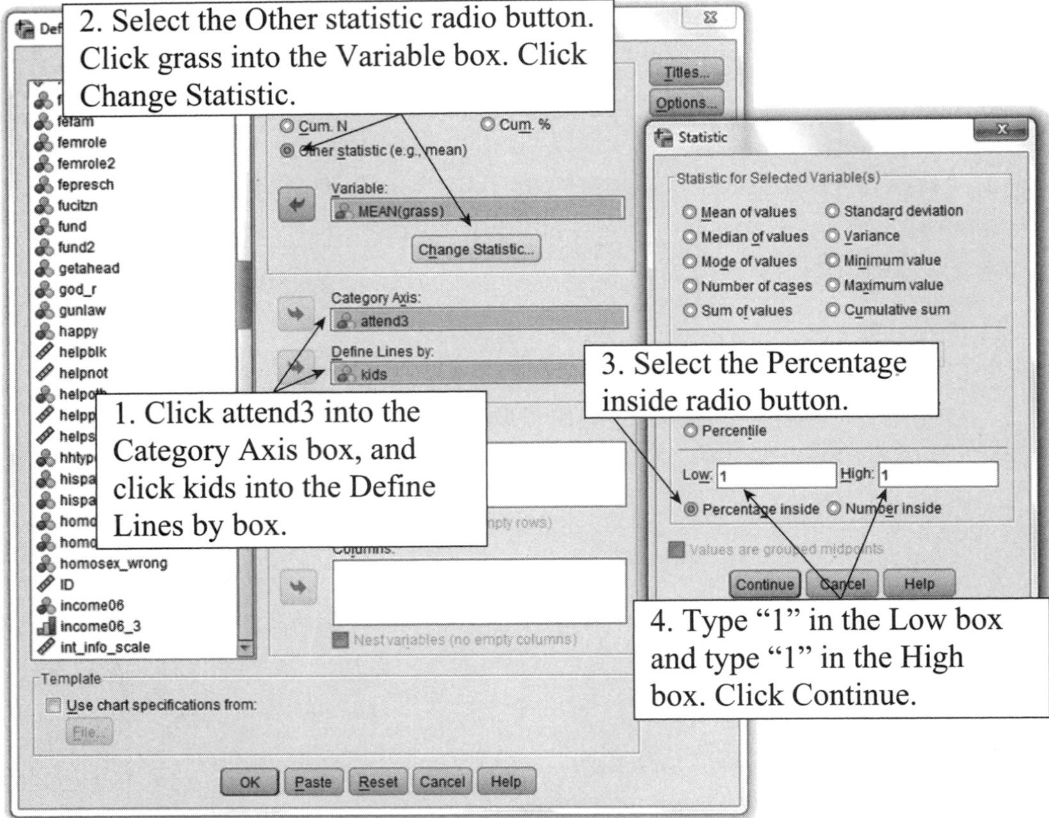

Figure 5-4 Multiple Line Chart of Additive Relationships with Negative Tendency

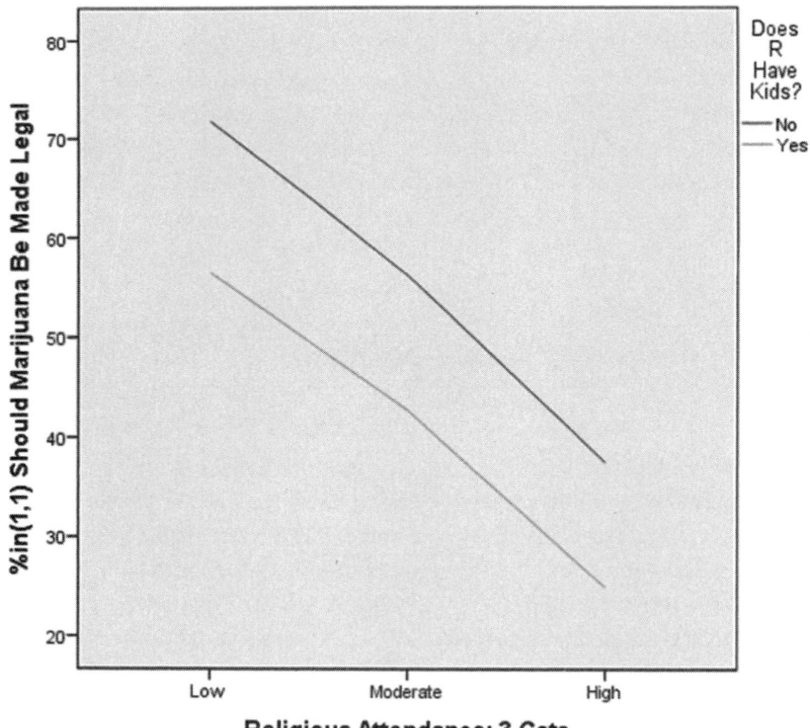

Figure 5-5 Changing the Y-axis Title

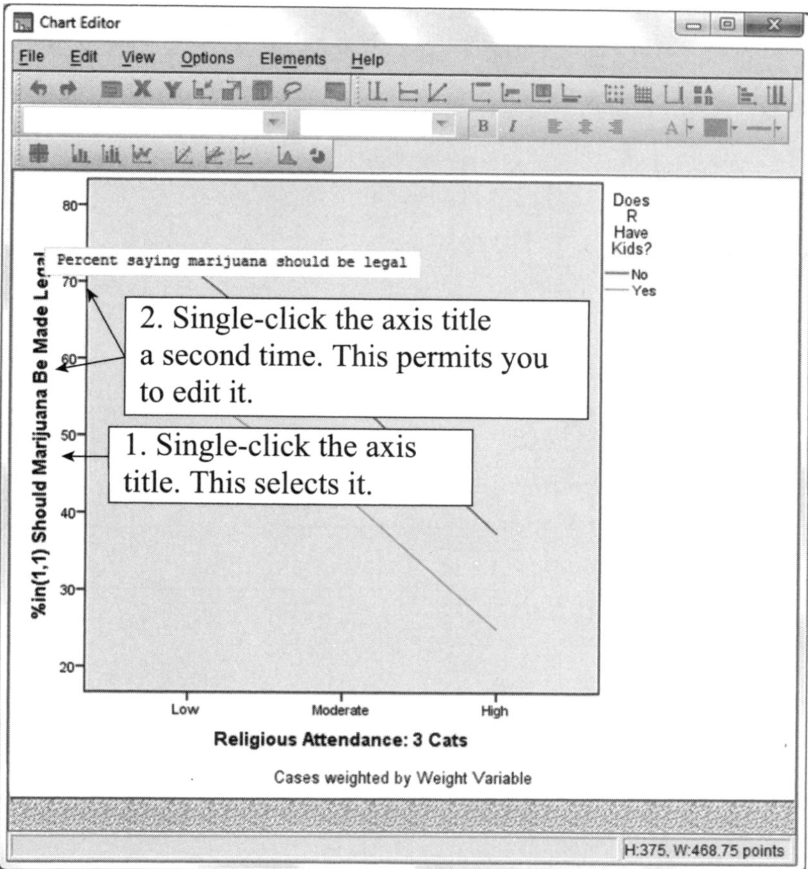

Figure 5-6 Changing Line Weights

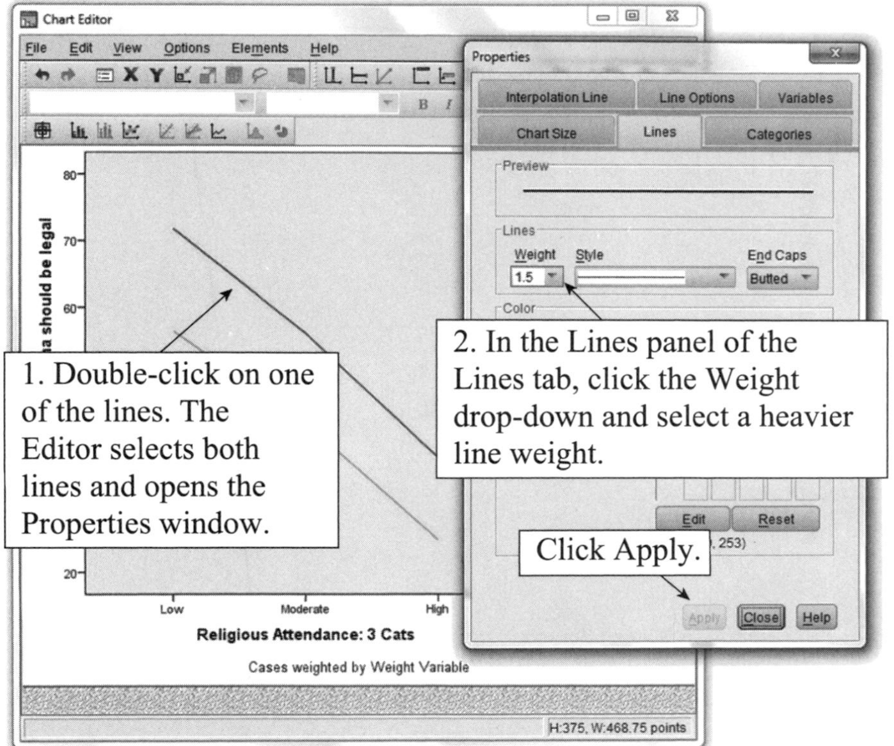

Figure 5-7 Changing Line Style

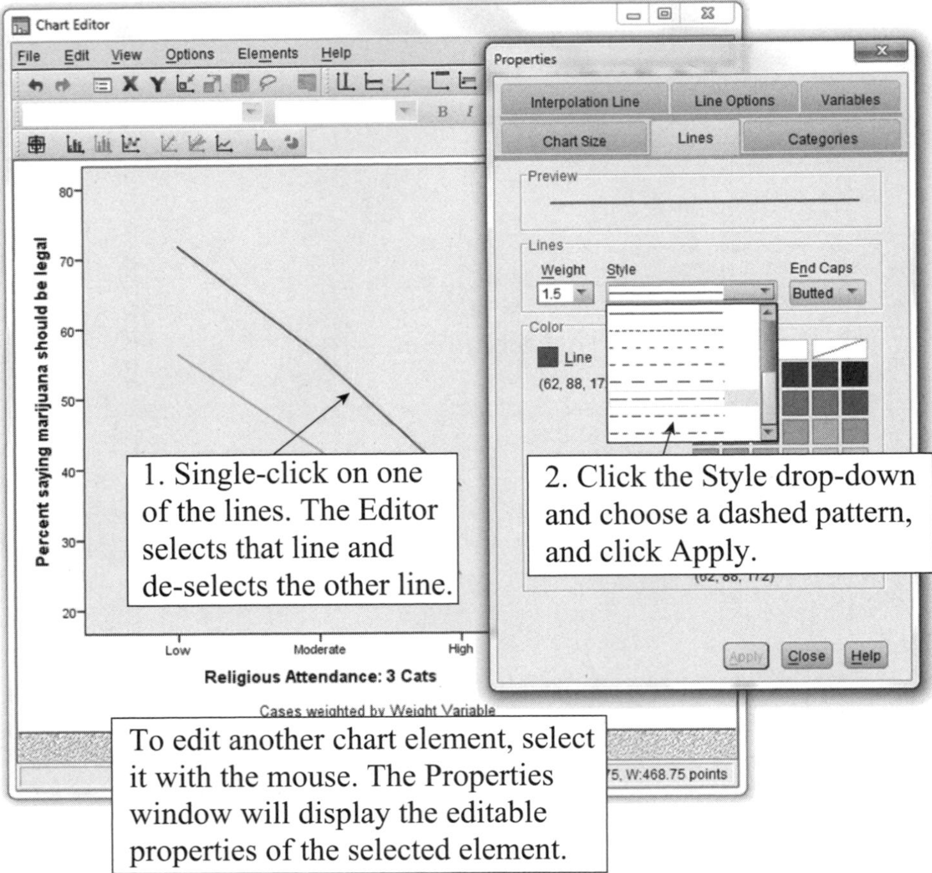

Figure 5-8 Multiple Line Chart of Additive Relationships with Negative Tendency (edited)

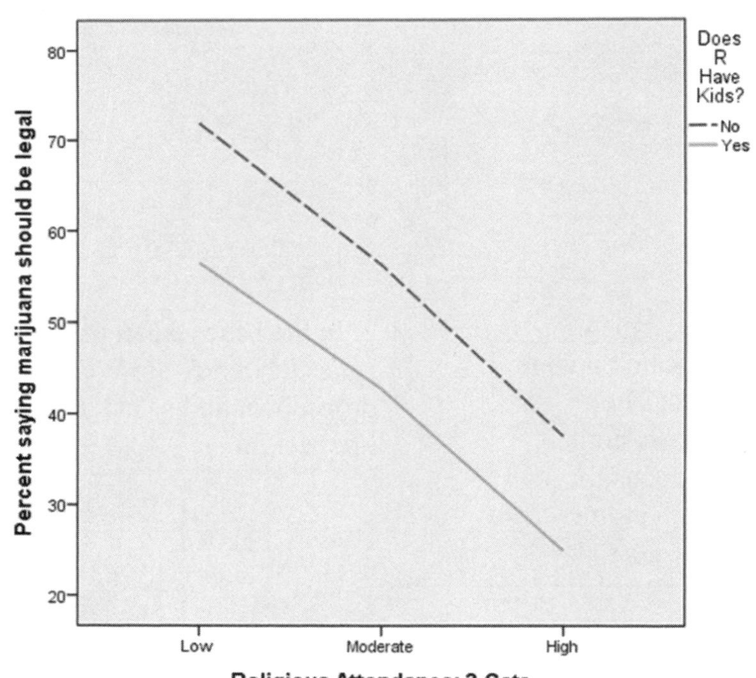

MEAN COMPARISON ANALYSIS WITH A CONTROL VARIABLE

Mean comparison analysis is used when the dependent variable is interval level and the independent variable and the control variable are nominal or ordinal level. In most ways, the procedure for using Compare Means with layers to obtain controlled comparisons is similar to that for using Crosstabs. However, the two procedures differ in one important way. We will work through two guided examples using NES2012. The first example shows an interesting pattern of interaction. The second example gives you a chance to identify a set of additive relationships. Open NES2012 and let's begin the first guided example.

Example of an Interaction Relationship

It has become an article of faith that women are more strongly attracted to the Democratic Party than are men. Indeed, on NES2012's Democratic Party feeling thermometer (ft_dem), women's ratings are five "degrees" warmer than men's: 54 degrees versus 49 degrees. We might wonder, however, whether this gap is the same for married and unmarried people. Plausibly, shared beliefs and values (perhaps including party affiliation) are of key importance to couples who marry. And evidence suggests that married couples become politically more similar over time.[4] Let's investigate the relationship between Democratic ratings and gender, controlling for marital status.

As you know, NES2012 contains a number of feeling thermometer variables, which record respondents' ratings of different political groups and personalities on a scale from 0 (cold or negative) to 100 (warm or positive). One of these variables, ft_dem, which gauges feelings toward the Democratic Party, will be the dependent variable in the current example. The independent variable is gender. For the control variable we will use married, which you created in Chapter 3. We will use Analyze → Compare Means → Means to produce mean values of ft_dem for each value of gender, controlling for married.

Click Analyze → Compare Means → Means. Find ft_dem in the variable list and click it into the Dependent List box. Now we want SPSS to proceed as follows. First, we want it to separate respondents into two groups, unmarried and married, on the basis of the control variable, married. Second, we want SPSS to calculate mean values of ft_dem for each category of the independent variable, gender. SPSS handles mean comparisons by first separating cases on the variable named in the first Layer box. It then calculates means of the dependent variable for variables named in subsequent Layer boxes. For this reason, it is best to put the control variable in the first layer and to put the independent variable in the second layer. Because married is the control variable, locate married in the variable list and click it into the Layer 1 of 1 box (Figure 5-9). Click Next. The next Layer box, labeled "Layer 2 of 2," opens. The independent variable, gender, goes in this box. Click gender into the Layer 2 of 2 box (Figure 5-10). One last thing: Click Options. In Cell Statistics, click Standard Deviation back into the left-hand Statistics box, and then click Continue. You are ready to go. Click OK. The following control table appears in the Viewer:

ft_dem PRE: Feeling Thermometer: Democratic Party

married Is R married?	gender Gender	Mean	N
0 No	1 Male	53.07	1219
	2 Female	62.08	1295
	Total	57.71	2513
1 Yes	1 Male	46.14	1602
	2 Female	48.03	1731
	Total	47.13	3333
Total	1 Male	49.13	2821
	2 Female	54.04	3026
	Total	51.67	5847

Figure 5-9 Means Window with Dependent Variable and Control Variable

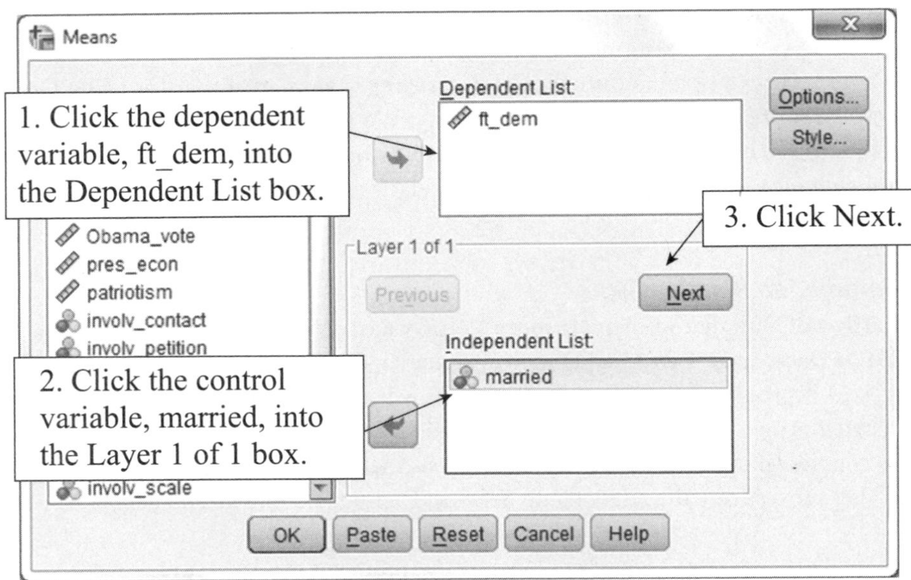

The values of the control variable, married, appear along the left-hand side of the table. The topmost set of mean comparisons shows the mean Democratic Party thermometer ratings for married respondents, the next set is for unmarried respondents, and the bottom set (labeled "Total") shows the uncontrolled relationship between ft_dem and gender—for unmarried and married respondents combined. This is a compact table, yet it contains a wealth of information. From the "Total" table we can retrieve the overall relationship between gender and the feeling thermometer: 49.13 for males and 54.04 for females, about a 5-point gender gap. (The "Total" row of the "Total" table tells us the overall mean for the entire sample: 51.67 degrees.) Notice, too, that we have obtained the overall means for unmarried (57.71) and married (47.13) individuals—more than a 10-point "marriage gap."

Figure 5-10 Means Window with Independent Variable in Layer Box

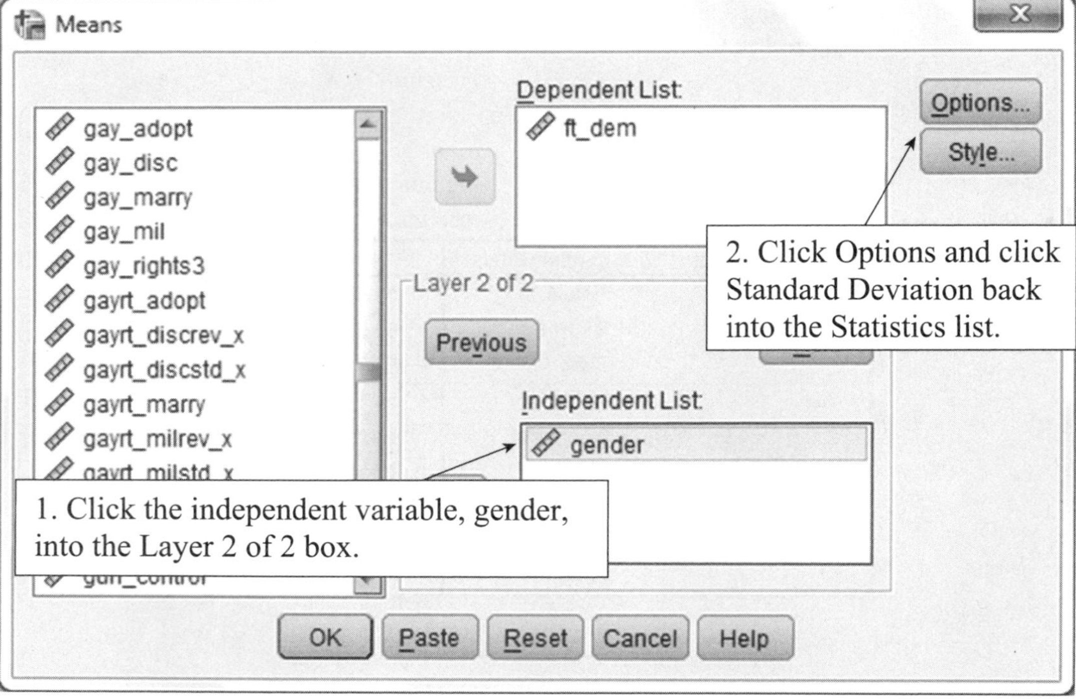

Now, to evaluate the controlled effect of the independent variable, we would compare the mean ratings of women with the mean ratings of men for unmarried and for married respondents. What do these comparisons reveal? Consider respondents who are not married. The mean Democratic Party rating for unmarried men is 53.07. This mean increases to 62.08 for unmarried women. So, for the unmarried, the thermometer gets 9 degrees warmer as we move from males to females. Now shift your attention to married respondents. Here we see a gender gap of less than 2 degrees: 46.14 for men and 48.03 for women. Does the gender–Democratic thermometer relationship have the same tendency at both values of the control? Yes, for both unmarried and married respondents, women feel more warmly toward the Democratic Party than do men. Do the relationships have the same (or similar) strengths at both values of the control? No, the gender gap is almost five times larger for unmarried people than for married people. Again, a situation such as this—same tendency, different strengths—is one form of interaction.

Confirm the interaction interpretation by determining how the control variable, married, affects Democratic ratings for each gender. For males, for instance, there is a difference of about 7 degrees: 53.07 for unmarried men compared with 46.14 for married men. The marriage effect, however, is 14 degrees for women: 62.08 compared with 48.03. Again, the relationship has the same tendency (unmarried people rate the Democrats higher than do married people), but different strengths (the effect is substantially larger for women than for men).

A line chart will illuminate the interaction relationships we have been discussing. The steps for obtaining a multiple line chart for an interval-level dependent variable are the same steps you learned earlier, with one work-saving exception.

1. Click Graphs → Legacy Dialogs→ Line. This opens the Line Charts window.
2. In the Line Charts window, click Multiple, and then click Define. This opens the Define Multiple Line window.
3. Click the independent variable, gender, into the Category Axis box.
4. Click the control variable, married, into the Define Lines by box.
5. In the Lines Represent panel of the Define Multiple Line window, select the Other statistic radio button. This activates the Variable box.
6. Click the dependent variable, ft_dem, into the Variable box. SPSS moves ft_dem into the Variable box with its default designation, "MEAN(ft_dem)." For an interval-level dependent variable, this default is precisely what you want.
7. Click OK.

We now have a tailor-made line chart of the relationships (Figure 5-11).

You can see why line charts are essential for correctly interpreting controlled comparisons. By tracing along each line, from male to female, you can see the effect of gender on thermometer ratings. Among married people, the line slopes up mildly, signaling a narrow gender gap. Among unmarried respondents, by contrast, the line rises more sharply—a wider gender gap. Notice, too, the relationship between marital status and the dependent variable, separately for men and women: about a 7-point marriage effect for males, compared with a 14-point effect for females.

Thus far in this chapter we found two instances of interaction: the divlaw2–attend3–kids relationships and the ft_dem–gender–married relationships. Both cases revealed a common form of interaction. The relationship between the independent and dependent variables had the same tendency for both values of the control variable, but the relationship was stronger for one value than for the other value. Interaction can assume other forms, too. Interaction has two field marks, though, that will give it away. First, when you examine the relationship between the independent variable and the dependent variable at different values of the control variable, you may find that the relationship varies in tendency or direction, perhaps positive for one value of the control variable, zero or negative for other control values. Second, the relationship may have the same tendency for all control values but differ in strength, negative-weak versus negative-strong or positive-weak versus positive-strong. In identifying interaction, practice makes perfect. And, believe it or not, statistics can help (see Chapter 9).

Figure 5-11 Multiple Line Chart of Interaction Relationships

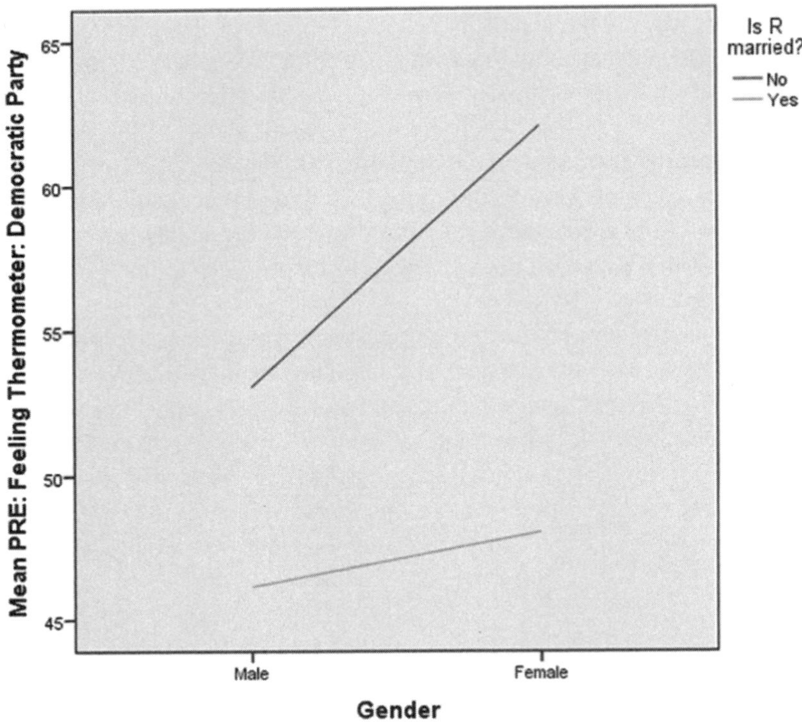

Example of an Additive Relationship

Compared with the protean complexity of interaction, additive relationships are the soul of symmetry. In a set of additive relationships, both the independent and the control variables help to explain the dependent variable. More than this, the effect of the independent variable is the same or very similar—same tendency, same strength—for all values of the control variable. Interaction relationships assume several forms. Additive relationships assume only one.

NES2012 contains several measures of "linked fate," the extent to which individual members of identifiable groups feel attached to other members of the same group. For example, link_wom_scale measures the extent to which female respondents sense a connection between themselves and other women in society. Female respondents are measured as feeling "Weak," "Moderate," or "Strong" ties to other females. NES2012 also contains modsex_scale, which measures the extent to which individuals perceive that women are discriminated against and have few opportunities for achievement. Modsex_scale runs from 0 (the respondent perceives little discrimination against women and more opportunities for achievement) to 16 (a great deal of discrimination, few opportunities). It seems reasonable to hypothesize that women with a stronger sense of linked fate (higher values on link_wom_scale) will be more likely to perceive higher levels of sexism (higher values on modsex_scale) than will women with a weaker sense of linked fate. It is an interesting question, however, whether the relationship will be the same for white females and African American females. Blacks are likely to perceive greater discrimination than are whites, regardless of their feelings of link fate with other women. In this example, you will analyze the modsex_scale–link_wom_scale relationship, controlling for race (dem_raceeth2).

Click Analyze → Compare Means → Means. Everything is still in place from our ft_dem–gender–married analysis. Click Reset. Click modsex_scale into the Dependent list. Click the control variable, dem_raceeth2, into the first Layer box. Click Next. Click the independent variable, link_wom_scale, into the second Layer box. Click Options and remove the Standard Deviation from Cell Statistics. Click OK. Another information-rich table is at hand:

modsex_scale Modern sexism

dem_raceeth2 White/Black	link_wom_scale Linked fate: other Women	Mean	N
1 White	0 Weak	7.99	599
	1 Moderate	8.60	857
	2 Strong	9.34	421
	Total	8.57	1878
2 Black	0 Weak	8.99	123
	1 Moderate	9.73	139
	2 Strong	10.36	82
	Total	9.61	343
Total	0 Weak	8.16	722
	1 Moderate	8.75	996
	2 Strong	9.50	503
	Total	8.73	2221

Does linked fate work as hypothesized? Yes. For both whites and blacks, mean values of modsex_scale ascend as we move from "Weak" to "Moderate" to "Strong." Indeed, the magnitude of the end-to-end increase is virtually identical for both races: 1.35 for white females (9.34 – 7.99) and 1.37 for black females (10.36 – 8.99). And notice the consistent effects of race. At each value of the independent variable, African American women are about 1 point higher on the discrimination scale than their white counterparts: 1 point among those having "Weak" linked fate, 1.13 points among the "Moderate" group, and 1.02 points among women who feel "Strong" ties to other women. Thus, regardless of race, the "linked-fate effect" is about 1.35. And regardless of feelings of linked fate, the "race effect" is about 1.

By now, obtaining a multiple line chart of the modsex_scale–link_wom_scale–dem_raceeth2 relationships is a straightforward exercise.

1. Click Graphs → Legacy Dialogs → Line.
2. In the Line Charts window, click Multiple, and then click Define. (Click Reset to clear the panels.)
3. Click the independent variable, link_wom_scale, into the Category Axis box.
4. Click the control variable, dem_raceeth2, into the Define Lines by box.
5. In the Lines Represent panel of the Define Multiple Line window, select the Other statistic radio button.
6. Click the dependent variable, modsex_scale, into the Variable box.
7. Click OK.

You can see how this line chart (Figure 5-12) communicates the additive relationship. Moving from left to right, from weaker link to stronger link, each line rises by about 1.35 units. That's the linked-fate effect. The effect of race is conveyed by the distance between the lines. Despite a very slight widening at the middle category of the linked-fate measure, the racial difference is quite consistent. Now, you might encounter additive relationships in which the lines slope downward, imparting a negative relationship between the independent and dependent variables. And the lines might "float" closer together, suggesting a consistent but weaker effect of the control variable on the dependent variable, controlling for the independent variable. But you will always see symmetry in the relationships. The effect of the independent variable on the dependent variable will be the same or very similar for all values of the control variable, and the effect of the control variable on the dependent variable will be the same or very similar for all values of the independent variable.

Invoke the Chart Editor and make some improvements to this multiple line chart. Experiment with the Chart Editor. Ask the Properties window to do new things. Figure 5-13 may serve as an example. (Advanced chart editing is covered in Chapter 8.)

Figure 5-12 Multiple Line Chart of Additive Relationships with Positive Tendency

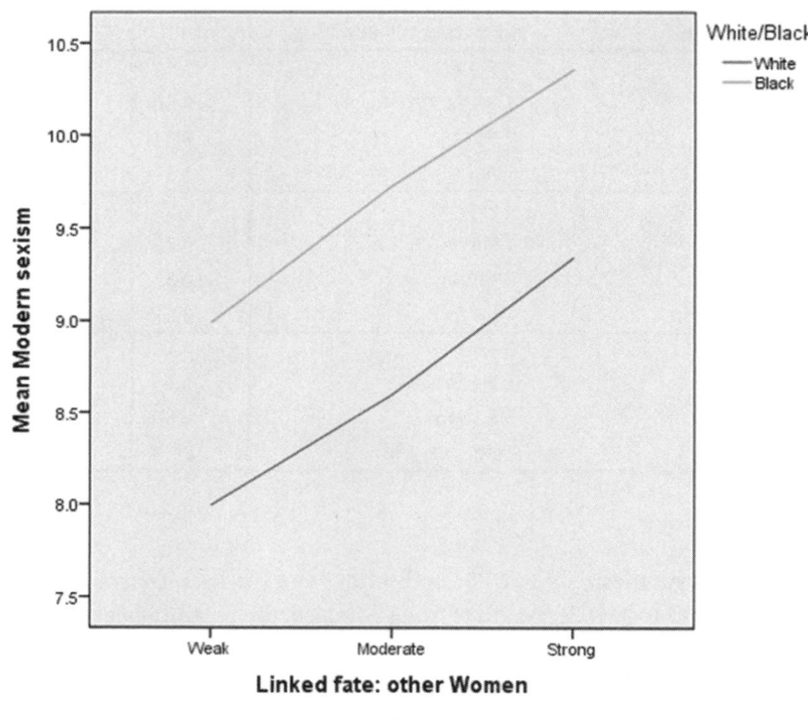

Figure 5-13 Multiple Line Chart of Additive Relationships with Positive Tendency (edited)

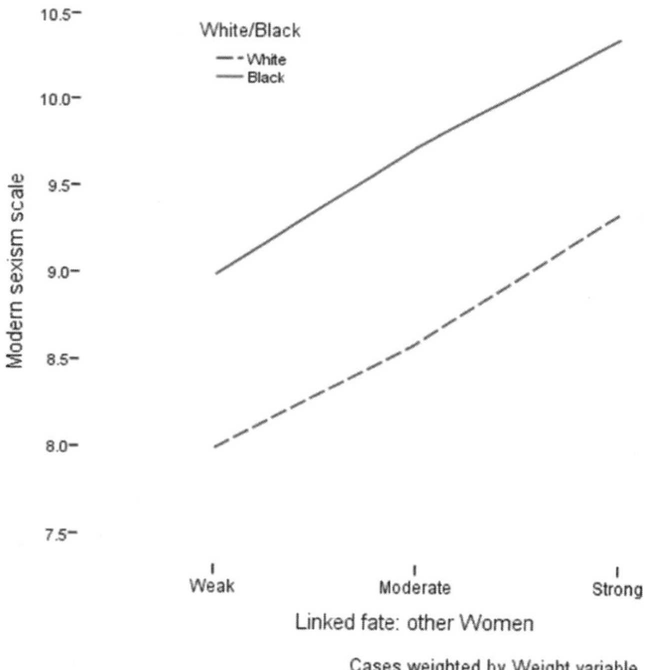

EXERCISES

1. (Dataset: World. Variables: democ_regime08, frac_eth3, gdpcap2_08.) Some countries have democratic regimes, and other countries do not. What factors help to explain this difference? One idea is that the type of government is shaped by the ethnic and religious diversity in a country's population. Countries

that are relatively homogeneous, with most people sharing the same language and religious beliefs, are more likely to develop democratic systems than are countries having more linguistic conflicts and religious differences. Consider the ethnic heterogeneity hypothesis: Countries with lower levels of ethnic heterogeneity will be more likely to be democracies than will countries with higher levels of ethnic heterogeneity.

A. According to the ethnic heterogeneity hypothesis, if you were to compare countries having lower heterogeneity with countries having higher heterogeneity, you should find (check one):

- ❑ a lower percentage of democracies among countries having lower heterogeneity.
- ❑ a higher percentage of democracies among countries having lower heterogeneity.
- ❑ no difference between the percentage of democracies among countries having lower heterogeneity and the percentage of democracies among countries with higher heterogeneity.

B. World contains the variable democ_regime08, which classifies each country as a democracy (coded 1 and labeled "Yes") or a nondemocracy (coded 0 and labeled "No"). This is the dependent variable. World also contains frac_eth3, which classifies countries according to their level of ethnic heterogeneity: low (coded 1), medium (coded 2), or high (coded 3). This is the independent variable. Run Crosstabs, testing the ethnic heterogeneity hypothesis. Fill in the percentages of democracies:

	Ethnic heterogeneity		
	Low	Medium	High
Percentage of democracies	?	?	?

C. Based on these results, does it appear that the ethnic heterogeneity hypothesis is correct or incorrect?

Correct Incorrect

D. Explain your answer in C, making specific reference to the percentage of democracies:

___

___

___

___

E. A country's level of economic development might also be linked to its type of government. According to this perspective, countries with higher levels of economic development are more likely to be democracies than are countries with lower levels. The World dataset contains the variable gdpcap2_08. This variable, based on gross domestic product (GDP) per capita, is an indicator of economic development. Countries are classified as low (coded 1) or high (coded 2). Obtain a cross-tabulation analysis of the democ_regime08–frac_eth3 relationship, controlling for gdpcap2_08. Fill in the percentages of democracies:

	Ethnic heterogeneity		
	Low	Medium	High
Low GDP per capita percentage of democracies	?	?	?
High GDP per capita percentage of democracies	?	?	?

F. Obtain a multiple line chart depicting the percentage of democracies for each value of frac_eth3, controlling for gdpcap2_08. (Remember that democracies are coded 1 on democ_regime08.) In the Chart Editor, give the scale axis this new title: "Percentage of democracies." Edit the line weights. Change the style of one of the lines. Make other desired changes to enhance appearance and readability. Print the chart you created.

G. Consider the evidence from parts E and F. Based on your analysis, how would you describe the relationship between ethnic heterogeneity and democracy, controlling for GDP per capita? (circle one)

Additive Interaction

H. Explain your answer in G, making specific reference to the evidence in parts E and F.

___

___

___

___

2. (Dataset: World. Variables: women13, pr_sys, womyear2). In Chapter 2 you analyzed the distribution of the variable women13, the percentage of women in the lower house of the legislatures in a number of countries. In this exercise you will analyze the relationship between women13 and two variables that could have an impact on the number of women serving in national legislatures.

First, consider the role of the type of electoral system. Many democracies have proportional representation (PR) systems. PR systems foster multiple parties having diverse ideological positions—and, perhaps, having diverse demographic compositions as well. Non-PR systems, like the system used in U.S. elections, militate in favor of fewer and more homogeneous parties. Thus you might expect that non-PR countries will have fewer women in their national legislatures than will countries with PR-based electoral systems.

Now consider the role of history and tradition. In some countries, women have had a long history of political empowerment. New Zealand, for example, gave women the right to vote in 1893. In other countries, such as Switzerland (where women were not enfranchised until 1971), women have had less experience in the electoral arena. Thus it seems reasonable to hypothesize that countries with longer histories of women's suffrage will have higher percentages of women in their national legislatures than will countries in which women's suffrage is a more recent development. In this exercise you will isolate the effect of the type of electoral system on the percentage of women in parliament, controlling for the timing of women's suffrage. However, before running any analyses, you will graphically depict different possible scenarios for the relationships you might discover.

Parts A, B, and C contain graphic shells showing the percentage of women in parliament along the vertical axis and the type of electoral system along the horizontal axis. Countries without PR systems are represented by the tick mark on the left, and countries with PR systems are represented by the tick mark on the right. For each shell, you will draw two lines within the graphic space, a solid line depicting the relationship for countries having a longer history of women's suffrage and a dashed line depicting the relationship for countries having a shorter history of women's suffrage.

A. Draw an additive relationship fitting this description: Countries with PR systems have higher percentages of women in parliament than do countries with non-PR systems, and countries with a longer history of women's suffrage have higher percentages of women in parliament than do countries with a shorter history of women's suffrage. (*Hint*: In additive relationships, the strength and tendency of the relationship is the same or very similar for all values of the control variable.) Remember to use a solid line to depict the relationship for countries having a longer history of women's suffrage and a dashed line to depict the relationship for countries having a shorter history of women's suffrage.

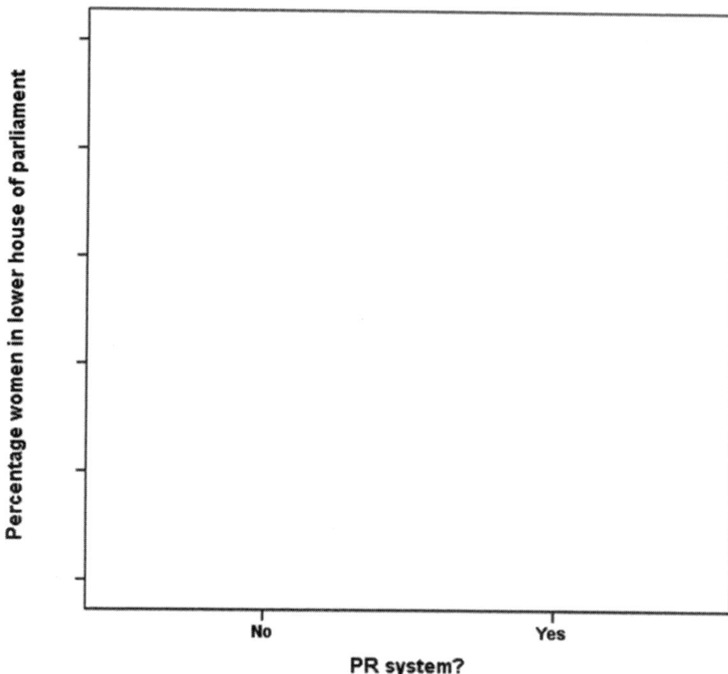

B. Draw a spurious relationship: Type of electoral system has no effect on the percentage of women in parliament; timing of women's suffrage has a big effect on the percentage of women in parliament.

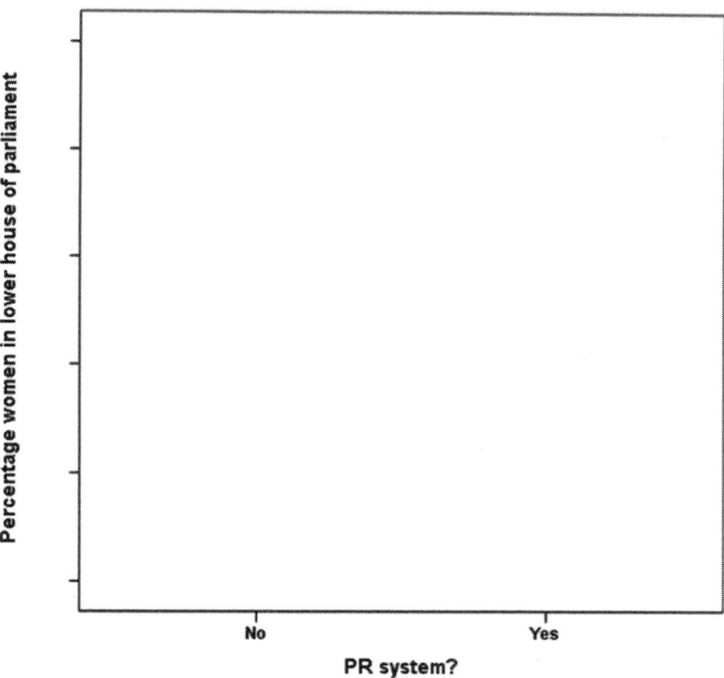

C. Draw a set of interaction relationships fitting this description: For countries with a longer history of women's suffrage, those with PR systems have higher percentages of women in parliament than do countries with non-PR systems. For countries with a shorter history of women's suffrage, the type of electoral system has no effect on the percentage of women in parliament.

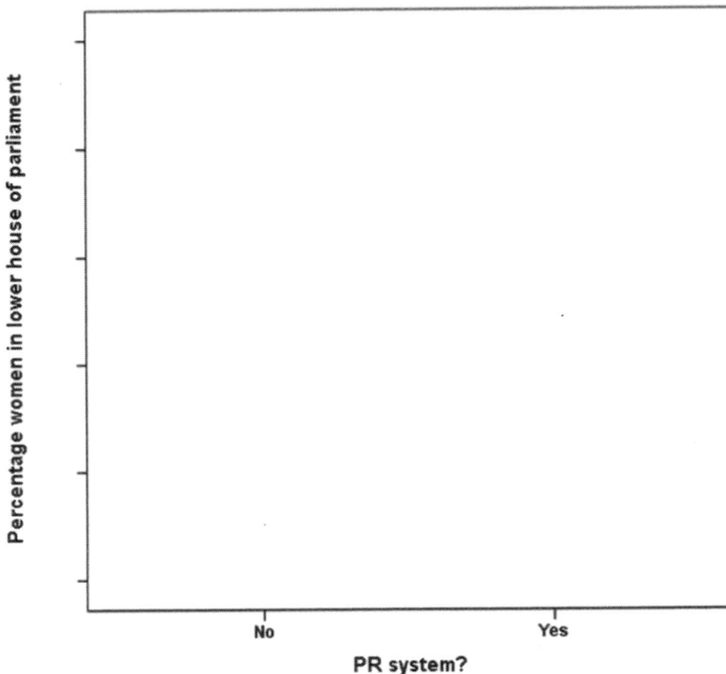

D. In addition to the dependent variable, women13, World contains pr_sys, coded 0 for countries with non-PR systems and coded 1 for those having PR systems. Use pr_sys as the independent variable. World also contains womyear2, which measures the timing of women's suffrage by two values: 1944 or before (coded 0) and after 1944 (coded 1). Use womyear2 as the control variable.

Run Compare Means to determine the mean of women13 for each value of pr_sys, controlling for womyear2. (Remember to put the control variable, womyear2, in the first Layer box.) Record the mean values in the table that follows:

Women's suffrage	PR system?	Mean
1944 or before	No	?
	Yes	?
After 1944	No	?
	Yes	?

E. Obtain a line chart of the relationship between women13 and pr_sys, controlling for womyear2. Open the Chart Editor. Edit the line weights, and change the style of one of the lines. Make other desired changes to enhance appearance and readability. Print the chart you created.

F. Examine the table (part D) and the chart (part E). Consider the women13–pr_sys relationship for countries that enfranchised women in 1944 or before. Examine the difference between the means for non-PR countries and PR countries. This difference shows that the mean for PR countries is (fill in the blank) ________ points (circle one)

lower than higher than the mean for non-PR countries.

Now consider the women13–pr_sys relationship for countries that enfranchised women after 1944. Examine the difference between the means for non-PR countries and PR countries. This difference shows that the mean for PR countries is (fill in the blank) ________ points (circle one)

lower than higher than the mean for non-PR countries.

G. Which of the following statements best characterizes the women13–pr_sys relationship, controlling for womyear2? (check one)

- ❑ The women13–pr_sys relationships have the same tendency and very similar strengths at both values of womyear2.
- ❑ The women13–pr_sys relationships have the same tendency but very different strengths at each value of womyear2.
- ❑ The women13–pr_sys relationships have different tendencies at each value of womyear2.

H. Review your artistic work in parts A to C. Examine the table (part D) and the line chart (part E). Consider your conclusions in parts F and G. Which possible scenario—the line chart you drew in A, B, or C—most closely resembles the pattern shown in the data? (circle one)

The line chart in A   The line chart in B   The line chart in C

3. (Dataset: NES2012. Variables: voted2012, income5, cses_GOTV.) A classic feature of American politics—and an enduring source of concern for democratic theory—is that low-income individuals are less likely to participate than are high-income individuals. In E.E. Schattschneider's legendary phrase, politics reflects the "mobilization of bias": People with economic resources are mobilized in, and those without resources are mobilized out.[5] Do get-out-the-vote (GOTV) campaigns ameliorate the income–participation relationship by causing lower-income people to vote at higher rates, bringing them into closer parity with higher-income people? Or do such campaigns actually make things worse by heightening the turnout of wealthier people, while having little effect among poorer Americans? Consider two Schattschneider-esque propositions:

Proposition One: Regardless of GOTV contact, higher-income people will be more likely to vote than will lower-income people.

Proposition Two: GOTV contact will cause a bigger boost in turnout among higher-income people than among lower-income people. Therefore, the income–turnout relationship will be stronger among those who were contacted than among those who were not contacted.

NES2012 contains voted2012, coded 0 for respondents who did not vote in the 2012 presidential election and coded 1 for respondents who did vote. This is the dependent variable. The independent variable is income5, which measures family income in quintiles. Codes range from 1 (the poorest quintile, labeled "Quint1") to 5 (the richest quintile, "Quint5"). The control variable is cses_GOTV, coded 0 for respondents who were not contacted by a party or candidate in 2012, and coded 1 for those who were contacted.[6]

A. Analyze the voted2012–income5 relationship, controlling for cses_GOTV. In the table that follows, record the percentages who voted:

	Income quintile				
Was R contacted by party/candidate?	1	2	3	4	5
No, not contacted					
Percentage who voted	?	?	?	?	?
Yes, contacted					
Percentage who voted	?	?	?	?	?

B. Produce a multiple line chart of the voted2012–income5 relationship, controlling for cses_GOTV. In the Chart Editor, give the y-axis a descriptive title. Edit the chart for style and appearance. Print the chart.

C. Consider the evidence you adduced in parts A and B. Is Proposition One supported or not supported by your findings? (circle one)

Proposition One is not supported.   Proposition One is supported.

D. Explain your answer in C, making specific reference to evidence from parts A and B.

____

____

____

____

E. Is Proposition Two supported or not supported by your findings? (circle one)

Proposition Two is not supported. Proposition Two is supported.

F. Explain your answer in E, making specific reference to evidence from parts A and B.

____

____

____

____

4. (Dataset: NES2012. Variables: polknow3, dhs_threat3, ftgr_tea). Given the Tea Party movement's deep skepticism of government activism, it seems plausible to hypothesize that individuals who regard the government as a threat would have warmer feelings toward the Tea Party than would those who do not think the government poses a threat. Of course, individuals would need to be reasonably well informed about politics to make the connection between their assessment of government threat and their evaluation of the Tea Party. When we control for political knowledge (control variable), we may find that the relationship between Tea Party ratings (dependent variable) and perceptions of government threat (independent variable) gets stronger as knowledge increases. In other words, interaction could be occurring in this set of relationships. Consider two propositions and an ancillary hypothesis.

Proposition One: At all levels of political knowledge (NES2012 variable polknow3), individuals who perceive the government as a threat (dhs_threat3) will give the Tea Party higher ratings (ftgr_tea) than will people who do not regard the government as a threat.

Proposition Two: The relationship between perceived threat and Tea Party ratings will be weaker for lower-knowledge respondents than for higher-knowledge respondents.

Ancillary Hypothesis: In a comparison of individuals, those with higher levels of political knowledge are less likely to regard the government as a threat than are those with lower levels of political knowledge.

The dependent variable: the Tea Party feeling thermometer (ftgr_tea), which runs from 0 (cold or negative feelings) to 100 (warm or positive feelings). The independent variable: dhs_threat3, which captures assessments of government's threat with three ordinal values—government represents no threat ("None"), a moderate threat ("Mod"), or an extreme threat ("Extrm"). Political knowledge is also a three-category ordinal: low ("Low know"), moderate ("Mid know"), and high knowledge ("High know").

A. Obtain a table of mean values of ftgr_tea for each combination of dhs_threat3 and polknow3. Record the means next to the question marks in the following table.

	Feeling thermometer: Tea Party	
Political knowledge	Federal government a threat?	Mean
Low knowledge	None	?
	Moderate	?
	Extreme	?
	Total	?

Political knowledge	Feeling thermometer: Tea Party	
	Federal government a threat?	Mean
Moderate knowledge	None	?
	Moderate	?
	Extreme	?
	Total	?
High knowledge	None	?
	Moderate	?
	Extreme	?
	Total	?

B. Is Proposition One supported or not supported by your findings? (circle one)

Proposition One is not supported. Proposition One is supported.

C. Explain your answer in B, making specific reference to evidence in part A.

____

____

____

____

D. Is Proposition Two supported or not supported by your findings? (circle one)

Proposition Two is not supported. Proposition Two is supported.

E. Explain your answer in D, making specific reference to evidence from part A.

____

____

____

____

F. Perform a cross-tabulation analysis to test the ancillary hypothesis. Use dhs_threat3 as the dependent variable and polknow3 as the independent variable. Print the cross-tabulation table.

G. Is the ancillary hypothesis supported by your findings in part F? (circle one)

The Ancillary Hypothesis is not supported. The Ancillary Hypothesis is supported.

H. Explain your answer in G, making specific reference to the cross-tabulation percentages.

____

____

____

____

5. (Dataset: GSS2012. Variables: race_2, intethn_2, natrace, natfare, natsci.) For an exercise in Chapter 4, you tested for the presence of preference falsification, the tendency for respondents to offer false opinions that they nonetheless believe to be socially desirable under the circumstances. You evaluated the hypothesis that respondents are more likely to express support for government policies aimed at helping blacks (such as "government spending to improve the conditions of blacks") when questioned by a black interviewer than when questioned by a white interviewer. But you did not control for the respondent's race. That is, you did not look to see whether whites are more (or less) likely than blacks to misrepresent their support for racial policies, depending on the race of the interviewer.[7]

   Furthermore, it may be that whites, and perhaps blacks as well, will engage in the same preference-falsifying behavior for policies that do not explicitly reference race but that may *symbolize* race, such as "government spending for welfare." Although "welfare" does not mention "blacks," it may be that whites see "welfare" through a racially tinged lens and will respond *as if* the question refers to a racial policy. Of course, some policies, such as "government spending for scientific research," do not evoke such symbolic connections. Questions about these race-neutral policies should not show the same race-of-interviewer effects as questions that make explicit—or implicit—reference to race.[8]

   In this exercise you will extend your Chapter 4 analysis in two ways. First, you will analyze the relationship between interviewer race (intethn_2, the independent variable) and three dependent variables: opinions on an explicitly racial policy (natrace, which measures attitudes toward spending to improve the conditions of blacks), a symbolically racial policy (natfare, opinions on spending for welfare), and a race-neutral policy (natsci, spending for scientific research). Second, you will perform these analyses while controlling for the respondent's race (race_2).

   Based on previous research in this area, what might you expect to find? Here are two plausible expectations:

   Expectation 1: For both white and black respondents, the race-of-interviewer effect will be strongest for the explicitly racial policy (natrace), weaker for the symbolically racial policy (natfare), and weakest for the race-neutral policy (natsci).

   Expectation 2: For the explicitly racial policy (natrace) and for the symbolically racial policy (natfare), the race-of-interviewer effect will be greater for white respondents than for black respondents. For the race-neutral policy (natsci), the race-of-interviewer effect will be the same (or close to 0) for both white respondents and black respondents (see Expectation 1).

   A. Run the appropriate cross-tabulation analyses. In the table that follows, record the percentages of respondents saying that we are spending "too little" in each of the policy areas. For each policy, obtain the race-of-interviewer effect by subtracting the percentage of respondents saying "too little" when interviewed by a white questioner from the percentage saying "too little" when interviewed by a black questioner. (For example, if 50.0 percent of respondents said we are spending "too little" when questioned by a white interviewer and 70.0 percent said "too little" when questioned by a black interviewer, then the race-of-interview effect would be 70.0 percent minus 50.0 percent, or 20.0 percent.)

		Race of interviewer		
Race of respondent	Percent saying we are spending "too little" on:	White	Black	Race-of-interviewer effect (black % – white %)
White:	Improving the conditions of blacks (natrace)	?	?	?
	Welfare (natfare)	?	?	?
	Supporting scientific research (natsci)	?	?	?
Black:	Improving the conditions of blacks (natrace)	?	?	?
	Welfare (natfare)	?	?	?
	Supporting scientific research (natsci)	?	?	?

B. Examine the data closely. Among white respondents, would you say that Expectation 1 is or is not supported by the evidence? (circle one)

Expectation 1 is not supported. Expectation 1 is supported.

Explain your reasoning, making specific reference to the percentages in the table in part A.

____

____

____

____

____

____

Among black respondents, would you say that Expectation 1 is or is not supported by the evidence? (circle one)

Expectation 1 is not supported. Expectation 1 is supported.

Explain your reasoning, making specific reference to the percentages in the table in part A.

____

____

____

____

____

____

C. Now compare the race-of-interviewer effects between respondents of different races. That is, compare the race-of-interviewer effect on natrace among white respondents with the race-of-interviewer effect on natrace among black respondents. Do the same for natfare and natsci. Generally speaking, would you say that Expectation 2 is supported or is not supported by the evidence? (circle one)

Expectation 2 is not supported. Expectation 2 is supported.

Explain your reasoning, making specific reference to the percentages in the table in part A.

____

____

____

____

____

____

D. Produce and edit a line chart of the relationship between the percentage saying "too little" on natrace and intethn_2, controlling for race_2. (*Hint*: Respondents who think we are spending "too little" are coded 1 on natrace.) Print the chart.

E. Based on the tabular data and on the chart, how would you describe the relationship between the interviewer's race and expressed opinions about spending to help blacks, controlling for race of respondent?

Additive Interaction

F. Explain your answer in E, making specific reference to the evidence you have gathered in this exercise.

____

____

____

____

That concludes the exercises for this chapter.

NOTES

1. According to GSS2012, 82.8 percent of "High" attenders have children, compared with 62.0 percent of "Low" attenders—a 20-percentage-point difference.
2. Edward R. Tufte, *The Visual Display of Quantitative Information,* 2nd ed. (Cheshire, Conn.: Graphics Press, 2001), 93.
3. The Graphs → Legacy Dialogs → Bar (Clustered) interface is identical to the multiple line chart interface in every detail. If you prefer clustered bar charts, you can directly apply the skills you will learn in this chapter.
4. M. Kent Jennings and Laura Stoker, "Political Similarity and Influence Between Husbands and Wives," in *The Social Logic of Politics*, ed. Alan S. Zuckerman (Philadelphia: Temple University Press, 2005), 51–74.
5. E.E. Schattschneider, *The Semisovereign People* (Boston: Wadsworth, 1960).
6. Here is the 2012 American National Election Study's note regarding the meaning of the *cses* prefix: "Comparative Study of Electoral Systems (CSES) is a battery of questions common to many national election surveys around the world."
7. See Darren W. Davis and Brian D. Silver, "Stereotype Threat and Race of Interviewer Effects in a Survey of Political Knowledge," *American Journal of Political Science* 47, no. 1 (January 2003): 33–45.
8. There is a large body of literature on "symbolic racism." For an excellent review and analysis, see Stanley Feldman and Leonie Huddy, "Racial Resentment and White Opposition to Race-Conscious Programs: Principles or Prejudice?," *American Journal of Political Science* 49, no. 1 (January 2005): 168–183.

Making Inferences about Sample Means*

Watch a screencast of the guided examples in this chapter.
edge.sagepub.com/pollock

Procedures Covered

Analyze → Descriptive Statistics → Descriptives

Analyze → Compare Means → One-Sample T Test

Analyze → Compare Means → Independent-Samples T Test

Political research has much to do with observing patterns, creating explanations, framing hypotheses, and analyzing relationships. In interpreting their findings, however, researchers often operate in an environment of uncertainty. This uncertainty arises, in large measure, from the complexity of the political world. As we have seen, when we infer a causal connection between an independent variable and a dependent variable, it is hard to know for sure whether the independent variable is causing the dependent variable. Other, uncontrolled variables might be affecting the relationship, too. Yet uncertainty arises, as well, from the simple fact that research findings are often based on random samples. In an ideal world, we could observe and measure the characteristics of every element in the population of interest—every voting-age adult, every student enrolled at a university, every bill introduced in every state legislature, and so on. In such an ideal situation, we would enjoy a high degree of certainty that the variables we have described and the relationships we have analyzed mirror what is really going on in the population. But of course we often do not have access to every member of a population. Instead we rely on a sample, a subset drawn at random from the population. By taking a random sample, we introduce random sampling error. In using a sample to draw inferences about a population, therefore, we never use the word *certainty.* Rather, we talk about *confidence* or *probability.* We know that the measurements we make on the sample will reflect the characteristics of the population, within the boundaries of random sampling error.

What are those boundaries? If we calculate the mean income of a random sample of adults, for example, how confident can we be that the mean income we observe in our sample is the same as the mean income in the population? The answer depends on the standard error of the sample mean, the extent to which the mean income of the sample departs by chance from the mean income of the population. If we use a sample to calculate a mean income for women and a mean income for men, how confident can we be that the difference between these two sample means reflects the true income difference between women and men in the population? Again, the answer depends on the standard error—in this case, the standard error of the *difference* between the sample means, the extent to which the difference in the sample departs from the difference in the population.

*Special note to SPSS Student Version users: For the guided examples and exercises in Chapters 6 through 9, you will analyze NES2012_Student_B or GSS2012_Student_B.

In this chapter you will use three procedures to explore and apply inferential statistics. First, you will learn to use Descriptives to obtain basic information about interval-level variables. Second, using the One-Sample T Test procedure, you will obtain the 95 percent confidence interval (95% CI) for a sample mean. The 95% CI will tell you the boundaries within which there is a .95 probability that the true population mean falls. Third, using the Independent-Samples T Test procedure, you will test for statistically significant differences between two sample means.

DESCRIPTIVES AND ONE-SAMPLE T TEST

To gain insight into the properties and application of inferential statistics, we will work through an example using NES2012. We begin by looking at the Descriptives procedure, which yields basic information about interval-level variables. We then demonstrate the fundamentals of inference using the One-Sample T Test procedure.

NES2012 contains ftgr_gay, a feeling thermometer scale measuring attitudes toward gays. As you know, the National Election Study (NES) feeling thermometers range in value from 0 (cold or negative feelings) to 100 (warm or positive feelings). We can use Descriptives to obtain summary information about ftgr_gay. Open NES2012. Click Analyze → Descriptive Statistics → Descriptives. In the main Descriptives window, scroll down the left-hand variable list until you find ftgr_gay. Click ftgr_gay into the Variable(s) list (Figure 6-1). Click the Options button. Now you can specify which descriptive statistics you would like SPSS to produce. These defaults should already be checked: mean, standard deviation, minimum, and maximum. That's fine. Also check the box beside "S.E. mean," which stands for "standard error of the mean," as shown in Figure 6-1. Click Continue, and then click OK.

Figure 6-1 Descriptives Window and Descriptives: Options Window (modified)

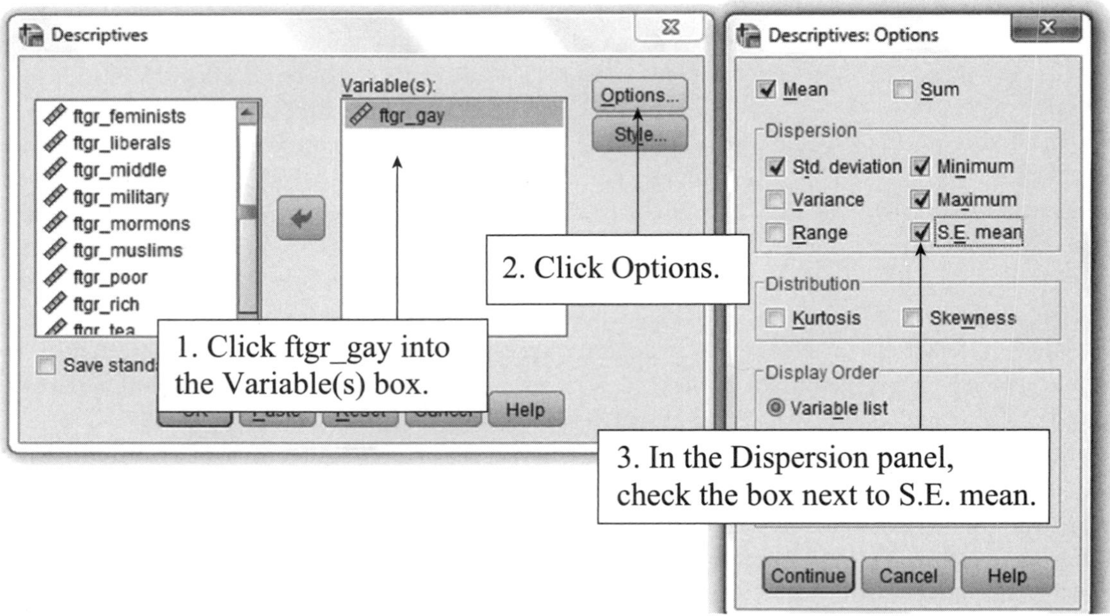

Descriptive Statistics

	N	Minimum	Maximum	Mean		Std. Deviation
	Statistic	Statistic	Statistic	Statistic	Std. Error	Statistic
ftgr_gay POST: Feeling thermometer: GAY MEN AND LESBIANS	5424	0	100	51.63	.377	27.784
Valid N (listwise)	5424					

SPSS has reported the requested statistics for ftgr_gay: number of cases analyzed (N), minimum and maximum observed values for ftgr_gay, mean value of ftgr_gay, standard error of the mean, and standard deviation. Among the 5,424 respondents, scores on ftgr_gay range from 0 to 100. The mean value of ftgr_gay is 51.63, with a standard deviation of 27.784 (which rounds to 27.78).[1] How closely does the mean of 51.63 reflect the true mean in the population from which this sample was drawn? If we had measured the gay thermometer for every U.S. citizen of voting age and calculated a population mean, how far off the mark would our sample estimate of 51.63 be?

The answer depends on the standard error of the sample mean. The standard error of a sample mean is based on the standard deviation and the size of the sample. SPSS determines the standard error just as you would—by dividing the standard deviation by the square root of the sample size. For ftgr_gay, the standard error is the standard deviation, 27.78, divided by the square root of 5,424. Performed with a hand calculator: 27.78/sqrt(5425) = 27.78/73.65 ≈ .377 ≈ .38.

This number, .38, tells us the extent to which the sample mean of 51.63 departs by chance from the population mean. The standard error is the essential ingredient for making inferences about the population mean. But let's get SPSS to help us make these inferences. Specifically, we will use the One-Sample T Test procedure to do two things: find the 95% CI of the mean, and use the confidence interval to test a hypothetical claim about the population mean. Click Analyze → Compare Means → One-Sample T Test, causing the One-Sample T Test window to open (Figure 6-2). The user supplies SPSS with information in two places: the Test Variable(s) panel and the Test Value box, which currently contains the default value of 0. Now, One-Sample T Test is not naturally designed to report the 95% CI for a mean. Rather, it is set up to compare the mean of a variable in the Test Variable(s) panel with a hypothetical mean (provided by the user in the Test Value box)

Figure 6-2 One-Sample T Test Window

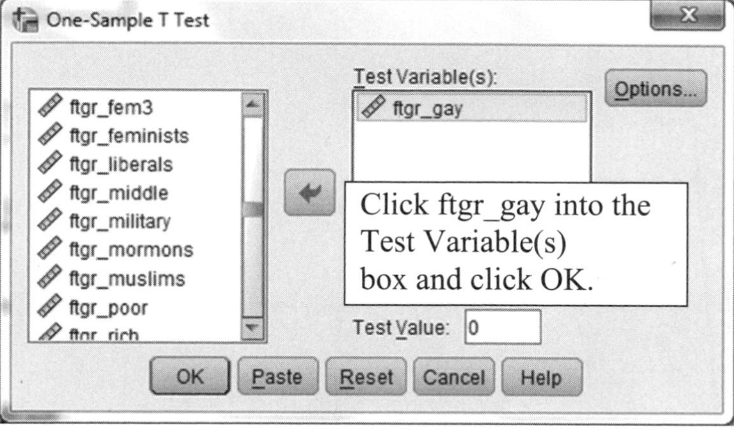

One-Sample Statistics

	N	Mean	Std. Deviation	Std. Error Mean
ftgr_gay POST: Feeling thermometer: GAY MEN AND LESBIANS	5424	51.63	27.784	.377

One-Sample Test

	Test Value = 0					
					95% Confidence Interval of the Difference	
	t	df	Sig. (2-tailed)	Mean Difference	Lower	Upper
ftgr_gay POST: Feeling thermometer: GAY MEN AND LESBIANS	136.842	5423	.000	51.627	50.89	52.37

and to see if random error could account for the difference. (We will discuss this calculation below.) However, if you run One-Sample T Test on its defaults, it will provide the 95% CI. Simply click the variable into the Test Variable(s) panel, as shown in Figure 6-2, and click OK.

The output for One-Sample T Test includes two tables. In the One-Sample Statistics table, SPSS reports summary information about ftgr_gay. This information is similar to the Descriptives output discussed earlier. Again, we can see that ftgr_gay has a mean of 51.63, a standard deviation of 27.78, and a standard error of .38 (which, reassuringly, is the same number we calculated by hand). We are interested mainly in the second table, the One-Sample Test table. In fact, when using One-Sample T Test to obtain confidence intervals, you may safely ignore all the information in the One-Sample Test table except for the rightmost cells. The values appearing under the label "95% Confidence Interval of the Difference," 50.89 and 52.37, define the lower and upper boundaries of the 95% CI.

It is an established statistical rule that 95 percent of all possible population means will fall in this interval:

$$\text{Sample mean} \pm 1.96(\text{Standard error of sample mean}).$$

By this rule, the lower boundary is 51.63 – 1.96(.38) = 50.89; and the upper boundary is 51.63 + 1.96(.38) = 52.37. There is a high probability, a 95 percent probability, that the true population mean lies in the region between 50.89 at the low end and 52.37 at the high end.

Figure 6-3 graphically depicts the One-Sample T Test results. The observed sample mean, 51.63, is represented by a dot. The two horizontal "whiskers" define the 95% CI, which lies between 50.89 and 52.37. The 95% CI is the foundation for the .05 level of statistical significance, the basic standard of hypothesis testing using inferential statistics. Any hypothetical claim stating that the true population mean is less than 50.89, or greater than 52.37, can be rejected as statistically unlikely. There is a probability of .05 or less (≤.05) that the population mean is below the lower boundary (one-half of .05, equal to .025) or above the upper boundary (the remaining half of .05, equal to .025). By the same token, any hypothetical claim that the true population mean is anywhere within the 95% CI

Figure 6-3 Error Bar Chart (One Sample Mean)

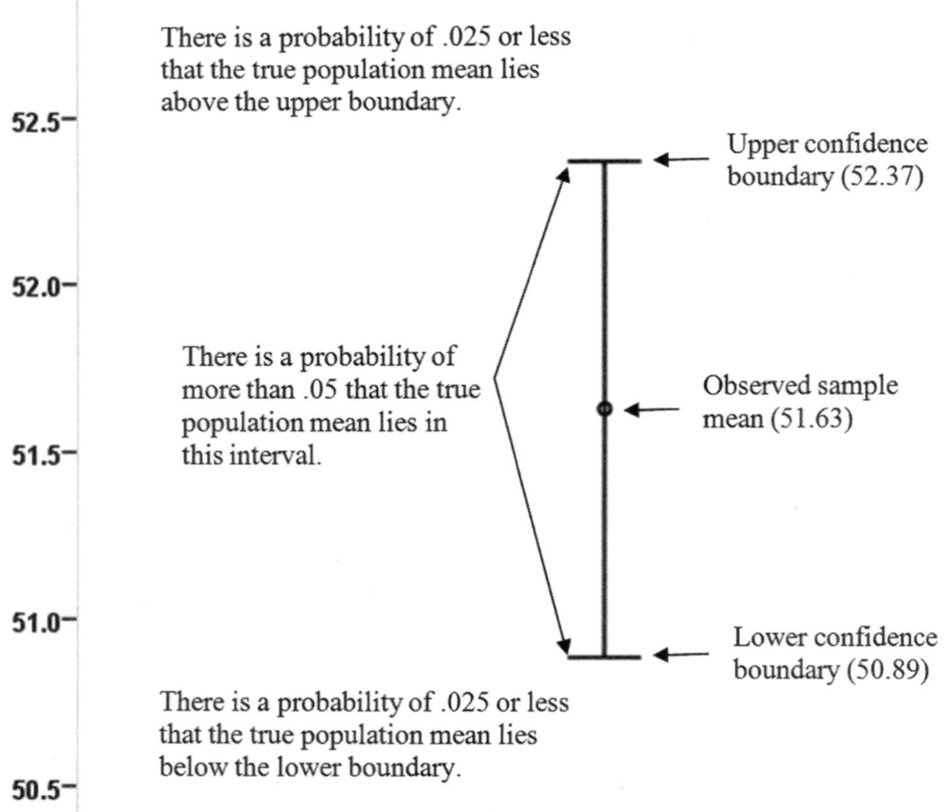

must be accepted as statistically likely—*likely* being defined as an event that would occur more frequently than 5 times out of 100 (>.05). Of course, not all hypothetical claims within the 95 percent bandwidth are equally probable. Proposed population means that are closer to the observed sample mean (in our example, around 51.63) are much more likely than population means farther out, on the frontier near the upper or lower boundaries.

The 95% CI—and the .05 standard—also comes into play when making inferences about the difference between a sample mean and a hypothetical population mean. Suppose that someone claimed that the true population mean is 52, not the observed NES sample mean of 51.63. The proposed mean of 52 falls within the 95% CI, between 50.89 and 52.37. Thus, there is a probability of greater than .05 that the claim is correct, and so we cannot reject it. Now, the fact that the hypothetical mean falls within the 95% CI directly implies that the *difference* between the observed mean (51.63) and the proposed mean (52) is not statistically significant; that is, it would occur by chance more than 5 times out of 100. Framed in the same language used earlier to describe the 95% CI of a single sample mean, we can say that 95 percent of all possible differences between an observed sample mean and a hypothetical population mean will fall in this interval:

(Sample mean – Hypothetical population mean) ± 1.96(Standard error of sample mean).

Furthermore, if 0 falls within the 95% CI, then we must infer that the difference is statistically indistinguishable from zero. Logically enough, if the 95% CI does not include 0, then we conclude that the difference is statistically significant. Applied to the example, the difference between the sample mean and the hypothetical mean is equal to 51.63 – 52 = –.37. The 95% CI's lower boundary = –.37 – 1.96(.38) = –1.11. The upper boundary = –.37 + 1.96(.38) = .37. Figure 6-4 displays the 95% CI for this example. Notice that the 95% CI includes 0. Thus, even though the two numbers, 51.63 and 52, appear to us to be different, from a statistical standpoint they are not different at all. If the NES were to draw its sample again, there is a probability of greater than .05 that ftgr_gay's new mean could be 52 instead of 51.63.

We have seen that the 95% CI is a simple yet effective inferential tool. But it is blunt. It tells us that there is a probability of greater than .05 that the population mean—or the difference between two means—lies within

Figure 6-4 Error Bar Chart (Difference between Sample Mean and Hypothetical Population Mean)

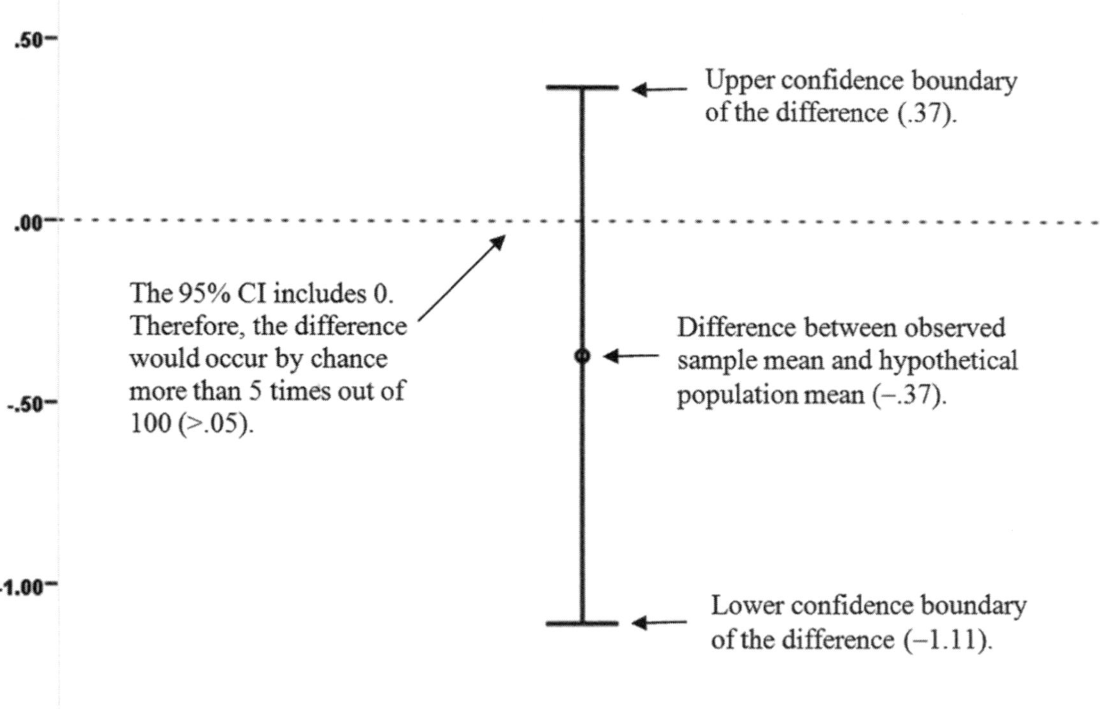

the interval's lower and upper limits. In fact, the "greater than .05 interval" would be a more descriptive term for the 95% CI. A more precise inferential method, the *P*-value approach, allows the researcher to determine the exact probability associated with a hypothetical claim about the population mean. For example, our confidence interval analysis of the hypothetical population mean of 52 revealed that a random sample would yield such a result more than 5 times out of 100. But how many times, *exactly*? Six times? Twenty-six times? Thirty-six times? Put differently, we know that the probability is greater than .05 that 51.63 and 52 come from the same distribution of population means. What, precisely, is that probability? Run One-Sample T Test on ftgr_gay again to determine the *P*-value associated with the hypothetical mean of 52. Click Analyze → Compare Means → One-Sample T Test. Ftgr_gay should still be in the Test Variable(s) panel. Now click in the Test Value box and type "52" (Figure 6-5). SPSS will calculate the difference between the mean of the test variable, ftgr_gay, and the test value, 52. SPSS will then report the probability that the test value, 52, could have come from the same population as did the mean of the test variable, ftgr_gay. Click OK. Again, we have One-Sample T Test output (Figure 6-6).

Notice that the numbers from our earlier analysis appear in the "Mean Difference" column and "95% Confidence Interval of the Difference" column. Now, however, we are after the exact probability that 51.63 and 52 reside in the same distribution of possible population means. To address this inferential issue, SPSS calculates a Student's *t*-test statistic, or *t*-ratio. A *t*-statistic is calculated using this formula:

$$t = (\text{Sample mean} - \text{Hypothetical population mean}) \,/\, (\text{Standard error of the sample mean}).$$

This value of *t*, −.99, appears in the leftmost cell of the One-Sample Test table.[2] Thus, ftgr_gay's mean falls .99 standard errors below the hypothetical mean of 52. Turn your attention to the cell labeled "Sig. (2-tailed),"

Figure 6-5 Testing a Hypothetical Claim about a Sample Mean

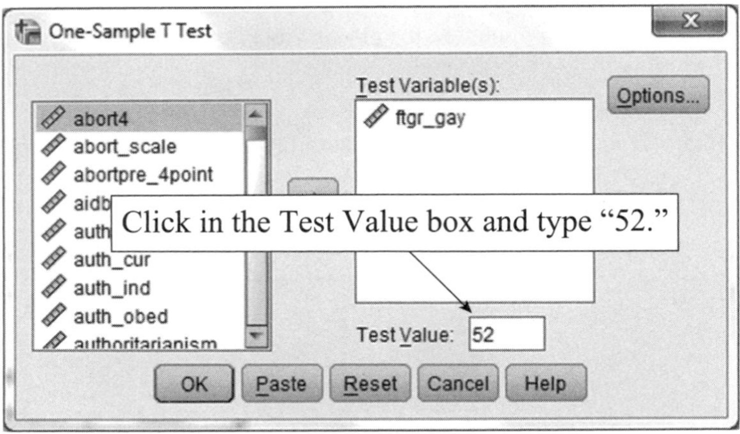

Figure 6-6 Testing for Statistical Significance

One-Sample Test

	Test Value = 52					
					95% Confidence Interval of the Difference	
	t	df	Sig. (2-tailed)	Mean Difference	Lower	Upper
ftgr_gay POST: Feeling thermometer: GAY MEN AND LESBIANS	-.989	5423	.323	-.373	-1.11	.37

SPSS calculates a *t*-statistic for the difference between the means, and it uses the *t*-statistic to calculate the *P*-value.

Here are the statistics from the confidence-interval analysis: The mean difference (−.37) and the 95% CI of the difference (−1.11 to .37).

which contains the number .323. This is the *P*-value associated with the *t*-statistic, and it may be interpreted this way: There is a probability of .323 that the sample mean and the hypothetical mean were drawn from the same distribution of means. A less intuitive, but technically more proper, interpretation is as follows: If the difference between the two means is assumed to be 0, then random sampling error would produce the observed difference 32.3 percent of the time, by chance. So, the no-difference hypothesis holds up. From the 95% CI, we already knew that 51.63 and 52 were not significantly different. The *P*-value approach puts a finer point on this inference.[3]

INDEPENDENT-SAMPLES T TEST

The 95% CI approach and the *P*-value approach are essential tools for testing hypotheses about the difference between two sample means. Someone investigating the gender gap, for example, might test a series of hypotheses about the political differences between men and women. In the next guided example, we test two gender gap hypotheses:

> Hypothesis 1: In a comparison of individuals, men will give gays lower feeling thermometer ratings than will women.
>
> Hypothesis 2: In a comparison of individuals, men will give the Republican Party higher feeling thermometer ratings than will women.

The first hypothesis suggests that when we divide the sample on the basis of the independent variable, gender, and compare mean values of the gay feeling thermometer, the male mean will be lower than the female mean. The second hypothesis suggests that when we compare men and women on the Republican Party feeling thermometer, the male mean will be higher than the female mean.

The researcher always tests his or her hypotheses against a skeptical foil, the null hypothesis, labeled H_0. The null hypothesis claims that, regardless of any group differences that a researcher observes in a random sample, no group differences exist in the population from which the sample was drawn. How does H_0 explain apparently systematic patterns that might turn up in a sample, such as a mean difference between women and men on the gay feeling thermometer? It points to random sampling error. In essence the null hypothesis says, "You observed such and such a difference between two groups in your random sample. But, in reality, no difference exists in the population. When you took the sample, you introduced random sampling error. Thus random sampling error accounts for the difference you observed." For both Hypothesis 1 and Hypothesis 2 above, the null hypothesis says that there are no real differences between men and women in the population, that men do not give lower ratings to gays or higher ratings to the Republican Party. The null hypothesis asserts further that any observed differences in the sample can be accounted for by random sampling error.

The null hypothesis is so central to the methodology of statistical inference that we always begin by assuming it to be correct. We then set a high standard for rejecting it. The researcher's hypotheses—such as the feeling thermometer hypotheses—are considered alternative hypotheses, label H_A. The Independent-Samples T Test procedure permits us to test each alternative hypothesis against the null hypothesis and to decide whether the observed differences between males and females are too large to have occurred by random chance when the sample was drawn. For each mean comparison, the Independent-Samples T Test procedure will give us a *P*-value: the probability of obtaining the sample difference under the working assumption that the null hypothesis is true.

To reject the null hypothesis, we must be confident that the mean difference could not occur by chance more than 5 times out of 100. Thus, for *P*-values of less than or equal to .05 (≤.05), reject H_0. For *P*-values of greater than .05 (>.05), do not reject H_0. This probabilistic decision rule may strike you as decidedly out of sync with ordinary life experiences. If you were planning an outdoor activity, and the weather forecast called for a 10 percent chance of rain, you would not change your plans—.10 is a low probability. Indeed, a 25 percent chance of rain (a probability equal to .25) would not even cause you to carry an umbrella. When it comes to testing H_0, however, the definition of a "high" probability is much more stringent. Suppose we have every expectation that our analysis will confirm our hypothesis, H_A. Suppose further that we obtain a set of results telling us that random sampling error, H_0's favorite process, would produce our results 6 times out of 100. Now, a probability of .06 seems quite low. But it is not low enough to reject the null hypothesis. The idea behind the decision rule is to minimize the probability of rejecting the null hypothesis when, in the population from which our sample was randomly drawn, the null hypothesis is in fact true. This is called Type I error. If we are going to get it wrong, we want to accept the null hypothesis when, in fact, it is false. This is called Type II error, and the inferential rule is freighted toward committing Type II error and away from committing Type I error.

With these principles in mind, let's ask SPSS to test the two gender gap hypotheses. Click Analyze → Compare Means → Independent-Samples T Test. The Independent-Samples T Test window appears (Figure 6-7). SPSS wants to know two things: the name or names of the test variable(s) and the name of the grouping variable. SPSS will calculate the mean values of the variables named in the Test Variable(s) panel for each category of the variable named in the Grouping Variable box. It will then test to see if the differences between the means are significantly different from 0.

We want to compare the means for men and women on two feeling thermometers: ftgr_gay (gays) and ft_rep (Republican Party). Find ftgr_gay and ft_rep in the variable list and click both of them into the Test Variable(s) panel. (See Figure 6-8.) Because you want the means of these variables to be calculated separately for each sex, gender is the grouping variable. When you click gender into the Grouping Variable box, SPSS moves it into the box with the designation "gender(? ?)." The Define Groups button is activated (Figure 6-8). SPSS

Figure 6-7 Independent-Samples T Test Window

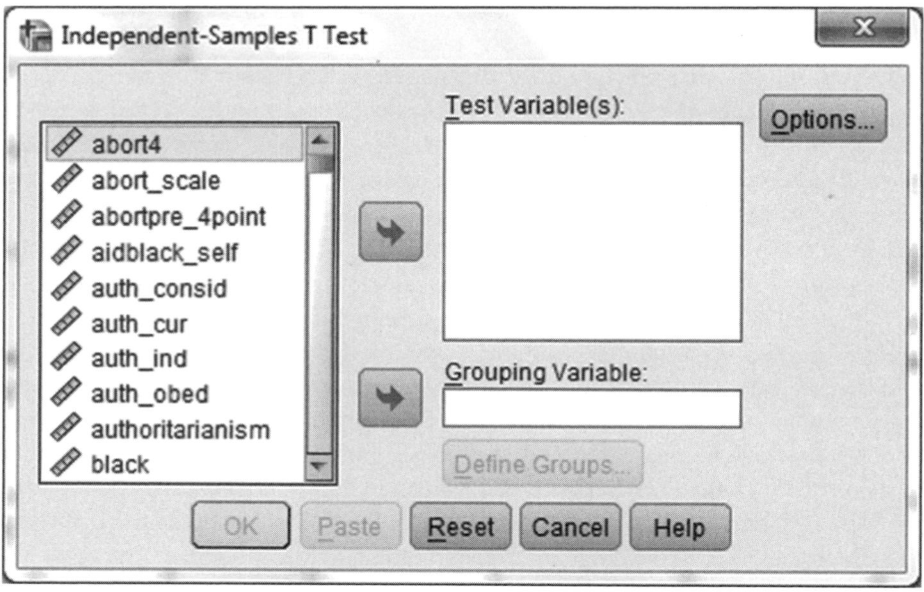

Figure 6-8 Specifying Test Variables and Defining the Grouping Variable

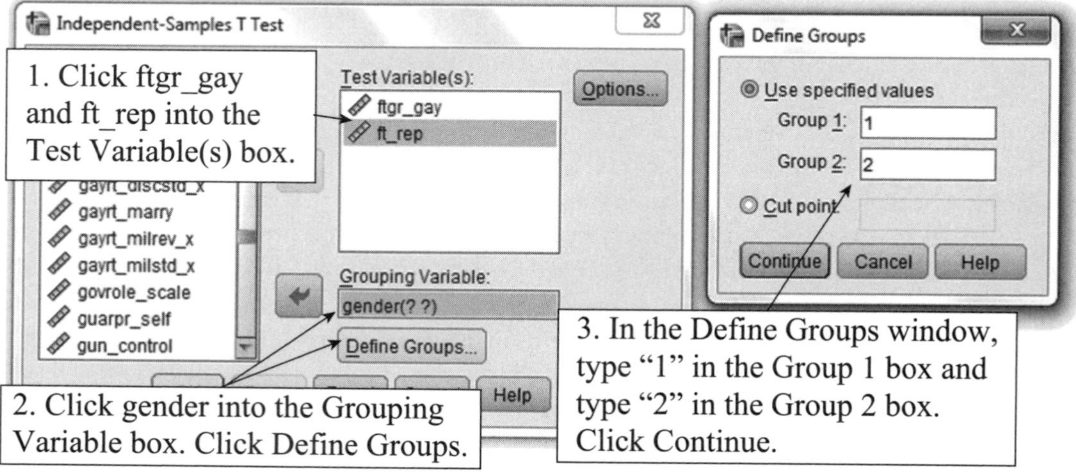

needs more information. It needs to know the codes of the two groups you wish to compare. Men are coded 1 on gender and women are coded 2. (Recall that by right-clicking on a variable you can reacquaint yourself with that variable's codes.) Click Define Groups (Figure 6-8). There are two ways to define the groups you want to compare: Use specified values (the default) and Cut point. The choice depends on the situation. If you opt for Use specified values, then SPSS will divide the cases into two groups based on the codes you supply for Group 1 and Group 2. If the grouping variable has more than two categories, then you may wish to use Cut point. SPSS will divide the cases into two groups based on the code entered in the Cut point box—one group for all cases having codes equal to or greater than the Cut point code and one group having codes less than the Cut point code. (You will use Cut point in one of the exercises at the end of this chapter.) Because gender has two codes—1 for males and 2 for females—we will go with the Use specified values option in this example. Click in the Group 1 box and type "1," and then click in the Group 2 box and type "2." Click Continue, as shown in Figure 6-8. Notice that SPSS has replaced the question marks next to gender with the codes for males and females. Click OK.

SPSS runs both mean comparisons and reports the results in the Viewer (Figure 6-9). The top table, labeled "Group Statistics," shows descriptive information about the means of ftgr_gay and ft_rep. The bottom table, "Independent Samples Test," tests for statistically significant differences between men and women on each dependent variable.

We will evaluate the gender difference on the gay feeling thermometer first. From the Group Statistics table we can see that males, on average, rated gays at 47.37, whereas females had a higher mean, 55.67. It would appear that our alternative hypothesis has merit. The difference between these two sample means is 47.37 minus 55.67, or −8.30. (SPSS always calculates the difference by subtracting the Group 2 mean from the Group 1 mean. This value appears in the "Mean Difference" column of the Independent-Samples Test table.) The null hypothesis claims that this difference is the result of random sampling error and, therefore, that the true male–female difference in the population is equal to 0. Using the information in the Independent-Samples Test table, we test the null hypothesis (H_0) against the alternative hypothesis (H_A) that the male mean is lower than the female mean.

Notice that there are two rows of numbers for each dependent variable. One row is labeled "Equal variances assumed" and the other is "Equal variances not assumed." The statistics along "Equal variances not assumed" are generally more conservative, so it is a safer bet to use them.[4] In comparing two sample means, SPSS calculates a t-statistic using the following formula:

(Group 1 mean – Group 2 mean) / (Standard error of the mean difference).[5]

Figure 6-9 Results of Independent-Samples T Test

Group Statistics

	gender Gender	N	Mean	Std. Deviation	Std. Error Mean
ftgr_gay POST: Feeling thermometer: GAY MEN AND LESBIANS	1 Male	2641	47.37	26.932	.524
	2 Female	2783	55.67	27.981	.530
ft_rep PRE: Feeling Thermometer: Republican Party	1 Male	2821	44.57	27.120	.511
	2 Female	3034	44.32	28.522	.518

1. SPSS subtracts the female mean from the male mean.

2. SPSS reports the mean difference here.

Independent Samples Test

		Levene's Test for Equality of Variances		t-test for Equality of Means					95% Confidence Interval of the Difference	
		F	Sig.	t	df	Sig. (2-tailed)	Mean Difference	Std. Error Difference	Lower	Upper
ftgr_gay POST: Feeling thermometer: GAY MEN AND LESBIANS	Equal variances assumed	14.864	.000	-11.123	5422	.000	-8.302	.746	-9.765	-6.839
	Equal variances not assumed			-11.134	5420.558	.000	-8.302	.746	-9.764	-6.840
ft_rep PRE: Feeling Thermometer: Republican Party	Equal variances assumed	7.891	.005	.344	5853	.731	.251	.729	-1.177	1.679
	Equal variances not assumed			.345	5849.742	.730	.251	.727	-1.175	1.676

3. Use the statistics along the "Equal variances not assumed" row.

4. SPSS reports the t-statistics for each mean difference.

5. Find P-values here.

6. Does the 95% CI contain H_0's favorite number?

For the ftgr_gay hypothesis, SPSS returns a huge *t*-statistic, –11.134. If you happened to glance at the boundaries of the 95% CI—from –9.76 at the low end to –6.84 at the high end—you already knew that the results would be bad news for the null hypothesis. It comes as no surprise, then, that SPSS reports a *P*-value of .000. Is .000 equal to or less than .05? Yes, it is. Safe conclusion: Under the assumption that the null hypothesis is correct, random sampling error would yield an observed mean difference of –8.30 very nearly 0 percent of the time. Reject the null hypothesis.[6]

However, H_0 carries the day on the gender–ft_rep relationship. Trouble brews early for H_A: The male mean, 44.57, and the female mean, 44.32, are only .25 units apart, hardly a robust gender gap. The anemic *t*-statistic (.345) and its gargantuan *P*-value (.730) end the debate: Under the assumption that the null hypothesis is correct, random error would produce a mean difference about 73 percent of the time. Do not reject the null hypothesis. Adding insult to H_A's injury, H_0 fans will no doubt be pleased to learn that the 95% CI of the mean difference, –1.18 to 1.68, includes H_0's winning number, 0.

EXERCISES

1. (Dataset: GSS2012. Variable: egalit_scale.) The 2012 General Social Survey (GSS) asked people a series of questions designed to measure how egalitarian they are—that is, the extent to which they think economic opportunities and rewards should be distributed more equally in society. The GSS2012 variable egalit_scale ranges from 1 (low egalitarianism) to 35 (high egalitarianism). The 2012 GSS, of course, is a random sample of U.S. adults. In this exercise, you will analyze egalitarianism using One-Sample T Test. You then will draw inferences about the population mean.

   A. Egalitarianism has a sample mean of (fill in the blank) ________________.

   B. There is a probability of .95 that the true population mean falls between an egalitarianism score of (fill in the blank) ____________ at the low end and a score of (fill in the blank) ____________ at the high end.

   C. A student researcher hypothesizes that social work majors will score significantly higher on the egalitarianism scale than the typical adult. The student researcher also hypothesizes that business majors will score significantly lower on the egalitarianism scale than the average adult. After administering the scale to a number of social work majors and a group of business majors, the researcher obtains these results: social work majors' mean, 20.10; business majors' mean, 18.8.

   Using the confidence interval approach to apply the .05 test of statistical significance, based on your answer in B, you can infer that (check one)

   ❑ social work majors probably are not more egalitarian than most adults.

   ❑ social work majors probably are more egalitarian than most adults.

   Using the confidence interval approach to apply the .05 test of statistical significance, based on your answer in B, you can infer that (check one)

   ❑ business majors probably are not less egalitarian than most adults.

   ❑ business majors probably are less egalitarian than most adults.

   D. Obtain a *P*-value from your analysis of the business majors' mean. The *P*-value tells you that there is a probability equal to (fill in the blank) __________ that (complete the sentence) ____________

   ____.

2. (Dataset: GSS2012. Variables: int_info_scale, age.) Are older people interested in a wider variety of social, economic, political, and scientific issues than are younger people? Or do younger people and older people not differ significantly in the scope of their interests? In this exercise you will use Independent-Samples T Test to test this hypothesis: In a comparison of individuals, people who are 30 years or older are interested in a wider range of current issues than are people who are younger than 30 years.

   GSS2012 contains int_info_scale, which measures respondents' level of interest in ten different issue areas. Scores on int_info_scale range from 0 (low interest) to 20 (high interest). This is the dependent variable and will go in the Test Variable(s) panel. The independent variable, age, goes in the Grouping Variable box. You want SPSS to create two groups from age: a group of respondents who are 30 or older and a group of respondents who are younger than 30. You can tell SPSS to do so by using Cut point in the Define Groups window. When you open the Define Groups window, click the radio button next to "Cut point" and type "30" in the Cut point box. Click Continue.

A. Examine the results of your analysis. Fill in the table below:

Statistics for level of interest in current issues (int_info_scale)	
Mean for older group (≥30 years old)	?
Mean for younger group (<30 years old)	?
Mean difference	?
Lower 95% CI boundary of mean difference	?
Upper 95% CI boundary of mean difference	?
Does 95% CI contain 0? (Yes or No)	?
t-statistic	?
P-value	?

B. According to the null hypothesis, in the population from which the sample was drawn, the difference between the mean for people 30 or older and the mean for people younger than 30 is equal to (fill in the blank) ____.

C. Based on your tabular entries in part A, can you infer that the older age group scores significantly higher on the level of interest scale than does the younger age group? (circle one)

No, the older group does not score significantly higher.
Yes, the older group scores significantly higher.

D. Explain your answer in C, making specific reference to relevant statistics in part A.

____

____

____

____

3. (Dataset: GSS2012. Variables: childs, attend3.) The role of religion lies at the center of an interesting debate about the future of U.S. partisan politics. Republican presidential candidates do much better among people who frequently attend religious services than among people who are less observant. However, religious attendance has been waning. This growing secularization, according to some observers, portends a weakening of the Republican base and a growing opportunity for the Democratic Party.[7] But we also know that religious beliefs and affiliations (or the lack thereof) are strongly shaped by childhood socialization. Are less-religious people raising and socializing children at the same rate as the more religious? In this exercise, you will test this hypothesis: In a comparison of individuals, those with lower levels of religiosity will have fewer children than will those with higher levels of religiosity. This hypothesis says that as religious attendance goes up, so will the average number of children.

   Dataset GSS2012 contains childs, the respondent's number of children. This is the dependent variable. The independent variable is attend3, which measures religious attendance by three ordinal categories: "Low" (coded 1), "Moderate" (coded 2), and "High" (coded 3).

   A. Exercise a familiar skill you acquired in Chapter 4. Perform a mean comparison analysis, obtaining mean values of childs (and numbers of cases) for each value of attend3. Fill in the following table:

	Summary of number of children	
Religious attendance	Mean	N
Low	?	?
Moderate	?	?
High	?	?
Total	?	?

B. Do these findings support the childs–attend3 hypothesis? (circle one)

Yes No

Explain your answer, making specific reference to the data in part A.

____

____

____

____

C. Focus your analysis on a comparison between respondents with low attendance (coded 1) and respondents with high attendance (coded 3). Run Independent-Samples T Test to find out if high attenders have significantly more children than do low attenders. Apply the .05 level of significance. (fill in the blanks)

"Low" attendance mean: ______________________________

"High" attendance mean: ______________________________

Mean difference: ______________________________

95% CI of the mean difference: between ______________ and ______________.

t-statistic for mean difference: ______________________________.

P-value of the mean difference: ______________________________.

D. Does the statistical evidence support the hypothesis that people who are more religious have significantly more children than do people who are less religious? (check one)

- ❑ Yes, the statistical evidence supports the hypothesis.
- ❑ No, the statistical evidence does not support the hypothesis.

E. Explain your answer in E, making specific reference to the statistics in part C.

____

____

____

____

4. (Dataset: GSS2012. Variables: sibs, relig, authoritarianism, sex.) Here are two bits of conventional wisdom, beliefs that are accepted widely as accurate descriptions of the world.

Conventional Wisdom 1: Catholics have bigger families than do Protestants.

Conventional Wisdom 2: Men have stronger authoritarian tendencies than do women.

In this exercise, you will test these ideas and see how well they stand up to the statistical evidence. Test Conventional Wisdom 1 by comparing the average number of siblings (GSS2012 variable sibs) for Protestants and Catholics (relig). Test Conventional Wisdom 2 by comparing mean authoritarianism scale scores (authoritarianism) for males and females (sex). The authoritarianism scale ranges from 0 (low authoritarianism) to 7 (high authoritarianism).

A. Run the analyses. Record the results in the following table:

	Conventional Wisdom 1	Conventional Wisdom 2
Mean difference	?	?
Lower 95% CI boundary of mean difference	?	?
Upper 95% CI boundary of mean difference	?	?
Does 95% CI contain 0? (Yes or No)	?	?
t-statistic	?	?
P-value	?	?

B. Consider the following statement: "According to the statistical evidence, we can reject H_0 for Conventional Wisdom 1." Is this statement correct or incorrect? (circle one)

Incorrect Correct

Explain your answer, making specific reference to the statistics in part A.

____

____

____

____

C. Consider the following statement: "The statistical evidence supports Conventional Wisdom 2." Is this statement correct or incorrect? (circle one)

Incorrect Correct

Explain your answer, making specific reference to the statistics in part A.

____

____

____

____

That concludes the exercises for this chapter.

NOTES

1. To simplify the presentation of the material in this part of the chapter, values will be rounded to two decimal places.
2. SPSS performs this calculation at 32-decimal precision. So if you were to check SPSS's math, using the mean difference and standard error that appear in the SPSS Viewer, you would arrive at a slightly different *t*-ratio than the value of t reported in the One-Sample Test table.

3. SPSS returns two-tailed *P*-values (labeled "Sig."), not one-tailed values. Two-tailed values report the probability associated with the absolute value of *t*, or $|t|$. For the current example, even though SPSS puts a negative sign on the *t*-ratio, −.99, the accompanying significance value, .323, combines *P*-values for the region of the Student's *t*-distribution below $t = -.99$ *and* above $t = +.99$. Because most hypotheses are directional—for example, we would properly hypothesize that women score *higher* than men on ftgr_gay, not that women and men *differ* on ftgr_gay—two-tailed *P*-values impose a stringent .025 one-tailed test of statistical significance. However, such stringency is statistically acceptable, because it biases inference in favor of Type II error. Moreover, as far as the author is aware, the two-tailed standard is universal in political research, and so it is followed in this book.
4. One of the statistical assumptions of mean comparisons is that the amount of variation in the dependent variable is the same for the groups being compared—for example, that the amount of variation in ftgr_gay is the same in the female subsample and the male subsample. If this assumption holds up, then it is safe to use the "Equal variances assumed" row. If it does not hold up, then the "Equal variances not assumed" row must be used. SPSS tests the equal-variances assumption by reporting statistics for Levene's test. Technically, if the significance value for Levene's test is greater than or equal to .05, you can use the "Equal variances assumed" row. If Levene's significance value is less than .05, then you must use the "Equal variances not assumed" row. As a practical matter, the two rows of numbers are never wildly different. But it is statistically prudent (and simpler) to assume that the variances are not equal.
5. The standard error of the difference is derived by squaring each subsample's standard error, summing the squares, and then taking the square root of the sum.
6. A *P*-value cannot exactly equal 0. There is always some chance, however remote, that random error produced the difference observed in the sample. Although the editing of SPSS tabular output is not covered in this book, it is possible to double-click on a table (SPSS refers to tabular objects as "pivot tables") to make appearance-enhancing changes or to look at the mind-numbingly precise numbers that SPSS rounds to produce the digits on display in the table. Double-clicking on the Independent-Samples T Test output shown in Figure 6-8, and then double-clicking on the "Sig. (2-tailed)" value just discussed (the value .000), reveals this number: 1.7448E-28. That's scientific notation for .000000000000000000 00000000017448.
7. John B. Judis and Ruy Teixeira, *The Emerging Democratic Majority* (New York: Scribner, 2002).

Chi-square and Measures of Association*

Watch a screencast of the guided examples in this chapter.
edge.sagepub.com/pollock

Procedures Covered

Analyze → Descriptive → Crosstabs → Statistics

In the preceding chapter you learned how to test for mean differences on an interval-level dependent variable. But what if you are not dealing with interval-level variables? What if you are doing cross-tabulation analysis and are trying to figure out whether an observed relationship between two nominal or ordinal variables mirrors the true relationship in the population? Just as with mean differences, the answer depends on the boundaries of random sampling error, the extent to which your observed results "happened by chance" when you took the sample. The Crosstabs procedure can provide the information needed to test the statistical significance of nominal or ordinal relationships, and it will yield appropriate measures of association.

You are familiar with the Crosstabs procedure. For analyzing datasets that contain a preponderance of categorical variables—variables measured by nominal or ordinal categories—cross-tabulation is by far the most common mode of analysis in political research. In this section we will revisit Crosstabs and use the Statistics subroutine to obtain the oldest and most widely applied test of statistical significance in cross-tabulation analysis, the chi-square test. With rare exceptions, chi-square can always be used to determine whether an observed cross-tabulation relationship departs significantly from the expectations of the null hypothesis. In the first guided example, you will be introduced to the logic behind chi-square, and you will learn how to interpret SPSS's chi-square output.

In this chapter you will also learn how to obtain measures of association for the relationships you are analyzing. If both are ordinal-level variables, then Somers's *d* is the appropriate measure of association. Somers's *d* is an *asymmetrical* measure. It reports different measures of the strength of a relationship, depending on whether the independent variable is used to predict the dependent variable or the dependent variable is used to predict the independent variable. Asymmetrical measures of association generally are preferred over *symmetrical* measures, which yield the same value, regardless of whether the independent variable is used to predict the dependent variable or the dependent variable is used to predict the independent variable.[1]

Somers's *d* is a proportional reduction in error (PRE) measure of the strength of a relationship. A PRE measure tells you the extent to which the values of the independent variable predict the values of the dependent variable. A value close to 0 says that the independent variable provides little predictive leverage;

*Special note to SPSS Student Version users: For the guided examples and exercises in Chapters 6 through 9, you will analyze NES2012_Student_B or GSS2012_Student_B.

the relationship is weak. Values close to the poles—to −1 for negative associations or to +1 for positive relationships—tell you that the independent variable provides a lot of help in predicting the dependent variable; the relationship is strong.[2]

For measuring the strength of nominal-level relationships, the choices are more limited. A nominal-level PRE measure, lambda, is sometimes used. Granted, PRE measures are generally preferred over measures that do not permit a PRE interpretation. Even so, lambda frequently underestimates the strength of relationships, a problem that is especially acute when one of the variables has low variation. Therefore, when you are analyzing a relationship in which one or both of the variables are nominal, you will request Cramer's V. Cramer's V, one of a variety of chi-square–based measures, does not measure strength by the PRE criterion. However, it is bounded by 0 (no relationship) and 1 (a perfect relationship). Cramer's V is particularly useful in evaluating controlled comparisons.

ANALYZING AN ORDINAL-LEVEL RELATIONSHIP

We will begin by using NES2012 to analyze an ordinal-level relationship. Consider this hypothesis: In a comparison of individuals, those having higher levels of education will have stronger pro-environmental attitudes than will those having lower levels of education. Dataset NES2012 has envjob_3, an ordinal variable that measures the extent to which respondents think that we should "regulate business to protect the environment and create jobs," or have "no regulation, because it will not work and will cost jobs."[3] Responses are classified as pro-environment ("Envir," coded 1), a middle position ("Mid," 2), or pro-jobs ("Jobs," 3). Envjob_3 is the dependent variable. NES2012 variable, dem_educ3, is the independent variable. Dem_educ3's ordinal categories: high school or less ("HS or less," 1), some college ("Some coll," 2), or college degree or higher ("Coll+," 3). Open NES2012 and let's perform the analysis.

First we will test the envjob_3–dem_educ3 hypothesis the old-fashioned way—by getting a cross-tabulation and comparing column percentages. Click Analyze → Descriptive Statistics → Crosstabs. Remember to put the dependent variable, envjob_3, on the rows and the independent variable, dem_educ3, on the columns. Request column percentages. Run the analysis and consider the output.

envjob_3 Envir or Jobs? * dem_educ3 Education Crosstabulation

			dem_educ3 Education			
			1 HS or less	2 Some coll	3 Coll+	Total
envjob_3 Envir or Jobs?	1 Envir	Count	694	571	656	1921
		% within dem_educ3 Education	38.1%	37.8%	41.3%	39.1%
	2 Mid	Count	646	562	561	1769
		% within dem_educ3 Education	35.5%	37.2%	35.3%	36.0%
	3 Jobs	Count	482	377	370	1229
		% within dem_educ3 Education	26.5%	25.0%	23.3%	25.0%
Total		Count	1822	1510	1587	4919
		% within dem_educ3 Education	100.0%	100.0%	100.0%	100.0%

How would you evaluate the envjob_3–dem_educ3 hypothesis in light of this analysis? Focus on the column percentages in the "Envir" row. According to the hypothesis, as we move along this row, from lower education to higher education, the percentage of pro-environment respondents should increase. Is this what happens? The percentages run from 38.1 among the least educated, drop slightly, to 37.8, among the middle group, and then rise again, to 41.3, among those with a college education or higher. So, there is something on the order of a 3-percentage-point difference between the least- and most-educated respondents, not a terribly robust relationship between the independent and dependent variables. The 3-point gradient is similar—perhaps slightly more systematic—along the "Jobs" row: 26.5 percent, 25.0 percent, 23.3 percent. Indeed, two political analysts might offer conflicting interpretations of these results. The first analyst might conclude that, yes, as education increases, pro-environment sentiments grow stronger, and pro-jobs attitudes become weaker.

The other might declare the relationship too weak to support the hypothesis. Inferential statistics, of course, is designed to settle such arguments.

Let's reconsider the envjob_3–dem_educ3 cross-tabulation in the way that the chi-square test of statistical significance would approach it. Chi-square begins by looking at the "Total" column, which contains the distribution of the entire sample across the values of the dependent variable, envjob_3. Thus, 39.1 percent of the sample is pro-environment, 36.0 percent takes a middle position, and 25.0 percent is pro-jobs. Chi-square then frames the null hypothesis, which claims that, in the population, envjob_3 and dem_educ3 are not related to each other, that individuals' levels of education are unrelated to their opinions about the environment. If the null hypothesis is correct, then a random sample of people with a high school education or less would produce the same distribution of opinions as the total distribution: 39.1 percent "Envir" / 36.0 percent "Mid" / 25.0 percent "Jobs." By the same token, a random sample of people with some college would yield a distribution that looks just like the total distribution: 39.1 percent "Envir" / 36.0 percent "Mid" / 25.0 percent "Jobs." A random sample of individuals with college or higher would produce the same result: 39.1 percent "Envir" / 36.0 percent "Mid" / 25.0 percent "Jobs." Thus, if the null hypothesis is correct, then the distribution of cases down each column of the table will be the same as the "Total" column. Of course, the null hypothesis asserts that any departures from this monotonous pattern resulted from random sampling error.

Now reexamine the table and make a considered judgment. Would you say that the observed distribution of cases within each category of dem_educ3 conforms to the expectations of the null hypothesis? For those with high school or less, the distribution is very close to the total distribution, with modest departures—for example, a somewhat lower percentage in the "Envir" category than the null would expect and a slightly higher percentage in the "Jobs" category. The distribution for those with some college corresponds quite well to the total distribution, as does the distribution for the most-educated respondents. Thus, for each value of dem_educ3, there is fairly close conformity to what we would expect to find if the null hypothesis is true. The small departures from these expectations, furthermore, might easily be explained by random sampling error, H_0's explanation for everything.

Let's rerun the analysis and find out if our considered judgment is borne out by the chi-square test. We will also obtain a measure of association for the relationship. Return to the Crosstabs window. Click Statistics. The Crosstabs: Statistics window pops up (Figure 7-1). There are many choices here, but we know what we want: We would like SPSS to perform a chi-square test on the table. Check the Chi-square box. We also know which measure of association to request. Because both envjob_3 and dem_educ3 are ordinal-level variables, we will request Somers's *d*. Check the box next to "Somers' *d*." Click Continue, and then click OK.

Figure 7-1 Requesting Statistics (ordinal-level relationship)

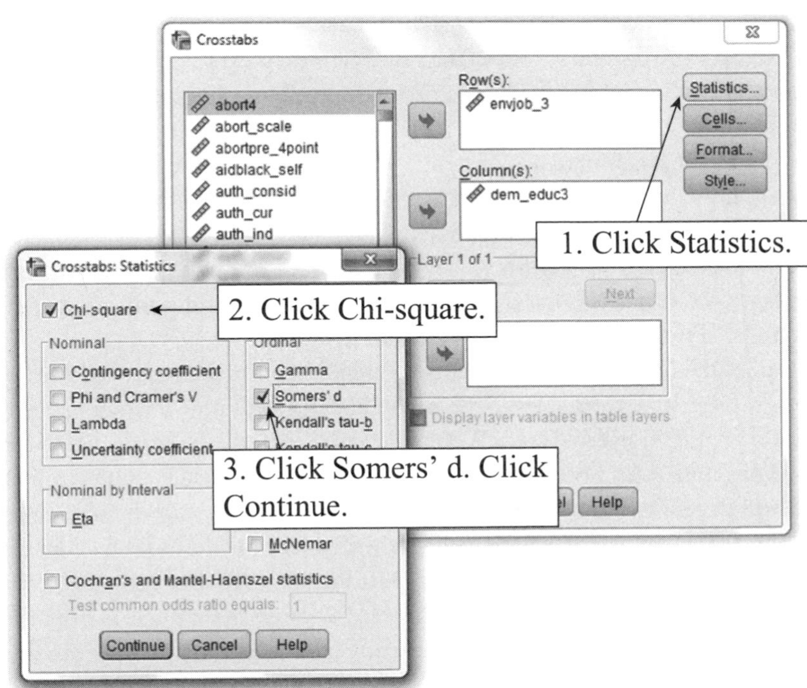

Figure 7-2 Chi-square Tests and Directional Measures Results (ordinal-level relationship)

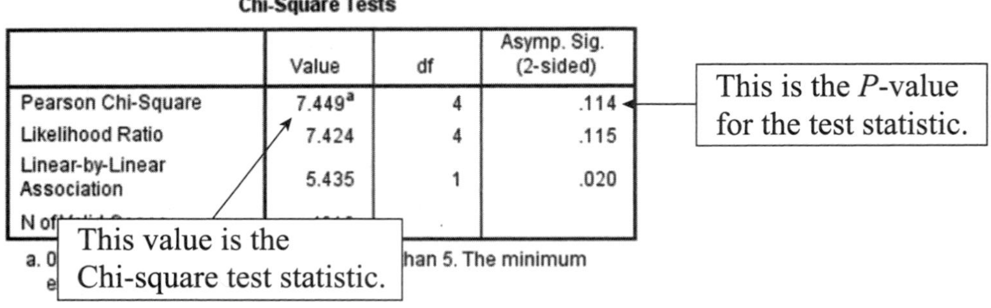

Chi-Square Tests

	Value	df	Asymp. Sig. (2-sided)
Pearson Chi-Square	7.449[a]	4	.114
Likelihood Ratio	7.424	4	.115
Linear-by-Linear Association	5.435	1	.020
N of [illegible]			

a. 0 [illegible] han 5. The minimum e[illegible]

This value is the Chi-square test statistic.
This is the *P*-value for the test statistic.

Directional Measures

			Value	Asymp. Std. Er[illegible]		
Ordinal by Ordinal	Somers' d	Symmetric	-.029			
		envjob_3 Envir or Jobs? Dependent	-.029			
		dem_educ3 Education Dependent	-.029			

a. Not assuming the null hypothesis.

b. Using the asymptotic standard error assuming the null hypothesis.

Use the dependent variable in your hypothesis to pick the appropriate value of Somers's *d*.

SPSS runs the cross-tabulation analysis again, and this time it has produced two additional tables of statistics: Chi-Square Tests and Directional Measures (Figure 7-2). Given the parsimony of our requests, SPSS has been rather generous in its statistical output. In the Chi-Square Tests table, focus exclusively on the row labeled "Pearson Chi-Square." The first column, labeled "Value," provides the chi-square test statistic. A test statistic is a number that SPSS calculates from the observed data. Generally speaking, the larger the magnitude of a test statistic, the less likely that the observed data can be explained by random sampling error. The smaller the test statistic, the more likely that the null's favorite process—random chance—accounts for the observed data. So, if the observed data perfectly fit the expectations of the null hypothesis, then the chi-square test statistic would be 0. As the observed data depart from the null's expectations, this value grows in size, allowing the researcher to begin entertaining the idea of rejecting the null hypothesis.

For the envjob_3–dem_educ3 cross-tabulation, SPSS calculated a chi-square test statistic equal to 7.449. Is this number, 7.449, statistically different from 0, the value we would expect to obtain if the null hypothesis were true? Put another way: If the null hypothesis is correct, how often will we obtain a test statistic of 7.449 by chance? The answer is contained in the rightmost column of the Chi-Square Tests table, under the label "Asymp. Sig. (2-sided)." For the chi-square test of significance, this value is the *P*-value. In our example SPSS reports a *P*-value of .114. If the null hypothesis is correct in its assertion that no relationship exists between the independent and dependent variables, then we will obtain a test statistic of 7.449, by chance, about 11 percent of the time. Because .114 exceeds the .05 standard, the null hypothesis is on safe ground. From our initial comparison of percentages, we suspected that the relationship might not trump the null hypothesis. The chi-square test has confirmed that suspicion. Accept the null hypothesis.

Turn your attention to the Directional Measures table, which reports the requested measure of Somers's *d*. In fact, three Somers's *d* statistics are displayed. Because SPSS doesn't know how we framed the hypothesis, it provided values of Somers's *d* for every scenario: symmetric (no hypothetical expectations about the relationship), envjob_3 dependent (envjob_3 is the dependent variable and dem_educ3 is the independent variable), and dem_educ3 dependent (dem_educ3 is the dependent variable and envjob_3 is the independent variable). Always use the dependent variable in your hypothesis to choose the correct value of Somers's *d*. Because envjob_3 is our dependent variable, we would report the Somers's *d* value, –.029.

What does this value, –.029, tell us about the relationship? Because the statistic is negative, it tells us that increasing codes on dem_educ3 are associated with decreasing codes on envjob_3. We can discern a faint pattern: More-educated respondents (coded 3 on dem_educ3) are slightly more likely to fall into the "Envir" category (coded 1 on envjob_3), and less-educated respondents (coded 1 on dem_educ3) are slightly more likely to fall into the "Jobs" category (coded 3 on envjob_3). Because the statistic is puny—it has a magnitude (absolute value) of .029 on a scale that runs from 0.000 to 1.000—it tells us that the relationship is weak. More specifically, because Somers's *d* is a PRE measure of association, we can say this: Compared to how well we can predict environmental opinions without knowing respondents' levels of education, we can improve our prediction by 2.9 percent by knowing respondents' levels of education.

There's not much going on there. Obviously, we need to frame another hypothesis, using different variables, and see if our luck changes. But before moving on, let's quickly review the interpretation of the chi-square statistic and Somers's *d*. This is also a good place to introduce templates that will help you describe your findings.

Summary

SPSS reports a chi-square test statistic, labeled "Pearson Chi-Square." This test statistic is calculated from the observed tabular data. Values close to 0 are within the domain of the null hypothesis. As chi-square increases in magnitude (the chi-square statistic cannot assume negative values), H_0's explanation for the observed data—"it all happened by chance"—becomes increasingly implausible.

The chi-square statistic is accompanied by a *P*-value, which appears beneath the label "Asymp. Sig. (2-sided)." Here is a template for writing an interpretation of the *P*-value:

> If the null hypothesis is correct that, in the population from which the sample was drawn, there is no relationship between [independent variable] and [dependent variable], then random sampling error will produce the observed data [*P*-value] of the time.

For our example: "If the null hypothesis is correct that, in the population from which the sample was drawn, there is no relationship between education and environmental opinions, then random sampling error will produce the observed data .114 of the time." (If you prefer percentages, you can make this substitution: ". . . will produce the observed data 11.4 percent of the time.") Use the .05 benchmark. If the *P*-value is less than or equal to .05, then reject the null hypothesis. If the *P*-value is greater than .05, accept the null hypothesis.

For ordinal-by-ordinal relationships, request Somers's *d*. Somers's *d* is a directional measure, ranging from −1 to +1. Somers's *d* has a PRE interpretation. Here is a template for writing an interpretation of Somers's *d* or, for that matter, any PRE measure:

> Compared to how well we can predict [dependent variable] by not knowing [independent variable], we can improve our prediction by [value of PRE measure] by knowing [independent variable].

Our example: "Compared to how well we can predict environmental opinions by not knowing respondents' levels of education, we can improve our prediction by .029 by knowing respondents' levels of education." (Actually, percentages may sound better here: ". . . we can improve our prediction by 2.9 percent by knowing respondents' levels of education.") Note that a negative sign on a PRE measure imparts the direction of the relationship, but it does not affect the PRE interpretation.

ANALYZING AN ORDINAL-LEVEL RELATIONSHIP WITH A CONTROL VARIABLE

The education–environmental attitudes hypothesis did not fare well against the null hypothesis. Here is a hypothesis that sounds more promising: In a comparison of individuals, liberals will be more supportive of gay rights than will conservatives. For the dependent variable, we will use gay_rights3, which measures attitudes toward gay rights by three categories: "Low" support (coded 1), a middle position ("Mid," 2), and "High" support (3). The independent variable is libcon3: liberal ("Lib," 1), moderate ("Mod," 2), and conservative ("Cons," 3). Because education might also affect attitudes toward gay rights, we will use dem_educ3 (from the previous example) as the control variable.

By this point in the book, cross-tabulation analysis has become routine. Return to the Crosstabs window. Click envjob_3 back into the variable list and click gay_rights3 into the Row(s) panel. Because dem_educ3 will be the control variable, click dem_educ3 back into the variable list, and then click it into the Layer 1 of 1 panel. Find libcon3 and click it into the Column(s) panel. The other necessary choices—column percentages in Cells, Chi-square and Somers' d in Statistics—should still be in place from the previous analysis. Click OK.

gay_rights3 Gay Rights Support * libcon3 Ideology * dem_educ3 Education Crosstabulation

				libcon3 Ideology			
dem_educ3 Education				1 Lib	2 Mod	3 Cons	Total
1 HS or less	gay_rights3 Gay Rights Support	1 Low	Count	61	108	258	427
			% within libcon3 Ideology	20.9%	44.4%	51.6%	41.3%
		2 Mid	Count	99	82	169	350
			% within libcon3 Ideology	33.9%	33.7%	33.8%	33.8%
		3 High	Count	132	53	73	258
			% within libcon3 Ideology	45.2%	21.8%	14.6%	24.9%
	Total		Count	292	243	500	1035
			% within libcon3 Ideology	100.0%	100.0%	100.0%	100.0%
2 Some coll	gay_rights3 Gay Rights Support	1 Low	Count	46	53	220	319
			% within libcon3 Ideology	17.5%	33.8%	53.8%	38.5%
		2 Mid	Count	81	51	142	274
			% within libcon3 Ideology	30.8%	32.5%	34.7%	33.1%
		3 High	Count	136	53	47	236
			% within libcon3 Ideology	51.7%	33.8%	11.5%	28.5%
	Total		Count	263	157	409	829
			% within libcon3 Ideology	100.0%	100.0%	100.0%	100.0%
3 Coll+	gay_rights3 Gay Rights Support	1 Low	Count	31	23	200	254
			% within libcon3 Ideology	9.7%	20.4%	49.6%	30.5%
		2 Mid	Count	78	47	156	281
			% within libcon3 Ideology	24.5%	41.6%	38.7%	33.7%
		3 High	Count	209	43	47	299
			% within libcon3 Ideology	65.7%	38.1%	11.7%	35.9%
	Total		Count	318	113	403	834
			% within libcon3 Ideology	100.0%	100.0%	100.0%	100.0%
Total	gay_rights3 Gay Rights Support	1 Low	Count	138	184	678	1000
			% within libcon3 Ideology	15.8%	35.9%	51.7%	37.1%
		2 Mid	Count	258	180	467	905
			% within libcon3 Ideology	29.6%	35.1%	35.6%	33.5%
		3 High	Count	477	149	167	793
			% within libcon3 Ideology	54.6%	29.0%	12.7%	29.4%
	Total		Count	873	513	1312	2698
			% within libcon3 Ideology	100.0%	100.0%	100.0%	100.0%

It would appear that, at all levels of education, ideology plays a big role in gay rights attitudes. Among the least-educated group, there is a sizable 30-point decline in the percentages professing "High" support across the values of libcon3, from 45.2 among liberals to 14.6 percent among conservatives. Yet the drop is even steeper among those with some college: from 51.7 percent to 11.5 percent, a 40-point drop. The gap increases to over 50 points among the most highly educated: 65.7 percent for liberals and 11.7 percent for conservatives. Thus, the "ideology effect" is either 30 points, 40 points, or over 50 points, depending on education level.[4] Although the direction of the gay_rights3–dem_educ3 relationship is the same at all levels of education—conservatives are less supportive than liberals—the relationship becomes stronger as education increases. Interaction would seem the best way to describe this set of relationships.

Reading tables and discussing patterns are familiar tasks. But do the statistics support our interpretation? First let's check for statistical significance by examining the Chi-Square Tests table.

Chi-Square Tests

dem_educ3 Education		Value	df	Asymp. Sig. (2-sided)
1 HS or less	Pearson Chi-Square	113.431[b]	4	.000
	Likelihood Ratio	113.384	4	.000
	Linear-by-Linear Association	103.362	1	.000
	N of Valid Cases	1035		
2 Some coll	Pearson Chi-Square	149.556[c]	4	.000
	Likelihood Ratio	156.868	4	.000
	Linear-by-Linear Association	144.579	1	.000
	N of Valid Cases	829		
3 Coll+	Pearson Chi-Square	255.299[d]	4	.000
	Likelihood Ratio	272.629	4	.000
	Linear-by-Linear Association	239.196	1	.000
	N of Valid Cases	834		
Total	Pearson Chi-Square	501.653[a]	4	.000
	Likelihood Ratio	518.122	4	.000
	Linear-by-Linear Association	478.484	1	.000
	N of Valid Cases	2698		

Judging from the chi-square tests at all values of the control—for the least educated (chi-square = 114.431, *P*-value = .000), for those with some college (chi-square = 149.556, *P*-value =.000), and for the most educated (chi-square = 255.299, *P*-value = .000)—it is extremely unlikely that the observed patterns were produced by random sampling error. So the chi-square statistics invite us to reject the null hypothesis. How strong is the relationship between gay_rights3 and libcon3 for each education group? Refer to the Directional Measures table.

Directional Measures

dem_educ3 Education				Value	Asymp. Std. Error[a]	Approx. T[b]	Approx. Sig.
1 HS or less	Ordinal by Ordinal	Somers' d	Symmetric	-.273	.026	-10.287	.000
			gay_rights3 Gay Rights Support Dependent	-.277	.027	-10.287	.000
			libcon3 Ideology Dependent	-.268	.026	-10.287	.000
2 Some coll	Ordinal by Ordinal	Somers' d	Symmetric	-.372	.027	-13.582	.000
			gay_rights3 Gay Rights Support Dependent	-.384	.029	-13.582	.000
			libcon3 Ideology Dependent	-.360	.026	-13.582	.000
3 Coll+	Ordinal by Ordinal	Somers' d	Symmetric	-.491	.025	-19.796	.000
			gay_rights3 Gay Rights Support Dependent	-.516	.027	-19.796	.000
			libcon3 Ideology Dependent	-.468	.024	-19.796	.000
Total	Ordinal by Ordinal	Somers' d	Symmetric	-.373	.015	-24.401	.000
			gay_rights3 Gay Rights Support Dependent	-.386	.016	-24.401	.000
			libcon3 Ideology Dependent	-.362	.015	-24.401	.000

Again note the negative signs on the Somers's *d* statistics. At each education level, as the coded values of libcon3 increase from "Lib" to "Cons," gay_rights3's codes decline from "High" support to "Low" support. Thus, the negative signs are consistent with the hypothesis that conservatives are less supportive of gay rights than are liberals.

Focus on the Somers's *d* magnitudes. Somers's *d* has a magnitude (absolute value) of .277 for the least-educated group, .384 for the middle group, and .516 for the most-educated group. So the values of Somers's *d* capture the strengthening relationship between gay_rights3 and libcon3 as education increases. Plus, because Somers's *d* is a PRE measure, we can give a specific answer to the "how strong?" question. For least-educated respondents we would say that, compared to how well we can predict their opinions on gay rights without knowing their ideology, we can improve our prediction by 27.7 percent by knowing their ideology. The predictive leverage of the independent variable strengthens to 38.4 percent for the middle group, and increases to 51.6 percent for those at the highest level of educational attainment.

ANALYZING A NOMINAL-LEVEL RELATIONSHIP WITH A CONTROL VARIABLE

All of the variables analyzed thus far have been ordinal level. Many social and political characteristics, however, are measured by nominal categories—gender, race, region, or religious denomination, to name a few. In this example, we will use race to help frame the following hypothesis: In a comparison of individuals, blacks are more likely than are whites to be Democrats. To make this remarkably pedestrian hypothesis marginally more interesting, we will control for another variable that might also affect partisanship, whether the respondent resides in the South. Would the racial difference on partisanship be the same for southerners and nonsoutherners? Or might the racial divide be stronger in the South than the non-South? Let's investigate.

Dataset NES2012 contains pid_3, with values "Dem" (code1), "Ind" (2), and "Rep" (3). Pid_3 is the dependent variable. The independent variable is dem_raceeth2: "White" (1) and "Black" (2). For the control variable we will use South: "Non-south" (0) and "South" (1). The analytic task at hand is, by now, abundantly familiar.

Click Analyze → Descriptive Statistics → Crosstabs. Click Reset to clear the panels. Now set up our new analysis: pid_3 on the rows, dem_raceeth2 on the columns, and South in the Layer panel (Figure 7-3).

Figure 7-3 Requesting Chi-square and Cramer's V (nominal-level relationship)

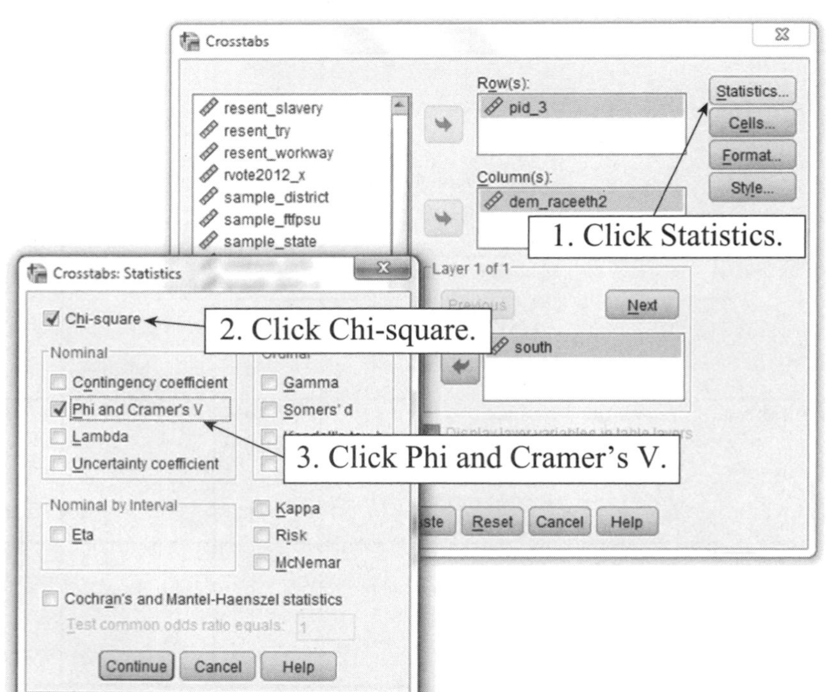

Click Cells and request column percentages. Click Statistics. Again we want chi-square, so make sure that the Chi-square box is checked. Because race is a nominal-level variable, we can't use any of the ordinal statistics. But we can use Cramer's V. In the Nominal panel, check the box next to "Phi and Cramer's V." Click Continue, and then click OK.

pid_3 Party ID: 3 cats * dem_raceeth2 White/Black * south South Crosstabulation

				dem_raceeth2 White/Black		
south South				1 White	2 Black	Total
0 Non-south	pid_3 Party ID: 3 cats	1 Dem	Count	885	224	1109
			% within dem_raceeth2 White/Black	29.5%	71.1%	33.5%
		2 Ind	Count	1177	83	1260
			% within dem_raceeth2 White/Black	39.3%	26.3%	38.0%
		3 Rep	Count	935	8	943
			% within dem_raceeth2 White/Black	31.2%	2.5%	28.5%
	Total		Count	2997	315	3312
			% within dem_raceeth2 White/Black	100.0%	100.0%	100.0%
1 South	pid_3 Party ID: 3 cats	1 Dem	Count	209	296	505
			% within dem_raceeth2 White/Black	18.0%	76.9%	32.7%
		2 Ind	Count	487	80	567
			% within dem_raceeth2 White/Black	41.9%	20.8%	36.7%
		3 Rep	Count	465	9	474
			% within dem_raceeth2 White/Black	40.1%	2.3%	30.7%
	Total		Count	1161	385	1546
			% within dem_raceeth2 White/Black	100.0%	100.0%	100.0%
Total	pid_3 Party ID: 3 cats	1 Dem	Count	1094	520	1614
			% within dem_raceeth2 White/Black	26.3%	74.3%	33.2%
		2 Ind	Count	1664	163	1827
			% within dem_raceeth2 White/Black	40.0%	23.3%	37.6%
		3 Rep	Count	1400	17	1417
			% within dem_raceeth2 White/Black	33.7%	2.4%	29.2%
	Total		Count	4158	700	4858
			% within dem_raceeth2 White/Black	100.0%	100.0%	100.0%

Before examining the statistics, consider the substantive relationships depicted in the cross-tabulations. Are there inter-regional differences in the patterns of the relationships? Among nonsoutherners, 29.5 percent of whites are Democrats, compared with 71.1 percent of blacks—a more than 40-percentage-point gap. What happens when we switch to respondents who reside in the South? Among southerners, the percentage of black Democrats increases to 76.9, whereas the percentage of white Democrats drops by about 11 points, to 18.0 percent. These dynamics produce a racial gap that is considerably wider in the South (about 60 points) than in the non-South (about 40 points). Because the effect of race on partisanship is stronger in the South than in the non-South, we can conclude that interaction best describes this situation. Now let's see what the statistics have to say.

Chi-Square Tests

south South		Value	df	Asymp. Sig. (2-sided)
0 Non-south	Pearson Chi-Square	241.921[b]	2	.000
	Likelihood Ratio	261.122	2	.000
	Linear-by-Linear Association	227.834	1	.000
	N of Valid Cases	3312		
1 South	Pearson Chi-Square	476.322[c]	2	.000
	Likelihood Ratio	499.768	2	.000
	Linear-by-Linear Association	426.008	1	.000
	N of Valid Cases	1546		
Total	Pearson Chi-Square	660.149[a]	2	.000
	Likelihood Ratio	694.302	2	.000
	Linear-by-Linear Association	604.066	1	.000
	N of Valid Cases	4858		

According to the Chi-Square Tests table, the party identification–race relationship defeats the null hypothesis in the non-South cross-tabulation (chi-square = 241.921, *P*-value = .000) and in the South cross-tabulation (chi-square = 476.322, *P*-value = .000). Let's see whether Cramer's V backs up our interaction interpretation. Scroll down to the next table, Symmetric Measures.

Symmetric Measures

south South			Value	Approx. Sig.
0 Non-south	Nominal by Nominal	Phi	.270	.000
		Cramer's V	.270	.000
	N of Valid Cases		3312	
1 South	Nominal by Nominal	Phi	.555	.000
		Cramer's V	.555	.000
	N of Valid Cases		1546	
Total	Nominal by Nominal	Phi	.369	.000
		Cramer's V	.369	.000
	N of Valid Cases		4858	

For the non-South, we obtain a V of .270; for the South, .555. Cramer's V does not have a PRE interpretation. However, it varies between 0 (weak relationship) and 1 (strong relationship). V is particularly useful in interpreting controlled comparisons. In reassuring support of our interaction interpretation, the V for southern respondents is much stronger than the V for nonsouthern respondents.

EXERCISES

1. (Dataset: States. Variables: Abort_rank3, Gun_rank3, cook_index3.) Pedantic pontificator is pondering a potential partisan paradox of public policy.

   "Think about two sorts of policies that figure prominently in cultural debate: laws restricting abortion and laws restricting guns. For both policies, fewer restrictions mean more choices and greater freedom, whereas more restrictions mean fewer choices and less freedom. Because choice and freedom are the touchstone values, one would think that partisan elites would be consistent in their positions on these policies. If Republicans favor fewer gun restrictions, then they ought to favor fewer abortion restrictions, too. By the same logic, if Democrats favor fewer abortion restrictions, then they should also support less gun control. As a keen observer of state politics, however, it is my impression that Republican-controlled states have less restrictive gun laws but more restrictive abortion laws. Democrat-controlled states are just the reverse: less restrictive abortion laws and more restrictive gun laws. I am sure that when you analyze the States dataset, you will discover this odd partisan paradox."

The states dataset contains these two policy measures, which will serve as dependent variables: Abort_rank3 and Gun_rank3. Both variables are identically coded, three-category ordinals. Codes range from 1 (states having more restrictions) to 3 (states having fewer restrictions). Another three-category ordinal, cook_index3, measures states' partisan balance in three codes: 1 (Republican states), 2 (states with even balance), and 3 (Democratic states). This is the independent variable.

A. If pedantic pontificator is correct, as you compare states across increasing values of cook_index3—from Republican states, to even states, to Democratic states—the percentage of states having more restrictive abortion policies should (circle one)

decrease. stay the same. increase.

The percentage of states having more restrictive gun policies should (circle one)

decrease. stay the same. increase.

B. If pedantic pontificator is correct, you should find that states having higher codes on cook_index3 will have (circle one)

lower higher

codes on Abort_rank3. You should also find that states having higher codes on cook_index3 will have (circle one)

lower higher

codes on Gun_rank3.

C. Think about how SPSS calculates Somers's *d*. If pedantic pontificator is correct, the Somers's *d* statistic for the Abort_rank3–cook_index3 relationship will have a (circle one)

negative positive

sign. The Somers's *d* statistic for the Gun_rank3–cook_index3 relationship will have a (circle one)

negative positive

sign.

D. Obtain the appropriate cross-tabulation analyses of the Abort_rank3–cook_index3 relationship and the Gun_rank3–cook_index3 relationship. Make sure to request chi-square and Somers's *d*. Browse the cross-tabulation results. In the table below, enter the percentage of Democratic states, even states, and Republican states having more-restrictive policies. In the Abort_rank3 row, for example, record the percentage states that are "more restrictive." Similarly, in the Gun_rank3 row, enter the percentage of states that are "more restrictive." For each relationship, record chi-square, chi-square's *P*-value, and Somers's *d*.

Dependent variable	More Republican	Even	More Democratic	Chi-square	*P*-value	Somers's *d*
Abort_rank3 % more restrictive	?	?	?	?	?	?
Gun_rank3 % more restrictive	?	?	?	?	?	?

E. Consider Somers's *d* for the Gun_rank3–cook_index3 relationship. This value of Somers's *d* means that, compared to how well we can predict Gun_rank3 without knowing cook_index3 (complete the sentence)

____

____

F. Consider the chi-square *P*-value for the Abort_rank3–cook_index3 relationship. This *P*-value means that, under the assumption that the null hypothesis is correct, (complete the sentence)

____

____

Therefore, you should (circle one)

reject not reject

the null hypothesis.

G. Consider all the evidence from your analysis. The evidence suggests that pedantic pontificator is (circle one)

correct. incorrect.

Explain your reasoning, making specific reference to the statistical evidence in part D.

____

____

____

____

____

2. (Dataset: GSS2012. Variables: abhlth, femrole2, sex.) Interested student has joined pedantic pontificator in a discussion of the gender gap in U.S. politics.

Interested student: "On what sorts of issues or opinions are men and women most likely to be at odds? What defines the gender gap, anyway?"

Pedantic pontificator: "That's easy. A couple of points seem obvious, to me anyway. First, we know that the conflict over abortion rights is the defining gender issue of our time. Women will be more likely than men to take a strong pro-choice position on this issue. Second—and pay close attention here—on more mundane cultural questions, such as whether women should take nontraditional roles outside the home, men and women will not differ at all."

A. Pedantic pontificator has suggested the following two hypotheses about the gender gap: (check two)

- ☐ In a comparison of individuals, women will be less likely than men to think that abortion should be allowed.
- ☐ In a comparison of individuals, women and men will be equally likely to think that abortion should be allowed.
- ☐ In a comparison of individuals, women will be more likely than men to think that abortion should be allowed.
- ☐ In a comparison of individuals, women will be less likely than men to think that women should play nontraditional roles.
- ☐ In a comparison of individuals, women and men will be equally likely to think that women should play nontraditional roles.
- ☐ In a comparison of individuals, women will be more likely than men to think that women should play nontraditional roles.

B. GSS2012 contains two variables that will serve as dependent variables. Abhlth, which asks respondents whether an abortion should be allowed if the pregnancy endangers the woman's health, is coded "Yes" and "No." The variable femrole2, which measures attitudes toward the role of women, has values labeled "Traditional" and "NonTrad." The independent variable is sex, "Male" or "Female." Request chi-square. Sex is a nominal variable, so request Cramer's V. In the abhlth–sex cross-tabulation, focus on the percentage saying "Yes." In the femrole2–sex cross-tabulation, focus on the "NonTrad" category. Record your results in the table that follows.

Dependent variable	Male	Female	Chi-square	*P*-value	Cramer's *V*
Percent "Yes" (abhlth)	?	?	?	?	?
Percent "NonTrad" (femrole2)	?	?	?	?	?

C. Based on these results, you may conclude that (check three)

- ❑ a statistically significant gender gap exists on abortion opinions.
- ❑ pedantic pontificator's hypothesis about the femrole2–sex relationship is not supported by the analysis.
- ❑ under the assumption that the null hypothesis is correct, the abhlth–sex relationship could have occurred by chance more frequently than 5 times out of 100.
- ❑ pedantic pontificator's hypothesis about the abhlth–sex relationship is supported by the analysis.
- ❑ a higher percentage of females than males think that women belong in nontraditional roles.

D. The *P*-value of the chi-square statistic in the femrole2–sex cross-tabulation tells you that, under the assumption that the null hypothesis is correct (complete the sentence) ______________________________

____

3. (Dataset: GSS2012. Variables: polview3, racial_liberal3, social_cons3, spend3.) While having lunch together, three researchers are discussing what the terms *liberal*, *moderate*, and *conservative* mean to most people. Each researcher is touting a favorite independent variable that may explain the way survey respondents describe themselves ideologically.

Researcher 1: "When people are asked a question about their ideological views, they think about their attitudes toward government spending. If people think the government should spend more on important programs, they will respond that they are 'liberal.' If they don't want too much spending, they will say that they are 'conservative.'"

Researcher 2: "Well, that's fine. But let's not forget about social policies, such as abortion and pornography. These issues must influence how people describe themselves ideologically. People with more permissive views on these sorts of issues will call themselves 'liberal.' People who favor government restrictions will label themselves as 'conservative.'"

Researcher 3: "Okay, you both make good points. But you're ignoring the importance of racial issues in American politics. When asked whether they are liberal or conservative, people probably think about their opinions on racial policies, such as affirmative action. Stronger proponents of racial equality will say they are 'liberal,' and weaker proponents will say they are 'conservative.'"

In Chapter 3 you created an ordinal measure of ideology, polview3, which is coded 1 for "Liberal," 2 for "Moderate," and 3 for "Conservative." This is the dependent variable. GSS2012 also contains Researcher 1's favorite independent variable, spend3, a three-category ordinal measure of attitudes toward government spending. Spend3 is coded 0 ("Conserv," spend on fewer programs), 1 ("Mod," middle position), or 2 ("Liberal," spend on more programs). Researcher 2's favorite independent variable is social_cons3, a three-category ordinal measure of attitudes on social issues. Social_cons3 is coded 0 ("Liberal," respondent has the most permissive views on social issues), 1 ("Mod," middle), or 2 ("Conserv," respondent has the least permissive views). Researcher 3's favorite independent variable is racial_liberal3, also a three-category ordinal variable. Racial_liberal3 is coded 0 ("Conserv," respondent has least liberal positions on racial policies), 1 ("Mod," middle), or 2 ("Liberal," respondent has the most liberal positions on racial policies).

A. Think about how SPSS calculates Somers's *d*. Assuming that each researcher is correct, SPSS should report (check all that apply)

- ❑ a negative sign on Somers's *d* for the polview3–spend3 relationship.
- ❑ a positive sign on Somers's *d* for the polview3–social_cons3 relationship.
- ❑ a negative on Somers's *d* for the polview3–racial_liberal3 relationship.

B. Run a cross-tabulation analysis for each of the relationships, using polview3 as the dependent variable and spend3, social_cons3, and racial_liberal3 as independent variables. Obtain Somers's *d* for each relationship. Summarize your results in the following table. In the first three columns, enter the percentage of self-identified "conservatives" on polview3 for each value of the independent variable. For example, from the spend3 cross-tabulation, record the percentage of conservatives among respondents who are "Conserv" (code 0 of spend3), the percentage of conservatives among respondents taking the "Mod" position (code 1 on spend3), and the percentage of conservatives among respondents who are "Liberal" (code 2 on spend3). For each relationship, record chi-square, chi-square's *P*-value, and Somers's *d*.

	Code on independent variable*					
	0	1	2	Chi-square	*P*-value	Somers's *d*
Percent "Conservative" (spend3 cross-tabulation)	?	?	?	?	?	?
Percent "Conservative" (social_cons3 cross-tabulation)	?	?	?	?	?	?
Percent "Conservative" (racial_liberal3 cross-tabulation)	?	?	?	?	?	?

*For spend3, code 0 = "Conserv," code 1 = "Mod", and code 2 = "Liberal." For social_cons3, code 0 = "Liberal," code 1 = "Mod," and code 2 = "Conserv." For racial_liberal3, code 0= "Conserv," code 1 = "Mod," and code 2 = "Liberal."

C. Consider the evidence you have assembled. Your analysis supports which of the following statements? (check three)

- ❑ As values of spend3 increase, the percentage of respondents describing themselves as conservative decreases.
- ❑ As values of social_cons3 increase, the percentage of respondents describing themselves as conservative increases.
- ❑ The polview3–racial_liberal3 relationship is not statistically significant.
- ❑ If the null hypothesis is correct, you will obtain the polview3–spend3 relationship less frequently than 5 times out of 100 by chance.
- ❑ If the null hypothesis is correct, you will obtain the polview3–racial_liberal3 relationship more frequently than 5 times out of 100 by chance.

D. Somers's *d* for the polview3–social_cons3 relationship is equal to (fill in the blank) ________________. Thus, compared with how well we can predict polview3 by not knowing (complete the sentence) ________________

____

E. The three researchers make a friendly wager. The researcher whose favorite independent variable does the worst job predicting values of the dependent variable has to buy lunch for the other two. Who pays for lunch? (circle one)

Researcher 1 Researcher 2 Researcher 3

4. (Dataset: GSS2012. Variables: partyid_3, egalit_scale3, educ_2.) Certainly you would expect partisanship and egalitarian attitudes to be related: In a comparison of individuals, those with stronger egalitarian beliefs are more likely to be Democrats than those with weaker egalitarian beliefs. Yet it also seems reasonable to hypothesize that the relationship between egalitarianism (independent variable) and party identification (dependent variable) will not be the same for all education groups (control variable). It may be that, among people with less education, the party identification–egalitarianism relationship will be weaker than among those with higher levels of education. This idea suggests a set of interaction relationships: As education increases, the relationship between the independent variable and the dependent variable becomes stronger. In this exercise, you will test for this set of interaction relationships.

   GSS2012 contains partyid_3, which measures party identification: "Dem," "Ind," and "Rep." This is the dependent variable. (For this exercise, treat partyid_3 as an ordinal-level variable, with higher codes denoting stronger Republican identification.) The independent variable is egalit_scale3: "Less egal," "Middle," or "More egal." The control variable is educ_2: "0-12 yrs" (coded 1) and "13+ yrs" (coded 2).

   Run Crosstabs, using partyid_3 as the dependent variable, egalit_scale3 as the independent variable, and educ_2 as the control. Request the relevant statistics.

   A. In the controlled comparison cross-tabulations, focus on the percentages of Democrats across the values of egalit_scale3. Fill in the table that follows.

Education level	Less egalitarian (% Democrat)	Middle (% Democrat)	More egalitarian (% Democrat)	Chi-square	*P*-value	Somers's *d*
0 –12 years	?	?	?	?	?	?
13 + years	?	?	?	?	?	?

   B. Which of the following inferences are supported by your analysis? (check all that apply)

   ❑ At both levels of education, people with stronger egalitarian beliefs are more likely to be Democrats than are people with weaker egalitarian beliefs.

   ❑ For the less-educated group, random sampling error would produce the observed relationship between egalitarianism and partisanship less frequently than 5 times out of 100.

   ❑ The partisanship–egalitarianism relationship is stronger for the more-educated group than for the less-educated group.

   C. Focus on the value of Somers's *d* for those who have 13 or more years of education. This value of Somers's *d* says that, compared to how well you can predict (complete the sentence) ______________________________

   ____

   D. Based on your analysis of these relationships, you can conclude that (check one)

   ❑ The partisanship–egalitarianism–education relationships are not a set of interaction relationships.

   ❑ The partisanship–egalitarianism–education relationships are a set of interaction relationships.

   Explain your reasoning, making specific reference to the statistical evidence in part A.______________________

   ____

   ____

   ____

   ____

   ____

5. (Dataset: World. Variables: protact3, gender_equal3, vi_rel3, pmat12_3.) Ronald Inglehart offers a particularly elegant and compelling idea about the future of economically advanced societies. According to Inglehart, the cultures of many postindustrial societies have been going through a value shift—the waning importance of materialist values and a growing pursuit of postmaterialist values. In postmaterialist societies,

economically based conflicts—unions versus big business, rich versus poor—are increasingly supplanted by an emphasis on self-expression and social equality. Postmaterialist societies are also marked by rising secularism and elite-challenging behaviors, such as boycotts and demonstrations. In this exercise you will investigate Inglehart's theory.[5]

The World variable pmat12_3 measures the level of postmaterialism values by a three-category ordinal measure: low postmaterialism (coded 1), moderate postmaterialism (coded 2), and high postmaterialism (coded 3). Higher codes denote a greater prevalence of postmaterial values. Use pmat12_3 as the independent variable. Here are three dependent variables, all of which are three-category ordinals: gender_equal3, which captures gender equality (1 = low equality, 2 = medium equality, 3 = high equality); protact3, which measures citizen participation in protests (1 = low, 2 = moderate, 3 = high); and vi_rel3, which gauges religiosity by the percentage of the public saying that religion is "very important" (1 = less than 20 percent, 2 = 20–50 percent, 3 = more than 50 percent). Higher codes on the dependent variables denote greater gender equality (gender_equal3), more protest activity (protact3), and higher levels of religiosity (vi_rel3).

A. Using pmat12_3 as the independent variable, three postmaterialist hypotheses can be framed:

   Gender equality hypothesis (fill in the blanks): In a comparison of countries, those with higher levels of postmaterialism will have ____________________ levels of gender equality than will countries having lower levels of postmaterialism.

   Protest activity hypothesis (fill in the blanks): In a comparison of countries, those with ____________________ levels of postmaterialism will have ____________________ levels of protest activity than will countries having ____________________ levels of postmaterialism.

   Religiosity hypothesis (complete the sentence): In a comparison of countries, those with ____________________

   ____

   ____

   ____

B. Consider how the independent variable is coded and how each dependent variable is coded. In the way that SPSS calculates the appropriate measure of association, which one of the three hypotheses implies a negative sign on the measure of association? (check one)

   ❑ The gender equality hypothesis

   ❑ The protest activity hypothesis

   ❑ The religiosity hypothesis

C. Test each hypothesis using cross-tabulation analysis. Obtain chi-square and the appropriate measure of association. In the table that follows, record the percentages of countries falling into the highest category of each dependent variable. Also, report chi-square statistics, *P*-values, and measures of association.

	Level of postmaterialism					
Dependent variable	Low	Moderate	High	Chi-square	*P*-value	Measure of association
Percentage high gender equality	?	?	?	?	?	?
Percentage high protest activity	?	?	?	?	?	?
Percentage high religiosity	?	?	?	?	?	?

D. Which of the following inferences are supported by your analysis? (check all that apply)

   ❑ The gender equality hypothesis is supported.

   ❑ Compared with how well we can predict gender equality by not knowing the level of postmaterialism, we can improve our prediction by 21.3 percent by knowing the level of postmaterialism.

- ❑ The protest activity hypothesis is supported.
- ❑ If the null hypothesis is correct, the postmaterialism–protest activity relationship would occur, by chance, less frequently than 5 times out of 100.
- ❑ The religiosity hypothesis is supported.
- ❑ If the null hypothesis is correct, the postmaterialism–religiosity relationship would occur, by chance, more frequently than 5 times out of 100.

That concludes the exercises for this chapter.

NOTES

1. Asymmetry is the essence of hypothetical relationships. Thus, one would hypothesize that income causes opinions on welfare policies, but one would not hypothesize that welfare opinions cause income. We would prefer a measure of association that tells us how well income (independent variable) predicts welfare opinions (dependent variable), not how well welfare opinions predict income. Or, to cite Warner's tongue-in-cheek example: "There are some situations where the ability to make predictions is asymmetrical; for example, consider a study about gender and pregnancy. If you know that an individual is pregnant, you can predict gender (the person must be female) perfectly. However, it you know that an individual is female, you cannot assume that she is pregnant." Rebecca M. Warner, *Applied Statistics* (Los Angeles: SAGE, 2008), 316.
2. Somers's *d* may be used for square tables (in which the independent and dependent variables have the same number of categories) and for non-square tables (in which the independent and dependent variables have different numbers of categories). Because of its other attractive properties, some methodologists prefer Somers's *d* to other measures, such as Gamma, Kendall's tau-b, or Kendall's tau-c. See George W. Bohrnstedt and David Knoke, *Statistics for Social Data Analysis*, 2nd ed. (Itasca, Ill.: Peacock Publishers, 1988), 325.
3. This question wording represents a noteworthy departure from the traditional "environment vs. jobs" tradeoff question in the American National Election Studies (ANES or NES). In the 2008 ANES (question V083154), the strongest pro-environment position on the 7-point scales is "protect environment, *even if it costs jobs* and standard of living," and the strongest pro-jobs position is "jobs and standard of living are more important than environment." (Emphasis added.) The 2012 ANES 7-point scale on which envjob_3 is based, envjob_self, allows the respondent to support the protection of the environment *and* the creation of jobs: "regulate business to protect the environment *and create jobs*." (Emphasis added.) This have-your-cake-and-eat-it-too proposition was hard to resist. In 2012, 20.6 percent took the strongest pro-environment position, compared with only 8.1 percent in 2008.
4. Notice that the "education effect" is quite pronounced for liberals, yet it is virtually nonexistent for conservatives. For liberals, gay rights support increases from 45.2 percent, to 51.7 percent, to 65.7 percent—about 20 points from low education to high education. By contrast, education has practically no effect for conservatives: 14.6 percent, 11.5 percent, and 11.7 percent.
5. Inglehart has written extensively about cultural change in postindustrial societies. For example, see his *Culture Shift in Advanced Industrial Society* (Princeton: Princeton University Press, 1990).

Correlation and Linear Regression*

Watch a screencast of the guided examples in this chapter.
edge.sagepub.com/pollock

Procedures Covered

Analyze → Correlate → Bivariate

Analyze → Regression → Linear

Graphs → Legacy Dialogs → Scatter/Dot

Correlation and regression are powerful and flexible techniques used to analyze interval-level relationships. Pearson's correlation coefficient (Pearson's *r*) measures the strength and direction of the relationship between two interval-level variables. Pearson's *r* is not a proportional reduction in error (PRE) measure, but it does gauge strength by an easily understood scale—from −1, a perfectly negative association between the variables, to +1, a perfectly positive relationship. A correlation of 0 indicates no relationship. Researchers often use correlation techniques in the beginning stages of analysis to get an overall picture of the relationships between interesting variables.

Regression analysis produces a statistic, the regression coefficient, that estimates the effect of an independent variable on a dependent variable. Regression also produces a PRE measure of association, *R*-square, which indicates how completely the independent variable (or variables) explains the dependent variable. In regression analysis the dependent variable is measured at the interval level, but the independent variable can be of any variety—nominal, ordinal, or interval. Regression is more specialized than correlation. Researchers use regression analysis to model causal relationships between one or more independent variables and a dependent variable.

In the first part of this chapter, you will learn to perform correlation analysis using the Correlate procedure, and you will learn to perform and interpret bivariate regression using Regression → Linear. Bivariate regression uses one independent variable to predict a dependent variable. We will then turn to Scatter/Dot, an SPSS graphic routine that yields a scatterplot, a visual depiction of the relationship between two interval-level variables. With generous use of the Chart Editor, you will learn how to add a regression line to the scatterplot and how to edit the graph for elegance and clarity. Finally, you will use Regression → Linear to perform multiple regression analysis. Multiple regression, which uses two or more independent variables to predict a dependent variable, is an essential tool for analyzing complex relationships.

*Special note to SPSS Student Version users: For the guided examples and exercises in Chapters 6 through 9, you will analyze NES2012_Student_B or GSS2012_Student_B.

CORRELATION AND BIVARIATE REGRESSION

Suppose that a student of state politics is interested in the gender composition of state legislatures. Using Descriptives to analyze the States dataset, this student finds that state legislatures range from 12.5 percent female to 42 percent female. Why is there such variation in the female composition of state legislatures? The student researcher begins to formulate an explanation. Perhaps states with lower percentages of college graduates have lower percentages of women legislators than do states with more college-educated residents. And maybe a cultural variable, the percentage of states' residents who frequently attend religious services, plays a role. Perhaps states with higher percentages of frequent attenders have lower percentages of female lawmakers. Correlation analysis would give this researcher an overview of the relationships among these variables. Let's use Correlate and Regression → Linear to investigate.

Open the States dataset. Click Analyze → Correlate → Bivariate. The Bivariate Correlations window is a no-frills interface (Figure 8-1). We are interested in three variables: the percentage of frequent church attenders (attend_pct), the percentage of college graduates (BA_or_more), and the percentage of female state legislators (womleg_2015). Click each of these variables into the Variables panel, as shown in Figure 8-1.

Figure 8-1 Bivariate Correlations Window (modified)

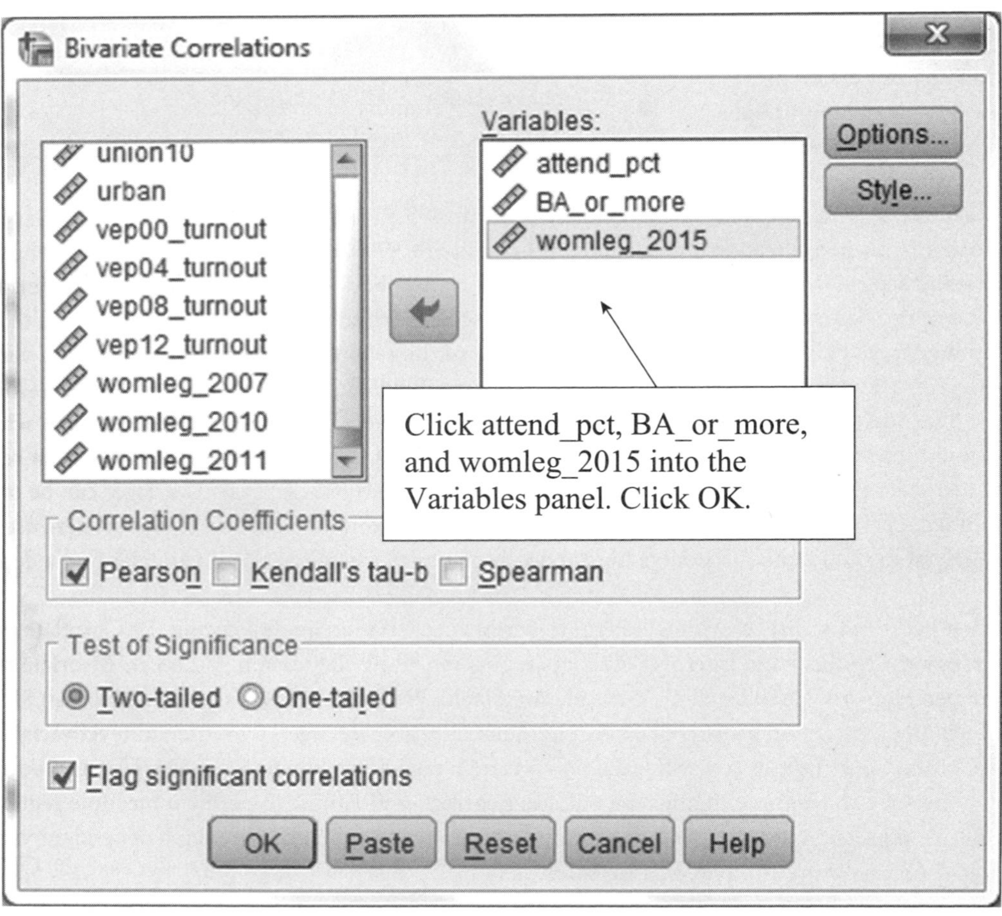

By default, SPSS will return Pearson's correlation coefficients. So the Pearson box, which is already checked, suits our purpose. Click OK. SPSS reports the results in the Viewer.

Correlations

		attend_pct Percent frequently attend relig serv (Pew)	BA_or_more Percent college or higher	womleg_2015 Percent women state legislators, 2015
attend_pct Percent frequently attend relig serv (Pew)	Pearson Correlation	1	-.519**	-.716**
	Sig. (2-tailed)		.000	.000
	N	50	50	50
BA_or_more Percent college or higher	Pearson Correlation	-.519**	1	.593**
	Sig. (2-tailed)	.000		.000
	N	50	50	50
womleg_2015 Percent women state legislators, 2015	Pearson Correlation	-.716**	.593**	1
	Sig. (2-tailed)	.000	.000	
	N	50	50	50

The Correlations table, called a correlation matrix, shows the correlation of each variable with each of the other variables—it even shows the correlation between each variable and itself. Each of the correlations in which we are interested appears twice in the table: once above the upper-left-to-lower-right diagonal of 1's, and again below the diagonal. The correlation between womleg_2015 and attend_pct is –.716, which tells us that increasing values of one of the variables is associated with decreasing values of the other variable. So as the percentage of frequent church attenders goes up, the percentage of female legislators goes down. How strong is the relationship? We know that Pearson's *r* is bracketed by –1 and +1, so we could say that this relationship is a strong negative association. The correlation between womleg_2015 and BA_or_more, .593, indicates a positive relationship: As states' percentages of college graduates increase, so do their percentages of women legislators. Again, this is a fairly strong association. Finally, attend_pct and BA_or_more, with a Pearson's *r* of –.519, show a moderately strong negative relationship. As the percentage of college graduates increases, the percentage of frequent attenders declines. Thus, as we compare states with fewer college graduates to states with more college graduates, we are also comparing states with more frequent attenders to states with fewer frequent attenders. (This relationship becomes important later.)

Correlation analysis is a good place to start when analyzing interval-level relationships. Even so, a correlation coefficient is agnostic on the question of which variable is the cause and which the effect. Does an increase in the percentage of frequent church attenders somehow cause lower percentages of women in state legislatures? Or do increasing percentages of women in state legislatures somehow cause states to have lower percentages of church attenders? Either way, correlation analysis reports the same measure of association, a Pearson's *r* of –.716.

Regression is more powerful than correlation, in part because it helps us investigate causal relationships—relationships in which an independent variable is thought to affect a dependent variable. Regression analysis will (1) reveal the precise nature of the relationship between an independent variable and a dependent variable, (2) test the null hypothesis that the observed relationship occurred by chance, and (3) provide a PRE measure of association between the independent variable and the dependent variable. To illustrate these and other points, we will run two separate bivariate regressions. First we will examine the relationship between attend_pct and womleg_2015, and then we will analyze the relationship between BA_or_more and womleg_2015.

Click Analyze → Regression → Linear. The Linear Regression window appears (Figure 8-2). Click womleg_2015 into the Dependent box. Find attend_pct in the variable list and click it into the Independent(s) box. Click OK.

SPSS regression output includes four tables: Variables Entered/Removed, Model Summary, ANOVA (which stands for analysis of variance), and Coefficients. For the regression analyses you will perform in this book, the Model Summary table and the Coefficients table contain the most important information. Let's examine them.

Figure 8-2 Linear Regression Window

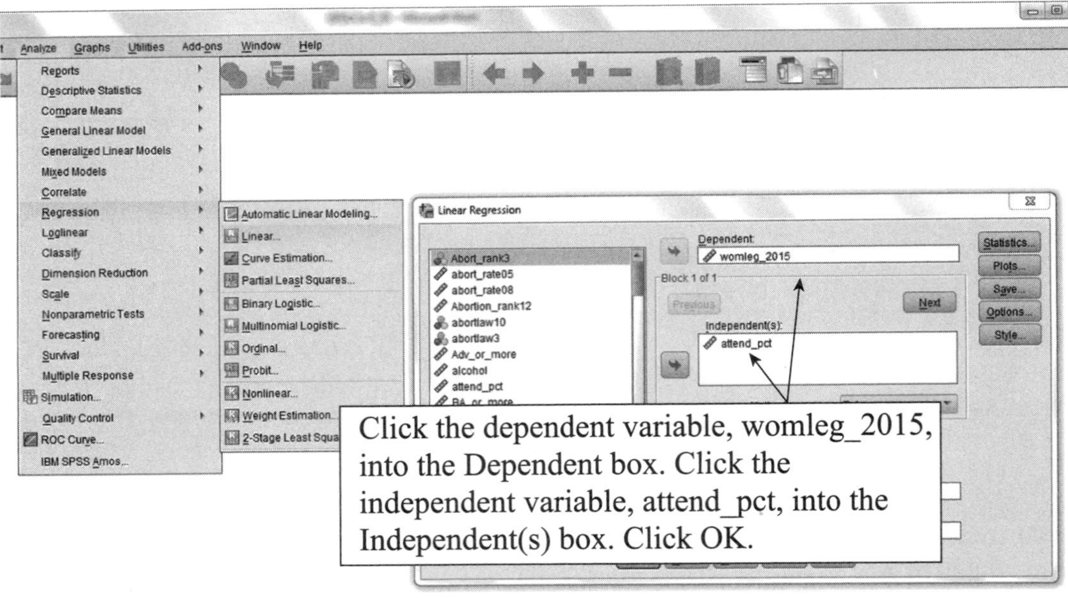

Model Summary

Model	R	R Square	Adjusted R Square	Std. Error of the Estimate
1	.716[a]	.512	.502	4.94540

a. Predictors: (Constant), attend_pct Percent frequently attend relig serv (Pew)

Coefficients[a]

Model		Unstandardized Coefficients		Standardized Coefficients	t	Sig.
		B	Std. Error	Beta		
1	(Constant)	44.990	3.018		14.908	.000
	attend_pct Percent frequently attend relig serv (Pew)	-.535	.075	-.716	-7.097	.000

a. Dependent Variable: womleg_2015 Percent women state legislators, 2015

First, consider the Coefficients table. The leftmost column, under the heading "Model," contains the names of the key elements in the regression equation. "Constant" is the Y-intercept of the regression line, and "Percent frequently attend relig serv" is the label of the independent variable. The numbers along the "Constant" row report statistics about the Y-intercept, and the numbers along the "Percent frequently attend relig serv" row report statistics about the independent variable. Now look at the first column of numbers, which shows the regression coefficient for each parameter. According to these values, the Y-intercept is equal to 44.99, and the regression coefficient is –.535. The regression equation for estimating the effect of attend_pct on womleg_2015, therefore, is as follows (to make the numbers a bit simpler, we will round to two decimal places):

Percent of state legislators who are women = 44.99 – 0.535*attend_pct.

The constant, 44.99, is the estimated value of Y when X equals 0. If you were using this equation to estimate the percentage of women legislators for a state, you would start with 44.99 percent and then subtract .535, or about one-half a percentage point, for each percentage of the state's population who are frequent attenders. So your estimate for a state with, say, 50 percent frequent attenders would be 44.99 – .535*(50) = 44.99 – 26.75 ≈ 18 percent female legislators. The main statistic of interest, then, is the regression coefficient, –.535, which estimates the average change in the dependent variable for each unit change in the independent variable. A regression coefficient of –.535 tells us that for each one-unit increase in the percentage of frequent attenders, there is a .535-unit decrease in the percentage of female legislators. So a 1-percentage-point increase in attend_pct is associated with a .535-percentage-point decrease in womleg_2015.[1]

What would the null hypothesis have to say about all this? Of course, we are not analyzing a random sample here, since we have information on the entire population of 50 states. But let's assume, for illustrative purposes, that we have just analyzed a random sample and that we have obtained a sample estimate of the effect of attend_pct on womleg_2015. The null hypothesis would say what it always says: In the population from which the sample was drawn, there is no relationship between the independent variable (in this case, the percentage of frequent attenders) and the dependent variable (the percentage of female legislators). In the population the true regression coefficient is equal to 0. Furthermore, the regression coefficient that we obtained, –.535, occurred by chance.

In SPSS regression results, you test the null hypothesis by examining two columns in the Coefficients table—the column labeled "t," which reports *t*-ratios, and the column labeled "Sig.," which reports *P*-values. Informally, to safely reject the null hypothesis, you generally look for *t*-ratios with magnitudes (absolute values) of 2 or greater. According to the results of our analysis, the regression coefficient for attend_pct has a *t*-ratio of –7.097, well above the informal 2-or-greater rule. A *P*-value, which tells you the probability of obtaining the results if the null hypothesis is correct, helps you to make more precise inferences about the relationship between the independent variable and the dependent variable. If "Sig." is greater than .05, then the observed results would occur too frequently by chance, and you must not reject the null hypothesis. By contrast, if "Sig." is equal to or less than .05, then the null hypothesis represents an unlikely occurrence and may be rejected. The *t*-ratio for attend_pct has a corresponding *P*-value of .000. If the null is correct, then random sampling error would have produced the observed results zero times in a thousand. Reject the null hypothesis. It depends on the research problem at hand, of course, but for most applications you can ignore the *t*-ratio and *P*-value for the constant.[2]

How strong is the relationship between attend_pct and womleg_2015? The answer is provided by the *R*-square statistics, which appear in the Model Summary table. SPSS reports two values, one labeled "R Square," and one labeled "Adjusted R Square." Which one should you use? Most research articles report the adjusted value, so let's rely on adjusted *R*-square to provide the best overall measure of the strength of the relationship.[3] Adjusted *R*-square is equal to .502. *R*-square communicates the proportion of the variation in the dependent variable that is explained by the independent variable. Like any proportion, *R*-square can assume any value between 0 and 1. Thus, of all the variation in womleg_2015 between states, .502, or 50.2 percent, is explained by attend_pct.

So that you can become comfortable with bivariate regression—and to address a potential source of confusion—let's do another run, this time using BA_or_more as the independent variable. Click Analyze → Regression → Linear. Leave womleg_2015 in the Dependent box, but click attend_pct back into the Variables list. Click BA_or_more into the Independent(s) box and click OK. Examine the Coefficients table and the Model Summary table.
What is the regression line for the effect of BA_or_more on womleg_2015? It is

Percent female state legislators = .292 + 0.878*BA_or_more.

Model Summary

Model	R	R Square	Adjusted R Square	Std. Error of the Estimate
1	.593[a]	.352	.338	5.69975

a. Predictors: (Constant), BA_or_more Percent college or higher

Coefficients[a]

Model		Unstandardized Coefficients		Standardized Coefficients	t	Sig.
		B	Std. Error	Beta		
1	(Constant)	.292	4.745		.062	.951
	BA_or_more Percent college or higher	.878	.172	.593	5.104	.000

a. Dependent Variable: womleg_2015 Percent women state legislators, 2015

First, consider the weak magnitude of the constant, .292. For states in which 0 percent of residents have college degrees, the estimated percentage of female legislators is merely three-tenths of a percent, an implausibly low number.[4] In fact, you will sometimes obtain regression results in which the constant is a negative number, which leaves the realm of the implausible and enters the realm of the impossible, at least for dependent variables, such as womleg_2015, that cannot assume negative values. (In one of this chapter's exercises, you will obtain a negative constant, even though the dependent variable cannot take on negative values.) Simply stated, SPSS anchors the line at the Y-intercept that produces the best estimates for the data. Of course, you can use the equation to arrive at a more realistic estimate for cases having the lowest observed value on the independent variable. For example, for states in which 20 percent of the population has a college degree—a value that is quite close to the actual minimum of BA_or_higher—we would estimate a value on womleg_2015 of about 18 percent: .292 + .878*20 ≈ 18 percent.

The regression coefficient, .878, says that for each percentage-point increase in BA_or_more, there is an average increase of .878 of a percentage point in the percentage of female legislators. Again, increase the percentage of BA_or_more graduates by 1, and the percentage of women legislators goes up by almost nine-tenths of a percentage point, on average. In the population, could the true value of the regression coefficient be 0? Probably not, according to the *t*-ratio (5.104) and the *P*-value (0.000). And, according to the adjusted *R*-square, the independent variable does a fair amount of work in explaining the dependent variable. About 33 percent of the variation in womleg_2015 is explained by BA_or_more. As bivariate regressions go, that's not too bad.

SCATTERPLOTS

An SPSS graphic routine, Scatter/Dot, adds a visual dimension to correlation and regression and thus can help you paint a richer portrait of a relationship. Consider Figure 8-3, created using Graphs → Legacy Dialogs → Scatter/Dot and edited in the Chart Editor. This graph, generically referred to as a scatterplot, displays the cases in a two-dimensional space according to their values on the two variables. The horizontal axis (X-axis) is defined by the independent variable, BA_or_more, and the vertical axis (Y-axis) is defined by the dependent variable,

Figure 8-3 Scatterplot with Regression Line

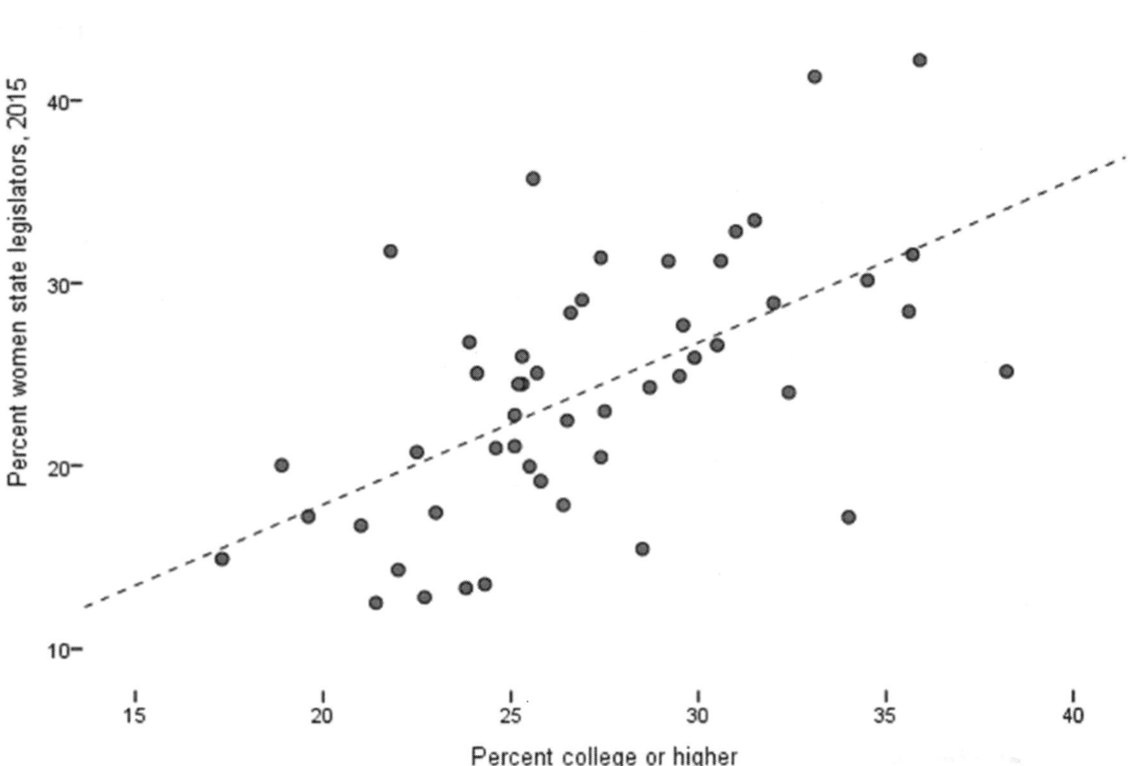

womleg_2015. We know from our correlation analysis that Pearson's r for this relationship is .593. We can now see what the correlation "looks like." Based on Figure 8-3, states with lower percentages of college graduates tend to have lower percentages of women legislators. As you move from left to right along the X-axis, values on the Y-axis generally increase, just as the positive correlation coefficient suggested.

The scatterplot has other interesting features. Notice that the dots have been overlaid by the linear regression line obtained from the analysis we just performed.

Estimated percentage of women legislators = .292 + .878*BA_or_more.

Thanks to this visual depiction, we can see that the linear summary of the relationship, while reasonably coherent, is far from perfect. Notice the sparse clarity of the graph. The dots are solid, but the background is white, both inside and outside the data space. The axis lines have been removed, leaving only the tick marks, which are labeled in round numbers, without decimal points. The two key data elements—the dots representing each case and the regression line summarizing the relationship—do not compete for our eye with any other lines, colors, or text. The scatterplot in Figure 8-3 comes close to what Edward R. Tufte calls an "erased" graph, a graph in which nonessential elements have been deleted. In Chapter 5, we touched on Tufte's definition of the data/ink ratio, the proportion of a graph's total ink devoted to depicting the information contained in the data. Tufte, a leading expert on the visual communication of quantitative information, recommends that the greatest share of a graph's elements should be devoted to data ink—graphic features that convey the essence of the relationship.[5] Let's recreate this graphic.

Click Graphs → Legacy Dialogs → Scatter/Dot. In the Scatter/Dot window, select Simple Scatter and click Define, opening the Simple Scatterplot dialog (Figure 8-4). Click the independent variable (BA_or_more) into the X Axis box, click the dependent variable (womleg_2015) into the Y Axis box, and click OK. SPSS summons its defaults and cranks out a scatterplot (Figure 8-5). This is a good start, but improvement is always possible. Double-click on the image, opening the Chart Editor (Figure 8-6). First we will complement or enhance the data elements—add the regression line, make the dots more prominent—and then we will deemphasize the graph's nondata features by whiting out the scatterplot's fill, border, and axes. Also, we will need to un-bold the axis titles. (In SPSS's default rendering, the bolded axis titles are the first thing one looks at.) Perhaps we also will want to modify the X Axis title to make it more presentable.

Figure 8-4 Opening Scatter/Dot

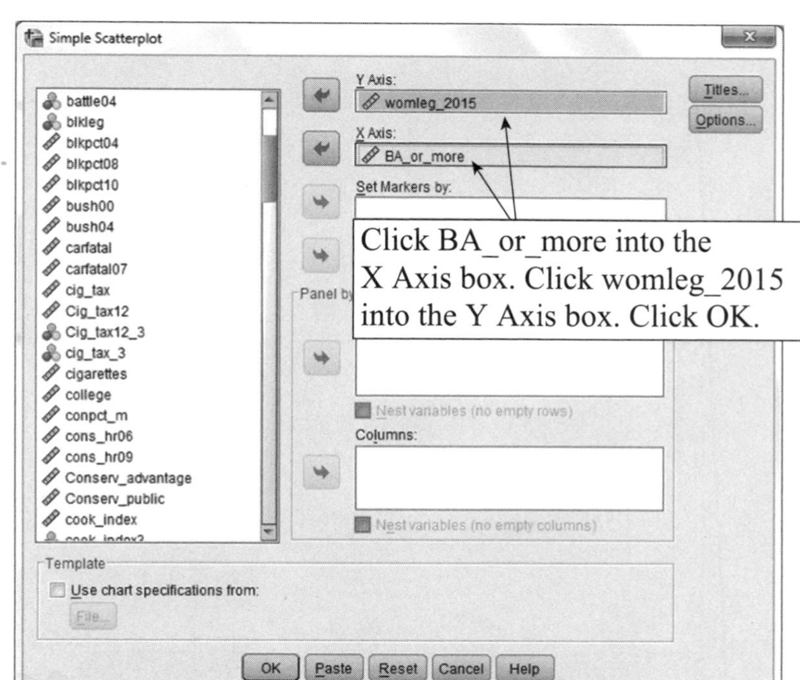

Figure 8-5 Unedited Scatterplot in the Viewer

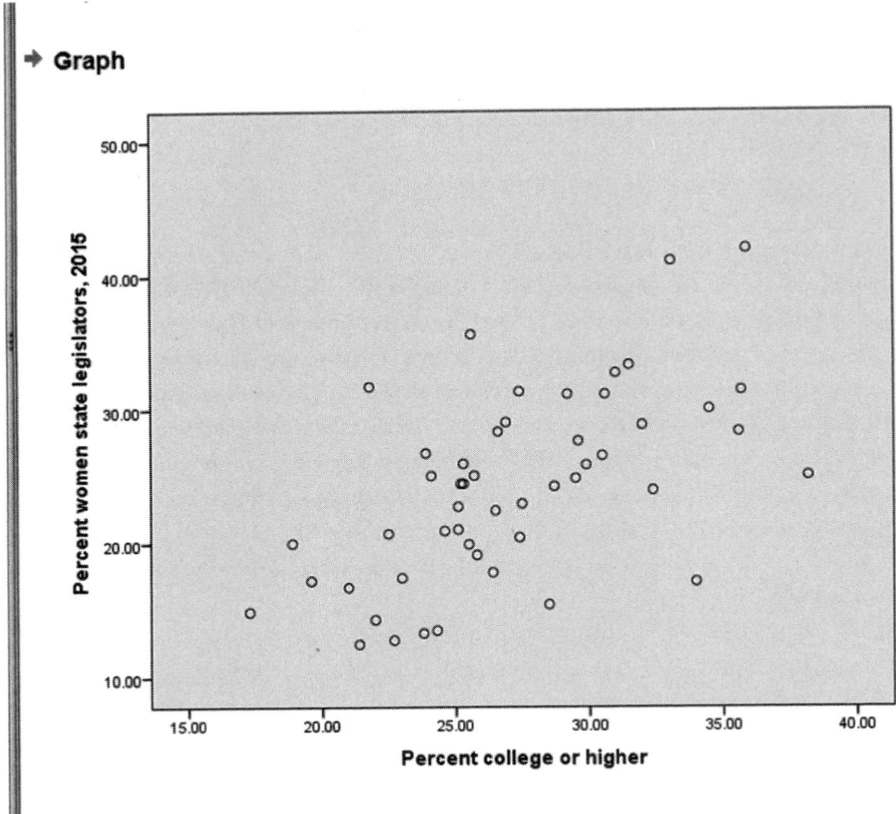

To add the regression line, click the Add Fit Line at Total button (see Figure 8-7). SPSS superimposes the line, selects it, and automatically opens the Properties window. The Fit Line tab (the opening tab) does not require our attention. Click the Lines tab. In its solid-black attire, the regression line looks more like a sure thing than a probabilistic estimate. Click the Style drop-down and pick one of the dashed-line options. Click Apply,

Figure 8-6 Scatterplot Ready for Editing

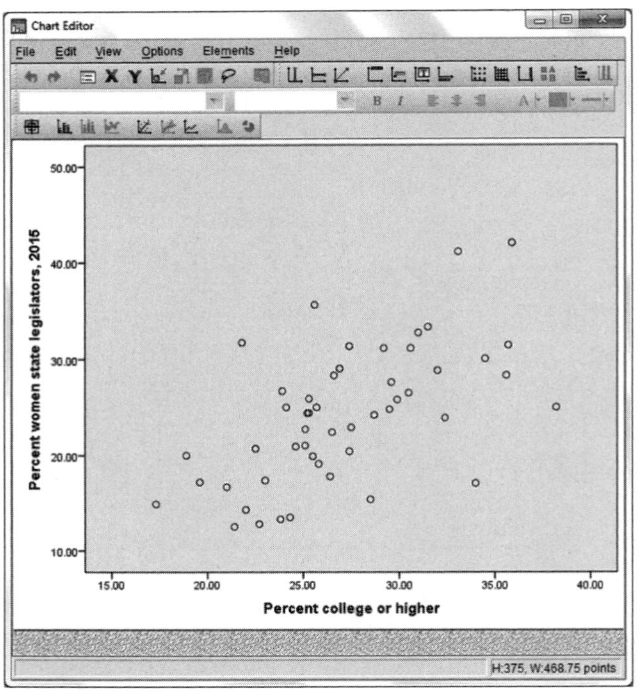

Figure 8-7 Adding a Regression Line to the Scatterplot

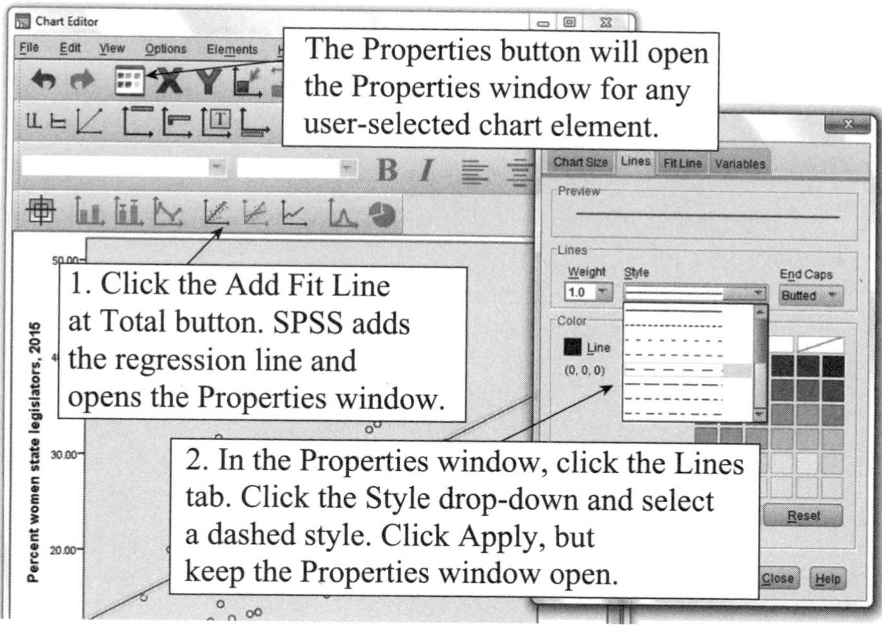

but be sure to keep the Properties window open.[6] Now click on any one of the hollow circles in the cloud of points or "markers." SPSS selects all of the markers (Figure 8-8). In the Color panel of the Marker tab, click Fill. The default setting, a diagonal line through a white background, means "transparent." This won't do. Make a color choice in the palette, and then click Apply. SPSS fills the dots with your selected choice.

Compared with the effort involved in enhancing the scatterplot's data-related information, the task of erasing the nonessential elements of the graph is rather more labor intensive. But with a little practice it becomes second nature. To whiten the graphic background (and dim but not whiten the axes), click anywhere on the empty gray space inside the graph (Figure 8-9). The Properties window adapts, telling us which elements are editable. In the Color panel of the Fill & Border tab, click Fill and select white, click Border and select white,

Figure 8-8 Adding a Fill Color to Scatterplot Markers

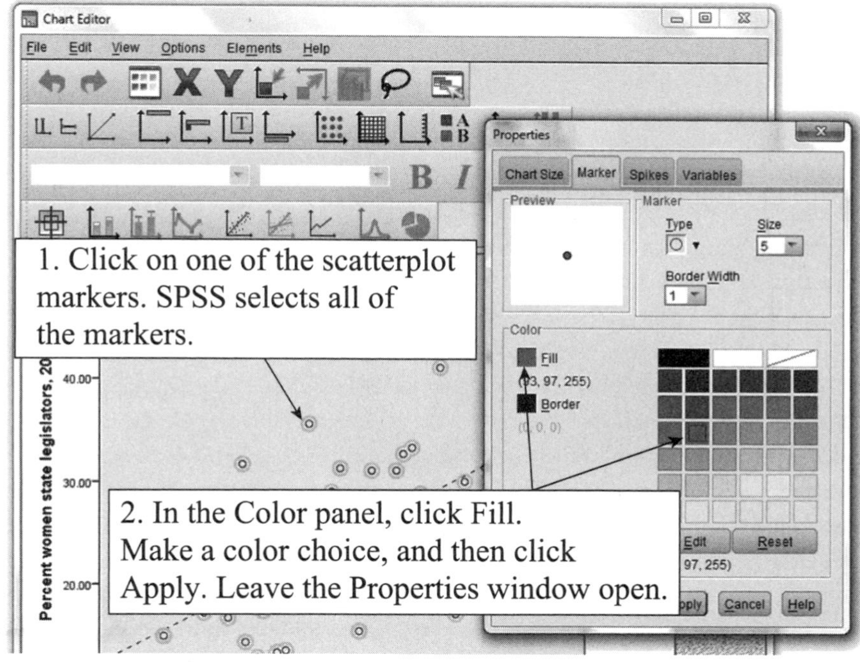

Figure 8-9 Whiting Out the Border and Fill

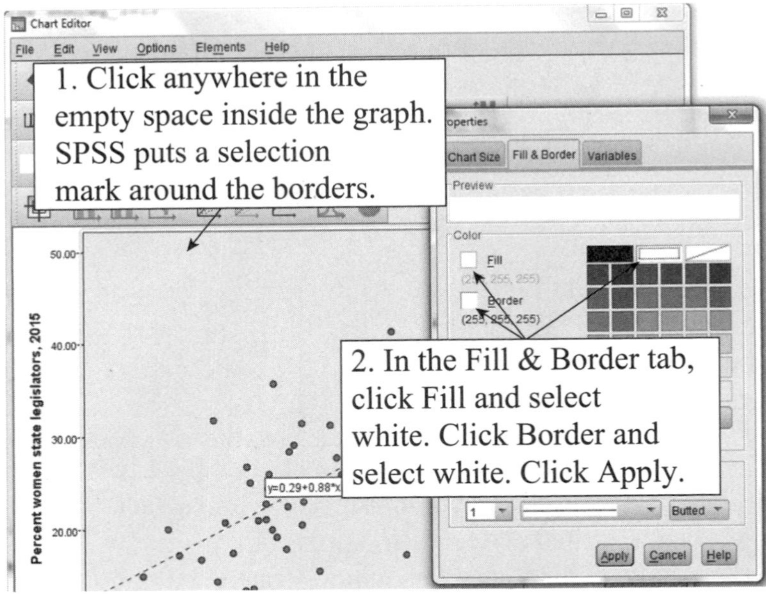

and click Apply. Now we will blank out the newly dimmed axes. Carefully click on the X-axis, but make sure not to click on one of the tick labels (Figure 8-10). Depress the Control key and keep it depressed. Click on the Y-axis. Now both axes are selected. In the Color panel of the Lines tab, click Line, select white, and click Apply. While we are here, we will also delete the unnecessary and distracting digits to the right of the decimal points in the axes tick-mark labels. Click the Number Format tab (refer to Figure 8-10). Click in the Decimal Places box (which may be empty) and type 0. Click Apply.

By default, SPSS bolds its graphic axis titles. This draws us away from the data and directs us toward a less important text element. Click on the X-axis title. Hold down the Control key and click on the Y-axis title (Figure 8-11). Both axis titles should now be selected. Click the Preferred Size drop-down and select 10. Click the Style drop-down and select Normal. Click Apply. There are two additional text elements to clean up. Click on the equation. In Properties, select the Reference Line tab. Uncheck the Attach label to line box (Figure 8-12). Select the R^2 Linear text box, as shown in Figure 8-12. Hit the delete key. Before exiting the Chart Editor, you may want to save your chart preferences as a template, which can be opened and applied to future scatterplot-editing tasks.[7]

MULTIPLE REGRESSION

Before proceeding, let's review what we have learned thus far about the womleg_2015–attend_pct and womleg_2015–BA_or_more relationships. The womleg_2015–attend_pct regression revealed a statistically significant negative relationship: The percentage of female legislators declines by .535 of a percentage point, on average, for every 1-percentage-point increase in religious attendance. The womleg_2015–BA_or_more regression revealed a significantly positive relationship: The percentage of female legislators increases by .878 of a percentage point, on average, for every 1-percentage-point increase in college graduates. A researcher who performed these analyses to test two separate hypotheses, the "religiosity hypothesis" and the "college hypothesis," might be tempted to conclude that each coefficient (–.535 for religiosity and .878 for college degrees) captures the true effect of each variable on the dependent variable. However, this conclusion would be unwarranted. Recall this result, revealed in the correlation analysis: The two independent variables are themselves rather strongly related ($r = -.519$). Thus, when we compare states having lower percentages of college graduates with states having higher percentages of college graduates, we are also comparing states having more highly religious residents with states having fewer highly religious residents. Do states with more college graduates have higher percentages of female legislators because they have more college graduates, or because they have lower religiosity? How much of the "college effect" is attributable to the "religiosity effect?" Multiple regression analysis is designed to disentangle the confounding effects of two (or more) independent variables.

Figure 8-10 Editing the Axes of a Scatterplot

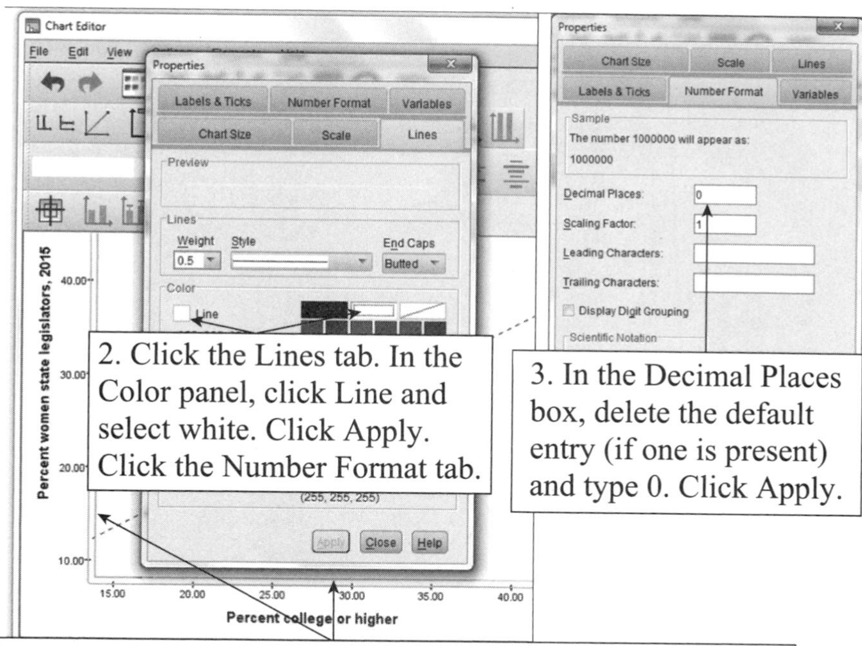

Figure 8-11 Editing the Axis Titles

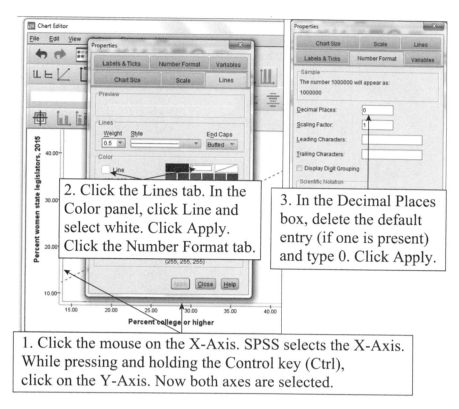

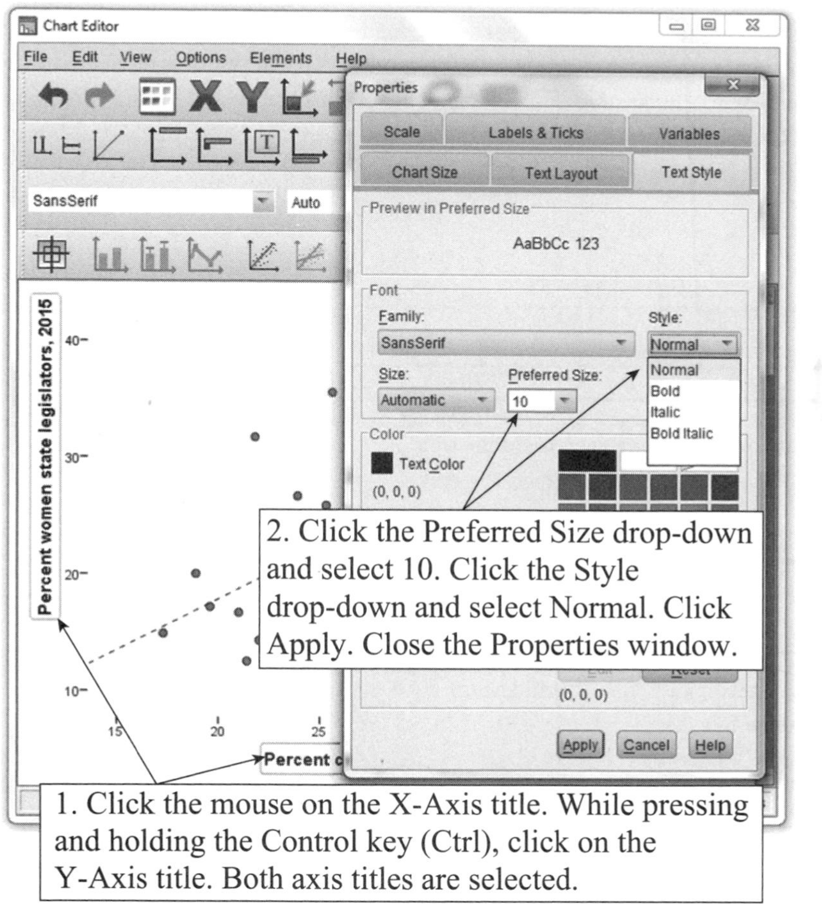

Figure 8-12 Deleting Distracting Text Elements

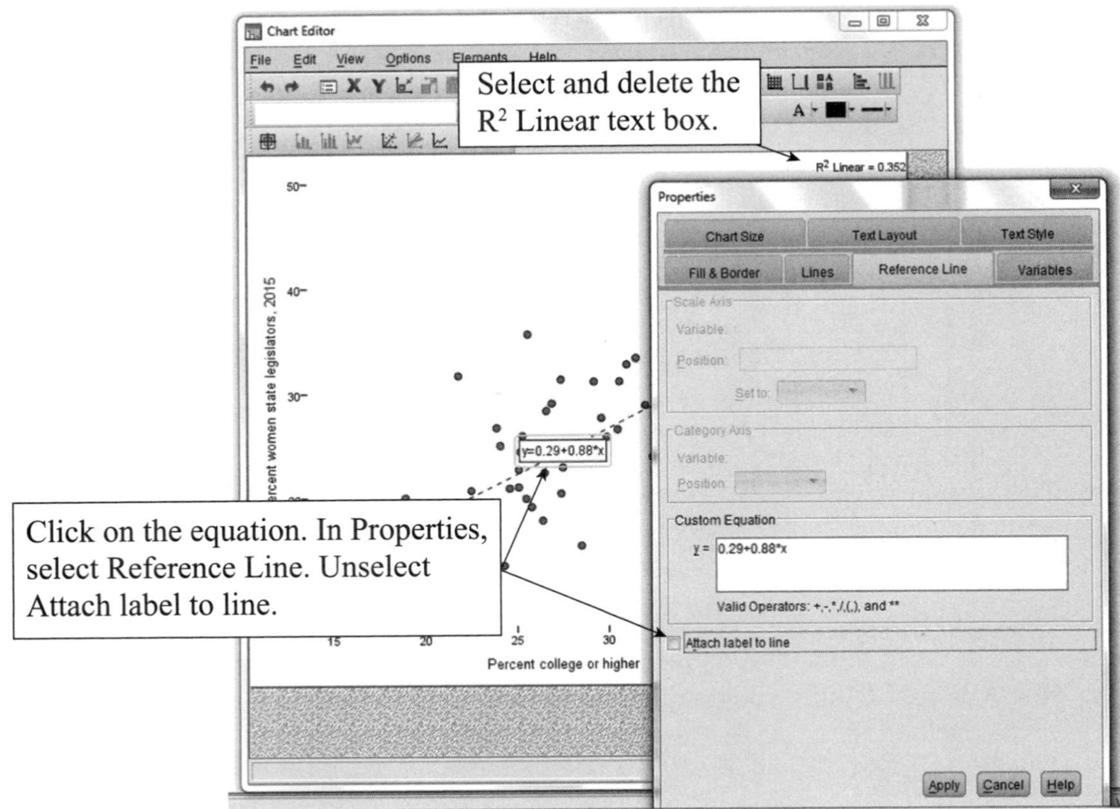

Multiple regression will estimate the effect of each independent variable on the dependent variable, controlling for the effects of all other independent variables in the model. We will perform such an analysis, again using womleg_2015 as the dependent variable and entering *both* BA_or_more and attend_pct as independent variables. Return to the Regression window. Leaving BA_or_more in place from the earlier bivariate regression, click attend_pct into the Independent(s) box and click OK.

Model Summary

Model	R	R Square	Adjusted R Square	Std. Error of the Estimate
1	.761[a]	.579	.561	4.64021

a. Predictors: (Constant), attend_pct Percent frequently attend relig serv (Pew), BA_or_more Percent college or higher

Coefficients[a]

Model		Unstandardized Coefficients		Standardized Coefficients	t	Sig.
		B	Std. Error	Beta		
1	(Constant)	28.191	6.748		4.178	.000
	BA_or_more Percent college or higher	.449	.164	.304	2.743	.009
	attend_pct Percent frequently attend relig serv (Pew)	-.417	.083	-.558	-5.042	.000

a. Dependent Variable: womleg_2015 Percent women state legislators, 2015

This analysis provides the information we need to isolate the partial effect of each independent variable on the dependent variable. The multiple regression equation is as follows:

Percent female state legislators = 28.191 + .449*(BA_or_more) – .417*(attend_pct)

Focus on the regression coefficients for each of the independent variables. The coefficient on BA_or_more, .449, tells us the effect of BA_or_more on womleg_2015, controlling for attend_pct. Recall that in the bivariate analysis, a 1-percentage-point increase in BA_or_more was associated with a .878-unit increase in the percentage of female legislators. When we control for religious attendance, however, we find a reduction in this effect—to a .449-unit increase in womleg_2015. Even so, the regression coefficient on BA_or_more, with a *t*-statistic of 2.743 and a *P*-value of .009, remains statistically significant. The partial effect of attend_pct tells a similar story. The uncontrolled effect of religious attendance, –.535, weakens to –.417 but remains significant ($t = -5.042$, *P*-value = .000). In multiple regression, adjusted *R*-square communicates how well all of the independent variables explain the dependent variable. So by knowing two things about states—percentage of college graduates and level of religious attendance—we can account for about 56.1 percent of the variation across states in the percentage of female legislators. This is an improvement over the explanatory leverage of attend_pct (.502) or BA_or_more (.338) considered separately.

EXERCISES

1. (Dataset: States. Variables: demHR11, demstate13, union10.) Consider a plausible scenario for the relationships between three variables: the percentages of a state's U.S. House and U.S. Senate delegations who are Democrats, the percentage of state legislators who are Democrats, and the percentage of workers in the state who are unionized. One could hypothesize that, compared with states with few Democrats in their state legislatures, states having larger percentages of Democratic legislators would also have greater proportions of Democrats in their U.S. congressional delegations. Furthermore, because unions tend to support Democratic candidates, one would also expect more heavily unionized states to have higher percentages of Democratic legislators at the state and national levels. The States dataset contains three variables: demHR11, the percentage of House and Senate members who are Democrats; demstate13, the percentage of state legislators who are Democrats; and union10, the percentage of workers who are union members.

   A. Run Analyze → Correlate → Bivariate to find the Pearson correlation coefficients among demHR11, demstate13, and union10. Next to the question marks, write in the correlation coefficients.

		Percent US House and Senate Democratic (demHR11)	Percent of state legislators who are Democrats (demstate13)	Percent workers who are union members (union10)
Percent US House and Senate Democratic (demHR11)	Pearson correlation	1		
Percent of state legislators who are Democrats (demstate13)	Pearson correlation	?	1	
Percent workers who are union members (union10)	Pearson correlation	?	?	1

   B. According to the correlation coefficient, as the percentage of unionized workers increases, the percentage of Democratic U.S. House members and U.S. Senators (circle one)

   increases. decreases.

C. According to the correlation coefficient, as the percentage of unionized workers decreases, the percentage of Democratic U.S. House members and U.S. Senators (circle one)

increases. decreases.

D. Which two of the following statements describe the relationship between the percentage of unionized workers and the percentage of state legislators who are Democrats? (check two)

- ☐ The relationship is negative.
- ☐ The relationship is positive.
- ☐ The relationship is stronger than the relationship between the percentage of unionized workers and the percentage of Democratic U.S. House representatives and U.S. senators.
- ☐ The relationship is weaker than the relationship between the percentage of unionized workers and the percentage of Democratic U.S. House representatives and U.S. senators.

2. (Dataset: States. Variables: HR_conserv11, Conserv_public.) Two congressional scholars are discussing the extent to which members of the U.S. House of Representatives stay in touch with the voters in their states.

Scholar 1: "When members of congress vote on important public policies, they are closely attuned to the ideological make-ups of their states. Members from states having many liberals will tend to cast votes in the liberal direction. Representatives from states with mostly conservative constituencies, by contrast, will take conservative positions on important policies."

Scholar 2: "You certainly have a naïve view of congressional behavior. Once they get elected, members of congress adopt a 'Washington, D.C. state of mind,' perhaps voting in the liberal direction on one policy and in the conservative direction on another. One thing is certain: The way members vote has little to do with the ideological composition of their states."

Think about an independent variable that measures the percentage of self-described "conservatives" among the mass public in a state, with low values denoting low percentages of conservatives and high values denoting high percentages of conservatives. And consider a dependent variable that gauges the degree to which the state's House delegation votes in a conservative direction on public policies. Low scores on this dependent variable tell you that the delegation tends to vote in a liberal direction and high scores say that the delegation votes in a conservative direction.

A. Below is an empty graphic shell showing the relationship between the independent variable and the dependent variable. Draw a regression line inside the shell that depicts what the relationship should look like if Scholar 1 is correct.

B. Below is another graphic shell showing the relationship between the independent variable and the dependent variable. Draw a regression line inside the shell that depicts what the relationship should look like if Scholar 2 is correct.

HR conservative rating

Percent Mass Public Conservative

C. The States dataset contains the variable Conserv_public, the percentage of the mass public calling themselves conservative. This is the independent variable. The dataset also contains HR_conserv11, a measure of conservative votes by states' House members. Scores on this variable can range from 0 (low conservatism) to 100 (high conservatism). This is the dependent variable. Perform a regression analysis.

According to the regression equation, a 1-percentage-point increase in conservatives in the mass public is associated with (check one)

- ❑ about a 27-point decrease in House conservatism scores.
- ❑ about a 2-point increase in House conservatism scores.
- ❑ about a 8-point increase in House conservatism scores.

D. If you were to use this regression to estimate the mean House conservatism score for states having 30 percent conservatives, your estimate would be (circle one)

a score of about 35.   a score of about 45.   a score of about 55.

E. The adjusted *R*-squared for this relationship is equal to ______. This tells you that about ______ percent of the variation in HR_conserv11 is explained by Conserv_public.

F. Use Graphs → Legacy Dialogs → Scatter/Dot to create a scatterplot of the relationship between Conserv_public (X-axis) and HR_conserv11 (Y-axis). In the Chart Editor, add a linear regression line to the scatterplot. Enhance the graph's data-ink ratio by following the procedures described in this chapter for creating an erased graph. Print the graph.

G. Based on your inspection of the regression results, the scatterplot and linear prediction line, and adjusted *R*-squared, which congressional scholar is more correct? (check one)

- ❑ Scholar 1 is more correct.
- ❑ Scholar 2 is more correct.

H. Explain your answer in G, making specific reference to the statistical and graphic evidence.

____

____

____

____

____

____

3. (Dataset: States. Variables: TO_0812, Obama2012.) An article of faith among Democratic Party strategists (and a source of apprehension among Republican strategists) is that high voter turnouts help Democratic candidates. Why should this be the case? According to the conventional wisdom, Democratic electorates are less likely to vote than are Republican voters. Thus, low turnouts naturally favor Republican candidates. As turnouts push higher, the reasoning goes, a larger number of potential Democratic voters will go to the polls, creating a better opportunity for Democratic candidates. Therefore, as turnouts go up, so should the Democratic percentage of the vote.[8]

   A. Use regression to test this conventional wisdom. The States dataset contains TO_0812, the percentage-point change in presidential election turnout between 2008 and 2012. States in which turnout declined between 2008 and 2012 have negative values on TO_0812, whereas states in which turnout increased have positive values on TO_0812. (For example, Utah's turnout increased by a bit more than 2 percentage points between 2008 and 2012, giving Utah a score of 2.1 on TO_0812. Florida's turnout dropped by 4 points, giving a value of –4 on TO_0812.) TO_0812 is the independent variable. Another variable, Obama2012, the percentage of the vote cast for Democratic candidate Barack Obama, is the dependent variable.

   Based on your results, the regression equation for estimating the percentage voting for Obama is: (put the constant in the first blank)

   __________ + ____________ * TO_0812.

   B. The *P*-value for the regression coefficient on TO_0812 is ______________, and the adjusted *R*-squared is ______________________.

   C. Consider your findings in A and B. One may conclude that (check one)

   ❑ the conventional wisdom is correct

   ❑ the conventional wisdom is incorrect

   D. Explain your answer in C, making specific reference to the regression results.

   ____

   ____

   ____

   ____

   ____

   ____

4. (Dataset: States. Variables: abortlaw10, ProChoice.) As you are no doubt aware, in its momentous decision in *Roe v. Wade* (1973), the U.S. Supreme Court declared that states may not outlaw abortion. Even so, many state legislatures have enacted restrictions and regulations that, while not banning abortion, make an abortion more difficult to obtain. Other states, however, have few or no restrictions. What factors might explain these differences in abortion laws among the states? We know that the mass public remains divided on this issue. Public opinion in some states is more favorable toward permitting abortion, whereas in other states public opinion is less favorable. Does public opinion guide state policy on this issue?

   The States dataset contains abortlaw10, which measures the number of abortion restrictions a state has enacted into law. Values on abortlaw10 range from 0 (least restrictive) to 10 (most restrictive). This is the dependent variable. The dataset also has the variable ProChoice, the percentage of the mass public that is pro-choice. This is the independent variable.

   A. If you were to use regression analysis to test the idea that public opinion on abortion affects state abortion policy, you would expect to find (check one)

   ❑ a negative sign on ProChoice's regression coefficient

   ❑ a positive sign on ProChoice's regression coefficient

B. Using regression, analyze the abortlaw10–ProChoice relationship. According to the results, the regression equation for estimating the number of abortion restrictions is (fill in the blanks)

______________ ______________________*ProChoice.

(constant) (regression coefficient)

C. The *P*-value for the regression coefficient is __________. The value of adjusted *R*-squared is __________.

D. According to States, about 60 percent of Colorado residents are pro-choice. In Arkansas, by contrast, only about 40 percent of the public holds this view. Based on the regression equation: (fill in the blanks)

- ❑ You would estimate that Colorado would have about __________________ abortion restrictions.
- ❑ You would estimate that Arkansas would have about __________________ abortion restrictions.

E. Adjusted *R*-squared is equal to __________________. This means that (complete the sentence)

____

____

F. Use Graphs → Legacy Dialogs → Scatter/Dot to create a scatterplot of the relationship between ProChoice (X-axis) and abortlaw10 (Y-axis). In the Chart Editor, add a linear regression line to the scatterplot. Enhance the graph's data/ink ratio by following the procedures described in this chapter for creating an erased graph. Print the graph.

5. Suppose that a critic, upon examining the variables in States, and viewing your results in Exercise 4, expresses skepticism about the relationship between mass-level abortion attitudes and the number of state-level restrictions on abortion:

"There is a key aspect of state governance that you have not taken into account: the percentage of state legislators who are women (womleg_2015). If you were to examine the correlation coefficients among abortlaw10, ProChoice, and womleg_2015, you will find two things. First, the womleg_2015–abortlaw10 correlation will be negative and pretty strong . . . say, at least –.50. Second, the womleg_2015–ProChoice correlation will be positive and fairly strong—at least +.50. Third, when you perform a multiple regression analysis of abortlaw10, using ProChoice and womleg_2015 as independent variables, you will find that womleg_2015 is statistically significant, while ProChoice will fade to statistical insignificance."

A. Obtain the correlation matrix that will allow you to test the critic's claim. Record the correlations in the following table:

		No. of abortion restrictions (abortlaw10)	Percent mass public pro-choice (ProChoice)	Percent female legislators (womleg_2015)
No. of abortion restrictions (abortlaw10)	Pearson Correlation	1		
Percent mass public pro-choice (ProChoice)	Pearson Correlation	?	1	
Percent female legislators (womleg_2015)	Pearson Correlation	?	?	1

B. Consider the skeptical critic's first claim regarding the relationship between womleg_2015 and abortlaw10. According to the correlation coefficient, this claim is:

❑ Correct because ____

____

❑ Incorrect because ______________________________

____

C. Consider the skeptical critic's second claim regarding the relationship between womleg_2015 and ProChoice. According to the correlation coefficient, this claim is:

❑ Correct because ______________________________

____

❑ Incorrect because ______________________________

____

D. Run the multiple regression suggested by the critic. Write the correct values next to the question marks in the following table:

Number of restrictions (abortlaw10)	Coefficient	*t*-statistic	*P*-value
Percent mass public pro-choice (ProChoice)	?	?	?
Percent female legislators (womleg_2015)	?	?	?
Constant	?		

E. Based on the evidence in part D, is the critic's third claim regarding the multiple regression analysis correct? This claim is

❑ Correct because ______________________________

____

____

❑ Incorrect because ______________________________

____

____

6. (Dataset: GSS2012. Variables: tolerance, educ, age, polviews.) What factors affect a person's level of tolerance of unpopular groups? Consider three hypotheses:

   Hypothesis 1: In a comparison of individuals, older people will be less tolerant than younger people.

   Hypothesis 2: In a comparison of individuals, those with higher levels of education will have higher levels of tolerance than those with lower levels of education.

   Hypothesis 3: In a comparison of individuals, conservatives will be less tolerant than liberals.

GSS2012 includes the following variables, as described in the following table:

GSS2012 variable	Label	Coding	Status in this exercise
Tolerance	Tolerance	0 (low) to 15 (high)	Dependent variable
Age (age)	R's age (years)	18 to 89	Independent variable
Education (educ)	Highest year of school	0 to 20	Independent variable
Political views (polviews)	Ideological self-placement	1 (extremely liberal) to 7 (extremely conservative)	Independent variable

A. Run Correlate. Focus on the correlations between the dependent variable and each of the independent variables. Write the correlations in the following table:

	Tolerance
Age (age)	?
Education (educ)	?
Political views (polviews)	?

B. Based on the *direction* of each correlation coefficient, does it appear that each hypothesis has merit? Answer yes or no and explain:

____

____

____

____

____

C. Run multiple regression analysis. Fill in the following table:

Tolerance	Coefficient	*t*-statistic	*P*-value
Age (age)	?	?	?
Education (educ)	?	?	?
Political views (polviews)	?	?	?
Constant	?		
Adjusted *R*-squared	?		

D. Consider whether each hypothesis—Hypothesis 1, Hypothesis 2, and Hypothesis 3—is supported by your analysis. For each hypothesis, check the correct box and explain your answer.

❑ Hypothesis 1 is supported because ______________________________

____

❑ Hypothesis 1 is not supported because ______________________________

____

❑ Hypothesis 2 is supported because ______________________________

____

❑ Hypothesis 2 is not supported because ______________________________

____

❑ Hypothesis 3 is supported because ______________________________

____

❑ Hypothesis 3 is not supported because ______________________________

____

E. Use the regression equation to estimate the tolerance score for the typical respondent, which we will define as a person having the mean values of all the independent variables. Run Descriptives to obtain the mean values for each independent variable. Write the means in the table that follows:

	Age (age)	Education (educ)	Political views (polviews)
Mean	?	?	?

F. When you use the mean values to estimate the tolerance score for the typical person, you obtain an estimate equal to (fill in the blank) ____________.

That concludes the exercises for this chapter.

NOTES

1. Regression analysis on variables measured by percentages can be confusing. Always stay focused on the exact units of measurement. One percentage point would be 1.00. So if attend_pct increases by 1.00, then womleg_2015 decreases, on average, by .535, or about one-half of a percentage point.
2. The *t*-ratio for the Y-intercept permits you to test the null hypothesis that, in the population, the Y-intercept is 0. In this case, we have no interest in testing the hypothesis that states having 0 frequent attenders have 0 percent women in their state legislatures.
3. Most data analysis programs, SPSS included, provide two values of *R*-square—a plain version, which SPSS labels "R Square," and an adjusted version, "Adjusted R Square." Adjusted *R*-square is often about the same as (but is always less than) plain *R*-square. What is the difference? Just like a sample mean, which provides an estimate of the unseen population mean, a sample *R*-square provides an estimate of the true value of *R*-square in the population. And just like a sample mean, the sample *R*-square is equal to the population *R*-square, give or take random sampling error. However, unlike the random error associated with a sample mean, *R*-square's errors can assume only positive values—squaring any negative error, after all, produces a positive number—introducing upward bias into the estimated value of *R*-square. This problem, which is more troublesome for small samples and for models with many independent variables, can be corrected by adjusting plain *R*-square "downward." For a sample of size *N* and a regression model with *k* predictors, adjusted *R*-square is equal to: $1 - (1 - R\text{-square})[(N - 1)/(N - k - 1)]$. See Barbara G. Tabachnick and Linda S. Fidell, *Using Multivariate Statistics*, 3rd ed. (New York: HarperCollins, 1996), 164–165.
4. Of course, the smallest value of BA_or_more in the actual data is substantially higher than 0. If you do a quick Descriptives run, you will find that the lowest value of BA_or_more is 17.3 percent.
5. Edward R. Tufte, *The Visual Display of Quantitative Information*, 2nd ed. (Cheshire, Conn.: Graphics Press, 2001). Tufte's work has inspired other excellent treatments of visual communication. For example, see Stephen Few, *Show Me the Numbers: Designing Tables and Graphs to Enlighten* (Oakland, Calif.: Analytics Press, 2004); and Howard Wainer, *Graphic Discovery: A Trout in the Milk and Other Visual Adventures* (Princeton: Princeton University Press, 2005).
6. You will want to keep the Properties window open for your entire excursion into the Chart Editor. Each time you select a different part of the graph for editing, SPSS automatically adjusts the Properties window to reflect the editable features of the graphic element you have selected. Naturally, you can open the Properties window upon entering the Chart Editor by clicking the Properties button.
7. With the Chart Editor still open, click File → Save Chart Template. In the Save Chart Template window, click in the All Settings box, which selects all chart features. Now uncheck the box next to Text Content. (You don't want SPSS to apply the same axis titles to all of your scatterplots.) Click Continue. Find a good place to save the template (and concoct a descriptive name for the file), which SPSS saves with the .sgt extension. To apply the template to future editing projects: In the Chart Editor, click File → Apply Chart Template, find the .sgt file, and click Open. Experience teaches that SPSS will apply most of the template's features to the new graphic, although some minor editing may still be required.
8. See Michael D. Martinez and Jeff Gill, "The Effects of Turnout on Partisan Outcomes in U.S. Presidential Elections 1960–2000," *Journal of Politics* 67, no. 4 (November 2005): 1248–1274. Martinez and Gill find that the Democratic advantage from higher turnouts has declined over time.

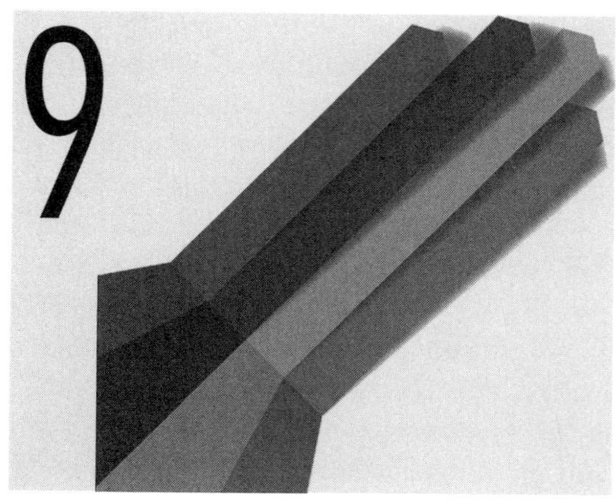

Dummy Variables and Interaction Effects*

Watch a screencast of the guided examples in this chapter.
edge.sagepub.com/pollock

Procedures Covered

Transform → Recode into Different Variables (dummy variables)

Analyze → Regression → Linear (with dummy variables)

Transform→ Compute → If (optional case selection condition)

Analyze → Regression → Linear (with interaction variable)

You can adapt regression analysis to different research situations. In one situation you might have nominal or ordinal independent variables. Provided that these variables are dummy variables, you can run a regression analysis, using categorical variables to predict values of an interval-level dependent variable. In this chapter you will learn how to construct dummy variables and how to use them in regression analysis. In a second research situation you might suspect that the effect of one independent variable on the dependent variable is not the same for all values of another independent variable—in other words, that interaction is going on in the data. Provided that you have created an interaction variable, you can use multiple regression to estimate the size and statistical significance of interaction effects. In this chapter you will learn how to create an interaction variable and how to perform and interpret multiple regression with interaction effects.

REGRESSION WITH DUMMY VARIABLES

A dummy variable can take on only two values, 1 or 0. Each case being analyzed either has the characteristic being measured (a code of 1) or does not have it (a code of 0). For example, a dummy variable for gender might code females as 1 and males as 0. Everybody who is coded 1 has the characteristic of being female, and everybody who is coded 0 does not have that characteristic. To appreciate why this 0 or 1 coding is the essential feature of dummy variables, consider the following regression model. The model, which uses data gathered during the 2012 presidential campaign, is designed to test the hypothesis that women gave Democratic presidential candidate Barack Obama higher feeling thermometer ratings than did men:

$$\text{Obama feeling thermometer} = a + b(\text{female})$$

In this formulation, gender is measured by a dummy variable, female, which is coded 0 for males and 1 for females. Since males are scored 0 on the dummy, the constant or intercept, a, will tell us the average Obama

---

* Special note to SPSS Student Version users: For the guided examples and exercises in Chapters 6 through 9, you will analyze NES2012_Student_B or GSS2012_Student_B.

rating among men. Substituting 0 for the dummy yields: a + b*0 = a. In the language of dummy variable regression, males are the "omitted" or "excluded" category, the category whose mean value on the dependent variable is captured by the intercept, a. The regression coefficient, b, will tell us how much to adjust the intercept for women—that is, when the dummy switches from 0 to 1. Thus, just as in any regression, b will estimate the average change in the dependent variable for a unit change in the independent variable. Since in this case a unit change in the independent variable is the difference between men (coded 0 on female) and women (coded 1 on female), the regression coefficient will reflect the mean difference in Obama thermometer ratings between males and females.

It is important to be clear on this point: The coefficient, b, does not communicate the mean Obama rating among females. Rather, it estimates the mean difference between males and females. (Of course, an estimated value of the dependent variable among females can be arrived at easily by summing a and b: a + b*1 = a + b.) As with any regression coefficient, we can rely on the coefficient's *t*-ratio and *P*-value to test the null hypothesis that there is no statistically meaningful gender difference in thermometer ratings of Obama.

Open NES2012 and figure out how to use gender as an independent variable in a regression analysis of Obama thermometer ratings. Obama_therm is the dependent variable. The independent variable, gender, is a nominal-level measure, coded 1 for males and 2 for females. Because of the way it is currently coded, gender could not be used in regression analysis. How can we create a dummy variable, female, coded 0 for males and 1 for females? We could assign these values by using Transform → Recode into Different Variables and applying this recoding scheme:

Respondent's gender	Old value (gender)	New value (female)
Male	1	0
Female	2	1
	Missing	Missing

You know how to use Transform → Recode into Different Variables, so go ahead and create female, which you can label "Female dummy." (Figure 9-1 helps to reacquaint you with the Recode procedure.)

To check your work, run Frequencies on gender and female to ensure that the distributions are the same.

gender Gender

		Frequency	Percent	Valid Percent	Cumulative Percent
Valid	1 Male	2836	47.9	47.9	47.9
	2 Female	3080	52.1	52.1	100.0
	Total	5916	100.0	100.0	

female Female dummy

		Frequency	Percent	Valid Percent	Cumulative Percent
Valid	.00	2836	47.9	47.9	47.9
	1.00	3080	52.1	52.1	100.0
	Total	5916	100.0	100.0	

The 3,080 respondents coded 2 on gender are coded 1 on female, and the 2,836 respondents coded 1 on gender are coded 0 on female. Return to the Variable View and assign value labels to the dummy variable you have created ("Male" for value 0, "Female" for value 1).

Figure 9-1 Recoding to Create a Dummy Variable

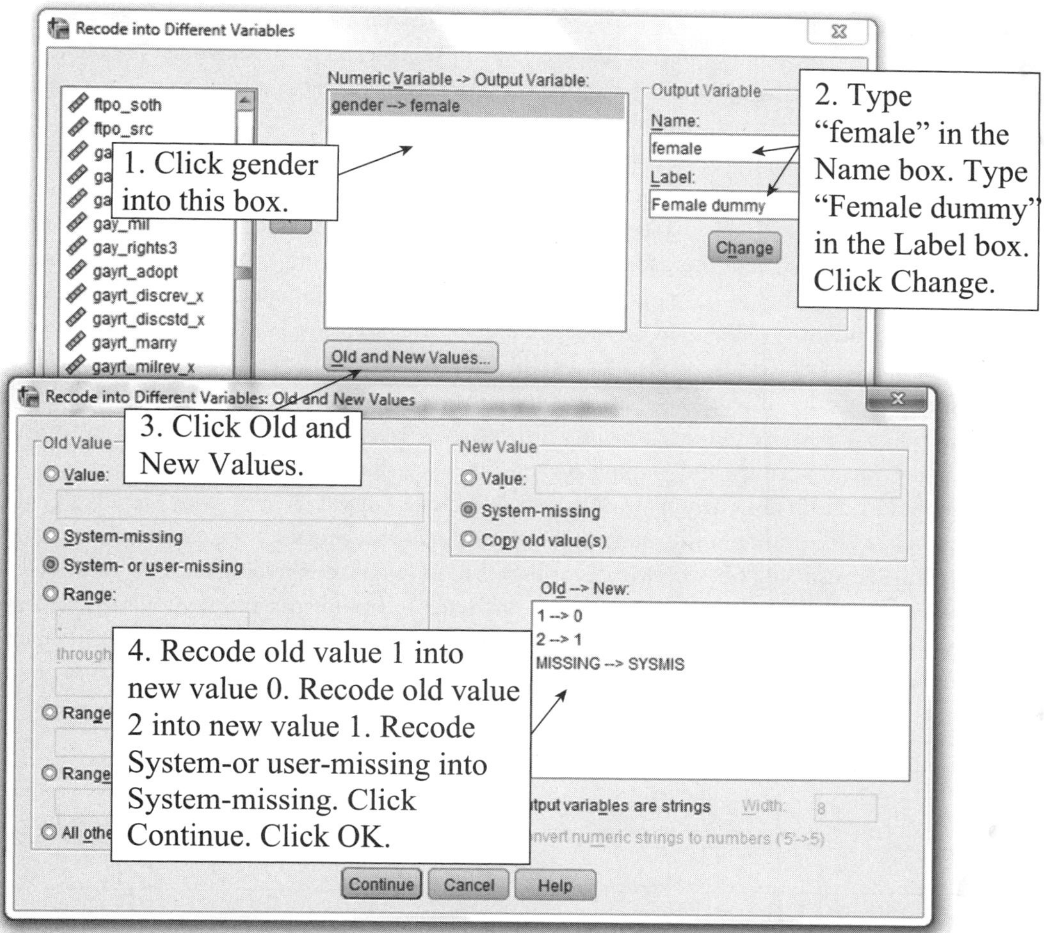

Now run linear regression, using the Barack Obama feeling thermometer (Obama_therm) as the dependent variable and female as the independent variable. Click Analyze → Regression → Linear. Click Obama_therm into the Dependent box, and click female into the Independent(s) box. Click OK.

Model Summary

Model	R	R Square	Adjusted R Square	Std. Error of the Estimate
1	.084[a]	.007	.007	34.203

a. Predictors: (Constant), female Female dummy

Coefficients[a]

Model		Unstandardized Coefficients B	Unstandardized Coefficients Std. Error	Standardized Coefficients Beta	t	Sig.
1	(Constant)	53.441	.664		80.510	.000
	female Female dummy	5.777	.925	.084	6.248	.000

a. Dependent Variable: Obama_therm Obama Rating

According to the Coefficients table, the regression equation is as follows:

Obama feeling thermometer = 53.441 + 5.777*Female dummy

How would we interpret these estimates? As always, the constant estimates the value of the dependent variable when the independent variable is 0. Because males have a value of 0 on female, the mean thermometer rating of Barack Obama for males is 53.441, the intercept. The regression coefficient on female communicates the mean change in the dependent variable for each unit change in the independent variable. So when the dummy switches from 0 to 1, the Obama rating goes up, on average, about 5.8 degrees. We can use this value to estimate the mean rating for females: 53.441 + 5.777 = 59.218. So men rated Obama at about 53 and women rated him at about 59. Was this gender difference produced by random sampling error? Not according to the *P*-value, .000. Do gender differences account for a big chunk of the variation in Barack Obama thermometer ratings? Not exactly. According to the adjusted *R*-square, gender alone accounts for seven-tenths of 1 percent of the variation in the dependent variable. There must be other variables that contribute to the explanation of Obama's ratings. Let's expand the model.

We would expect partisanship to have a big effect on the Obama thermometer scale. Democrats should score higher on the dependent variable than do Independents or Republicans. Plus, we know that women are more likely than men to be Democrats, so the Obama_therm–female relationship might be the spurious result of partisan differences, not gender differences. NES2012 contains pid_3, which codes Democrats as 1, Independents as 2, and Republicans as 3. Because pid_3 is a categorical variable, we cannot use it in a regression—not in its present form, anyway. But we can use pid_3 to create a dummy variable for partisanship.

Actually, we need to create not one but two dummy variables from pid_3. Why two? Here is a general rule about dummy variables: If the variable you want to "dummify" has *k* categories, then you need *k* – 1 dummies to measure the variable. Because pid_3 has three categories, we need two dummy variables. One of these variables, which we will call demdum, is equal to 1 for Democrats and 0 for Independents and Republicans. The second dummy variable, repdum, is equal to 1 for Republicans and 0 for Democrats and Independents. Independents, then, are uniquely identified by their exclusion from both dummies. Independents have values of 0 on demdum and 0 on repdum. Consider this recoding protocol:

Party ID, 3 categories	Old value (pid_3)	New value (demdum)	New value (repdum)
Democrat	1	1	0
Independent	2	0	0
Republican	3	0	1
	Missing	Missing	Missing

We will create demdum and repdum one at a time. To create demdum, click Transform → Recode into Different Variables. (The gender recode is still in the window, so click Reset.) Follow these steps:

1. Click pid_3 into the Numeric Variable → Output Variable panel.
2. Click in the Name box and type "demdum."
3. Click in the Label box and type "Democrat dummy." Click Change.
4. Click Old and New Values.

In the Recode into Different Variables: Old and New Values window, recode old value 1, the pid_3 code for Democrats, into new value 1, the code for Democrats on demdum. Old values 2 and 3, the pid_3 codes for Independents and Republicans, are equal to new value 0, the code for Independents and Republicans on demdum. You can use the Range boxes in the Old Value panel to accomplish this change. Make sure that you recode missing values on pid_3 into missing values on demdum. The Old and New Values window should now look like the upper panel of Figure 9-2.

Repeat the recoding procedure, using pid_3 to create repdum. Return to the Transform → Recode into Different Variables window. To avoid confusion, click the Reset button first and then follow these steps:

1. Click pid_3 into the Numeric Variable → Output Variable panel.
2. Type "repdum" in the Name box.

3. Type "Republican dummy" in the Label box and click Change.
4. Click Old and New Values.

This time, recode old value 3 on pid_3 into new value 1 on repdum. Old values 1 and 2 become 0 in the new values of repdum. Again, make sure to recode missing values on pid_3 into missing values on repdum (see the lower panel of Figure 9-2).

Figure 9-2 Creating Two Dummy Variables from a Three-Category Ordinal

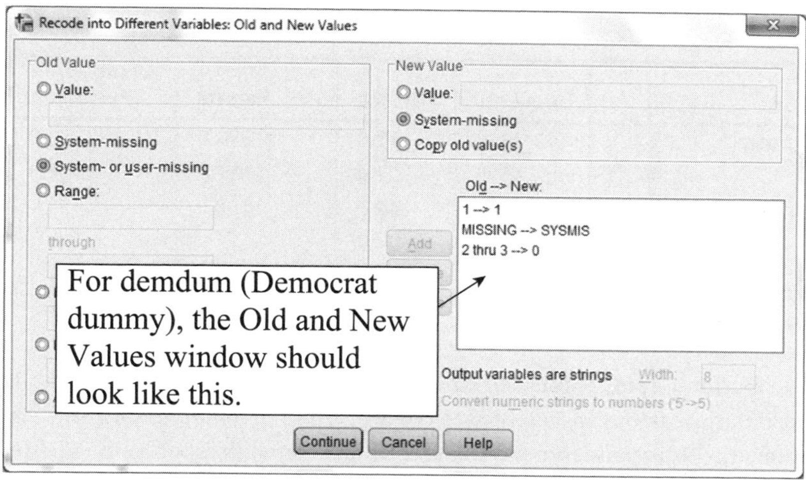

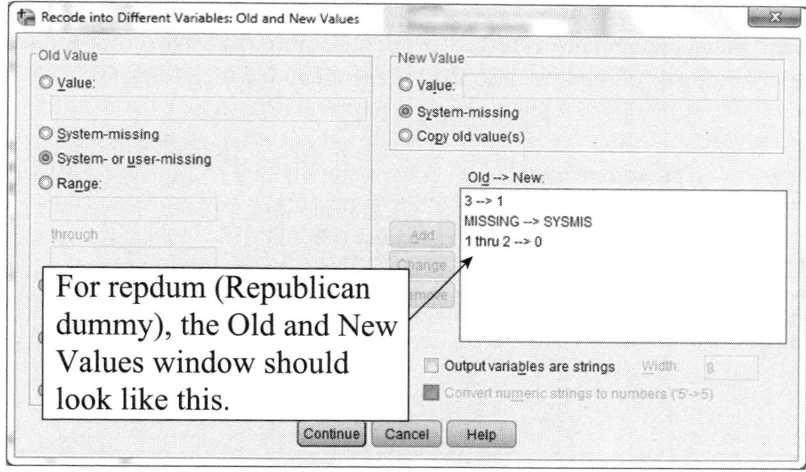

Before analyzing these new variables, it would be prudent to check your work. Run a quick Frequencies on pid_3, demdum, and repdum.

pid_3 Party ID: 3 cats

		Frequency	Percent	Valid Percent	Cumulative Percent
Valid	1 Dem	2046	34.6	34.7	34.7
	2 Ind	2251	38.0	38.2	72.9
	3 Rep	1599	27.0	27.1	100.0
	Total	5896	99.7	100.0	
Missing	System	20	.3		
Total		5916	100.0		

demdum Democrat dummy

		Frequency	Percent	Valid Percent	Cumulative Percent
Valid	.00	3850	65.1	65.3	65.3
	1.00	2046	34.6	34.7	100.0
	Total	5896	99.7	100.0	
Missing	System	20	.3		
Total		5916	100.0		

repdum Republican dummy

		Frequency	Percent	Valid Percent	Cumulative Percent
Valid	.00	4297	72.6	72.9	72.9
	1.00	1599	27.0	27.1	100.0
	Total	5896	99.7	100.0	
Missing	System	20	.3		
Total		5916	100.0		

According to the distribution of pid_3, NES2012 has 2,046 Democrats and 1,599 Republicans. According to the distribution of demdum, 2,046 respondents are coded 1 on the Democrat dummy. And according to the distribution of repdum, 1,599 respondents are coded 1 on the Republican dummy. The recodes check out.

Now we are ready to run a multiple regression analysis of Obama_therm, using female, demdum, and repdum as independent variables. Click Analyze → Regression → Linear. The variable Obama_therm should still be in the Dependent panel and female in the Independent(s) panel, so leave it in place. Click both of the partisanship dummies, demdum and repdum, into the Independent(s) panel. Click OK.

Model Summary

Model	R	R Square	Adjusted R Square	Std. Error of the Estimate
1	.654[a]	.428	.427	25.983

a. Predictors: (Constant), repdum Republican dummy, female Female dummy, demdum Democrat dummy

Coefficients[a]

Model		Unstandardized Coefficients		Standardized Coefficients	t	Sig.
		B	Std. Error	Beta		
1	(Constant)	52.021	.662		78.610	.000
	female Female dummy	2.897	.706	.042	4.102	.000
	demdum Democrat dummy	29.489	.828	.410	35.597	.000
	repdum Republican dummy	-27.215	.884	-.353	-30.795	.000

a. Dependent Variable: Obama_therm Obama Rating

The regression equation is as follows (to enhance readability, we will round to two decimals and shorten the variable names to "Female," "Democrat," and "Republican"):

Obama thermometer rating = 52.02 + 2.90*Female + 29.49*Democrat – 27.22*Republican.

First, get oriented by using the constant, 52.02, as a point of reference. Again, because this value estimates the dependent variable when all the independent variables are 0, 52.02 is the mean Obama rating for males who are Independents. Why so? Because all the dummies are switched to 0: Female is 0 (that's the "male" part of the intercept) and both the Democrat dummy and the Republican dummy are 0 (that's the "Independent" part of the intercept). The regression coefficient on Female tells us how much to adjust the "male" part of the intercept, controlling for partisanship. The regression coefficients on the partisanship dummies tell us how much to adjust the "independent" part of the intercept, controlling for gender. Thus, compared with Independents, Democrats average almost 30 degrees higher—and Republicans score more than 27 degrees lower—on the Obama thermometer. The partisan coefficients are large and statistically significant, with huge *t*-ratios and miniscule *P*-values. What about the effect of gender? The coefficient on Female, 2.90, tells us that women, on average, score about 3 degrees higher on the Obama scale, controlling for partisanship. This effect trumps the null hypothesis ($t = 4.102$ with *P*-value = .000). In the earlier regression, using the female dummy alone, we found a gender difference of nearly 6 degrees. That regression, of course, didn't account for the fact that women are more likely than men to be Democrats. After taking party differences into account, the gender difference weakens to about 3 degrees, although it remains statistically significant.

Overall, however, the model performs fairly well. The adjusted *R*-square value of .427 tells us that all the independent variables, taken together, account for about 43 percent of the variation in the dependent variable. Before going on to the next section, you may want to exercise your new skills by creating new dummies and further expanding the model. In any event, before proceeding be sure to save the dataset.

INTERACTION EFFECTS IN MULTIPLE REGRESSION

Multiple regression is a linear and additive technique. It assumes a linear relationship between the independent variables and the dependent variable. It also assumes that the effect of one independent variable on the dependent variable is the same for all values of the other independent variables in the model. In the regression we just estimated, for example, multiple regression assumed that the effect of being female is the same for all values of partisanship—that Democratic females are about 3 degrees warmer toward Barack Obama than are Democratic males and that Republican females and Independent females are also 3 degrees warmer than are their male counterparts. This assumption works fine for additive relationships. However, if interaction is taking place—if, for example, the gap between male and female ratings is significantly larger among Republicans than among Democrats or Independents—then multiple regression will not capture this effect. Before researchers model interaction effects by using multiple regression, they have usually performed preliminary analyses that suggest such effects are occurring in the data.

Consider an interesting theory in American public opinion. According to this perspective, which we will call the "polarization perspective," political disagreements are often more intense among people who are interested in and knowledgeable about public affairs than they are among people who are disengaged or who lack political knowledge.[1]

For example, it seems reasonable to hypothesize that individuals who oppose the legalization of marijuana would rate conservatives more highly than those who support legalization. So if we were to compare ratings on a conservative feeling thermometer for anti-pot and pro-pot respondents, we should find a higher mean among the anti-pot group. According to the polarization perspective, however, this relationship will be weaker for people with low political knowledge than for people with higher political knowledge. Among people with lower political knowledge, the mean difference in conservative ratings may be more modest, with legalization opponents giving conservatives somewhat higher average ratings than do legalization supporters. As political knowledge increases, however, this mean difference should increase, reflecting greater polarization between the anti- and pro-pot camps. Thus, the strength of the relationship between marijuana opinions and evaluations of conservatives will depend on the level of political knowledge.

The NES2012 dataset contains ftgr_cons, which records respondents' feeling thermometer ratings of "conservatives." Another variable, pot_legal3, is a 3-point gauge of respondents' legalization attitudes, coded 0 ("Favor"), 1 ("Middle"), and 2 ("Oppose"). A third variable, preknow3, measures each respondent's political knowledge by three values: 0 ("Low"), 1 ("Mid"), or 2 ("High"). A preliminary analysis will reveal whether the polarization perspective has merit. Following the methods covered in Chapter 5, we can obtain the results of a mean comparison analysis of the ftgr_cons–pot_legal3 relationship, controlling for preknow3:

ftgr_cons POST: Feeling thermometer: CONSERVATIVES

preknow3 Pol Knowledge	pot_legal3 Legalize Marijuana?	Mean	N
0 Low	0 Favor	49.28	485
	1 Middle	50.69	376
	2 Oppose	58.82	462
	Total	53.01	1323
1 Mid	0 Favor	47.91	742
	1 Middle	55.27	439
	2 Oppose	63.96	693
	Total	55.57	1874
2 High	0 Favor	44.42	877
	1 Middle	51.83	523
	2 Oppose	67.88	775
	Total	54.56	2174
Total	0 Favor	46.77	2104
	1 Middle	52.64	1338
	2 Oppose	64.31	1929
	Total	54.53	5371

In the way that the table is set up, we would assess the effect of the legalization attitudes variable, at each level of political knowledge, by reading down the column at each value of the control variable, preknow3. Examine the low-knowledge column. As we move from "Favor" to "Oppose," do mean conservative ratings increase? Yes, they do. Conservatives are rated at 49.28 degrees among pro-legalization respondents, 50.69 among those taking the middle position, and 58.82 among anti-legalization respondents. Top to bottom, this is a bit less than a 10-degree increase. The relationship is substantially stronger, however, at medium and high levels of political knowledge. For people with "Mid" knowledge, conservative ratings rise from 47.91 to 63.96, a 16-point increase. And the relationship is stronger still for individuals at the highest knowledge level, for whom the data show about a 23-point difference in ratings of conservatives, from 44.42 at the "Favor" end to 67.88 at the "Oppose" end. So, it looks like the ftr_cons–pot_legal3 relationship does indeed strengthen as political knowledge increases. How would we use regression analysis to estimate the size and statistical significance of these relationships?

We would begin building the model in a familiar way, by estimating the effects of each independent variable, pot_legal3 and preknow3, on the dependent variable, ratings of conservatives (ftgr_cons):

$$\text{Conservative rating} = a + b_1\text{*pot\_legal3} + b_2\text{*preknow3}$$

This is a simple additive model. The constant, a, estimates ftgr_cons for respondents who have a value of 0 on both independent variables—pro-legalization respondents who have low political knowledge. The parameter, b_1, estimates the effect of each unit increase in pot_legal3, from 0 to 2. The parameter, b_2, tells us the effect of each unit increase in preknow3, from 0 to 2.

Think about why the simple additive model does not adequately represent the complex relationships we discovered in the mean comparison analysis. For low-knowledge respondents, for whom preknow3 is equal to 0, the b_2*preknow3 term drops out, so the model reduces to:

$$\text{Conservative rating} = a + b_1\text{*pot\_legal3}$$

Our previous analysis revealed that, for low-knowledge people, conservative ratings increase from 49.28 (among pro-legalization respondents) to 58.82 (among anti-legalization respondents), about a 10-point effect. Based on those results, we know that the constant, a, will be equal to about 50 and that the coefficient, b_1, will be about 5. (Regression will linearize the 10-point distance, dividing it in half for each increment of pot_legal3.)

Now consider how the simple model would estimate the effect of pot_legal3 for medium-knowledge respondents, for whom preknow3 is equal to 1:

$$\text{Conservative rating} = a + b_1\text{*pot\_legal3} + b_2\text{*}1$$

which is the same as

$$\text{Conservative rating} = (a + b_2) + b_1\text{*pot\_legal3}$$

The coefficient, b_2, adjusts the constant. If b_2 is positive, we can say that higher-knowledge people give conservatives higher ratings, on average, than do lower-knowledge people. A negative sign on b_2 will mean that higher-knowledge people give conservatives lower average ratings than do lower-knowledge people. That's fine. But notice that, in the simple additive model, b_1 remains unaffected as knowledge goes up. Yet the mean comparison analysis clearly showed that the effect of pot_legal3 on conservative ratings—estimated by b_1—strengthens as knowledge increases. We need to add an adjustment to the regression, an adjustment that permits b_1 to change as preknow3 increases.

In multiple regression, this adjustment is accomplished by including an interaction variable as an independent variable. To create an interaction variable, you multiply one independent variable by the other independent variable. Consider how we would create an interaction variable for the problem at hand: pot_legal3*preknow3. All respondents who are coded 0 on preknow3 will, of course, have a value of 0 on the interaction variable. As political knowledge increases, however, so will the magnitude of the interaction variable. Let's include this term in the model just discussed and see what it looks like:

$$\text{Conservative rating} = a + b_1\text{*pot\_legal3} + b_2\text{*preknow3} + b_3(\text{pot\_legal3*preknow3})$$

The simple additive model did not permit b_1 to change as knowledge increased. Consider how the interaction term, "pot_legal3*preknow3," remedies this situation. Using medium-knowledge respondents (preknow3 equals 1) to illustrate, the interaction model would be

$$\text{Conservative rating} = a + b_1\text{*pot\_legal3} + b_2(1) + b_3(1\text{*pot\_legal3})$$

which is the same as

$$\text{Conservative rating} = (a + b_2) + (b_1 + b_3)\text{*pot\_legal3}$$

As in the simple model, b_2 tells us by how much to adjust the constant as knowledge increases. The key difference is the role of b_3, which tells us by how much to adjust the *effect* of pot_legal3 as knowledge increases. Because the positive relationship between conservative ratings and pot_legal3 gets stronger as preknow3 increases, we are expecting a positive sign on b_3. The *t*-ratio and *P*-value on b_3 will allow us to test the null hypothesis that the effect of pot_legal3 on the dependent variable is the same at all levels of political knowledge.

Let's work through the research problem and get SPSS to estimate the model for us. First we will use Compute to create an interaction variable. Then we will run Regression to estimate the additive effects and the interaction effect.

USING COMPUTE FOR INTERACTION VARIABLES

Because NES2012 does not have the interaction variable we need for our model, we will use Compute to calculate it. Click Transform → Compute. We will name the interaction variable "interact." Type "interact" in the Target Variable box (Figure 9-3). In the Numeric Expression box, type "pot_legal3*preknow3." Next, click Type & Label. In the Compute Variable: Type and Label window, type "pot_legal3*preknow3" in the Label box. Click Continue, returning to the Compute Variable window.

Before clicking OK and computing the variable, there is one more thing to do. Whenever you create a new variable by multiplying one variable by another (as we are doing), and at least one of the variables can take on

Figure 9-3 Computing an Interaction Variable

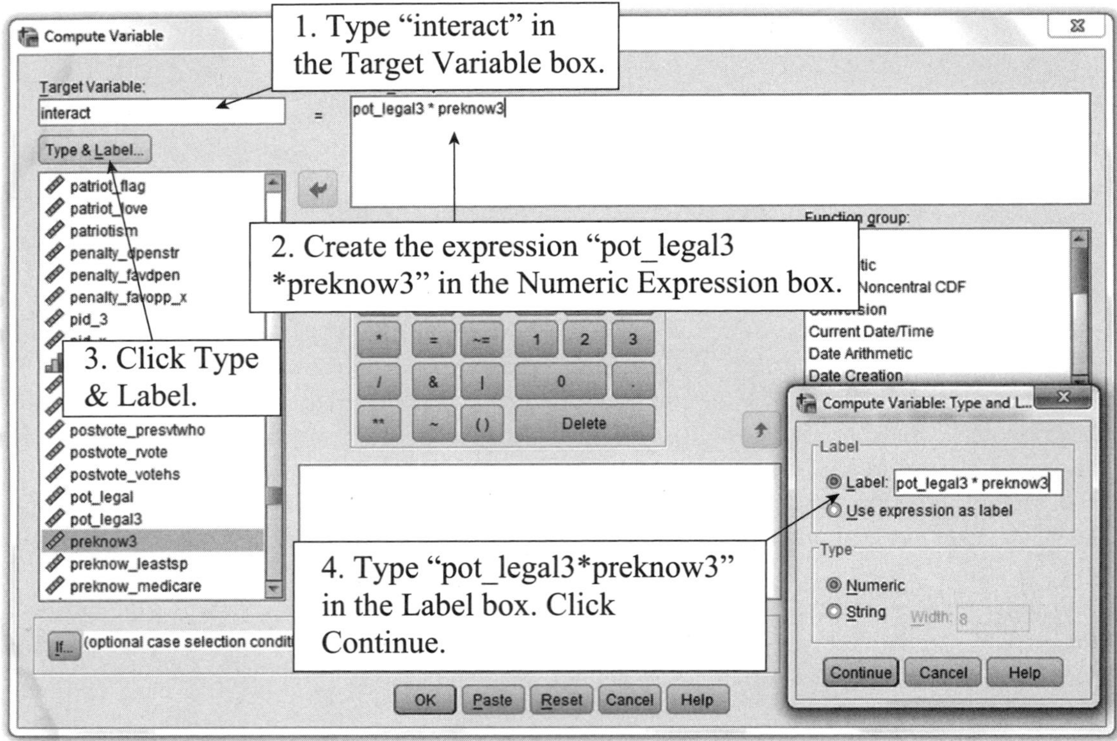

the value of 0 (as is the case here), you need to make sure that the computation is restricted to cases that have nonmissing values on both variables.[2] In the Compute Variable window, click the button labeled "If (optional case selection condition)," as shown in Figure 9-4. The grayed out Compute Variable: If Cases window appears. Select the radio button next to "Include if case satisfies condition." Doing so wakes up the window. Click in the box and type "not missing(pot_legal3) & not missing(preknow3)." Click Continue. Click OK. SPSS creates the interaction variable, interact.

Click Analyze → Regression → Linear. Click Reset to clear the panels for our new analysis. Click ftgr_cons into the Dependent box. Click pot_legal3, preknow3, and interact into the Independent(s) box, as shown in Figure 9-5. Click OK.

Model Summary

Model	R	R Square	Adjusted R Square	Std. Error of the Estimate
1	.330[a]	.109	.108	22.752

a. Predictors: (Constant), interact pot_legal3 * preknow3, preknow3 Pol Knowledge, pot_legal3 Legalize Marijuana?

Coefficients[a]

Model		Unstandardized Coefficients		Standardized Coefficients	t	Sig.
		B	Std. Error	Beta		
1	(Constant)	49.199	.839		58.661	.000
	pot_legal3 Legalize Marijuana?	4.651	.646	.167	7.201	.000
	preknow3 Pol Knowledge	-2.628	.592	-.086	-4.437	.000
	interact pot_legal3 * preknow3	3.488	.458	.208	7.621	.000

a. Dependent Variable: ftgr_cons POST: Feeling thermometer: CONSERVATIVES

Figure 9-4 Restricting Compute to Nonmissing Cases

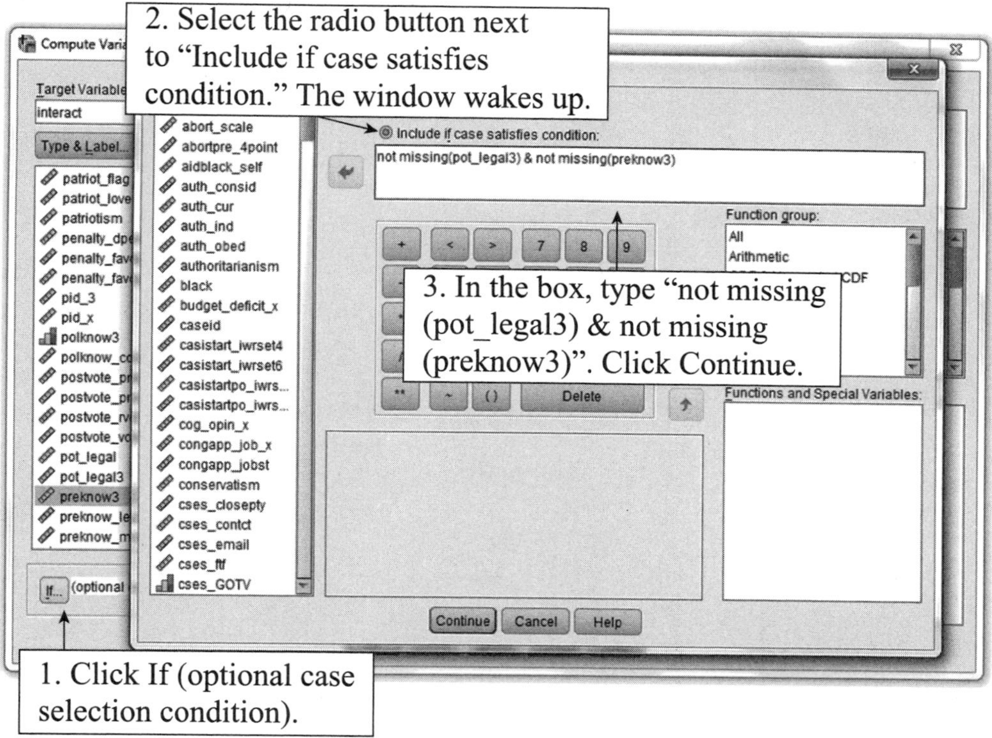
2. Select the radio button next to "Include if case satisfies condition." The window wakes up.
Include if case satisfies condition:
not missing(pot_legal3) & not missing(preknow3)
3. In the box, type "not missing (pot_legal3) & not missing (preknow3)". Click Continue.
Function group:
Functions and Special Variables:
Delete
Continue
Cancel
Help
1. Click If (optional case selection condition).

The regression equation for estimating conservative thermometer ratings (ftgr_cons) is shown below. (To simplify the discussion, coefficients are rounded to one decimal. Also, the interaction term is represented by its computational expression, "pot_legal3*preknow3.")

ftgr_cons = 49.2 + 4.7*pot_legal3 – 2.6*preknow3 + 3.5*(pot_legal3*preknow3)

Consider how this model applies to low-knowledge respondents, that is, when preknow3 = 0. For all these individuals, the third term is equal to zero (that is, –2.6*0 = 0), and the last term is zero as well (pot_legal3*0 = 0). So, for low-knowledge types, the first two terms, "49.2 + 4.7*pot_legal3," do all the predictive work. The constant, 49.2, is the estimated mean of ftgr_cons for those who favor legalization (code 0 on pot_legal3): 49.2 + 4.7*0 = 49.2. What about low-knowledge individuals who take a middle position on the issue? The estimate is: 49.2 + 4.7*1 = 53.9. For those in the "Oppose" camp: 49.2 + 4.7*2 = 58.6. Thus, at low levels of political knowledge, predicted ratings increase by approximately 10 points, from 49 to about 59, just as the mean comparison analysis suggested.

Now consider how this model applies to high-knowledge respondents, that is, when preknow3 = 2. Things get more complicated, but we can still use the simple additive model as a starting point. For example, high-knowledge legalization supporters "start" with the same estimate as their like-minded, low-knowledge counterparts: 49.2 + 4.7*0 = 49.2. In what ways do we need to adjust this initial estimate? Because marijuana supporters ("Favor") are coded 0 on pot_legal3, the interaction term drops out: 3.5*(0*2) = 0. No adjustment is required there. But notice that the negative coefficient on preknow3, –2.6, comes into play: –2.6*2 = –5.2. Thus, compared to their low-knowledge counterparts, high-knowledge/"Favor" respondents are 5.2 degrees chillier toward conservatives: 49.2 – 5.2 = 44.0.

Let's move to the other end of the marijuana issue—high-knowledge marijuana opponents, coded 2 on preknow3 and coded 2 on pot_legal3. To be sure, these respondents "start" where low-knowledge opponents ended: 49.2 + 4.7*2 = 58.6. However, two adjustments must be made. First, adjust the estimate downward to account for the effect of high knowledge: –2.6*2 = –5.2. Second, add the huge positive boost supplied by the interaction effect: 3.5*(2*2) = 14.0. Putting it all together: 58.6 – 5.2 + 14.0 = 67.4. Whereas, by our earlier estimate, the high knowledge/"Favor" group rated conservatives at 44.0, the high knowledge/"Oppose" group rated conservatives at 67.4. These estimates fit the results of the mean comparison analysis quite nicely.

Figure 9-5 Requesting Multiple Regression with an Interaction Variable

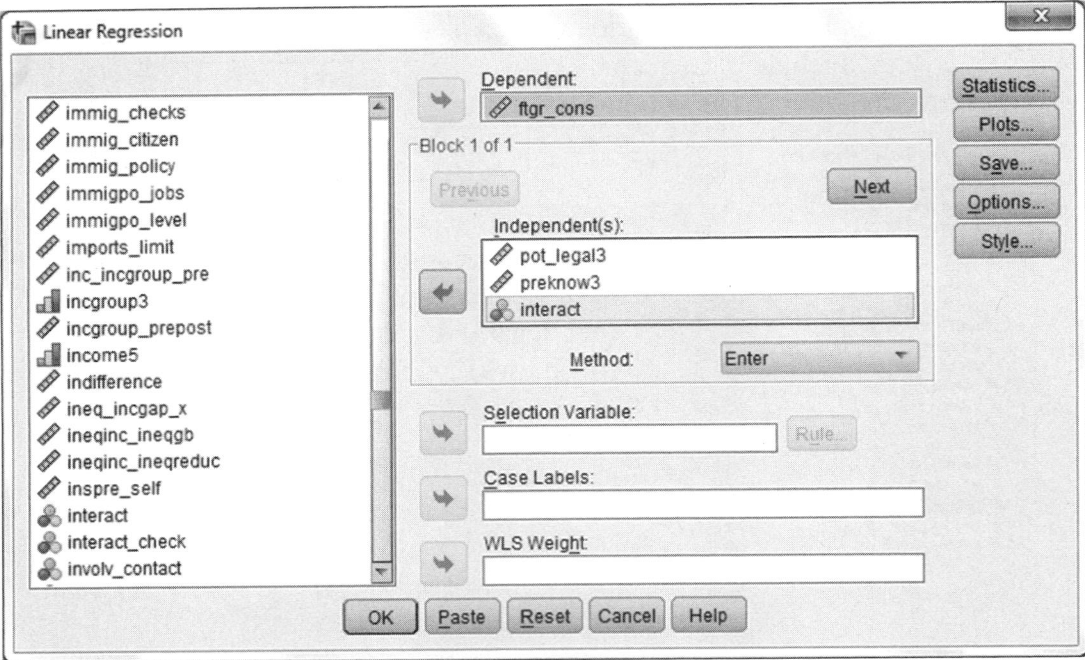

EXERCISES

1. (Dataset: World. Variables: Free_Overall, Gdp_Cap3.) In one of the exercises in Chapter 5, you used World to investigate the relationship between economic development and democracy. In this exercise, you will use multiple regression to reanalyze this relationship, using an interval-level measure of democracy (Free_Overall) and a set of dummy variables that you will create from Gdp_Cap3, a three-category ordinal measure of per-capita gross domestic product (GDP).

   A. World's Gdp_Cap3 is coded 1 for countries with "low" GDP per capita, 2 for countries in the "middle" category, and 3 for countries with "high" GDP per capita. Use Gdp_Cap3 to create two dummy variables, one named gdp_mid and labeled "mid-gdp dummy," and the other named gdp_high and labeled "high-gdp dummy." Follow this recoding scheme:

GDP per capita, 3 categories	Old value (Gdp_Cap3)	New value (gdp_mid)	New value (gdp_high)
Low	1	0	0
Middle	2	1	0
High	3	0	1
	Missing	Missing	Missing

   Check your recoding work by running Frequencies on Gdp_Cap3, gdp_mid, and gdp_high. In the table that follows, write the number of cases (raw frequencies) in the cells that have question marks:

GDP per capita, 3 categories	Frequency	gdp_mid	Frequency	gdp_high	Frequency
Low	53	0	?	0	?
Middle	?	1	?	1	?
High	?				
Valid total	149				

B. Imagine running a regression using gdp_mid and gdp_high to estimate a dependent variable: Dependent variable = Constant + b_1*gdp_mid + b_2*gdp_high. Complete the matching exercise below by drawing a line connecting the desired estimate on the left to the appropriate coefficient (or combination of coefficients) on the right.

Your estimate of the . . .	Would be provided by (the) . . .
mean difference between countries with the lowest GDP and the highest GDP . . .	constant
mean of the dependent variable for the highest GDP countries . . .	b_1
mean of the dependent variable for the lowest GDP countries . . .	constant + b_2
mean difference between the lowest GDP and the middle GDP countries . . .	b_2

C. World contains Free_Overall, a measure of democratic freedoms. The variable Free_Overall measures countries on a scale from 0 (least free) to 100 (most free). Run Regression → Linear, using Free_Overall as the dependent variable and gdp_mid and gdp_high as independent variables. The regression equation for estimating Free_Overall is as follows: (fill in the blanks, putting the constant in the first blank)

Free_Overall = ________________ + ________________*gdp_mid + ________________*gdp_high.

D. Use the regression coefficients to arrive at estimated mean values of Free_Overall for countries at each level of economic development. Write the estimates in the table that follows:

GDP per capita, 3 categories	Estimated mean on democratic freedoms scale
Low	?
Middle	?
High	?

E. Examine the *t*-ratio and *P*-value on gdp_mid. Do the middle GDP per capita countries score significantly higher on Free_Overall than do the lowest GDP per capita countries? (circle one)

Yes No

Explain your answer, making specific reference to the regression results.

____

____

____

____

F. Examine the *t*-ratio and *P*-value on gdp_high. Do the highest-GDP per capita countries score significantly higher on Free_Overall than do the lowest-GDP per capita countries? (circle one)

Yes No

Explain your answer, making specific reference to the regression results.

____

____

____

____

G. According to adjusted *R*-square, GDP per capita accounts for ________ percent of the variation in Free_Overall.

2. (Dataset: World. Variables: Gini10, Hi_Gdp, Democ_regime, Rich_Democ.) As a country becomes richer, do more of its citizens benefit economically? Or do economic resources become distributed inequitably across society? The answer may depend on the type of regime in power. Democratic regimes, which need to appeal broadly for votes, may adopt policies that redistribute wealth. Dictatorships, by contrast, are less concerned with popular accountability, and thus might hoard economic resources among the ruling elite, creating a less equitable distribution of wealth. This explanation suggests a set of interaction relationships. It suggests that, when we compare poorer democracies with richer democracies, richer democracies will have a more equal distribution of wealth. However, it also suggests that, when we compare poorer dictatorships with richer dictatorships, richer dictatorships will have a less equal distribution of wealth. In this exercise you will investigate this set of relationships.

World contains the variable Gini10, which measures the extent to which wealth is equally distributed in society. The variable can take on any value between 0 (equal distribution of wealth) and 100 (unequal distribution of wealth). So, lower values of Gini10 denote less economic inequality and higher values of Gini10 denote greater economic inequality. The dependent variable is Gini10. World also has a dummy variable, Hi_Gdp, that classifies each country as "low GDP" (coded 0) or "high GDP" (coded 1). Hi_Gdp will serve as the measure of the independent variable, level of wealth. Another dummy, Democ_regime, which categorizes each country as a democracy (coded 1 and labeled "yes" on Democ_regime) or dictatorship (coded 0 and labeled "no" on Democ_regime), is the control variable.

A. Exercise a skill you learned in Chapter 5. To see whether interaction is occurring, obtain a multiple line chart of the Gini10–Hi_Gdp–Democ_regime relationships. Click Graphs → Legacy Dialogs → Line → Multiple. Select Other statistic and click Gini10 into the Variable box in the Lines Represent panel. (SPSS will offer to graph the mean of Gini10, which suits your purpose.) The independent variable, Hi_Gdp, will go in the Category Axis box, and the control variable, Democ_regime, will go in the Define Lines by box. Edit the graph for clarity. For example, you will want the line styles to distinguish clearly between dictatorships and democracies. Print the multiple line chart you created.

B. Examine the chart you just created. It would appear that interaction (circle one)

is   is not

occurring in the data.

Explain your reasoning.

____

____

____

____

C. World contains Rich_Democ, an interaction variable computed by the expression Hi_Gdp*Democ_regime. Rich_Democ takes on the value of 1 for high-GDP democracies and the value of 0 for all other countries.

Run Regression → Linear, using Gini10 as the dependent variable and Hi_Gdp, Democ_regime, and Rich_Democ as independent variables. Fill in the following table:

Gini10	Coefficient	t-statistic	P-value
Hi_Gdp	?	?	?
Democ_regime	?	?	?
Rich_Democ	?	?	?
Constant	?		

D. Use the regression to arrive at estimated mean values of Gini10 for low-GDP and high-GDP democracies and dictatorships. Write your estimates in the table that follows:

Country GDP and regime	Estimated mean of Gini10
Low-GDP democracies	?
Low-GDP dictatorships	?
High-GDP democracies	?
High-GDP dictatorships	?

E. Suppose someone claimed that, from the standpoint of statistical significance, low-GDP dictatorships have a significantly more equal distribution of wealth than do low-GDP democracies. This claim is (circle one)

correct. incorrect.

Explain your reasoning, making specific reference to the regression results in part C.

______

______

______

______

______

______

F. Suppose someone claimed that, as GDP increases, wealth becomes significantly more equally distributed in democracies and significantly less equitably distributed in dictatorships. This claim is (circle one)

correct. incorrect.

Explain your reasoning, making specific reference to the regression results in parts C and D.

______

______

______

______

______

______

Before proceeding to the next exercise, be sure to save the World dataset.

3. (Dataset: NES2012. Variables: Prochoice_scale, relig_imp2, preknow3.) One of the examples in this chapter discussed the polarization perspective—the idea that political conflict is more pronounced among people who are more knowledgeable about politics than it is among less knowledgeable people. Perhaps the same pattern applies to the relationship between strength of religious attachment and abortion opinions. That is, it could be that religious commitment has a strong effect on abortion attitudes among politically knowledgeable people but that this effect is weaker for people who have lower knowledge about politics.

   NES2012 contains Prochoice_scale, which ranges from 1 to 65, with higher values denoting a stronger pro-choice position. A dummy variable, relig_imp2, captures the importance of religion: less important (coded 0 and labeled "No") or more important (coded 1 and labeled "Yes"). Just as in this chapter's example, use preknow3, which measures political knowledge by three values: 0 ("Low"), 1 ("Mid"), and 2 ("High"). In this exercise, you will compute an interaction variable. You will then run and interpret a multiple regression that includes the interaction variable you created.

   A. Use Transform → Compute to create a new variable, relig_inter, by multiplying relig_imp2 by preknow3. Make sure to restrict the computation of relig_inter to respondents having nonmissing values on relig_imp2 and preknow3. (If you are unsure how to do this, review this chapter's "Using Compute for Interaction Variables" section.) Think about relig_inter, the interaction variable you computed. A respondent with a weak religious affiliation (coded 0 on relig_imp2) has what value on relig_inter? (circle one)

   a value of 0   a value of 1   a value equal to his or her value on preknow3

   A respondent with a strong religious affiliation (coded 1 on relig_imp2) has what value on relig_inter? (circle one)

   a value of 0   a value of 1   a value equal to his or her value on preknow3

   B. Run regression, using Prochoice_scale as the dependent variable and relig_imp2, preknow3, and relig_inter as the independent variables. Fill in the following table:

Prochoice_scale	Coefficient	*t*-statistic	*P*-value
relig_imp2	?	?	?
preknow3	?	?	?
relig_inter	?	?	?
Constant	?		

   C. Use the regression coefficients to arrive at estimates of the dependent variable, Prochoice_scale, for each value of relig_imp2, by polknow3. Write the estimates in the following table.

	Is religion important to R?	
Political knowledge	No	Yes
Low	?	?
Mid	?	?
High	?	?

   D. Consider all of the evidence you have developed in this exercise. Think about the polarization perspective. Does the analysis support the idea that, as political knowledge increases, religiosity plays a larger role in shaping abortion opinions? Answer yes or no and explain your reasoning, making specific reference to the evidence in parts B and C.

   ____

   ____

____

____

____

____

____

Before proceeding to Exercise 4, be sure to save NES2012.

4. (Dataset: GSS2012. Variables: black, homosex2, partyid.) If one were trying to predict party identification on the basis of opinions on social issues, such as homosexuality, one would expect most African Americans to be Republicans. Indeed, blacks are considerably more likely to oppose homosexuality than are whites. According to the GSS2012 data, for example, over 70 percent of blacks say that homosexuality is "always wrong," compared with 50 percent of whites. Yet on the GSS2012's party identification scale (which ranges from 0 to 6, with higher scores denoting stronger Republican identifications), blacks average around 1, compared with an average of 3 for whites. Why? A plausible idea is that social issues lack *salience* for African Americans. Issues such as homosexuality may matter for whites—whites who think homosexuality is wrong are more likely to be Republicans than are whites who do not think it is wrong—but they have no effect for blacks. According to this argument, blacks who think homosexuality is wrong are no more likely to be Republican than are blacks who do not think homosexuality is wrong. Or so the argument goes. Is this idea correct? More research needs to be done on this question.[3]

   You can model salience with interaction variables. Consider the 7-point party identification scale (partyid) as a dependent variable, ranging from "Strong Democrat" at 0 to "Strong Republican" at 6. Now bring in two independent variables: a dummy variable for race (black, with blacks scored 1 and whites scored 0) and a dummy variable gauging opposition to homosexuality (homosex2, scored 1 if the respondent said homosexuality is "always wrong" and 0 for "not always wrong"). Finally, think about (but don't compute yet) an interaction variable, black_wrong, created by multiplying black and homosex2. Examine the regression model that follows.

$$\text{partyid} = a + b_1{*}\text{black} + b_2{*}\text{homosex2} + b_3{*}\text{black\_wrong}$$

A. The interaction variable, black_wrong, will take on a value of 1 for (check one)

- ❑ blacks who think that homosexuality is "always wrong."
- ❑ blacks who think that homosexuality is "not always wrong."
- ❑ all respondents.

B. To gauge the effect of homosex2 among whites, you would need to compare values of partyid for "not always wrong" whites and "always wrong" whites. Which of the following will estimate partyid for "not always wrong" whites? (check one)

❑ a   ❑ $a + b_1$ ❑ $a + b_2$

Which of the following will estimate partyid for "always wrong" whites? (check one)

❑ a   ❑ $a + b_1$ ❑ $a + b_2$

C. Remember that higher scores on partyid denote stronger Republican identifications. If the salience argument is correct—the idea that heightened opposition to homosexuality leads to stronger Republican leanings among whites but not blacks—then the sign on the coefficient, b_2, will be (circle one)

negative.   positive.   zero.

If the salience argument is correct, then the sign on the coefficient, b_3, will be (circle one)

negative.   positive.   zero.

D. Use Compute to create black_wrong. The multiplicative expression is homosex2*black. (Again, remember to restrict the computation to respondents who have nonmissing values on both variables, homosex2 and black.) Run a regression analysis to obtain estimates for the model. The regression equation for estimating partyid is as follows (fill in the blanks, putting the constant in the first blank):

partyid	Coefficient	*t*-statistic	*P*-value
black	?	?	?
homosex2	?	?	?
black_wrong	?	?	?
Constant	?		

E. Which of the variables in the model have statistically significant effects on partyid? Check all that apply.

❑ black ❑ homosex2 ❑ black_wrong

F. Use the model to estimate partyid for "not always wrong" whites and "always wrong" whites. For "not always wrong" whites you obtain ________________, and for "always wrong" whites you obtain ________________.

G. Use the model to estimate partyid for "not always wrong" blacks and "always wrong" blacks. For "not always wrong" blacks you obtain ________________, and for "always wrong" blacks you obtain ________________.

H. Consider all the evidence you have adduced. Based on the evidence, the salience idea appears to be (circle one)

correct. incorrect.

Explain your answer, making specific reference to the statistical evidence that you developed in this exercise.

____

____

____

____

____

____

____

That concludes the exercises for this chapter. Before exiting SPSS, be sure to save GSS2012.

NOTES

1. See John R. Zaller's influential work, *The Nature and Origins of Mass Opinion* (New York: Cambridge University Press, 1992).
2. In calculating a multiplicative product, SPSS will assign a valid code of 0 to any case that has a missing value on one of the variables and a value of 0 on the other variable. For example, a respondent who has a missing value on pot_legal3 and who has a value of 0 on preknow3 will be assigned a valid, analyzable value on the interaction variable—a value of 0. This respondent should be treated as missing but instead ends up in the analysis. SPSS also returns a valid code of 0 for any expression that divides 0 by a missing value: "Most numeric expressions receive the system-missing value when any one of the values in the expression is missing. Some arithmetic operations involving 0 *can be evaluated* even when the variables have missing values. These operations are: 0 * missing = 0; 0 / missing = 0," from *IBM SPSS Statistics 22 Command Syntax Reference* (Chicago: IBM Corporation, 2013), 95 (emphasis added). Avoid this flaw by restricting the Compute procedure to cases having nonmissing values on both variables.
3. See Quentin Kidd, Herman Diggs, Mehreen Farooq, and Megan Murray, "Black Voters, Black Candidates, and Social Issues: Does Party Identification Matter?," *Social Science Quarterly* 88, no. 1 (March 2007): 165–176.

Logistic Regression*

Watch a screencast of the guided examples in this chapter.
edge.sagepub.com/pollock

Procedures Covered

Analyze → Regression → Binary Logistic

Transform → Compute (Predicted probabilities)

Graphs → Legacy Dialogs → Line (Multiple/Summaries of separate variables)

You now have an array of SPSS skills that enable you to perform the appropriate analysis for just about any situation you will encounter. To analyze the relationship between two categorical variables—variables measured at the nominal or ordinal level—you would enlist Crosstabs. If the dependent variable is an interval-level scale and the independent variable is categorical, then mean comparison analysis would be one way to go. Alternatively, you might create a dummy variable (or variables), specify a linear regression model, and run Regression → Linear to estimate the effects of the categorical variable(s) on the dependent variable. Finally, if both the independent and dependent variables are interval level, then SPSS Correlate or Regression → Linear would be appropriate techniques. There is, however, a common research situation that you are not yet equipped to tackle.

In its most specialized application, logistic regression is designed to analyze the relationship between an interval-level independent variable and a binary dependent variable. A binary variable, as its name suggests, can assume only two values. Binary variables are just like the dummy variables you created and analyzed earlier in this book. Either a case has the attribute or behavior being measured or it does not. Voted/did not vote, married/not married, favor/oppose same-sex marriage, and South/non-South are examples of binary variables.

Consider a binary dependent variable of keen interest to students of political behavior: whether people voted in an election. This variable, of course, has only two values: Either individuals voted (coded 1 on the binary variable) or they did not vote (coded 0). Now think about an interval-level independent variable often linked to turnout, years of education. As measured by the General Social Survey, this variable ranges from 0 (no formal schooling) to 20 (20 years of education). We would expect a positive relationship between the independent and dependent variables. As years of education increase, the probability of voting should increase as well. So people with fewer years of schooling should have a relatively low probability of voting, and this probability should increase with each additional year of education. Now, we certainly can conceptualize this relationship as positive.

*For this chapter you will need access to a full-version SPSS installation that includes the SPSS Regression Models module. The full version of SPSS Base, by itself, does not permit the user to perform logistic regression. The SPSS Student Version does not contain the Regression Models module.

However, for statistical and substantive reasons, we cannot assume that it is linear—that is, we cannot assume that a 1-year change in education occasions a consistent increase in the probability of voting. Garden-variety regression, often called ordinary least squares or OLS regression, assumes a linear relationship between the independent and dependent variables.[1] Thus we cannot use Regression → Linear to analyze the relationship between education and the probability of voting. But as luck and statistics would have it, we can assume a linear relationship between education and the logged odds of voting. Let's put the relationship into logistic regression form and discuss its special properties:

$$\text{Logged odds (voting)} = a + b(\text{years of education})$$

This logistic regression model is quite OLS-like in appearance. Just as in OLS regression, the constant or intercept, a, estimates the dependent variable (in this case, the logged odds of voting) when the independent variable is equal to 0—that is, for people with no formal education. And the logistic regression coefficient, b, will estimate the change in the logged odds of voting for each 1-year increase in education. What is more, the analysis will produce a standard error for b, permitting us to test the null hypothesis that education has no effect on turnout. Finally, SPSS output for logistic regression will provide *R*-square–type measures, giving us an idea of the strength of the relationship between education and the likelihood of voting. In all these ways, logistic regression is comfortably akin to linear regression.

However, logistic regression output is more difficult to interpret than are OLS results. In ordinary regression, the coefficients of interest, the constant (a) and the slope (b), are expressed in actual units of the dependent variable. If we were to use OLS to investigate the relationship between years of education (X) and income in dollars (Y), the regression coefficient on education would communicate the dollar-change in income for each 1-year increase in education. With OLS, what you see is what you get. With logistic regression, by contrast, the coefficients of interest are expressed in terms of the logged odds of the dependent variable. The constant (a) will tell us the logged odds of voting when education is 0, and the regression coefficient (b) will estimate the change in the logged odds for each unit change in education. Logged odds, truth be told, have no intuitive appeal. Thus we often must translate logistic regression results into language that makes better intuitive sense.

USING REGRESSION → BINARY LOGISTIC

Let's run the voting–education analysis and clarify these points. GSS2012 contains voted08, coded 0 for respondents who did not vote in the 2008 election and coded 1 for those who voted.[2] GSS2012 also has educ, which records the number of years of schooling for each respondent. Click Analyze → Regression → Binary Logistic, opening the Logistic Regression window (Figure 10-1). Find voted08 in the variable list and click it into the Dependent box. Click educ into the Covariates box. (In logistic regression, independent variables are often called covariates.) For this run, we will do one additional thing. In the Logistic Regression window, click Options. The Logistic Regression: Options window opens (Figure 10-2). Click the box next to "Iteration history." This option will produce output that helps to illustrate how logistic regression works. Click Continue, returning to the main Logistic Regression window. Click OK.

In typical fashion, SPSS has given us a wealth of information. Eleven tables now populate the Viewer. For the essential purposes of this book, you need to be conversant with only three or four of these tables. Scroll to the bottom of the output, to the table labeled "Variables in the Equation." Here you will find the main results of the voted08–educ analysis (Figure 10-3).

Just as in Regression → Linear, the numbers in the column labeled "B" are the estimates for the constant and the regression coefficient. Plug these estimates into our model:

$$\text{Logged odds (voting)} = -2.068 + .226(\text{educ})$$

What do these coefficients tell us? Again, the constant says that, for people with no education, the estimated logged odds of voting is equal to −2.068. And the logistic regression coefficient on educ says that the logged odds of voting increases by .226 for each 1-year increase in education. So, as expected, as the independent variable increases, the likelihood of voting increases, too. Does education have a statistically significant

Figure 10-1 The Logistic Regression Window

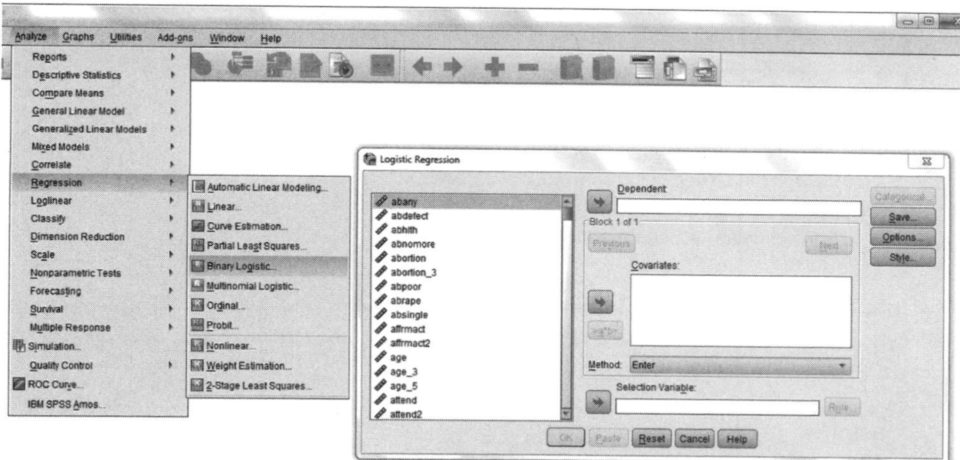

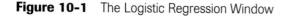

Figure 10-2 Requesting Logistic Regression with Iteration History

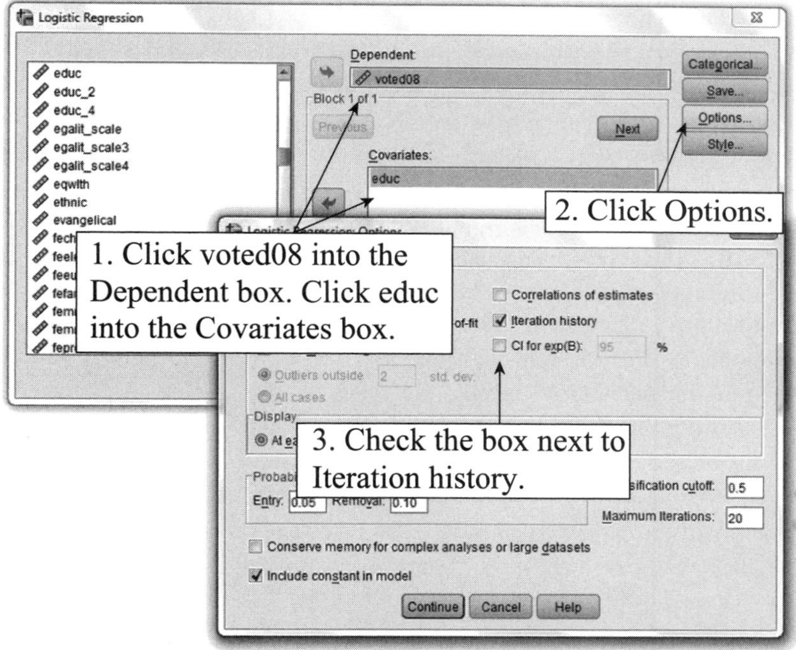
1. Click voted08 into the Dependent box. Click educ into the Covariates box.
2. Click Options.
3. Check the box next to Iteration history.

effect on the likelihood of voting? In OLS regression, SPSS determines statistical significance by calculating a *t*-statistic and an accompanying *P*-value. In logistic regression, SPSS calculates a Wald statistic (which is based on chi-square) and reports a *P*-value for Wald. Interpretation of this *P*-value, displayed in the column labeled "Sig.," is directly analogous to ordinary regression. If the *P*-value is greater than .05, then do not reject the null hypothesis. Conclude that the independent variable does not have a significant effect on the dependent variable. If the *P*-value is less than or equal to .05, then reject the null hypothesis and infer that the independent variable has a significant relationship with the dependent variable. In our output, the *P*-value for educ is .000, so we can conclude that, yes, education has a significant effect on voting turnout.

Return to the logistic regression coefficient, .226, and figure out how to make it more meaningful. Consider the rightmost column of the Variables in the Equation table, the column labeled "Exp(B)." Here SPSS has reported the value 1.254 for the independent variable, educ. Where did this number originate? SPSS obtained this number by raising the natural log base *e* (approximately equal to 2.72) to the power of the logistic regression coefficient, .226. This procedure translates the logged odds regression coefficient into an *odds ratio.* An odds ratio tells us by how much the odds of the dependent variable change for each unit change in the independent

Figure 10-3 Logistic Regression Output with One Independent Variable: Variables in the Equation and Model Summary

Model Summary

Step	-2 Log likelihood	Cox & Snell R Square	Nagelkerke R Square
1	1917.633[a]	.081	.117

a. Estimation terminated at iteration number 4 because parameter estimates changed by less than .001.

Note: Classification Table not shown.

Variables in the Equation

		B	S.E.	Wald	df	Sig.	Exp(B)
Step 1[a]	educ	.226	.020	124.760	1	.000	1.254
	Constant	-2.068	.270	58.517	1	.000	.126

a. Variable(s) entered on step 1: educ.

variable. An odds ratio of less than 1 says that the odds decrease as the independent variable increases (a negative relationship). An odds ratio equal to 1 says that the odds do not change as the independent variable increases (no relationship). And an odds ratio of greater than 1 says that the odds of the dependent variable increase as the independent variable increases (a positive relationship). An odds ratio of 1.254 means that respondents at a given level of education are 1.25 times more likely to have voted than are respondents at the next lower level of education. So people with, say, 10 years of education are 1.25 times more likely to have voted than are people with 9 years of education, people with 14 years are 1.25 times more likely to have voted than people with 13 years, and so on.

The value of Exp(B) is sometimes used to obtain an even more understandable estimate, the *percentage change in the odds* for each unit change in the independent variable. Simple arithmetic accomplishes this task. Subtract 1 from Exp(B) and multiply by 100. In our current example: (1.25 – 1) * 100 = 25. We can now say that each 1-year increment in education increases the odds of voting by 25 percent. As you can see, when the relationship is positive—that is, when the logistic regression coefficient is greater than 0 and the odds ratio is greater than 1—figuring out the percentage change in the odds requires almost no thought. Just subtract 1 from Exp(B) and move the decimal point two places to the right. But be alert for negative relationships, when the odds ratio is less than 1. (In the exercises at the end of this chapter, you will interpret negative relationships.) Suppose, for example, that Exp(B) were equal to .25, communicating a negative relationship between the independent variable and the probability of the dependent variable. The percentage change in the odds would be equal to (.25 – 1) * 100 = –75.0, indicating that a one-unit change in the independent variable decreases the odds of the dependent variable by 75 percent.

How strong is the relationship between years of education and the likelihood of voting? Consider the table labeled "Model Summary," also shown in Figure 10-3. OLS researchers are quite fond of *R*-square, the overall measure of strength that gauges the amount of variation in the dependent variable that is explained by the independent variable(s). For statistical reasons, however, the notion of "explained variation" has no direct analog in logistic regression. Even so, methodologists have proposed various "pseudo *R*-square" measures that gauge the strength of association between the dependent and independent variables, from 0 (no relationship) to 1 (perfect relationship). SPSS reports two of these: the Cox and Snell *R*-square and the Nagelkerke *R*-square. Cox–Snell is the more conservative measure—that is, its maximum achievable value is less than 1. The Nagelkerke measure adjusts for this, and so it generally reports a higher pseudo *R*-square than does Cox–Snell.[3] These two measures are never wildly different, and they do give the researcher a ballpark feel for the strength of the relationship. With values in the range of .081 to .117, you could conclude that education, although related to voting, by itself provides a less-than-complete explanation of it.

One other measure is reported in the Model Summary table, "–2 Log likelihood," equal to 1917.633. In some ways this is the most important measure of strength produced by logistic regression. By itself, however, the magnitude of –2 log likelihood doesn't mean very much. But scroll up a bit, so that you can view the tables labeled "Iteration History" and "Omnibus Tests of Model Coefficients" together on your screen (Figure 10-4).[4]

Figure 10-4 Logistic Regression Output with One Independent Variable: Iteration History and Omnibus Test of Model Coefficients

Iteration History[a,b,c,d]

Iteration		-2 Log likelihood	Coefficients	
			Constant	educ
Step 1	1	1931.010	-1.426	
	2	1917.751	-1.997	
	3	1917.633	-2.067	
	4	1917.633	-2.068	

a. Method: Enter

b. Constant is included in the model.

c. Initial -2 Log Likelihood: 2065.558

d. Estimation terminated at iteration number 4 be[cause] parameter estimates changed by less than .00[1].

This final-step "–2 Log likelihood" tells us how well we can predict voting *with* using education as a predictive tool.

This "Initial –2 Log likelihood" tells us how well we can predict voting *without* using education as a predictive tool.

Omnibus Tests of Model Coefficients

		Chi-square	df	Sig.
Step 1	Step	147.925	1	.000
	Block	147.925	1	.000
	Model	147.925	1	

This Chi-square statistic is the difference between the initial log likelihood and the final-step log likelihood.

Model Summary

Step	-2 Log likelihood	Cox & Snell R Square	Nagelkerke R Square
1	1917.633[a]	.081	.117

a. Estimation terminated at iteration number 4 because parameter estimates changed by less than .001.

In figuring out the most accurate estimates for the model's coefficients, logistic regression uses a technique called maximum likelihood estimation (MLE). When it begins the analysis, MLE finds out how well it can predict the observed values of the dependent variable without using the independent variable as a predictive tool. So MLE first determined how accurately it could predict whether individuals voted by not knowing how much education they have. The number labeled "Initial –2 Log Likelihood" (equal to 2065.558 and found beneath the Iteration History table) summarizes this "know-nothing" prediction. MLE then brings the independent variable into its calculations, running the analysis again—and again and again—to find the best possible predictive fit between years of education and the likelihood of voting. According to the Iteration History table, SPSS ran through four iterations, finally deciding that it had maximized its ability to predict voting by using education as a predictive instrument. This final-step log likelihood, 1917.633, is recorded in the Iteration History table and it also appears in the Model Summary table. This final number represents the "know something" model—that is, it summarizes how well we can predict voting by knowing education.

The amount of explanatory leverage gained by including education as a predictor is determined by subtracting the final-step –2 log likelihood (1917.633) from the initial –2 log likelihood (2065.558). If you performed this calculation by hand, you would end up with 147.925, which appears in the Omnibus Tests of Model Coefficients table next to "Model." This number, which could be succinctly labeled "Model chi-square," is a chi-square test statistic. In the "Sig." column of the Omnibus Tests of Model Coefficients table, SPSS has reported a *P*-value of .000 for this chi-square statistic. Conclusion: Compared with how well we can predict voting without knowing education, including education as a predictor significantly enhances the performance of the model.

By now you are aware of the interpretive challenges presented by logistic regression analysis. In running good old Regression → Linear, you had a mere handful of statistics to report and discuss: the constant, the regression coefficient(s) and accompanying *P*-value(s), and adjusted *R*-square. That's about it. With Regression → Binary Logistic, there are more statistics to record and interpret. Below is a tabular summary of the results of the voted08–educ analysis. You could use this tabular format to report the results of any logistic regressions you perform:

Model estimates and model summary: Logged odds (voting) = a + b(educ)				
Model estimates	Coefficient	Significance	Exp(B)*	Percentage change in odds
Constant	−2.068			
Education	.226	.000	1.254	25.4
Model summary	Value	Significance		
Chi-square**	147.925	.000		
Cox–Snell *R*-square	.081			
Nagelkerke *R*-square	.117			

*Alternatively, this column could be labeled "Odds ratio."

**Alternatively, this row could be labeled "Change in −2 log likelihood."

LOGISTIC REGRESSION WITH MULTIPLE INDEPENDENT VARIABLES

The act of voting might seem simple, but we know that it isn't. Certainly, education is not the only characteristic that shapes the individual's decision whether to vote or to stay home. Indeed, we have just seen that years of schooling, although clearly an important predictor of turnout, returned so-so pseudo–*R*-square statistics, indicating that other factors might also contribute to the explanation. Age, race, marital status, strength of partisanship, political efficacy—all these variables are known predictors of turnout. What is more, education might itself be related to other independent variables of interest, such as age or race. Thus you might reasonably want to know the partial effect of education on turnout, controlling for the effects of these other independent variables. When performing OLS regression, you can enter multiple independent variables into the model and estimate the partial effects of each one on the dependent variable. Logistic regression, like OLS regression, can accommodate multiple predictors of a binary dependent variable. Consider this logistic regression model:

$$\text{Logged odds (voting)} = a + b_1(\text{educ}) + b_2(\text{age})$$

Again we are in an OLS-like environment. As before, educ measures number of years of formal education. The variable age measures each respondent's age in years, from 18 to 89. From a substantive standpoint, we would again expect b_1, the coefficient on educ, to be positive: As education increases, so too should the logged odds of voting. We also know that older people are more likely to vote than are younger people. Thus we should find a positive sign on b_2, the coefficient on age. Just as in OLS, b_1 will estimate the effect of education on voting, controlling for age, and b_2 will estimate the effect of age on the dependent variable, controlling for the effect of education. Finally, the various measures of strength—Cox–Snell, Nagelkerke, model chi-square—will give us an idea of how well both independent variables explain turnout.

Let's see what happens when we add age to our model. Click Analyze → Regression → Binary Logistic. Everything is still in place from our previous run: voted08 is in the Dependent box and educ is in the Covariates box. Now locate age in the variable list and click it into the Covariates box. Click OK to run the analysis. Now scroll to the bottom of the output and view the results displayed in the Variables in the Equation and Model Summary tables.

Model Summary

Step	-2 Log likelihood	Cox & Snell R Square	Nagelkerke R Square
1	1768.617[a]	.153	.221

a. Estimation terminated at iteration number 5 because parameter estimates changed by less than .001.

Variables in the Equation

		B	S.E.	Wald	df	Sig.	Exp(B)
Step 1[a]	educ	.271	.022	153.677	1	.000	1.312
	age	.043	.004	121.614	1	.000	1.044
	Constant	-4.628	.371	155.917	1	.000	.010

a. Variable(s) entered on step 1: educ, age.

Plug these estimates into our model:

$$\text{Logged odds (voting)} = -4.628 + .271(\text{educ}) + .043(\text{age})$$

Interpretation of these coefficients follows a straightforward multiple regression protocol. The coefficient on educ, .271, tells us that, controlling for age, each additional year of education increases the logged odds of voting by .271. And notice that, controlling for education, age is positively related to the likelihood of voting. Each 1-year increase in age produces an increase of .043 in the logged odds of voting. According to Wald and accompanying *P*-values, each independent variable is significantly related to the dependent variable.

Now consider SPSS's helpful translations of the coefficients, from logged odds to odds ratios, which are displayed in the "Exp(B)" column. Interestingly, after controlling for age, the effect of education is somewhat stronger than its uncontrolled effect, which we analyzed earlier. Taking respondents' age differences into account, we find that each additional year of schooling increases the odds ratio by 1.312 and boosts the odds of voting by 31.2 percent: (1.312 – 1) * 100 = 31.2.[5] For age, too, the value of Exp(B), 1.044, is greater than 1, again communicating the positive relationship between age and the likelihood of voting. If you were to compare two individuals having the same number of years of education but who differed by 1 year in age, the older person would be 1.044 times more likely to vote than the younger person. Translating 1.044 into a percentage change in the odds: (1.044 – 1) * 100 = 4.4. Conclusion: Each additional year in age increases the odds of voting by 4.4 percent.[6]

According to Cox–Snell (.153) and Nagelkerke (.221), adding age to the model increased its explanatory power, at least when compared with the simple analysis using education as the sole predictor. The value of –2 log likelihood, 1768.617, is best viewed through the lens of the chi-square test, which you will find by scrolling up to the tables labeled "Omnibus Tests of Model Coefficients" and "Iteration History."

Iteration History[a,b,c,d]

Iteration		-2 Log likelihood	Coefficients		
			Constant	educ	age
Step 1	1	1805.386	-2.968	.182	.028
	2	1769.635	-4.333	.255	.041
	3	1768.618	-4.618	.271	.043
	4	1768.617	-4.628	.271	.043
	5	1768.617	-4.628	.271	.043

a. Method: Enter

b. Constant is included in the model.

c. Initial -2 Log Likelihood: 2058.528

d. Estimation terminated at iteration number 5 because parameter estimates changed by less than .001.

Omnibus Tests of Model Coefficients

		Chi-square	df	Sig.
Step 1	Step	289.911	2	.000
	Block	289.911	2	.000
	Model	289.911	2	.000

MLE's initial know-nothing model—estimating the likelihood of voting without using education or age as predictors—returned a –2 log likelihood of 2058.528. After bringing the independent variables into play and running through five iterations, MLE settled on a –2 log likelihood of 1768.617, an improvement of 289.911. This value, which is a chi-square test statistic, is statistically significant ("Sig." = .000). This tells us that, compared with the know-nothing model, both independent variables significantly improve our ability to predict the likelihood of voting.

WORKING WITH PREDICTED PROBABILITIES: MODELS WITH ONE INDEPENDENT VARIABLE

You now know how to perform basic logistic regression analysis, and you know how to interpret the logistic regression coefficient in terms of an odds ratio and in terms of a percentage change in the odds. No doubt, odds ratios are easier to comprehend than are logged odds. And percentage change in the odds seems more understandable still. Not surprisingly, most researchers prefer to think in terms of probabilities. One might reasonably ask, "What is the effect of a 1-year increase in education on the probability of voting?" Inconveniently, with logistic regression the answer is always, "It depends."

In the first analysis we ran, which examined the voting–education relationship, logistic regression assumed that a linear relationship exists between years of education and the logged odds of voting. This linearity assumption permitted us to arrive at an estimated effect that best fits the data. However, the technique also assumed a nonlinear relationship between years of education and the probability of voting. That is, it assumed that for people who lie near the extremes of the independent variable—respondents with either low or high levels of education—a 1-year increase in education will have a weaker effect on the probability of voting than will a 1-year increase for respondents in the middle range of the independent variable. Because people with low education are unlikely to vote, a 1-year change should not have a huge effect on this likelihood. Ditto for people with many years of schooling. They are already quite likely to vote, and a one-unit increase should not greatly enhance this probability. By contrast, in the middle range of the independent variable, education should have its most potent marginal impact, pushing individuals over the decision threshold from "do not vote" to "vote." So the effect of a 1-year change in education is either weaker or stronger, depending on where respondents "are" on the education variable.

In logistic regression models having more than one independent variable, such as the voted08–educ–age analysis, working with probabilities becomes even more problematic. The technique assumes that the independent variables have additive effects on the logged odds of the dependent variable. Thus, for any combination of values of the independent variables, we arrive at an estimated value of the logged odds of the dependent variable by adding up the partial effects of the predictor variables. However, logistic regression also assumes that the independent variables have interactive effects on the probability of the dependent variable. For example, in the case of younger respondents (who have a lower probability of voting), the technique might estimate a large effect of education on the probability of voting. For older respondents (who have a higher probability of voting), logistic regression might find a weaker effect of education on the probability of voting. So the effect of each independent variable on the probability of the dependent variable will depend on the values of the other predictors in the model.

Let's explore these issues one at a time, beginning with the simple model that used education alone to predict voting. Even though we cannot identify a single coefficient that summarizes the effect of education on the probability of voting, we can use SPSS to calculate a predicted probability of voting for respondents at each level of education. How does this work? Recall the logistic regression equation SPSS estimated in our first analysis:

$$\text{Logged odds (voting)} = -2.068 + .226(\text{educ})$$

SPSS would use this logistic regression model to obtain an estimated logged odds of voting for each respondent. It would plug in each respondent's education level, do the math, and calculate an estimated value of the dependent variable, the logged odds of voting. SPSS would then use the following formula to convert the estimated logged odds of voting into a predicted probability of voting:

$$\text{Probability of voting} = \text{Exp}(\text{Logged odds of voting})/(1 + \text{Exp}(\text{Logged odds of voting}))$$

According to this formula, we retrieve the probability of voting by first raising the natural log base *e* to the power of the logged odds of voting. We then divide this number by the quantity one plus *e* raised to the power of the logged odds of voting.[7] Clear as mud.

To get an idea of how SPSS calculates predicted probabilities, let's work through an example. Consider respondents who have a high school education: 12 years of schooling. Using the logistic regression equation obtained in the first guided example, we find the logged odds of voting for this group to be $-2.068 + .226(12) = -2.068 + 2.712 = .644$. What is the predicted probability of voting for people with 12 years of education? It would be $\text{Exp}(.644)/(1 + \text{Exp}(.644)) = 1.904/2.904 \approx .66$. So for respondents with a high school education, the estimated probability of voting is .66. At the user's request, SPSS will follow this procedure to calculate predicted probabilities for individuals at all values of education, and it will save these predicted probabilities as a new variable in the dataset.

Let's run the voted08–educ analysis again and request that SPSS calculate and save the predicted probability of voting for each respondent. Click Analyze → Regression→ Binary Logistic. All the variables are still in place from our previous run. This time, however, we want to use only one independent variable, educ. Select age with the mouse and click it back into the variable list, leaving educ in the Covariates box and voted08 in the Dependent box. Now click the Save button in the Logistic Regression window. This opens the Logistic Regression: Save window (Figure 10-5). In the Predicted Values panel, click the Probabilities box. Click Continue, which returns you to the Logistic Regression window. One more thing. We won't be discussing iteration history on this run, so click Options and uncheck the Iteration history box. Click Continue. You are ready to go. Click OK.

SPSS generates output that is identical (except for the iteration history) to our earlier run. So where are the predicted probabilities that we requested? Because we just ran the analysis, SPSS has taken us to the Viewer. Return to the Variable View of the Data Editor. Scroll to the bottom of the Variable View. As you know, this is where SPSS puts the new variables that you create using Recode or Compute. There you will find a new

Figure 10-5 Requesting Predicted Probabilities

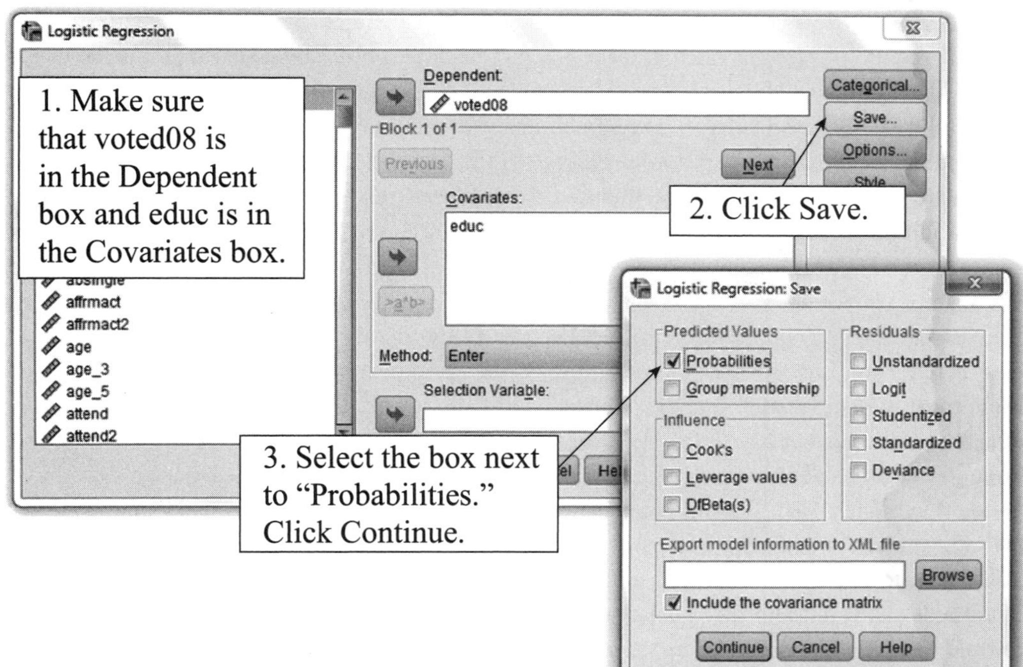

Figure 10-6 Predicted Probability Saved as a New Variable in the Data Editor

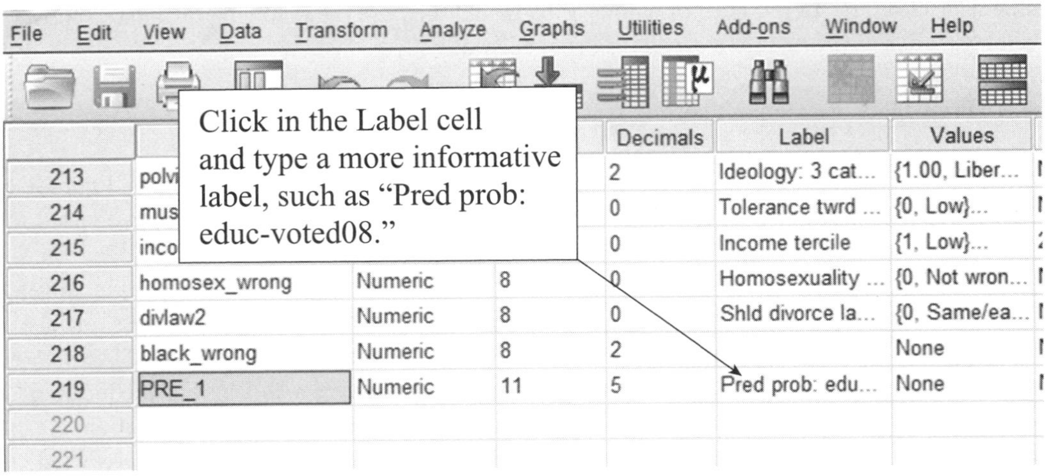

File Edit View Data Transform Analyze Graphs Utilities Add-ons Window Help

Click in the Label cell and type a more informative label, such as "Pred prob: educ-voted08."

				Decimals	Label	Values
213	polvi			2	Ideology: 3 cat...	{1.00, Liber...
214	mus			0	Tolerance twrd ...	{0, Low}...
215	inco			0	Income tercile	{1, Low}...
216	homosex_wrong	Numeric	8	0	Homosexuality ...	{0, Not wron...
217	divlaw2	Numeric	8	0	Shld divorce la...	{0, Same/ea...
218	black_wrong	Numeric	8	2		None
219	PRE_1	Numeric	11	5	Pred prob: edu...	None
220						
221						

variable bearing the name "PRE_1" and the label "Predicted probability" (Figure 10-6). SPSS has performed just as requested. It ran the analysis, generated the logistic regression output, and silently saved a new variable, the predicted probability of voting for each case in the dataset. We will want to have a look at PRE_1. But first we need to give it a more descriptive label. Click in the Label cell and type a more informative variable label, such as "Pred prob: educ-voted08."

In what ways can this new variable, PRE_1, help us to describe changes in the estimated probability of voting as education increases? Remember, SPSS now has a predicted probability of voting for respondents at each value of the education variable, from 0 years to 20 years. So there are two complementary ways to describe the relationship between education and PRE_1, the predicted probability of voting. First, we can perform Analyze → Compare Means → Means, asking SPSS to calculate the mean values of PRE_1 (dependent variable) for each value of educ (independent variable). This would show us by how much the estimated probability of voting increases between groups of respondents having different numbers of years of schooling. Second, we can obtain a line chart of the same information. To obtain a line chart, click Graphs → Legacy Dialogs → Line → Simple and click educ into the "Category Axis" box. Then select "Other statistic," and click PRE_1 into the Line Represents panel. This allows us to visualize the nonlinear relationship between education and the predicted probability of voting.

To you, both of these modes of analysis are old hat, so go ahead and perform the analyses. In the mean comparison results (Figure 10-7), the values of educ appear in ascending order down the left-hand column, and mean predicted probabilities (somewhat distractingly, to 7-decimal-point precision) are reported in the column labeled "Mean." The line chart (Figure 10-8) adds clarity and elegance to the relationship. To get a feel for what is going on, scroll back and forth between the tabular analysis and the graphic output. What happens to the predicted probability of voting as education increases? Notice that, in the lower range of the independent variable, between 0 years and about 6 years, the predicted probabilities are quite low (between .11 and about .33) and these probabilities increase on the order of .03 to .04 for each increment in education. Now shift your focus to the upper reaches of education and note much the same thing. Beginning at about 14 years of schooling, the estimated probability of voting is at or above about .75—a high likelihood of turning out—and so increments in this range have weaker effects on the probability of voting. In the middle range, from 7 to 13 years, the probabilities increase at a "faster" marginal rate, and within this range the graphic curve shows its steepest slope.

Although most political researchers like to get a handle on predicted probabilities, as we have just done, there is no agreed-upon format for succinctly summarizing logistic regression results in terms of probabilities. One commonly used approach is to report the so-called full effect of the independent variable on the probability of the dependent variable. The full effect is calculated by subtracting the probability associated with the lowest value of the independent variable from the probability associated with the highest value of the independent variable. According to our Compare Means analysis, the predicted probability of voting for people with no formal schooling is about .11, and the predicted probability for those with 20 years of education is .92. The full effect would be .92 – .11 = .81. So, measured across its full range of observed values, education boosts the probability of voting by .81.

Figure 10-7 Mean Comparison Table for Predicted Probabilities

Report

PRE_1 Pred prob: educ-voted08

educ Highest Year Of School	Mean	N
0 None	.1122621	7
1 1st grade	.1368860	2
2 2nd grade	.1659016	3
3 3rd grade	.1996450	6
4 4th grade	.2382909	11
5 5th grade	.2817839	4
6 6th grade	.3297782	34
7 7th grade	.3816039	5
8 8th grade	.4362724	38
9 9th grade	.4925350	48
10 10th grade	.5489873	59
11 11th grade	.6042061	103
12 12th grade	.6568896	528
13 1 yr coll	.7059731	165
14 2 years	.7506998	262
15 3 years	.7906404	106
16 4 years	.8256681	317
17 5 years	.8559034	82
18 6 years	.8816466	85
19 7 years	.9033102	39
20 8 years	.9213621	70
Total	.7117605	1974

Notice that, between 9 and 10 years of education, the predicted probability switches from less than .5 to greater than .5.

Figure 10-8 Line Chart for Predicted Probabilities

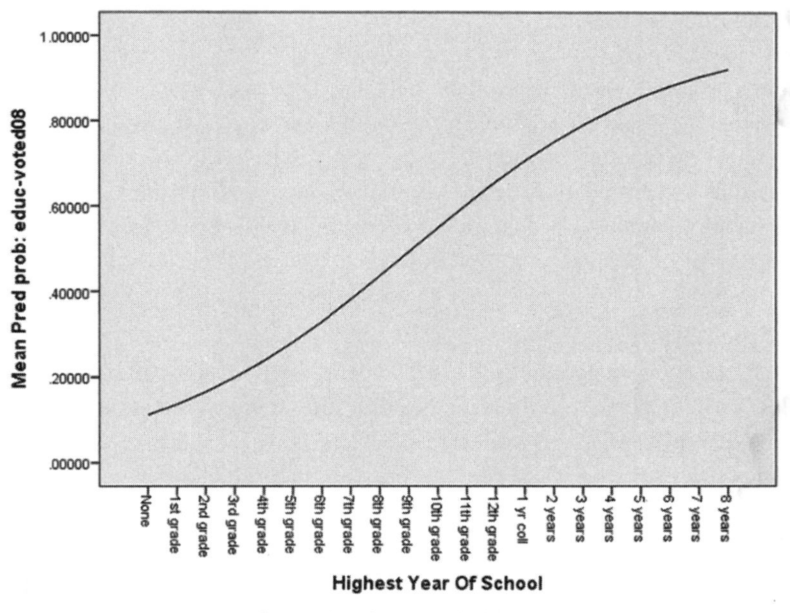

Another way of summarizing a relationship in terms of probabilities is to report the interval of the independent variable that has the biggest impact on the probability of the dependent variable. Suppose that you had to pick the 1-year increment in education that has the largest impact on the probability of voting. What would that increment be? Study the output and think about the phenomenon you are analyzing. Remember that voting is an up or down decision. A person either decides to vote or decides not to vote. But between which two values of education does a "vote" decision become more likely than a "do not vote" decision? You may have noticed that, between 9 years and 10 years, the predicted probabilities increase from .493 to .549, a difference of .056 and the largest marginal increase in the data. And it is between these two values of education that, according to the analysis, the binary decision shifts in favor of voting—from a probability of less than .50 to a probability of greater than .50. So the interval between 9 years and 10 years is the "sweet spot"—the interval with the largest impact on the probability of voting, and the interval in which the predicted probability switches from less than .50 to more than .50.[8]

WORKING WITH PREDICTED PROBABILITIES: MODELS WITH MULTIPLE INDEPENDENT VARIABLES

Saving predicted probabilities using the Logistic Regression: Save option works fine for simple models with one independent variable. By examining these predicted probabilities, you are able to summarize the full effect of the independent variable on the dependent variable. Furthermore, you can describe the interval of the independent variable having the largest impact on the probability of the dependent variable. Of course, SPSS will also gladly save predicted probabilities for logistic regression models having more than one independent variable. With some specialized exceptions, however, these predicted probabilities are not very useful for summarizing the effect of each independent variable on the probability of the dependent variable, controlling for the other independent variables in the model. As noted earlier, although logistic regression assumes that the independent variables have an additive effect on the logged odds of the dependent variable, the technique also assumes that the independent variables have an interactive effect on the probability of the dependent variable. Thus the effect of, say, education on the probability of voting will be different for younger people than for older people. And the effect of age will vary, depending on the level of education being analyzed. How can we summarize these interaction effects?

Researchers have proposed several intuitively accessible ways to represent probabilities.[9] One approach is to report changes in the probability of the dependent variable across the values of a particularly interesting independent variable, while holding all other independent variables constant at their sample-wide means. Thus, one retrieves "marginal effects at the means," or MEMs. In the current example, we might estimate the probability of voting at each value of educ_yrs, from 0 to 20, while holding age constant at its mean. This would allow us to answer the question, "For the 'average' respondent (in terms of age), how does the probability of voting change as education increases?"

A second approach is to report changes in the probability of the dependent variable across the range of an interesting independent variable—and to do so separately, for discrete categories of a another independent variable. Thus, one presents "marginal effects at representative values," or MERs. In the current example, we might estimate the probability of voting at each value of educ_yrs, from 0 to 20, for two different age groups: a young group (26 years old) and an older group (65 years old). This would enable us to answer these questions: "In what ways does education affect the probability of voting for younger people? How do these effects differ from education's effect for older people?"

Marginal Effects at the Means

In the MEMs approach, the analyst examines the effect of each independent variable while holding the other independent variables constant at their sample means. For example, we would ask and answer these questions: "For people of 'average' age, what effect does education have on the probability of voting?" and "For respondents with 'average' levels of education, what effect does age have on the probability of voting?" In this way, we can get an idea of the effect of each variable on individuals who are "average" on all the other variables being studied. Unfortunately, Regression → Binary Logistic will not calculate the predicted probabilities associated with each value of an independent variable while holding the other variables constant at their sample means.[10] That's the bad news. The good news is that the desired probabilities can be obtained using Transform → Compute, and they are readily analyzed using Compare Means.

Here is the logistic regression model that SPSS estimated for the voted08–educ–age relationships:

$$\text{Logged odds (voting)} = -4.628 + .271(\text{educ}) + .043(\text{age})$$

We can enlist this equation for two tasks. First, we can plug in the sample mean of age and calculate the full effect of educ on the probability of voting. Second, we can plug in the sample mean of educ and calculate the full effect of age on the probability of voting. Here we will work through the first task only—figuring out the full effect of education on the probability of voting for people of average age. Before proceeding, of course, we need to obtain the sample mean of age. A quick Descriptives run reveals that age has a mean value of 46.10 years. The following equation would permit us to estimate the logged odds of voting at any value of educ, holding age constant at its mean:

$$\text{Logged odds (voting)} = -4.628 + .271(\text{educ}) + .043(46.1)$$

We have already seen that probabilities may be retrieved from logged odds via this conversion:

$$\text{Probability of voting} = \text{Exp(Logged odds of voting)}/(1 + \text{Exp(Logged odds of voting)})$$

Figure 10-9 Computing a Predicted Probability for Different Values of an Independent Variable at the Mean Value of Another Independent Variable

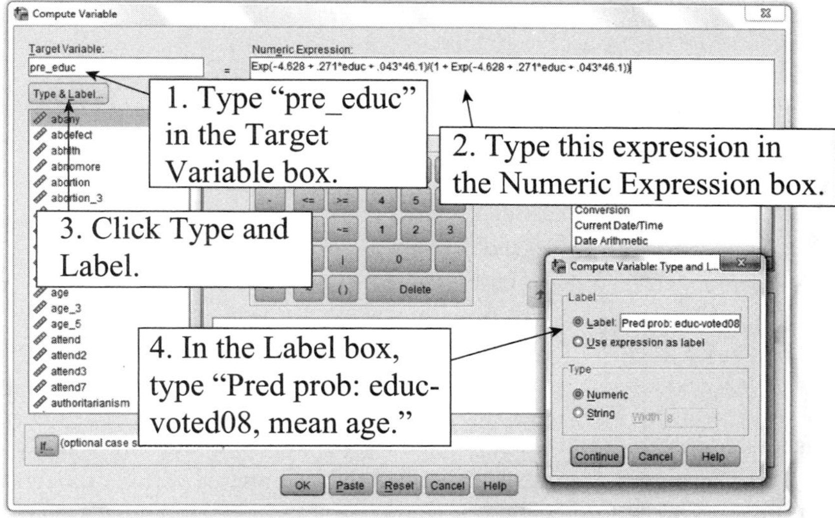

The following equation, therefore, would convert a logged odds of voting into a predicted probability of voting for any plugged-in value of educ, holding age constant at its mean of 46.1:

$$\text{Probability of voting} = \text{Exp}(-4.628 + .271{*}\text{educ} + .043{*}46.1)/$$
$$(1 + \text{Exp}(-4.628 + .271{*}\text{educ} + .043{*}46.1))$$

Of course, we could figure all this out using a hand calculator—first finding the predicted probability of voting for individuals having no formal schooling (educ = 0) and then calculating the predicted probability of people with 20 years of education (educ = 20). By subtracting the first probability (when educ = 0) from the second probability (when educ = 20), we would arrive at the full effect of educ at the mean value of age. But let's ask SPSS to do the work for us. Click Transform → Compute. What do we want SPSS to do? We want it to calculate the predicted probability of voting for respondents at each level of education, holding age constant at its sample mean. Because we are holding age constant but allowing educ to vary, we will name this variable "pre_educ." Type "pre_educ" in the Target Variable box. In the Numeric Expression box, type this expression: "Exp(−4.628 + .271*educ + .043*46.1)/(1 + Exp(−4.628 + .271*educ + .043*46.1))," as shown in Figure 10-9.[11] Click Type & Label. In the Label box, give pre_educ the descriptive label "Pred prob: educ-voted08, mean age." Click OK. SPSS computes a new variable, pre_educ, and enters this variable into the dataset.

Finally we have the estimates that permit us to examine the effect of education on the probability of voting for respondents of average age. Click Analyze → Compare Means → Means. Click our newly computed variable, pre_educ, into the Dependent List, and click educ into the Independent List. Click OK.

pre_educ Pred prob: educ-voted08, mean age

educ Highest Year Of School	Mean	N
0 None	.0663	7
1 1st grade	.0851	2
2 2nd grade	.1087	3
3 3rd grade	.1379	6
4 4th grade	.1734	11
5 5th grade	.2157	4
6 6th grade	.2651	34
7 7th grade	.3211	5
8 8th grade	.3828	38
9 9th grade	.4485	48
10 10th grade	.5161	59
11 11th grade	.5830	103
12 12th grade	.6471	528
13 1 yr coll	.7063	165
14 2 years	.7592	262
15 3 years	.8052	106
16 4 years	.8443	317
17 5 years	.8767	82
18 6 years	.9031	85
19 7 years	.9244	39
20 8 years	.9413	70
Total	.7105	1974

What is the full effect of education? Notice that people with 0 years of education have a probability of voting equal to about .07 (7 chances in 100 that the individual voted), compared with a probability of about .94 for individuals with 20 years of education (94 chances in 100 that the individual voted). Thus, holding age constant at its sample mean, we find that the full effect of education is equal to .94 − .07 = .87. Note that the largest marginal effect of education, a boost of nearly .07 in the probability of voting, occurs between 9 and 10 years of schooling.

Marginal Effects at Representative Values

The MEMs approach is perhaps the most prevalent methodology for describing predicted probabilities. However, for some research questions, MEMs may prove inadequate. Suppose that, based on a controlled cross-tabulation, we have reason to think that education works differently for younger people than for older people. If we were to estimate and compare the effects of education among two groups of respondents—those who are, say, 26 years of age, and those who are 65 years of age—what would the comparison reveal? Such questions require estimates of marginal effects at representative values, or MERs. Once again, here are the logistic regression estimates for the voted08–educ–age model:

$$\text{Logged odds (voting)} = -4.628 + .271(\text{educ}) + .043(\text{age})$$

In the MEMs method, we used these estimates to compute the probability of voting at each value of education while holding age constant at its sample mean. In the MERs method, we can ask SPSS to compute two estimated probabilities for the effect of education on voting—one while holding age constant at 26 years, and one while holding age constant at 65 years. Consider the two numeric expressions that follow:

Probability of voting, age 26:
pre_26 = Exp(−4.628 + .271*educ + .043*26)/(1 + Exp(−4.628 + .271*educ + .043*26))

Probability of voting, age 65:
pre_65 = Exp(−4.628 + .271*educ + .043*65)/(1 + Exp(−4.628 + .271*educ + .043*65))

The first command will estimate the probability of voting at each value of education, while holding age constant at 26 years. And it asks SPSS to save these predicted probabilities in a new variable, pre_26. The second statement estimates the probability of the dependent variable at each value of education, holding age constant at 65 years, and it too will save a new variable, pre_65. To obtain these estimates, we'll need to make two circuits through Transform → Compute, each requiring a fair amount of typing in the Numeric Expression box—although you may have already figured out a useful shortcut that greatly reduces the keyboard drudgery.[12] Figure 10-10 shows the Compute Variable window for obtaining pre_26. To get pre_65, modify the relevant details of the window: Change the Target Variable name to "pre_65," replace "26" with "65" in the Numeric Expression box, and alter Label to read "Pred prob: educ-voted08, age 65." Go ahead and run the Computes.

Figure 10-10 Computing a Predicted Probability for Different Values of an Independent Variable at a Fixed Value of Another Independent Variable

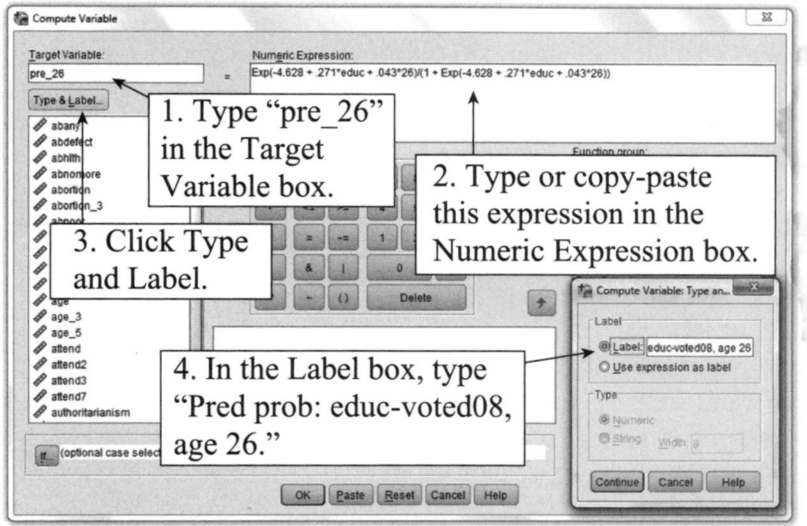

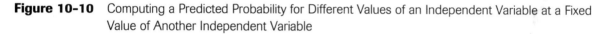

Run Means → Compare Means, putting educ in the Independent List and both pre_26 and pre_65 in the Dependent List. To enhance readability, in Options click Standard Deviation and Number of Cases back into the Statistics list. SPSS will return a bare-bones mean comparison table:

Mean

educ Highest Year Of School	pre_26 Pred prob: educ-voted08, age 26	pre_65 Pred prob: educ-voted08, age 65
0 None	.0290	.1379
1 1st grade	.0377	.1734
2 2nd grade	.0489	.2157
3 3rd grade	.0632	.2650
4 4th grade	.0812	.3210
5 5th grade	.1039	.3827
6 6th grade	.1319	.4484
7 7th grade	.1662	.5160
8 8th grade	.2072	.5830
9 9th grade	.2552	.6470
10 10th grade	.3100	.7062
11 11th grade	.3708	.7591
12 12th grade	.4359	.8052
13 1 yr coll	.5032	.8442
14 2 years	.5705	.8766
15 3 years	.6353	.9031
16 4 years	.6955	.9244
17 5 years	.7497	.9413
18 6 years	.7971	.9546
19 7 years	.8374	.9650
20 8 years	.8710	.9731
Total	.5357	.8341

Consider the dramatically different effects of education for these two age groups. To be sure, the full effect of education is about the same for 26-year-olds (.87 – .03 = .84) and 65-year-olds (.97 – .14 = .83). But the patterns of marginal effects are not the same at all. For younger people with low levels of education (between 0 and 10 years of schooling), the probability of voting is extraordinarily low, in the range of .03–.31. The educational increment with the largest marginal effect—the increment in which the probability of voting switches from less than .50 to more than .50—occurs between 12 and 13 years of schooling. Compare the probability profile of younger respondents—sluggish marginal effects in the lower range of education, a high "switchover" threshold—with the probability profile of older respondents. Does education work the same way as we read down the column labeled "pre_65"? Here the probabilities start at a higher level (about .14) and build quite rapidly, in increments of .04 to .05, crossing the .50 threshold at a low level of education, between 6 and 7 years of schooling.[13]

When you use the MERs method to explore complex relationships, you will want to complement your analyses with appropriate graphic support. Consider Figure 10-11, a multiple line chart that has spent some "erasing" time in the Chart Editor. This chart instantly communicates the remarkably different ways in which education affects turnout for 26-year-olds (dashed line) and 65-year-olds (solid line). With one minor exception, the skills you developed earlier in this book will allow you to obtain an unedited version of this graphic. By using the editing skills you already have—and acquiring additional skills through practice and experimentation—you can create the edited version. Click Graphs → Legacy Dialogs → Line (Figure 10-12). In the Line Chart window, select Multiple. Here is something new: Instead of the default setting, "Summaries for groups of cases," select the radio button next to "Summaries of separate variables," as shown in Figure 10-12. Click Define. The Summaries of Separate Variables window is a reasonably familiar-looking sight (Figure 10-13). The variable whose effects we want to display, educ, goes in the Category Axis box. The two predicted-probability variables, pre_26 and pre_65, go in the Lines Represent panel. SPSS offers to graph mean values of pre_26 and pre_65, which fits our purpose. Nothing more to it. Clicking OK produces the requested graphic result (Figure 10-14). This is a line chart with a lot of potential. Before moving on to the exercises, see what improvements you can make.[14]

Figure 10-11 Edited Multiple Line Chart of Two Logistic Regression Curves

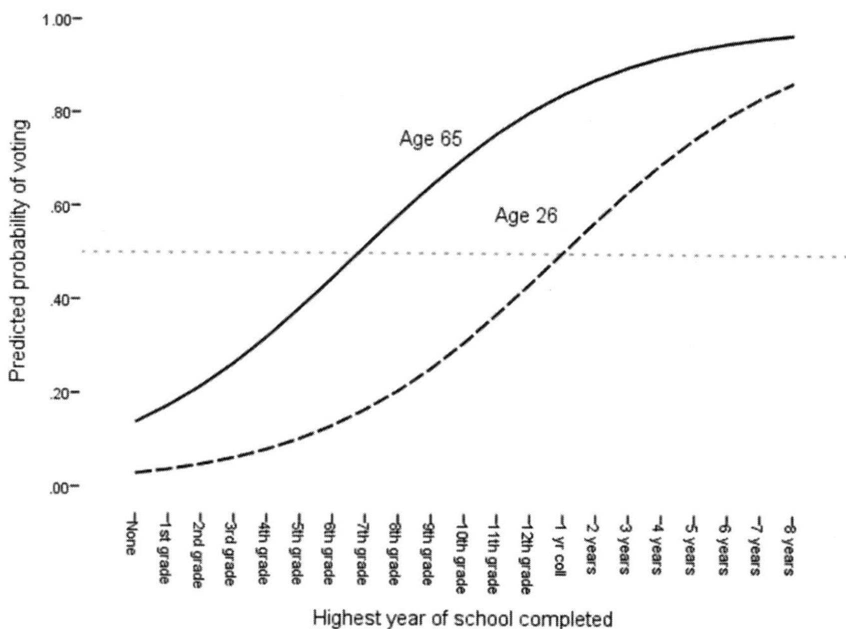

Figure 10-12 Changing the Defaults in the Line Chart Windows

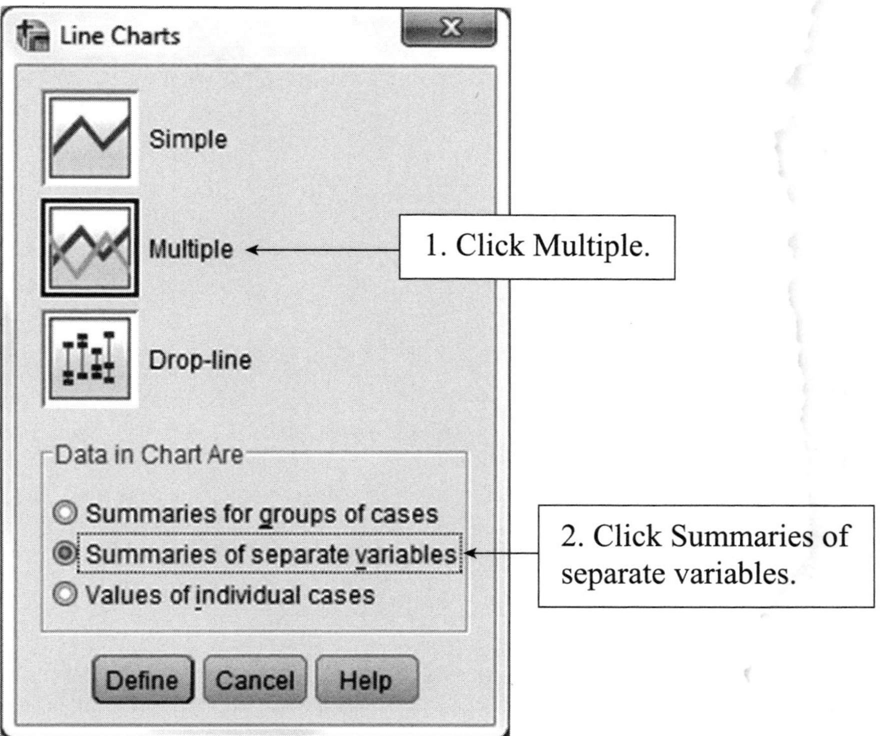

Figure 10-13 Define Multiple Line: Summaries of Separate Variables Window (modified)

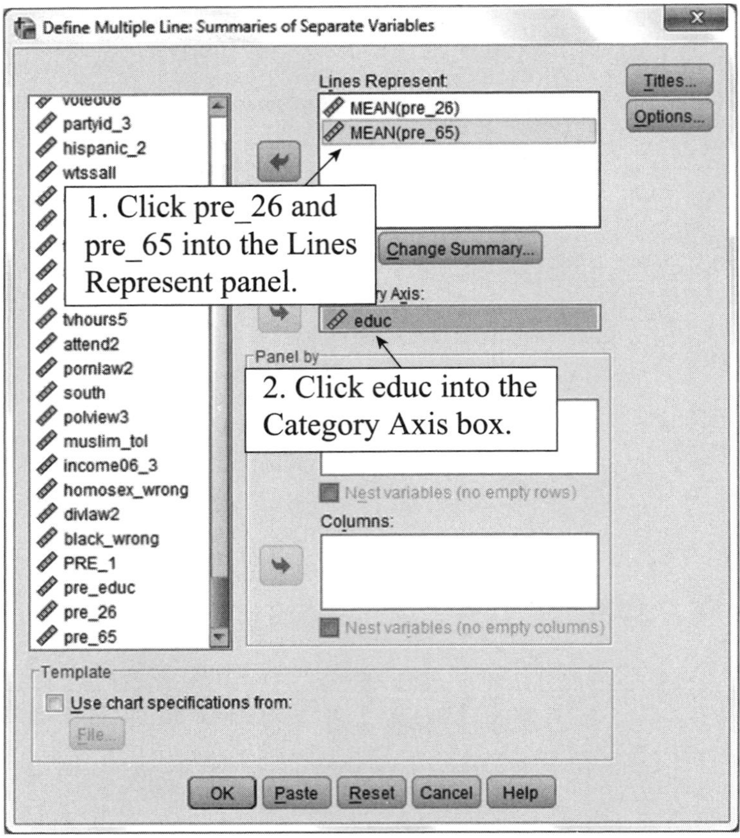

Figure 10-14 Multiple Line Chart of Two Logistic Regression Curves

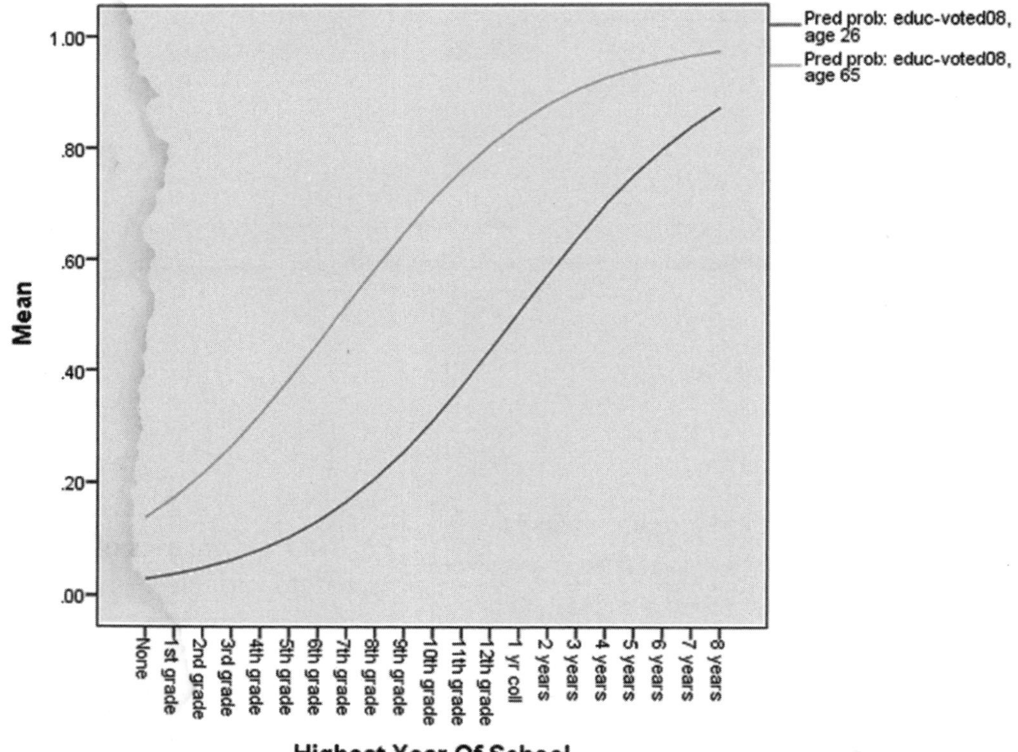

EXERCISES

1. (Dataset: States. Variables: Obama_win12, Relig_high, Gun_scale11.) As you know, presidential elections in the United States take place within an unusual institutional context. Naturally, candidates seek as many votes as they can get, but the real electoral prizes come in winner-take-all, state-sized chunks: The plurality-vote winner in each state receives all the electoral college votes from that state. Cast in logistic regression terms, each state represents a binary outcome—it goes either Democratic or Republican. What variables shape this outcome? As a candidate for the Democratic nomination, Barack Obama pointed toward several plausible variables. During a campaign appearance, Obama suggested that many voters, frustrated by the disappearance of economic opportunities, "cling to guns or religion or antipathy to people who aren't like them or anti-immigrant sentiment or anti-trade sentiment as a way to explain their frustrations." Obama said that these factors helped explain why his electoral support was weaker in certain geographical areas of the country.[15]

   Obama's remarks suggest the following hypothesis: In a comparison of states, those with higher percentages of residents who frequently attend religious services were less likely to have been won by Obama than were states having lower percentages of residents who frequently attend religious services.

   The States dataset contains Obama_win12, a binary variable coded 1 if the state's electoral vote went to Democratic candidate Barack Obama in 2012, and coded 0 if the state went to Republican Mitt Romney. This is the dependent variable. The dataset also has Relig_high, the percentage of state residents who frequently attend religious services. Relig_high is the independent variable. Run Regression → Binary Logistic, clicking Obama_win12 into the Dependent box and clicking Relig_high into the Covariates box. In Options, request iteration history. Click Save. In the Predicted Values panel of the Logistic Regression: Save window, select Probabilities.

   A. The following table contains seven question marks. Fill in the correct value next to each question mark.

Model estimates	Coefficient	Significance
Constant	?	
Relig_high	?	?
Model summary	Value	Significance
Chi-square	?	?
Cox–Snell *R*-square	?	
Nagelkerke *R*-square	?	

   Before proceeding to part B, review the procedure for converting an odds ratio into a percentage change in the odds for negative relationships.

   B. For the variable Relig_high, Exp(B) is equal to (fill in the blank) __________. After converting this number to a percentage change in the odds of an Obama win, you can say that a one-unit increase in Relig_high decreased the odds of an Obama win by __________ percent.

   C. Run Analyze → Compare Means → Means, obtaining mean values of the predicted probability of Obama_win12 (dependent variable, which SPSS saved as PRE_1) for each value of Relig_high (independent variable). Print the mean comparison table. Use the results to answer parts D, E, and F.

   D. For the state having the lowest value on Relig_high, the predicted probability of an Obama win was equal to ____________. For the state having the highest value on Relig_high, the predicted probability of an Obama win was equal to ____________. What is the full effect of Relig_high on the probability of Obama_win12? The full effect is equal to ____________. (*Hint:* Because the probability of an Obama win decreases as Relig_high increases, the full effect will be a negative number.)

   E. A Democratic strategist must decide in which states to concentrate her limited campaign resources. To achieve maximum effect, this strategist should concentrate her campaign on (check one)

   - ❑ a state in which 30 percent of its residents are highly religious.
   - ❑ a state in which 40 percent of its residents are highly religious.
   - ❑ a state in which 50 percent of its residents are highly religious.

F. Explain your reasoning in part E, making specific reference to the evidence in part C.

____

____

____

____

Suppose you want to improve the predictive performance of the Obama_win12–Relig_high model by adding a second independent variable, the Brady campaign's ranking of states' gun laws (Gun_scale11). Higher scores on Gun_scale11 denote more restrictions on firearms ownership. You reason that states having more firearms restrictions were more likely to have been won by Obama than states having fewer restrictions. You also think that the controlled effects of both variables, Relig_high and Gun_scale11, will be statistically significant. However, a critic plausibly suggests that the two independent variables, Relig_high and Gun_scale11, are themselves related—highly religious states will have fewer gun restrictions than will less religious states. This critic argues that only one of the variables, either Relig_high or Gun_scale11, will be significantly related to Obama_win12.

G. Run the Obama_win12 analysis again, using Relig_high and Gun_scale11 as independent variables. Click Save and uncheck Probabilities. In Options, uncheck Iteration history. Refer to the output. For the variable Gun_scale11, Exp(B) is equal to (fill in the blank) ______________. Convert this number to a percentage change in the odds of an Obama win. Controlling for Relig_high, you can say that a one-unit increase in Gun_scale11 decreased the odds of an Obama win by ______________ percent. Controlling for Gun_scale11, a one-unit increase in Relig_high decreased the odds of an Obama win by ______________ percent.

H. Recall the critic's suggestion that only one independent variable, either Relig_high or Gun_scale11, will be significantly related to Obama_win12. Your analysis shows that this critic is (circle one)

correct. incorrect.

I. Explain your answer in H, making specific reference to the logistic regression results you obtained in G.

____

____

____

____

2. (Dataset: World. Variables: Dem_Economist, Frac_Eth, Gdp_10_Thou.) In Chapter 5 you tested this hypothesis: In a comparison of countries, those having lower levels of ethnic heterogeneity will be more likely to be democracies than will those having higher levels of ethnic heterogeneity. This hypothesis says that, as heterogeneity goes up, the probability of democracy goes down. You then reran the analysis, controlling for a measure of countries' economic development, per-capita gross domestic product (GDP). For this independent variable, the relationship is thought to be positive: As economic development increases, so does the likelihood that a country will be democratic. In the current exercise, you will reexamine this set of relationships, using interval-level independent variables and a more powerful method of analysis, logistic regression.

World contains these three variables: Dem_Economist, Frac_Eth, and Gdp_10_Thou. Dem_Economist is coded 1 if the country is a democracy and coded 0 if it is not a democracy. This is the dependent variable. One of the independent variables, Frac_Eth, can vary between 0 (denoting low heterogeneity) and 1 (high heterogeneity). The other independent variable, Gdp_10_Thou, measures per-capita GDP in units of $10,000.

A. Run Regression → Binary Logistic, clicking Dem_Economist into the Dependent box and clicking Frac_Eth and Gdp_10_Thou into the Covariates box. In Options, request iteration history. (For this exercise, you will not be saving predicted probabilities.) Click OK to run the analysis. The following table contains eight question marks. Fill in the correct value next to each question mark.

Model estimates	Coefficient	Significance	Exp(B)
Constant	.103		
Frac_Eth	−2.253	?	?
Gdp_10_Thou	1.644	?	?
Model summary	Value	Significance	
Chi-square	?	?	
Cox–Snell R-square	?		
Nagelkerke R-square	?		

B. Use each value of Exp(B) to calculate a percentage change in the odds. Controlling for Gdp_10_Thou, a one-unit change in Frac_Eth, from low heterogeneity to high heterogeneity, (check one)

- ❑ increases the odds of democracy by about 11 percent.
- ❑ decreases the odds of democracy by about 90 percent.
- ❑ decreases the odds of democracy by about 105 percent.

Controlling for Frac_Eth, each $10,000 increase in per-capita GDP (check one)

- ❑ increases the odds of democracy by about 64 percent.
- ❑ increases the odds of democracy by about 418 percent.
- ❑ increases the odds of democracy by about 518 percent.

To respond to parts C, D, E, and F, you will need to use Compute to calculate a new variable, which you will name "pre_frac" and label "Pred prob: Frac_Eth-democ, mean gdp." Pre_frac will estimate the probability of democracy for each value of Frac_Eth, holding Gdp_10_Thou constant at its mean. Useful fact: The mean of Gdp_10_Thou is equal to .626. *Helpful hint:* The numeric expression for computing the predicted probability of democracy for each value of Frac_Eth is "Exp(.103 – 2.253*Frac_Eth + 1.644*.626)/(1 + Exp(.103 – 2.253*Frac_Eth + 1.644*.626))." After computing pre_frac, run Compare Means → Means, entering pre_frac as the dependent variable and Frac_Eth as the independent variable. You do not need to print the means table. However, you will need to refer to it for parts C, D, and E.

C. As an empirical matter, the most homogeneous country in the World dataset has a value of 0 on Frac_Eth, and the most heterogeneous country has a value of .93 on Frac_Eth. The predicted probability of democracy for a highly homogeneous country (Frac_Eth = 0) with an average level of Gdp_10_Thou is equal to (fill in the blank) ________________. The predicted probability of democracy for a highly heterogeneous country (Frac_Eth = .93) with an average level of Gdp_10_Thou is equal to (fill in the blank) ____________________.

D. As Frac_Eth increases, from low heterogeneity to high heterogeneity, the predicted probability of democracy (circle one)

decreases.   does not change.   increases.

E. At mean levels of Gdp_10_Thou, the full effect of Frac_Eth (from 0 to .93) on the probability of democracy is equal to (fill in the blank) ______________________.

F. Imagine a country that has average per-capita GDP and also has an average level of ethnic fractionalization: .45 on the Frac_Eth scale. This country (circle one)

is probably not a democracy.   is probably a democracy.

Write a sentence, explaining how you know:

____

____

____

____

3. (Dataset: NES2012. Variables: Obama_vote, pid_x, pres_econ.) When it comes to shaping vote choice in U.S. elections, party identification is preeminent—a powerful heuristic for deciding which candidate to support. Yet one can imagine circumstances in which the pull of party might be weaker. Retrospective evaluations, the approval or disapproval of an incumbent's performance, might work to alter the effect of partisanship. Consider two Democrats, one who thinks President Obama has done a good job of handling the economy, and another who thinks he's done a poor job. Would the poor-job Democrat be less likely than the good-job Democrat to vote for Obama? If so, how much less likely? And what about Independents, voters who lack partisan identifications. Do retrospective assessments have the largest impact among these voters? More generally, is the relationship between party identification and vote choice different for those with negative retrospective opinions than for those with positive retrospective opinions? The following NES2012 variables will help you answer these questions.

Variable	Definition	Coding
Obama_vote	Vote choice in 2012	0 = Romney vote; 1 = Obama vote
pid_x	Party identification	1 = Strong Democrat 2 = Weak Democrat 3 = Independent Democrat 4 = Independent 5 = Independent Republican 6 = Weak Republican 7 = Strong Republican
pres_econ	Approval of Obama's handling of economy	0 = Disapprove 1 = Approve

Run the appropriate logistic regression model to estimate the effects of pid_x and pres_econ on Obama_vote.

A. Consider the odds ratio (Exp(b)) on pres_econ. Controlling for party identification, when you compare an approver with a disapprover, the approver was about how many times more likely to have voted for Obama than the disapprover?

About ____________________ times more likely.

Before proceeding, compute two new variables, pid_app and pid_disapp. Pid_app will calculate estimated probabilities of an Obama vote for each value of party identification, among approvers (for whom pres_econ =1). Pid_disapp will calculate estimated probabilities of an Obama vote for each value of party identification, among disapprovers (for whom pres_econ = 0).

B. Run a Compare Means analysis, using pid_x as the independent variable and pid_app and pid_disapp as independent variables. In Options, request means only (click Number of Cases and Standard Deviation back into the Statistics list). Print the mean comparison table.

C. Compare the predicted probabilities in the pid_app column with the predicted probabilities in the pid_disapp column at each value of pid_x. Among which party identification group—Strong Democrats, Weak Democrats, Independent Democrats, Independents, Independent Republicans, Weak Republicans, or Strong Republicans—does presidential approval have its largest impact on the probability of an Obama vote?

The largest impact is among (fill in the blank) ________________. Explain how you know.

____

____

____

D. Among which party identification group does presidential approval have its smallest impact on the probability of an Obama vote?

The smallest impact is among (fill in the blank) ________________________. Explain how you know.

____

____

____

E. Use Graphs → Legacy Dialogs → Line to create a multiple line chart showing the relationship between party identification and predicted probabilities of an Obama vote among approvers and disapprovers. In the Line Charts window, make sure to request summaries of separate variables. Edit the graph for clarity. Strive for presentation quality. Print the line graph you created.

F. Examine the table you printed in part B and the graph you produced in part E. Consider this statement: "The effect of party identification on vote choice is stronger among disapprovers than among approvers." Does this statement appear to be correct or incorrect? (circle one)

Incorrect   Correct

Explain your answer, making specific reference to information contained in the table and the graph.

____

____

____

____

____

____

That concludes the exercises for this chapter.

NOTES

1. In arriving at the estimated effect of the independent variable on the dependent variable, linear regression finds the line that minimizes the square of the distance between the observed values of the dependent variable and the predicted values of the dependent variable—predicted, that is, on the basis of the independent variable. The regression line is often referred to as the "least squares" line or "ordinary least squares" line.
2. For all guided examples and exercises in this chapter, the binary dependent variables are naturally coded 0 or 1. To get logistic regression to work, SPSS must have 0/1 binaries. However, here is a bit of SPSS trivia. In running Regression → Binary Logistic, SPSS will check to make sure that the dependent variable has only two values. The values could be 0 and 1, 3 and 5, 2 and 6, or any two (but only two) unique values. If the two values are not 0 and 1, then SPSS will temporarily recode the variable for the immediate purposes of the analysis, encoding one value of the dependent as 0 and the other as 1. SPSS output informs you which natural code it changed to 0 and which it changed to 1. The encoding does not alter your permanent dataset codes.
3. Cox–Snell's maximum achievable value depends on the analysis at hand, but it can never exactly equal 1. For a binary dependent in which the probabilities of 0 and 1 are equal (probability of 0 = .5 and probability of 1 = .5), Cox–Snell reaches a maximum of only .75 for a model in which all cases are predicted perfectly. Nagelkerke's adjustment divides the

calculated value of Cox–Snell by the maximum achievable value of Cox–Snell, returning a coefficient that varies between 0 and 1. See D. R. Cox and E. J. Snell, *The Analysis of Binary Data* (London: Chapman and Hall, 1989); N. J. D. Nagelkerke, "A Note on a General Definition of the Coefficient of Determination," *Biometrika* 78, no. 3 (September 1991): 691–692.

4. When you request iteration history, SPSS will by default produce two histories—one appearing near the beginning of the output beneath the label "Block 0: Beginning Block" and one appearing later beneath the label "Block 1: Method = Enter." In most situations, all of the information you will need can be found under the Block 1 entry. Figure 10-4 portrays the information contained in the Block 1 entry.
5. Younger people tend to have higher levels of education than older people. Thus in the earlier analysis, in which we compared respondents having less education with respondents having more education (but in which we did not control for age), we were also comparing older respondents (who, on average, have fewer years of schooling) with younger respondents (who, on average, have more years of schooling). Because younger people are less likely to vote than are older people, the uncontrolled effect of age weakens the zero-order relationship between educ and voted08. In a situation like this, age is said to be a *suppressor variable,* because it suppresses or attenuates the true effect of education on turnout.
6. When using interval-level independent variables with many values, you will often obtain logistic regression coefficients and odds ratios that appear to be quite close to null hypothesis territory (coefficients close to 0 and odds ratios close to 1) but that nonetheless trump the null hypothesis. Remember that logistic regression, like OLS, estimates the marginal effect of a one-unit increment on the logged odds of the dependent variable. In the current example, logistic regression estimated the effect of a 1-year change in age (from, say, an age of 20 years to 21 years) on the logged odds of voting. The researcher may describe the relationship in terms of larger increments. Thus, if a 1-year increase in age (from 20 years to 21 years) increases the odds of voting by an estimated 4.4 percent, then a 10-year increase in age (from 20 years to 30 years) would produce a 44-percent increase in the odds of voting.
7. The expression "Exp(Logged odds of voting)" translates logged odds into odds: Exp(Logged odds of voting) = Odds of voting. You get from an odds to a probability by dividing the odds by the quantity one plus the odds: Probability of voting = Odds of voting/(1 + Odds of voting). Thus the formula for the probability of voting, "Exp(Logged odds of voting)/(1 + Exp(Logged odds of voting))," is equivalent to the formula "Odds of voting/(1 + Odds of voting)."
8. The largest marginal effect of the independent variable on the probability of the dependent variable is sometimes called the *instantaneous effect.* In our example, the instantaneous effect is equal to .056, and this effect occurs between 9 years and 10 years of education. The effect of a one-unit change in the independent variable on the probability of the dependent variable is always greatest for the interval containing a probability equal to .5. The instantaneous effect, calculated by hand, is equal to b*.5*(1 – .5), in which b is the value of the logistic regression coefficient. For a discussion of the instantaneous effect, see Fred C. Pampel, *Logistic Regression: A Primer,* SAGE University Papers Series on Quantitative Applications in the Social Sciences, series no. 07-132 (Thousand Oaks, Calif.: SAGE Publications, 2000), 24–26.
9. The discussion and terminology here draw on the insights of Richard Williams. See "Using the Margins Command to Estimate and Interpret Adjusted Predictions and Marginal Effects," *The Stata Journal* 12, no. 2 (2012): 308–331.
10. In calculating predicted probabilities for multivariate logistic regression models, SPSS returns estimated probabilities for subjects having each combination of values on the independent variables. It does not calculate the probabilities associated with each value of a given independent variable while holding the other predictors constant.
11. SPSS has a large repertoire of canned statistical functions. The function Exp(numerical expression) returns the natural log base *e* raised to the power of the numerical expression. This is precisely what we want here, because the estimated probability of voting is equal to Exp(Logged odds of voting)/(1 + Exp(Logged odds of voting)).
12. The Compute Variable window's micro-font Numeric Expression box is a tedious and error-prone place to work, especially if you wish to create long, nested expressions. On the plus side, the box accepts cut-and-paste editing, and it's not choosy about word processing software. In a word processor, you can type an expression just as you want it to appear in the Numeric Expression box, and then copy and paste it into the box. Because the current example's two expressions differ in only one detail—the pre_26 expression requires a "26" and the pre_65 expression requires a "65"—we could type the pre_26 statement, copy and paste it, and then compute pre_26. We would then return to Transform → Compute, change the Target Variable to pre_65, replace "26" with "65" in the Numeric Expression box, and compute pre_65.
13. See Raymond E. Wolfinger and Steven J. Rosenstone's classic study of turnout, *Who Votes?* (New Haven: Yale University Press, 1980). Using probit analysis, a technique that is very similar to logistic regression, Wolfinger and Rosenstone explored the effects of a range of demographic characteristics on the likelihood of voting.
14. You may want to experiment with a few choices in the Chart Editor's Options menu: Y Axis Reference Line, Text Box, and Hide Legend. SPSS sometimes produces charts that are too "square." A chart with a width of between 1.3 and 1.5 times its height may be more pleasing to the eye. In any event, you can alter the aspect ratio (the ratio of width to height) in the Chart Size tab of the Properties window. After unchecking the box next to "Maintain aspect ratio," click in the Width box and type a number that is between 1.3 and 1.5 times the value appearing in the Height box.
15. Obama reportedly made this remark at a fundraising event in San Francisco on April 6, 2008. See http://www.huffingtonpost.com/mayhill-fowler/obama-exclusive-audio-on_b_96333.html.

11 Doing Your Own Political Analysis

Watch a screencast of the guided examples in this chapter.
edge.sagepub.com/pollock

In working through the guided examples in this book, and in performing the exercises, you have developed some solid analytic skills. The datasets you have analyzed here could, of course, become the raw material for your own research. You would not be disappointed, however, if you were to look elsewhere for excellent data. High-quality social science data on a wide variety of phenomena and units of analysis—individuals, census tracts, states, countries—are easily accessible via the Internet and might serve as the centerpiece for your own research. Your school, for example, may be a member of the Inter-university Consortium for Political and Social Research (ICPSR), the premier organizational clearinghouse for datasets of all kinds.[1] In this chapter we will take a look at various sources of available data and provide practical guidance for inputting it into SPSS.

To get you thinking about doing your own research, we begin by laying out the stages of the research process and by offering some manageable ideas for original analysis. We then consider different data sources and procedures for inputting the data into the Data Editor. Finally, we describe a serviceable format for an organized and presentable research paper.

FIVE DOABLE IDEAS

Let's begin by describing an ideal research procedure and then discuss some practical considerations and constraints. In an ideal world you would

1. Observe an interesting behavior or relationship and frame a research question about it;
2. Develop a causal explanation for what you have observed and construct a hypothesis;
3. Read and learn from the work of other researchers who have tackled similar questions;
4. Collect and analyze the data that will address the hypothesis; and
5. Write a research paper or article in which you present and interpret your findings.

In this scenario, the phenomenon that you observe in stage 1 drives the whole process. First, think up a question, and then research it and obtain the data that will address it. As a practical matter, the process is almost never this clear cut. Often someone else's idea or assertion may pique your interest. For example, you might read articles or attend lectures on a variety of topics—democratization in developing countries, global environmental issues, ideological change in the Democratic or Republican Party, the effect of election laws on turnout and party competition, and so on—that suggest hypotheses you would like to examine. So you may begin the process at stage 3 and then return to stage 1 and refine your own ideas. Furthermore, the availability of relevant data, considered in stage 4, almost always plays a role in the sorts of questions we address. A doable project often requires a compromise between stage 1 and stage 4. What interesting question can you ask, given the available data? Fortunately, this compromise need not be as restrictive as it sounds. Consider five possibilities: political knowledge, economic performance and election outcomes, state courts and criminal procedure, electoral turnout in comparative perspective, and Congress.

Political Knowledge

As you may have learned in other political science courses, scholars continue to debate the levels of knowledge and political awareness among ordinary citizens. Do citizens know the length of a U.S. senator's term of office? Do they know what constitutional protections are guaranteed by the First Amendment? Do people tend to know more about some things—Internet privacy or abortion policy, for example—and less about other things, such as foreign policy or international politics? Political knowledge is a promising variable because the researcher is likely to find some people who know a lot about politics, some who know a fair amount, and others who know very little. One could ask, "What causes this variation?" Imagine constructing a brief questionnaire that asks eight or ten multiple-choice questions about basic facts and is tailored to the aspects of political knowledge you find most thought provoking.[2] After including questions that gauge some potentially important independent variables (partisanship, gender, liberalism/conservatism, college major, class standing), you could conduct an exploratory survey among perhaps fifty or one hundred of your classmates.

Economic Performance and Election Outcomes

Here is one of the most widely discussed ideas in political science: The state of the economy before an election has a big effect on the election result. If the economy is strong, the candidate of the incumbent party does well, probably winning. If the economy is performing poorly, the incumbent party's nominee pays the price, probably losing. This idea has a couple of intriguing aspects. For one thing, it works well—but not perfectly. Moreover, the economy–election relationship has several researchable layers. Focusing on presidential elections, you can imagine a simple two-category measure of the dependent variable—the incumbent party wins or the incumbent party loses. Now consider collecting information on some potential independent variables for each presidential election year: inflation rates, unemployment, economic growth, and so on. Alternatively, you could look at congressional or state-level elections, or elections in several different countries. Or you could modify and refine the basic idea, as many scholars have done, by adding additional noneconomic variables you believe to be important. Scandal? Foreign policy crises? With some hands-on data collection and guidance from your instructor, you can produce a well-crafted project.

State Courts and Criminal Procedure

To what extent does a justice's partisanship (or political ideology) affect his or her ruling in a case? This is a perennial question in the annals of judicial research. Original research on judicial proceedings, particularly at the federal level, is among the most difficult to conduct, even for seasoned scholars. But consider state judicial systems. Using an online resource available through most university servers, you could collect information about a large number of, say, criminal cases heard on appeal by the highest court in your state.[3] You could record whether the criminal defendant won or lost, and then determine the party affiliations of the justices. Additionally, you might compare judicial decision making in two states—one in which judges are appointed and one in which they are elected. You could make this comparison at the individual justice level at one point in time. Or you could look at the same set of courts over time, using aggregate units of analysis.

Electoral Turnout in Comparative Perspective

The record of voter turnout in American presidential elections, while showing an encouraging upward trend in the new millennium, remains relatively low. The situation in other democratic countries is strikingly different. Turnouts in some Western European countries average well above 70 percent. Why? More generally, what causes turnout to vary between countries? Some scholars have focused on legal factors. Unlike the United States, some countries may not require their citizens to register beforehand, or they may penalize citizens for not voting. Other scholars look at institutional differences in electoral systems. Many countries, for example, have systems of proportional representation in which narrowly focused parties with relatively few supporters nonetheless can gain representation in the legislature. Are citizens more likely to be mobilized to vote under such institutional arrangements? Using data sources available on the Internet,[4] you could gather information on a number of democratic countries. You could then look to see if different legal requirements and institutional arrangements are associated with differences in turnout. This area of research might also open the door for some informed speculation on your part. What sort of electoral reforms, if instituted in the United States, might enhance electoral turnout? What other (perhaps unintended) consequences might such reforms have?

Congress

Political scholars have long taken considerable interest in questions about the U.S. Congress. Some researchers focus on internal dynamics: the role of leadership, the power of party ties versus the pull of constituency. Others pay attention to demographics: Have the numbers of women and minorities who serve in Congress increased in the recent past? Still others look at ideology: Are Republicans, on average, becoming more conservative and Democrats more liberal in their congressional voting? The great thing about Congress is the rich data that are available. The U.S. House and the U.S. Senate are among the most-studied institutions in the world. Several annual or biannual publications chronicle and report a large number of attributes of members of the House and Senate.[5] And the Internet is rife with information about current and past Congresses. Liberal groups, such as Americans for Democratic Action, conservative groups, such as the American Conservative Union, and nonpartisan publications, such as the *National Journal*, regularly rate the voting records of elected officials and post these ratings on their Web sites.[6]

INPUTTING DATA

Each of these five possibilities represents a practical compromise between posing an interesting question, obtaining available data, and using SPSS to perform the analysis. However, as you will no doubt discover, data sources vary in their "input friendliness"—some data are easy to input into SPSS, and other data require more typing. This section reviews different data sources and input procedures.

SPSS Formatted Datasets

The least labor-intensive sources provide SPSS datasets that are ready to download and analyze. One such source, the ICPSR's data clearinghouse at the University of Michigan (http://www.icpsr.umich.edu), was mentioned at the beginning of this chapter. But many other sites exist, often maintained by scholars, academic departments, and private foundations. For example, if you are interested in international relations or comparative politics, visit Pippa Norris's Web site at Harvard's John F. Kennedy School of Government (http://www.pippanorris.com). For links to a number of SPSS datasets having a particular emphasis on Latino politics, see Prof. Matt A. Barreto's site at University of California, Los Angeles (http://mattbarreto.com/data/index.html). Are you interested in the political beliefs and civic behavior of young people? The Center for Information and Research on Civic Learning and Engagement (CIRCLE) provides excellent data (and links to data) in SPSS format (http://www.civicyouth.org/ResearchTopics/research-products-cat/data-sets/). More generally, University of California, Berkeley's Survey Documentation and Analysis (SDA) Web site—a clearinghouse for the General Social Surveys, the American National Election Studies, and Census Microdata—allows you to download customized datasets and codebooks in a variety of formats, including SPSS (http://sda.berkeley.edu/archive.htm).

Microsoft Excel Datasets

Internet data often are not SPSS-ready; rather, they are available in spreadsheet form, predominately Microsoft Excel format. In these situations, you can copy/paste the data from Excel into the SPSS Data Editor. There are a few caveats to keep in mind, however. To illustrate, consider a typical U.S. Census site (http://www.census.gov/compendia/statab/cats/elections/presidential.html), which links an Excel dataset that records presidential election outcomes by state (Figure 11-1). This set provides an instructive example of a common "gotcha" in transferring data from Excel to SPSS.

SPSS recognizes two basic forms of data, numeric and string. Numeric data contain only numbers, including numbers with decimals. String data contain letters, words, symbols, or commas. Although some string data are essential—case identifiers, such as state or country names, are obvious examples—SPSS much prefers to analyze numerics, not strings. In the current example, the data in the "Percent" columns, which contain only numbers and decimal points, will be read as numeric. However, the data in the vote total columns ("Total Vote," "Democratic Party," "Republican Party") contain commas, which SPSS will read as string data. SPSS would be happy to let you paste these values into the Data Editor, but it would not be at all happy to analyze them for you.

Figure 11-1 Opening an Excel Dataset and Evaluating Its SPSS-Friendliness

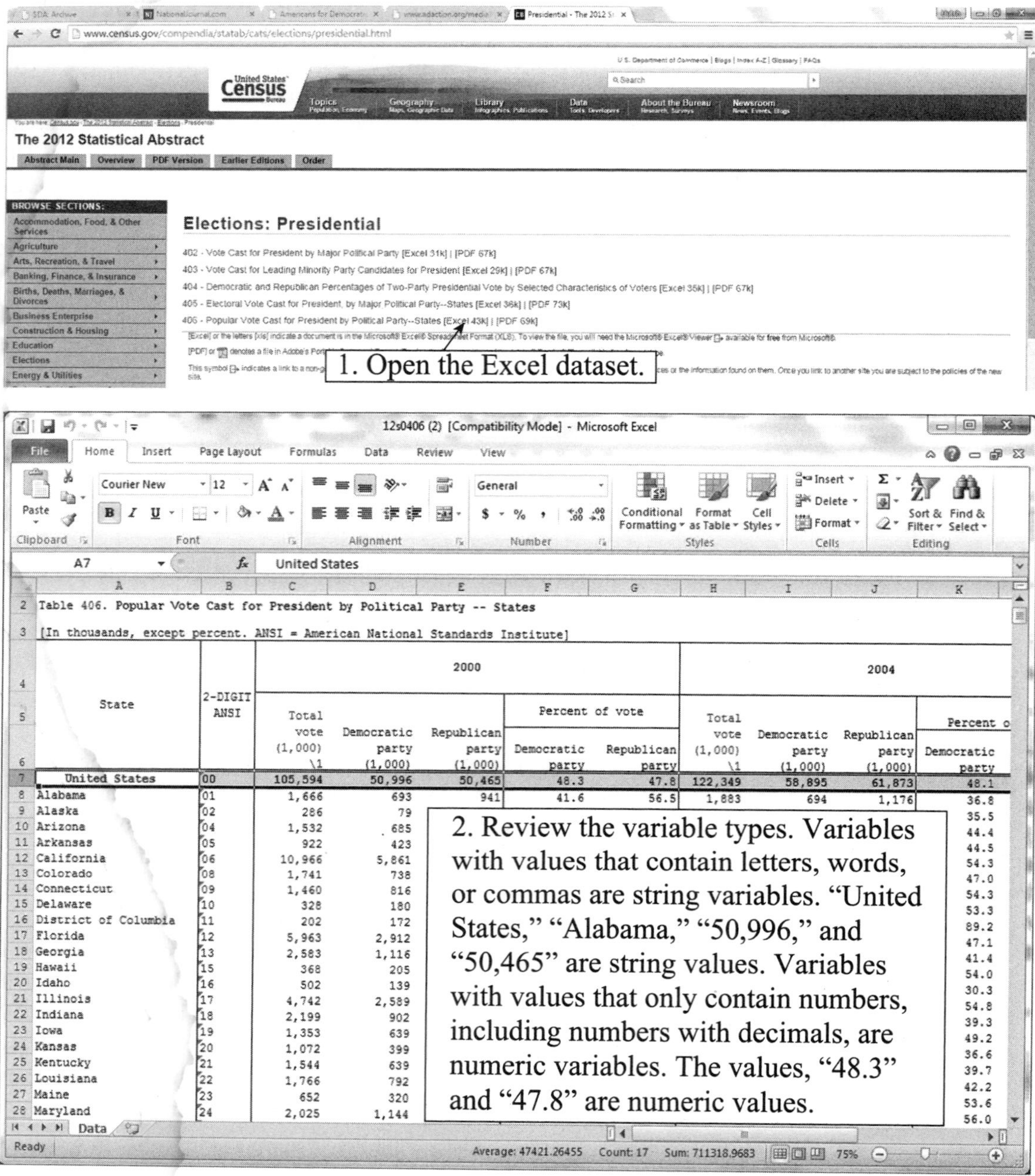

Source: United States Census Bureau.

To remove the commas, and thereby convert the data from string to numeric, follow these steps, which are illustrated in Figure 11-2.

1. Select the columns you wish to edit by clicking the column header. To select multiple nonadjacent columns, select the first column, press and hold the Control key, and then select the second column.
2. On Excel's main menu bar, click Format → Format Cells.
3. In the Category pane of the Format Cells window, select the Number tab.
4. In the Number tab, you will always want to uncheck the Use 1000 Separator box. Depending on the exact character of the data, you may want to modify the value in the Decimal places box. If the data contain decimals, then specify the number of decimal places. In the current example, the numbers in the edited columns do not contain decimals, so we would type "0" in the Decimal places box.

Figure 11-2 Removing Commas from Data Values Using Excel

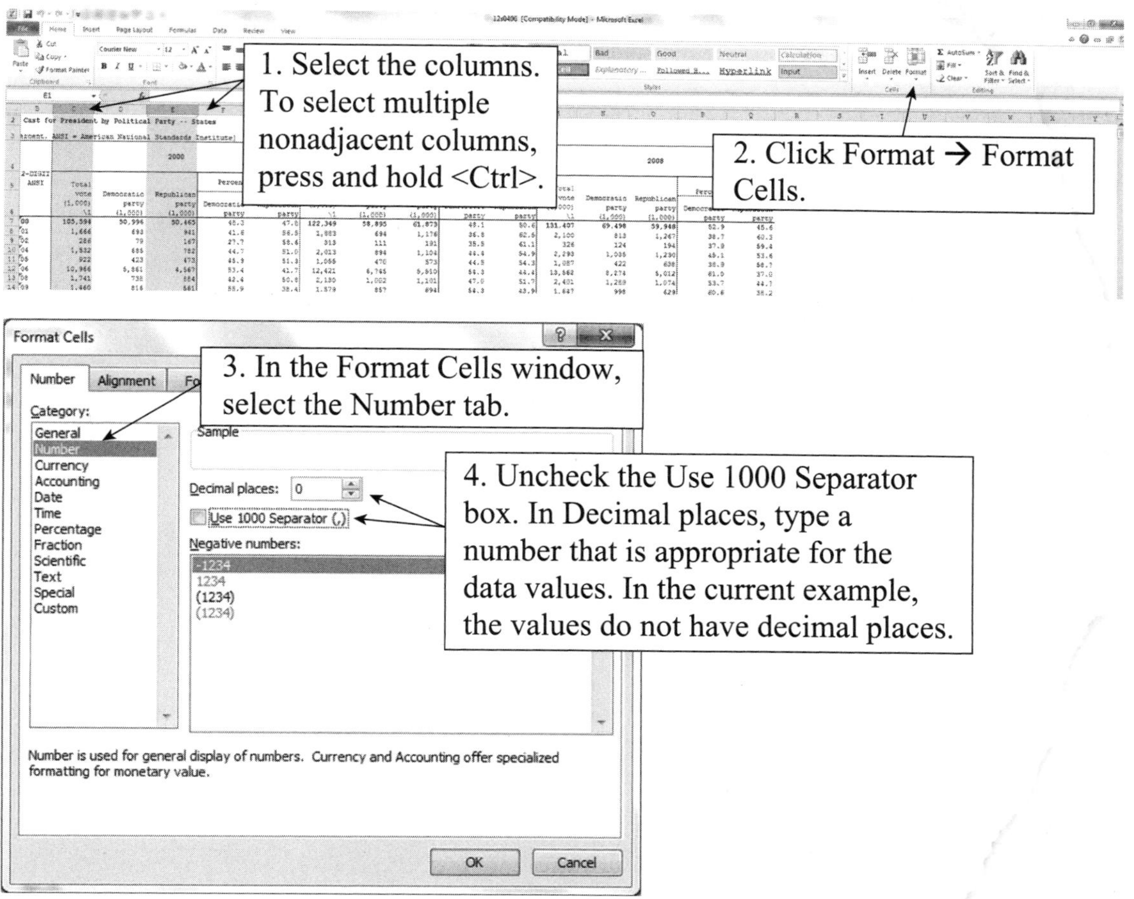

To copy/paste the edited Excel data into the SPSS Data Editor, follow these steps, which are illustrated in Figure 11-3.

1. Select the Excel data rows that you want to paste into SPSS. Make sure that the selection is square—that is, ensure that each row contains the same number of columns. Avoid selecting column headers and labels. Also, do not use Excel's row-number markers to make the selection. (This copies the desired columns, plus a number of empty columns.) Rather, select the data by clicking inside the matrix. In the current example, we would begin the selection by clicking on "Alabama," selecting the six columns to the right, and selecting down through the last state, "Wyoming." After completing the selection, click the Copy icon on the Excel menu bar.

2. On the SPSS menu bar, click File → New → Data.

3. If SPSS opens in the Variable View, select the Data View tab. Click in the upper-left cell of the Data View.

4. Click Edit → Paste. SPSS dumps the Excel data into the Data Editor and supplies generic variable names. Switch to the Variable View and provide descriptive names and labels for the variables.

As we have just seen, if the data are available in Excel format, it is a relatively simple matter to copy/paste into SPSS. If the data are in HTML format, it is also a relatively simple matter to copy/paste into Excel. By way of illustration, consider the American Conservative Union's data on members of the U.S. Senate.[7] As shown in Figure 11-4, we would select the data, copy it to the clipboard, and paste into Excel. Once in Excel (see Figure 11-5), inspect the data values for unwanted strings and undesirable text features, such as hyperlinks. In the current example, senators' votes are represented by strings: plus signs for positions favored by ACU and minus signs for positions not favored by ACU. Use Find/Replace to change these strings to numerics. Once you

Figure 11-3 Copy/Pasting from Excel into the SPSS Data Editor

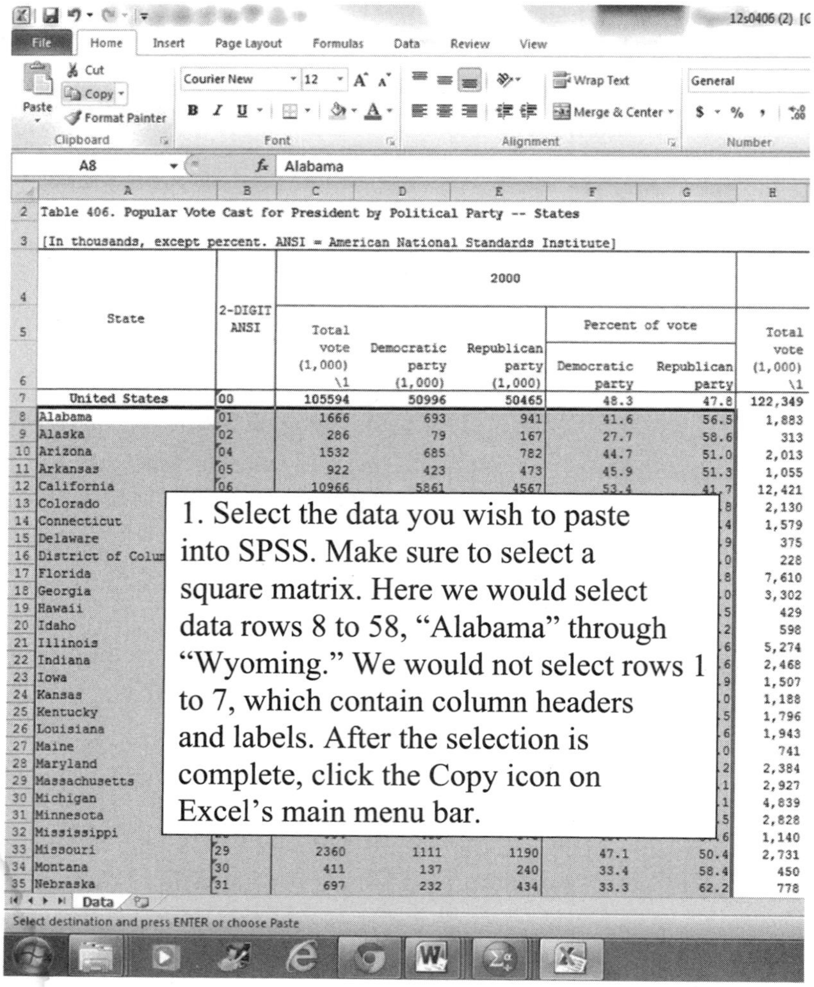

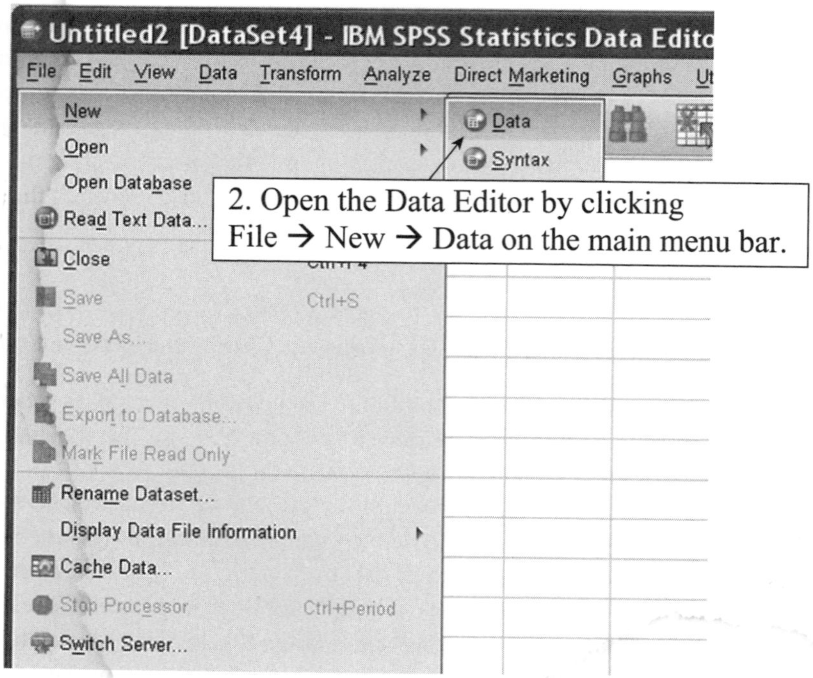

1. Select the data you wish to paste into SPSS. Make sure to select a square matrix. Here we would select data rows 8 to 58, "Alabama" through "Wyoming." We would not select rows 1 to 7, which contain column headers and labels. After the selection is complete, click the Copy icon on Excel's main menu bar.

2. Open the Data Editor by clicking File → New → Data on the main menu bar.

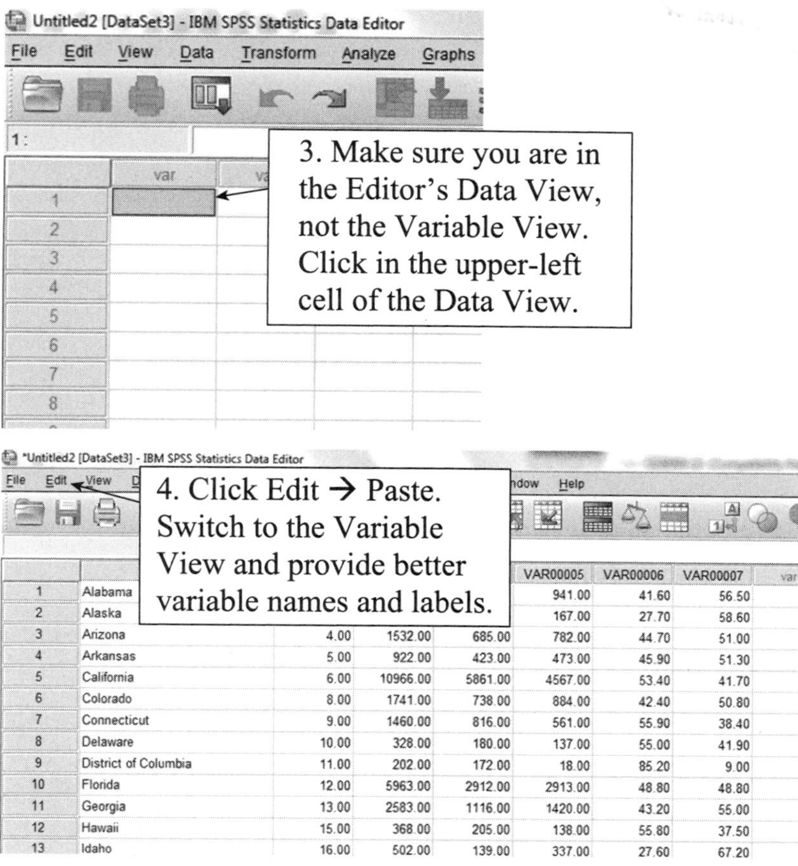

are satisfied that things look okay, follow the earlier-described procedure for copying Excel spreadsheets into the SPSS Data Editor (see Figure 11-3).

3. Make sure you are in the Editor's Data View, not the Variable View. Click in the upper-left cell of the Data View.
4. Click Edit → Paste. Switch to the Variable View and provide better variable names and labels.

WRITING IT UP

Several of the datasets described thus far would provide great raw material for analysis. After inputting your data, you can let the creative juices flow—describing the variables, performing cross-tabulation and mean comparison analyses, running linear regression and logistic regression models. Rewarding findings are guaranteed. Yet at some point the analysis ends, and the writing must begin. It is at this point, as well, that two contradictory considerations often collide. On one hand, you have an embarrassment of riches. You have worked on your research for several weeks, and you know the topic well—better, perhaps, than does anyone who will read the paper. There may be a large amount of material that you want to include in your paper. On the other hand, you want to get it written, and you do not want to write a book. Viewed from an instructor's perspective, the two questions most frequently asked by students are, "How should my paper be organized?" and "How long should it be?" (The questions are not necessarily asked in this order.)

Of course, different projects and instructors might call for different requirements. But here is a rough outline for a well-organized paper of 16–24 double-spaced pages (in 12-point font).

I. The research question (3–4 pages)

   A. Introduction to the problem (1 page)

   B. Theory and process (1–2 pages)

   C. Propositions (1 page)

II. Previous research (2–4 pages)

   A. Descriptive review (1–2 pages)

   B. Critical review (1–2 pages)

Figure 11-4 Data in HTML Format

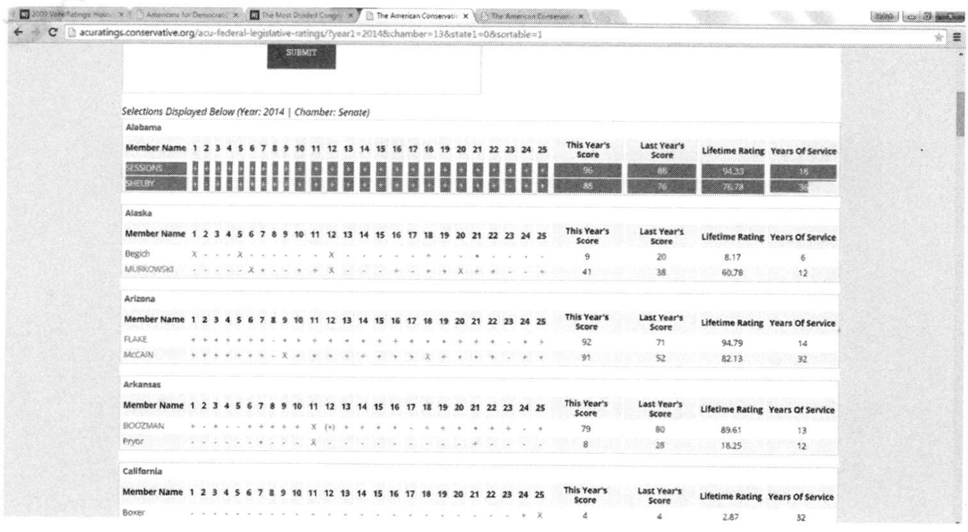

Source: Screenshot of federal legislative ratings from the American Conservative Union (http://acuratings.conservative.org/acu-federal-legislative-ratings/?year1=2014&chamber=13&state1=0&sortable=1).

Figure 11-5 Editing HTML Data in Excel before Copy/Pasting into SPSS

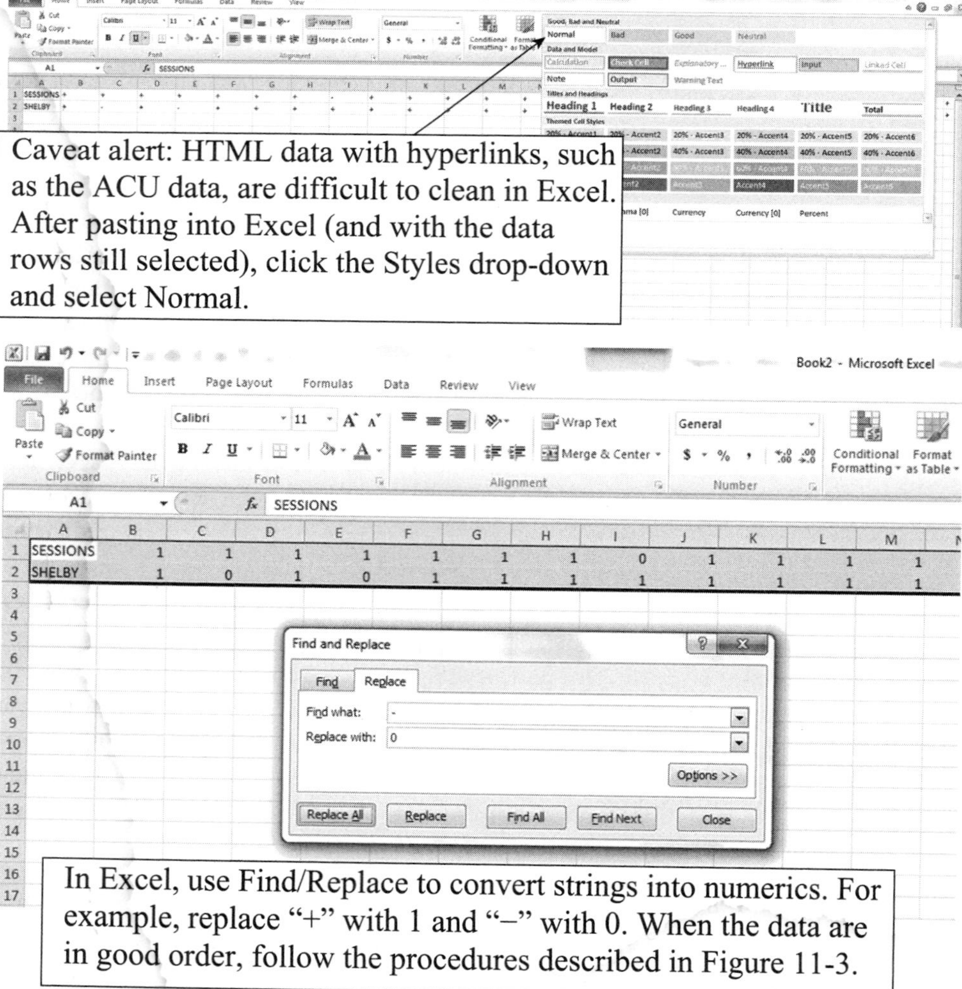

Caveat alert: HTML data with hyperlinks, such as the ACU data, are difficult to clean in Excel. After pasting into Excel (and with the data rows still selected), click the Styles drop-down and select Normal.
Book2 - Microsoft Excel
Find and Replace
Find what: -
Replace with: 0
In Excel, use Find/Replace to convert strings into numerics. For example, replace "+" with 1 and "–" with 0. When the data are in good order, follow the procedures described in Figure 11-3.

III. Data and hypotheses (3–4 pages)
   A. Data and variables (1–2 pages)
   B. Measurement (1 page)
   C. Hypotheses (1 page)

IV. Analysis (5–8 pages, including tables)
   A. Descriptive statistics (1–2 pages)
   B. Bivariate comparisons (2–3 pages)
   C. Controlled comparisons (2–3 pages)

V. Conclusions and implications (3–4 pages)
   A. Summary of findings (1 page)
   B. Implications for theory (1–2 pages)
   C. New issues or questions (1 page)

The Research Question

Because of its rhetorical challenges, the opening section of a paper is often the most difficult to write. In this section the writer must both engage the reader's interest and describe the purpose of the research. Here is a heuristic device that may be useful: In the first page of the write-up, place the specific research problem in the context of larger, clearly important issues or questions. For example, suppose your research is centered on the landmark health care legislation passed by Congress in 2010. A narrowly focused topic? Yes. A dry topic? Not at all. The opening page of this paper could frame larger questions about the sometimes conflicting roles of congressional party leadership and constituency interests in shaping the behavior of representatives and senators. Thus your analysis will advance our knowledge by illuminating one facet of a larger, more complex question.

Following the introduction, begin to zero in on the problem at hand. The "theory and process" section describes the logic of the relationships you are studying. Many political phenomena, as you have learned, have competing or alternative explanations. You should describe these alternatives, and the tension between them, in this section. Although a complete description of previous research does not appear in this section, you should give appropriate attribution to the most prominent work. These references tie your work to the scholarly community, and they raise the points you will cover in a more detailed review.

You should round out the introductory section of your paper with a brief statement of purpose or intent. Think about it from the reader's perspective. Thus far you have made the reader aware of the larger context of the analysis, and you have described the process that may explain the relationships of interest. If this process has merit, then it should submit to an empirical test of some kind. What test do you propose? The "Propositions" section serves this role. Here you set the parameters of the research—informing the reader about the units of analysis, the concepts to be measured, and the type of analysis to be performed.

Previous Research

In this section you provide an intellectual history of the research problem, a description and critique of the published research on which the analysis is based. You first would describe these previous analyses in some detail. What data and variables were used? What were the main findings? Did different researchers arrive at different conclusions? Political scientists who share a research interest often agree on many things. Yet knowledge is nourished through criticism, and in reviewing previous work you will notice key points of disagreement—about how concepts should be measured, what are the best data to use, or which variables need to be controlled. In the latter part of this section of the paper, you would review these points and perhaps contribute to the debate. A practical point: The frequently asked question "How many articles and books should be reviewed?" has no set answer. It depends on the project. However, here is an estimate: A well-grounded yet manageable review should discuss at least four references.

Data, Hypotheses, and Analysis

Together, the sections "Data and Hypotheses" and "Analysis" form the heart of the project, and they have been the primary concerns of this book. By now you are well versed in how to describe your data and variables and how to frame hypotheses. You also know how to set up a cross-tabulation or mean comparison table, and you can make controlled comparisons and interpret your findings.

In writing these sections, however, bear in mind a few reader-centered considerations. First, assume that the reader might want to replicate your study—collect the data you gathered, define and measure the concepts as you have defined and measured them, manipulate the variables just as you have computed and recoded them, and produce the tables you have reported. By explaining precisely what you did, your write-up should provide a clear guide for such a replication. Second, devote some space to a statistical description of the variables. Often you can add depth and interest to your analysis by briefly presenting the frequency distributions of the variables, particularly the dependent variable. Finally, exercise care in constructing readable tables. You can select, copy, and paste the tables generated by SPSS directly into a word processor, but they always require further editing for readability.

Conclusions and Implications

No section of a research paper can write itself. But the final section comes closest to realizing this optimistic hope. Here you discuss the analysis on three levels. First, you provide a condensed recapitulation. What are the main findings? Are the hypotheses borne out? Were there any unexpected findings? Second, you describe where the results fit in the larger fabric of scholarly research on the topic. In what ways are the findings consistent with the work of previous researchers? Does your analysis lend support to one scholarly perspective as opposed to another? Third, research papers often include obligatory "suggestions for further research." Indeed, you might have encountered some methodological problems that still must be worked out, or you might have unearthed a noteworthy substantive relationship that could bear future scrutiny. You should describe these new issues or questions. Here, too, you are allowed some room to speculate—to venture beyond the edge of the data and engage in a little "What if?" thinking. After all, the truth is still out there.

NOTES

1. You can browse ICPSR's holdings at www.icpsr.umich.edu.
2. For excellent guidance on the meaning and measurement of political knowledge, see Michael X. Delli Carpini and Scott Keeter, "Measuring Political Knowledge: Putting First Things First," *American Journal of Political Science* 37, no. 4 (November 1993): 1179–1206.
3. The cases are available from LexisNexis at www.lexis-nexis.com/academic/universe/Academic/. See also the National Center for State Courts, Court Statistics Project, at www.courtstatistics.org.
4. Pippa Norris of Harvard's John F. Kennedy School of Government has compiled excellent comparative and international data, which are available to the general public. These datasets are available in several formats, including SPSS. See www .pippanorris.com.
5. Examples include three books published by CQ Press: *Who's Who in Congress*, offered twice a year through 2001; *CQ's Politics in America*, published every two years; and *Vital Statistics on American Politics*, by Harold W. Stanley and Richard G. Niemi, which also appears every two years. *Vital Statistics* is an excellent single-volume general reference on American politics.
6. See www.adaction.org, www.conservative.org, and www.nationaljournal.com.
7. The American Conservative Union Federal Legislative Ratings are available at http://acuratings.conservative.org/ acu-federal-legislative-ratings/?year1=2014&chamber=13&state1=0&sortable=1.